Research in Social Work series

Series Editors: **Anna Gupta**, Royal Holloway, University of London, UK and **John Gal**, Hebrew University of Jerusalem, Israel

---

Published together with The European Social Work Research Association (ESWRA), this series examines current, progressive and innovative research applications of familiar ideas and models in international social work research

Also available in the series:

Social Work Research Using Arts-Based Methods
Edited by **Ephrat Huss** and **Eltje Bos**

Critical Gerontology for Social Workers
Edited by **Sandra Torres** and **Sarah Donnelly**

Involving Service Users in Social Work Education, Research and Policy
Edited by **Kristel Driessens** and **Vicky Lyssens-Danneboom**

Adoption from Care
Edited by **Tarja Pösö**, **Marit Skivenes** and **June Thoburn**

Interprofessional Collaboration and Service User Participation
Edited by **Kirsi Juhila**, **Tanja Dall**, **Christopher Hall** and **Juliet Koprowska**

The Settlement House Movement Revisited
Edited by **John Gal**, **Stefan Köngeter** and **Sarah Vicary**

Social Work and the Making of Social Policy
Edited by **Ute Klammer**, **Simone Leiber** and **Sigrid Leitner**

Research and the Social Work Picture
By **Ian Shaw**

Find out more at:

policy.bristoluniversitypress.co.uk/
research-in-social-work

Research in Social Work series

Series Editors: **Anna Gupta**, Royal Holloway, University of London, UK and **John Gal**, Hebrew University of Jerusalem, Israel

---

Forthcoming in the series:

Migration and Social Work

Edited by **Emilio J. Gómez-Ciriano, Elena Cabiati** and **Sofia Dedotsi**

Find out more at:

policy.bristoluniversitypress.co.uk/
research-in-social-work

Research in Social Work series

Series Editors: **Anna Gupta**, Royal Holloway, University of London, UK and **John Gal**, Hebrew University of Jerusalem, Israel

---

International Editorial Board:

Andrés Arias Astray,
Complutense University of Madrid, Spain
Isobel Bainton, Policy Press, UK
Inge Bryderup, Aalborg University, Denmark
Tony Evans, Royal Holloway, University of London, UK
Hannele Forsberg, University of Tampere, Finland
John Gal, Hebrew University of Jerusalem, Israel
Anna Gupta, Royal Holloway, University of London, UK
Todd I. Herrenkohl, University of Michigan, US
Ephrat Huss, Ben-Gurion University of the Negev, Israel
Stefan Köngeter, Eastern Switzerland University of Applied Science (OST), Switzerland
Manohar Pawar, Charles Sturt University, Australia
Ian Shaw, National University of Singapore and University of York, UK
Alessandro Sicora, University of Trento, Italy
Darja Zaviršek, University of Ljubljana, Slovenia

Find out more at:

policy.bristoluniversitypress.co.uk/research-in-social-work

THE ORIGINS OF SOCIAL CARE AND SOCIAL WORK
Creating a Global Future

Mark Henrickson

First published in Great Britain in 2024 by

Policy Press, an imprint of
Bristol University Press
University of Bristol
1-9 Old Park Hill
Bristol
BS2 8BB
UK
t: +44 (0)117 374 6645
e: bup-info@bristol.ac.uk

Details of international sales and distribution partners are available at
policy.bristoluniversitypress.co.uk

© Bristol University Press 2024

British Library Cataloguing in Publication Data
A catalogue record for this book is available from the British Library

ISBN 978-1-4473-5734-6 hardcover
ISBN 978-1-4473-5735-3 paperback
ISBN 978-1-4473-5736-0 ePub
ISBN 978-1-4473-5737-7 ePdf

The right of Mark Henrickson to be identified as author of this work has been asserted by him in accordance with the Copyright, Designs and Patents Act 1988.

All rights reserved: no part of this publication may be reproduced, stored in a retrieval system, or transmitted in any form or by any means, electronic, mechanical, photocopying, recording, or otherwise without the prior permission of Bristol University Press.

Every reasonable effort has been made to obtain permission to reproduce copyrighted material. If, however, anyone knows of an oversight, please contact the publisher.

The statements and opinions contained within this publication are solely those of the author and not of the University of Bristol or Bristol University Press. The University of Bristol and Bristol University Press disclaim responsibility for any injury to persons or property resulting from any material published in this publication.

Bristol University Press and Policy Press work to counter discrimination on
grounds of gender, race, disability, age and sexuality.

Scripture quotations are from the New Revised Standard Version Bible,
copyright © 1989 the Division of Christian Education of the National
Council of the Churches of Christ in the United States of America. Used by
permission. All rights reserved.

Cover design: Bristol University Press
Front cover image: iStock-1146749285

To Jack, who is incomprehensibly understanding, always

Contents

Acknowledgements		xi
1	Introduction	1
2	A royal responsibility	18
3	Inventing the poor	42
4	Reforming the poor	67
5	Capitalising the poor	94
6	Industrialising the poor	121
7	Liberalising the poor	154
8	Professionalising work with the poor	180
9	A global perspective	198
10	Creating a global future	214
References		224
Index		246

Acknowledgements

Writers and students know that writing is lonely work. Fortunately, I am blessed with a personality that thrives on isolation, and the forced isolation of COVID lockdowns during which much of this book was written was oddly helpful in that respect. Nevertheless, it would be beyond arrogant to assert that academic writing of any use can exist without the significant contributions and advice of others. Such contributions keep the writer from living in an echo chamber of their own voice, and from assuming that every thought is a fully formed pearl for which the world has been eagerly waiting. They also provide an informed critique to test whether an idea is expressed in a way that people from various disciplinary backgrounds can understand it. I am enormously grateful to these voices for their contributions and critiques:

- Professor Michael Belgrave, Professor in History, Massey University, Auckland, for his critique on my initial proposal. He said at the time, "I see you're trying to write a history of the universe", and at times it has felt a little like that.
- Professor Emerita In Young Han, Ewha Woman's University, Seoul, Korea who read the first chapters and provided early insight, direction, and encouragement.
- Professor John Bishop, Professor of Philosophy, University of Auckland, provided an incisive and rigorous critique from the perspective of a philosophy of theology.
- Professor Peter Lineham, MNZM, Professor Emeritus of History, Massey University, for his review of the historical aspects of the manuscript. I make no claims to be a historian, yet much of this work relies on history.
- Andrew Thompson (PhD candidate), University of Auckland, who provided a first-hand account of providing social care and social work in the United Kingdom during the Thatcher era and more general feedback on the professionalisation of social work.
- Valerie Sharpe, RSW, for feedback on the professionalisation of social work and for her ongoing professional support for which I am deeply grateful.
- Professor Tatsuru Akimoto, then-Head of the Asian Research Institute for International Social Work at Shukutoku University, Chiba, and his team for allowing me access to their important work on Buddhist and Islamic social work, and for his courageous and persistent critique of 'Western' social work.
- Massey University librarians, the unsung heroes of research, who ensured that the endless stream of resources I requested was delivered to my inbox

or letterbox at home in a timely and efficient way, even in the midst of lockdowns.
- And of course, my partner Jack, and Alex who lived through this with me.

In a more general way, I am grateful to my colleagues on the Board of the International Association of Schools of Social Work: during my time on the Board, they constantly challenged my assumptions about what social work should look like from a global perspective. It was my experiences on the Board and several of its working groups that created the seed that has grown into this book. I also thank my social work students for going along for the ride as we explored ideas together. To all of you, thank you. Errors, omissions, and opinions in the work are of course entirely my responsibility.

I believe strongly in the discipline and global future of social work, although I think that all of us are still trying to figure out what that future looks like. I only hope that this work is a useful contribution to that conversation.

1

Introduction

The origins of social work are usually said to be found in the slums of East London in the late nineteenth century (Younghusband, 1981), through the work of Octavia Hill and the Charity Organisation Society, and the founding of the Toynbee Hall Settlement by Samuel and Henrietta Barnett. Introductory classes in social work may make mention of these movements and allude to the Elizabethan Poor Law of 1601 (and if there is time, perhaps even English Poor Law reform in 1834) and its three classes of poor. American students will undoubtedly read about Jane Addams' Hull House and Mary Richmond's *Social Diagnosis*. While there can be no question that these approaches to poverty, deprivation, and social problems were important – even pioneering – events in the history of what we now understand as social work, to construct them as the origin of social work is to isolate them from the larger religious, philosophical, social, and political contexts in which they occurred. To focus exclusively on London, or even on the Settlement House Movement, or the various incarnations of the Charity Organisation Society in the UK and the US is also to take a very Anglophone, even colonial, view of the history of social work. Social work is a dynamic maturing discipline, occupation, and (in some places) profession around the world.

As we shall see, the roots of what we now call social work extend back through many millennia; contemporary constructions of poor and marginalised persons and the way policies are made and care is delivered remain remarkably consistent with those historical roots. A modern social worker would recognise the purpose and structure of the *Orphanotropheion* of Zotikos in 4th century Constantinople, and even policies to protect widows and orphans in ancient Mesopotamia (although fewer would recognise that the roots of contemporary residential care for older adults are found in the indoor relief workhouses of the 18th century, which were themselves modelled after 11th-century *gerocomeia*, which in turn referenced 4th-century poor houses and hospices). There is a significant push by international social work organisations and educational programmes to become internationalised (Healy, 2008; Noble et al, 2009; Cox and Pawar, 2013; Noble et al, 2014). This may seem desirable as we observe transnational migration, social workers sharing approaches to complex social problems, and social workers themselves migrating to different countries to live and work. However, in the internationalising process, and as the discipline establishes definitions, ethics, and standards in order to make social work consistent across borders, we must be very cautious not to simply replicate and impose liberal humanist theories and models of social work education and practice around the world. To do so would simply reproduce European colonialism of the 17th–19th centuries. We have also seen the dangers of exporting transiently fashionable political philosophies like neoliberalism and populism, which have exacerbated income inequalities and extremist agendas. Contemporary social workers have always identified closely with the poor and marginalised, and it is difficult to imagine ourselves as imperialists; yet that is the risk we face in the internationalising project as social workers and institutions in developed nations seek to provide leadership, support, and partnerships with social workers and institutions in developing nations (Cox and Pawar, 2013). One way to avoid this, of course, is for practitioners and educators to practice what we preach: to be willing to learn from those we wish to support.

At the same time, 'it is important that the profession be able to present to the outside world an understanding of its core nature, and of the relevance of that core nature to the fields of work on which the international community is focussed' (Cox and Pawar, 2013, p 4). If there is something at the core of social work as a method, discipline, or profession, it must remain recognisable regardless of the context in which it is practised. A strength of social work is its flexibility and adaptability to the multifarious contexts in which it is practised, the breadth of the scope of theory and practice on which social work draws. But social work should not be so flexible that non-social workers – including policymakers as well as allied disciplines such as psychologists, psychiatrists, nurses, teachers, occupational therapists, and so forth – fail to recognise and appreciate social work as an independent contemporary discipline with ancient origins. The roots of social work are found in policy and practical responses to the needs of vulnerabilised and marginalised persons and communities. If social work is to become truly global – a decision that has not yet been made – it is essential that we become aware of how those roots have shaped social work today so that in understanding its past, the social workers and organisations can make informed decisions about its future. The historical values, assumptions, and ways of understanding that are a part of contemporary Western social work are not shared around the world. European Enlightenment and liberal humanist values such as individualism do not have a natural home in cultures and societies that prioritise interdependence and relationships with each other, with their ancestors, or with the divine. It is a purpose of this book to identify and critique the theological foundations and Enlightenment values of contemporary social work in order to set out a vision for a future of global social work. In order to do that we must acknowledge the Western origins of the modern discipline of social work and the unavoidable influence of Western Christianity. As the historian Tom Holland writes:

> Two thousand years on from the birth of Christ, it does not require a belief that he rose from the dead to be stamped by the formidable – indeed the inescapable – influence of Christianity ... The West, increasingly empty though the pews may be, remains firmly moored to its Christian past. (Holland, 2019)

What I will argue in this book is that the roots of contemporary social work are found in Christian scriptures, the theologies of the 4th century CE, and Reformation Calvinism; it has as its primary purpose social stability through social control. In some places, this stability is called social harmony, but in all places, a primary goal has been social order relative to the way the local culture understands order and stability, and social care providers and social workers have been instrumental to governmental agendas of social order. Many contemporary social workers are not Christian, of course, and they, and even Christian social workers, may be troubled that their work embodies a patristic Christian theology that is more than 1,700 years old, or a Reformation expectation that the poor prove themselves worthy of assistance. Most social workers would see their role as a robustly secular one, drawing on post-Reformation European Enlightenment values such as self-determination, autonomy, human rights, and liberty. These humanistic values penetrated Europe at a time of colonialism and global capitalist exploitation and were exported around the world by European explorers, their priests and preachers, and state-supported corporations with vast powers. However, the theological foundations of contemporary social work reach much further into the past, and they are so much a part of how modern states manage the poor and marginalised that we may not be aware of that theological history.

When Emperor Constantine authorised Christianity in the eastern Roman Empire, he did so with the expectation that the Christian Church would provide assistance to the widow, the orphan, and the poor, and look after the sick. In this way, extreme poverty would be minimised, the poor would not riot, the wealthy would not have to look upon beggars in the street, and social stability and the reputation of the empire would be maintained. Church leaders drew on Hebrew and Christian scriptures and also Greek philanthropic practices to develop theologies about the poor, theologies and practices which remained more or less in place for a millennium. At the time of the Great Plague in the mid-14th century, the church's ability to respond to the poor was devastated: church workers were at least as affected by the plague as was the general population, and there were fewer labourers available to bring in the harvest. There was little assistance to offer, and few clergy to offer it. Great population movements throughout Europe generated by plague and hunger meant that civic authorities took over the responsibility for the poor in order to maintain social stability, and these authorities took over the theologies – which we might now call policies – and practices of the church more or less unchanged. In many countries,[1] responsibility for implementing those practices was delegated back to the churches and supplemented with civic resources. Those policies and practices have been shaped by new technologies, but the goal of social stability through social control has shaped civic – and theological – responses to the poor since the 14th century.

Cox and Pawar (2013) propose that social work has evolved to serve three areas of practice: as an arm of the welfare state; enhancing the social functioning or wellbeing of individuals and families; and by contributing to building health and cohesive communities, and so promoting the wellbeing of people. Broad stereotypes of social work hold that in some countries social work is constructed as an arm of government, and people with the occupational title of social worker (or benefit worker, eligibility worker, or similar) are effectively eligibility gatekeepers to benefits that are available from the state; these are social workers as an arm of the welfare state. In other countries, social workers, including public and private agencies that manage adoption and foster care, are focused on the care and protection of children and young people, and young people in trouble with the law; here again, social workers are effectively constructed as agents of the state. And in other places, social workers may work as independent clinicians trained and authorised to deliver mental health and related services under licence by boards and inspectorates. All of these kinds of social workers are positioned clearly within the tradition of maintaining social stability through social control. In the third example, while providing mental health or rehabilitative care may seem to be assisting an individual to enhance their social functioning, mental health, location (inpatient/indoor or community based/outdoor care), and the kind of care is largely defined by the state (or funder acting under the authority of the state). As in forensic work, a key stakeholder in mental health social work is the community, which primarily desires safety and stability. The social worker or care provider is once again an agent of the state. The third area, generally called community or social development, can include anything from organising a local community in order to accomplish specific goals to contributing to policy development in civil society. A key task of the social worker is to navigate the tension between a client's[2] 'rights' and wellbeing and that of the community or state. Any social worker who believes they are functioning independently needs

---

[1] I will use the anachronistic notion of 'countries' for the sake of simplicity, with the awareness that the notion of the modern nation-state dates only from the Treaty of Westphalia in 1648.

[2] A client, of course, can be an individual, family, group, or organisation.

to consider critically who is paying them, and who is regulating what they can do. Even where a social worker is working for a non-governmental organisation or even a for-profit organisation, the work may be funded by a government contract, outcomes may be defined, or practices regulated by a civic authority. Not all of these functions require the same level of educational qualification: some simply require training to a manual, while others require extensive education, independent decision-making, and critical thinking.

Ironically, at the same time that many contemporary social workers function as agents of the state, those same states can be reluctant to endorse or recognise social work as a profession because by the very nature of their work, which identifies and responds to the poor, marginalised, and vulnerabilised, social workers may represent a failure of state welfare policies to address poverty, inequalities, and other social problems. (The question of whether social work is or can be a profession, as opposed to an occupation, is one that we will consider.) Equally, as agents of the state, social workers may be reluctant to advocate for important policy reforms or on behalf of their clients because the authority to make meaningful change lies with those who sign the paycheques of the workers. Sometimes workers are prohibited contractually from speaking out on issues, particularly when their opinion differs from that of their employer, and workers are understandably anxious about putting their paycheques in jeopardy by doing so.

The use of the term or title 'social work' is claimed not only by people who engage in familiar social work settings but also by people who primarily engage in social development and social policy (throughout East and Southeast Asia, for instance). Legacy notions of social work may endure in many post-colonial nations and states. In other places, the title of social worker is not used, but instead, we find job titles like community worker, youth worker, community advocate, and similar; and the study of social work may be called community development, social pedagogy, social anthropology, and so forth. In some countries, the occupation of social work is not recognised at all, and in others, the use of the title of social worker is protected by law. The most comprehensive thing we can say about social work is that there is little we can say about it that is comprehensive. Governments and regulatory authorities struggle to come up with definitive scopes of practice to describe just what it is that social workers do, or do uniquely. As we shall see, this struggle is one of the challenges to social work's universal acceptance as a profession – and may be a reason why it cannot or should not be considered a profession.

Defining social work

In addition to the many different ways social work is recognised and practised around the world today, it would be entirely inappropriate to impose words like 'social work' or contemporary understandings of social work onto any period of history earlier than about 1870. Any history of social work, then, is vulnerable to the challenges of what we mean by social work. In this book, I take the position that activity, regardless of motivation, that improves the welfare of vulnerabilised and marginalised persons – which includes widows, orphans, the poor, and the stranger – is of interest in the history of contemporary social work. We may broadly describe these activities as social care. The complexity and diversity of social work have been recognised in the 2014 *Global Definition of Social Work*. A clear and unitary definition is important because it is the one thing that unifies the various ways that social work appears and is practised around the world. Although the *Global Definition* acknowledges that there is much that is common to contemporary social work around the world, the final critical sentence (too often omitted when the *Global Definition* is reproduced) recognises that there are also many regional and international differences in the way social work looks and is practised:

> Social work is a practice-based profession and an academic discipline that promotes social change and development, social cohesion, and the empowerment and liberation of people. Principles of social justice, human rights, collective responsibility, and respect for diversities are central to social work. Underpinned by theories of social work, social sciences, humanities and indigenous knowledges, social work engages people and structures to address life challenges and enhance wellbeing.
>
> The above definition may be amplified at national and/or regional levels. (International Association of Schools of Social Work and International Federation of Social Work, 2014)

That relatively (and deliberately) brief definition of social work is the result of four years of careful consultation with social practitioners, educators, and researchers around the world. With the addition of the important final sentence, the 2014 *Global Definition* takes into account that social work looks different in different parts of the world. Some regional social work organisations have taken up the challenge to amplify that high-level definition in their parts of the globe. At the time of writing, some nations are undertaking consultations to create national amplifications. As global social work undertakes this period of self-reflection and consultation, it is an exciting time because in some ways, for the first time, social work is coming to understand itself as truly global, and informed by the rich experiences and worldviews of cultures and societies around the world. I recall an occasion at the beginning of the *Definition* revision process when a colleague from an Anglophone country sat down next to me and I asked what they thought the new definition would look like; they replied that they thought there would be some tinkering and a few minor word changes, but the definition would, in the end, be much the same. A few years into the process I asked a venerable and highly respected social work academic from East Asia what they thought about the existing (previous) definition, and they replied that it was interesting but largely ignored in their country because its Western assumptions made it completely irrelevant. What happened in the 2014 *Global Definition* was a radical reconceptualisation and internationalisation of social work, which caught a few social workers by surprise and may have more fully engaged others. Still, other social workers felt it did not go far enough to engage global worldviews and agendas.

What we will see in this book is that what we now call social work includes activity that has been performed by people in different disciplines and professions throughout history, each informed by their own historical, theological, political, and social contexts. The history of social welfare, as opposed to social care and social work, has been the subject of a number of valuable explorations (which I have drawn on gratefully throughout the first part of this book), but there have been fewer attempts to capture the origins or history of the delivery of those theologies or policies of care: that is, how they were put into practice. Nevertheless, if we are to focus on the delivery of care and poor relief we must be mindful of the canonical or statutory authorities that require, permit, or constrain that delivery. In addition, we must be mindful of the influence of the theological, philosophical, and social realities that inform that authority. Any consideration of social care and social work, then, must be multidisciplinary and sensitive to the many contexts in which they are practised.

Much scholarship on the history of what we now call social work has been segregated into various disciplines such as history, economics, religion, philosophy, political science, sociology, and social anthropology, as well as the social work literature. While there have been many volumes that integrate contemporary understandings of international social work, there have been very few that interrogate the received notions of the origins of what we now call social work. The purpose of this book is to explore and interrogate these different histories and origin stories so as to create a clearer understanding of the state of social work today, and thereby establish a basis for a global future of social work. This book is not intended as a collection of histories of individuals, religions, or social movements – that work has been done at length in other places (see for instance Bowpitt, 1998; Handel, 2009; Day and Schiele, 2013, Bamford and Bilton, 2020, and any of the resources cited throughout this book). Nor is it an attempt to trace the various national histories of social work; such an undertaking would be encyclopaedic. Although I write in English, I will critique Anglophone and liberal humanist understandings of social work, for the future of social work, I believe, lies outside that epistemological framework. Nevertheless, a central contention of this exploration is that contemporary social work is rooted in the religious traditions of Europe and particularly Great Britain and North America (which form what we may term the North Atlantic axis), and from there exported by various means and motivations to the different national and cultural contexts in which we know it today. I call this a contention because this argument is unlikely to be well received by avowedly secular practitioners of social work today; and certainly, many contemporary social work contexts are non-religious, or even anti-religious. At the same time, I acknowledge that many social workers and students of social work are motivated by their religious and spiritual beliefs. But, I shall argue, to ignore the religious history of social work is to ignore the rich traditions of thought and motivations to care for the poor, the vulnerabilised, and the marginalised, which remain at the core of contemporary social work. It would also be to ignore the ways that these texts and traditions continue to influence contemporary social policy and social work in less obvious ways, and how social workers uncritically reproduce them. As Tierney (1959) writes, these roots are ancient:

> [T]he occasional fragments of secular legislation that one comes upon in the medieval period, insofar as they related to the relief of poverty and not to the suppression of vagrancy, were almost invariably mere reënactments of principles drawn from the [church's] canonistic works which contained the main body of medieval law in the field. In studying these works, therefore, we are exploring not only the prehistory of modern ecclesiastical charities but also the prehistory of modern public relief. (pp 5–6)

I shall develop this idea further in Chapter 3.

It is these Western religious roots that eventually led to Protestantism, the Enlightenment, and the rise of humanism and individualism, and created fundamental contemporary tensions with South and East Asian, Islamic, African, and other relational cultures, including indigenous cultures around the world. We are in an era where deconstructing the impact of colonialism, capitalism, and neoliberalism has become not only fashionable but necessary. The philosophical assumptions and values that underpin contemporary social work undeniably lie along the North Atlantic axis, and if we are to consider social work as a truly global discipline and profession then we must identify and critique these roots in order to allow and encourage the discipline to make choices about what it wishes to retain and what it wishes to change. What I am foreshadowing here, of course, is that social work as it is known and practised in liberal humanist nations may wish to – or need to – evolve. By allowing a more transparent critique of social work knowledge we may begin to navigate among these often-competing philosophical assumptions and values and create a global discipline and profession which addresses 'life challenges and enhances wellbeing', as the 2014 *Global Definition* says, using local vernaculars and epistemologies. At the same time, we can recognise that what the challenges are and the ways they are addressed, and the very notion of wellbeing, differ considerably in different national, regional, cultural, and relational contexts.

The received wisdom on the relationship between religion and social work is that social care was shaped by the Protestant Reformation, and then gradually became secularised as religious functions were transferred to the state or private charities. Slack (1990) argues that the intellectual roots of changing attitudes towards the poor did not begin only with European Protestantism, as historians once argued, but rather occurred, although in different ways, in Roman Catholic-dominated[3] countries as well. This argument is echoed and explored more thoroughly by Kahl (2009) and will be explored in Chapter 4. Nevertheless, Grell and Cunningham (1997) write that,

> Even if Protestantism and the Reformation cannot lay sole claim to having caused the reforms of poor relief and health care which occurred in the sixteenth and seventeenth centuries in Protestant Western Europe, the speed and thoroughness with which they were undertaken would not have been imaginable without the theological rationale which the Protestant reforms gave to these reforms. (p 3)

The so-called Elizabethan Poor Law of 1601 was not unique but was one in a series of British Poor Laws and one among many national poor laws and localised regulations that occurred in England and throughout Europe in a long tradition that stretches back to the Middle Ages. Slack reminds us of the elitist (and feudal) assumptions behind these laws, when 'poor' meant not simply those who were destitute but anyone who had to work for a living. Nor was Enlightenment humanism (Chapter 5) the exclusive motivation for these developments, although it was both directly and indirectly very important. The rise of Christian Evangelicalism in Britain, with its Calvinist and Arminian roots, was an essential element of the social response to extensive urban poverty in the late 18th and 19th centuries (Bowpitt, 1998). It was this Evangelical response which was exported to the US, and eventually, through colonisation and mercantilism, into social policies around the world. These distant religious roots make social work an

---

[3] Throughout this book I shall use 'Catholic' to refer to the Christian church prior to the Reformation, and 'Roman Catholic' to refer to that branch of Christendom during and after the Reformation.

uneasy fit in contemporary Asian, African, Islamic and indigenous contexts around the world whose social histories are very different. Nevertheless, these historical roots have shaped modern social work in the present and will continue to do so in both explicit and implicit ways as long as they are uncritically assumed. Critiquing these assumptions is a critical challenge of 21st-century social work.

The second oldest profession?

The name Andreas Hyperius may not be a familiar one to 21st-century social workers, but this professor of theology in Marburg, Germany, wrote a poor relief tract called *De publica in pauperes beneficentia* (published posthumously in 1570) advocating for shared responsibility for relief of the poor between the church and local government, and for the appointment of responsible people as overseers to visit the poor to 'assure themselves of their need and whether or not they needed further assistance such as medical care' (Grell and Cunningham, 1997). Hyperius's tract appears to have been inspired by the poor relief order introduced in Ypres/Ieper in 1525. Although we must be very cautious about imposing modernist constructions of social work onto history, we might identify Hyperius as one of the first advocates for assessment as we would recognise it in contemporary social work, arguably pushing the origins of contemporary social work back by some 350 years. We could conceivably push this history back even further to the Stele of Hammurabi, dating from the 18th century BCE, which established guidance in the Babylonian Empire on how the vulnerable persons were to be cared for (Day and Schiele, 2013). Subsequent Judaeo-Christian religious scriptures make many specific references to care for the poor (Chapter 2), and designated specific persons to provide that care. Tierney (1959) writes that medieval poor law required that bishops ensure that poor relief was available and administered by parish priests and almoners (distributors of alms) who knew the recipients of relief, their families, and situations intimately (Chapter 3). By becoming critically aware of our roots, social workers will be better positioned to strengthen the discipline of social work and make decisions about what we want social work to look like in an increasingly global future.

This book is appropriate now for several reasons. Firstly, social work is becoming increasingly global; indeed there has been an explosion of interest in social work in East and South Asia, and even in Islamic countries such as Indonesia and Bangladesh, although contemporary European frameworks of social work limit its development and acceptance in Islamic nations (Ragab, 2016). Many post-colonial African nations have retained the values of colonial religion and even surpassed their former colonisers in numbers and enthusiasm for those religions: the Anglican Communion (Church of

England), for instance, became majority Black African earlier this century (Pew Research Center, 2008; Goodhew, 2018). Black Africans have adopted and transformed the religion of their former colonisers and slave traders. The indigenisation of social work, however, has met with challenges including a lack of indigenous teaching materials and resources (Mupedziswa and Sinkamba, 2014). Latin American social workers undertook a far-reaching self-examination in the 1960s and adopted a critical perspective on capitalism based on a Marxist analysis which sought to transform social structures, critically analyse social work's daily practices, and question 'its servile disposition towards dominant social structures' (Muñoz-Guzmán et al, 2014). In the People's Republic of China, social work education programmes increased from 20 in 1994 to 150 by 2005 (Chi, 2005), more than a seven-fold increase in just nine years. Social work is increasingly aware of the need, and its professional responsibility, to define itself and develop practice models in a global context, as we have seen in the 2014 *Global Definition* and the 2018 *Global Social Work Statement of Ethical Principles* (International Association of Schools of Social Work and International Federation of Social Workers, 2018), but simply putting a linguistic varnish onto a fundamentally liberal humanist structure is insufficient to earn global acceptance or even to be relevant in non-Western contexts. Secondly, the challenges of transnational migrants and refugees on every continent and throughout most oceans presents an accumulating challenge to nations and international organisations. This challenge is particularly acute for social work, which seeks to respect human dignity and promote social justice. These social challenges have arisen before, and we can learn from our history both how to respond and how not to respond. Thirdly, increasing critiques of capitalism and its bastard child neoliberalism now demand that we develop alternative and thoughtful economic and social policy models and ways to address poverty and injustice at international, national, and local levels. In its *Global Definition*, social work has set itself the responsibility to prevent and ameliorate poverty and to enhance wellbeing. This is an enormous and compelling task, and one which requires careful reflection on what has happened in the past so that we can create a more equitable future.

The social imaginary

One of the inspirations for this book is the work of the Canadian philosopher Charles Taylor.[4] In his major work *A Secular Age* (2007), Taylor exhaustively

---

[4] I take up any summary of Taylor's extensive work with some trepidation and acknowledge that any such attempt will inevitably be incomplete. I have focused here on what I believe are the key elements that relate to the topic of this book and not to all of Taylor's undertaking.

considers what we mean by secularity. He argues that secularism is not merely the absence of religion but rather an entirely different epistemological framework that needs to be critiqued and understood in a historical context. His question is how the West moved from a culture where it was unthinkable not to believe in God to one where belief in God is one option among many, or even where non-belief is 'inescapable' (p 25). The commonly accepted view (which Taylor calls the 'subtraction' view of modernity) is that this shift was due to the Enlightenment and the rise of Darwinism, positivist science, and reason, over the numinous, sacramental, mysterious, and enchanted. This movement gave rise to the 'buffered' self, a modern self, which is, or attempts to be, impervious to external numinous forces; this in turn presumably leads to greater individual freedom to live in a disenchanted world. However, Taylor (2007) proposes that this subtraction view is inadequate, that 'the in fact very exigent demands of universal justice and benevolence which characterize modern humanism can't be explained just by the subtraction of earlier goals and allegiances' (p 572). He suggests that while early social and political structures such as feudalism were vertical, with elites as the top supported by the labour of the poor at the bottom, and only God above the monarch, a change in our social imaginary (the set of values, beliefs, laws, institutions and symbols which shape the way we think of, or imagine, our society) began from about 1400, and this change resulted in a more horizontal understanding of societies. This change required that political (monarchs and lords) and religious (monks, priests, and bishops) elites reconceptualised what a civilised country was: in particular, it required new and increasingly secular ways to ensure social order. We will also see that this reconceptualisation of social order had to do with responding to the crisis of social disorder brought about by the Great Plague (the bubonic plague of 1347–53 which killed between 30 per cent and 60 per cent of the population of Europe), the subsequent dissolution of feudalism, population movements, and the crisis of labour. Later, under the influence of religious reformers, particularly the Calvinists and their offshoots, each person was now responsible for living an ordered, civilised life. This expectation in turn required that elites increase their control over a number of segments of society, including (and perhaps especially) the poor; indeed, elites secured and maintained their position through social control. Taylor (2007) writes:

> But what is remarkable is how, gathering pace in the sixteenth century in the wake of the Reforms [sic], and then continuing at higher intensities, attempts are undertaken to make over the lower orders. They are precisely not left as they are, but badgered, bullied, pushed, preached at, drilled, and organized to abandon their lax and disordered folkways and conform to one or another feature of civil behaviour. (p 102)

Secular poor laws, which had emerged following the Great Plague and which regulated almost all aspects of the lives of the poor, were increasingly tightened and punitive. In this way, poverty was no longer a threat to order, and thus to civilisation, according to Taylor's construction of events: 'And by the end of this process we enter a world, ours, where everyone among us is supposed to be "civilized"' (p 102). In fact, Taylor himself suggests that the poor laws were a signal example of the imposition of order on an unruly world: conditions of relief for the indigent were strictly defined, begging forbidden or severely restricted, and vagabondage outlawed. In England, for instance, this urgency for social stability led to the curtailment of movement of individuals from one parish to another (brought about by people seeking work after the Great Plague) and the establishment of residency as a requirement in secular law for obtaining assistance. Civility and religious reform (whether Protestant or Roman Catholic) were seamlessly combined in practice, and the fruit of religious conversion was an ordered life, which contributed to civility and social stability. It is here that the break with the feudal elite was completed: no longer were only the elites expected to live up to the demands of the Christian gospel, but this expectation extended to all faithful people.

In the 16th century, there was also a reconceptualisation of the poor. During the feudal era, elites did not have contempt for the destitute and the powerless but rather saw them as an opportunity for sanctification or personal holiness. As Taylor notes, 'Following the discourse of Matthew 25, to help a person in need was to help Christ' (p 108). We will see that this salvific opportunism has much earlier origins in the 4th century. As a result of the Great Plague of the 14th century, attempts to control population movements, crop failures, labour shortages, and an eventual rise in population, a new attitude toward the poor emerged among the elites. It is here that more punitive poor laws emerged which built on medieval distinctions between the deserving and undeserving poor. The deserving poor, who were incapable of work (the so-called impotent poor), were more tightly controlled, often in indoor relief (workhouse) environments. The undeserving poor were either put to work (provided by secular authorities through parishes) or if they would not work, punished. It is these poor laws that largely remained in place, with various adjustments, for the next 300 years. We will consider this in more detail in Chapter 4.

The emergence of helping

It is the increasingly horizontal society and the accompanying drive to civility which problematised poverty and vulnerability (rather than simply accepting these things as realities or opportunities for sanctification, as happened in previous millennia) and led to the emergence of social work in the 20th century as a distinct role with the dual functions of seeking to enable all individuals to become full participants in their cultures and societies, and at the same time bearing responsibility for controlling the poor and vulnerable so as to maintain social order. Both of these roles were inherited from the religious establishments of the time, which, as we will see, very much influenced the social construction of the poor and destitute and the polity of their states and eras.

The shift to a more horizontal social imaginary led to increased democratisation, increased expectations of citizenship, and an expectation that each person live a holy life. A notionally horizontal society gives rise to the belief that each person is responsible for their own salvation and that each person should have access to sufficient education to read and understand scripture, participate in prayers (thus the publication of vernacular Bibles and liturgy), and to understand what a righteous life is so that they can live it. A horizontal society also requires that elites rethink the role of poverty and the poor in their societies. If the purpose of each order of society was no longer to support the one above it (eg, poor and landless villeins or peasants support the smaller landowners or vassals, the vassals the nobles, and the nobles the monarch, who is answerable only to God), then how should societies be structured? If divine right is challenged, if *Magna Carta* puts limits on the power of the monarch, and the structure of societies is no longer ordained by God, then the entire social structure must be reconsidered. This reconsideration began to emerge with the early Reformation and 18th and 19th century clergy and thinkers such as the Wesleys, Wilberforce, and Bosanquet, and which social reformers such as Booth, Octavia Hill, the Barnetts, the Webbs, Jane Addams, and Mary Richmond (among many others) addressed in their own ways, and which we shall consider in Chapter 6. Social reformers of the 19th century debated whether the cause of poverty – which only gradually became understood as a problem in itself, rather than as a problem of civil order – lay with the morality of the individual, or with oppressive environments, which included avaricious and callous landlords and employers, and controlling, later punitive, public policies such as poor laws. These poor laws throughout Europe and the US had their roots in various Reformation understandings of morality and poverty, and in both the developed and impoverished West, the residue of these religion-influenced poor laws effectively remains to this day.

The dual functions of charitable or philanthropic work – helping to alleviate genuine suffering while at the same time maintaining social order – remain threaded throughout the history of social work. These dual functions are in tension, and that tension will not sit comfortably with many 21st century Western social workers who would like to see themselves as emancipators and empowerers. Yet when we consider the many roles that social workers fill, including statutory eligibility workers, child protection workers, forensic social workers, mental health workers, community organisers, and community advocates, we find those lived tensions. If one of the challenges to social work is whether it is a profession or not, then the answer to that question may lie in how we conceptualise the social control function of social work. Is the role of a social worker merely to be a gatekeeper to a collection of resources, working to a regulatory regime, to be regulated by, and be an agent of a state charged with the responsibility of maintaining social order? Is the role of a social worker to create a working relationship with a client, to undertake a skilled, theory-based collaborative assessment, or to develop a plan and to help the client implement that plan as an act of personal liberation? Our decision about professionalism may rely on how we answer those questions.

The struggle between vertical and horizontal understandings of societies remains today. Although medieval feudalism has been replaced by capitalism (in some form) in most of the world, the assumption that the poorer orders of society exist largely to support the wealthier ones, and that the new elites (at this time of writing found mostly in the financial, technological, and extraction industries) deserve the rewards they extract from the labour of the poor is a familiar one. The notion that through right living, sacrifice, and hard work one can rise from poverty to privilege is also a familiar one. But these quasi-religious beliefs only hold when societies are truly horizontal, truly meritocratic, and truly equitable, and where every person has equal access to resources (such as clean water and sufficient food, adequate housing, education, a just and non-violent political environment free from corruption, and a stable climate). The awful truth is that such environments are rare in the 21st century if indeed they exist at all. Social work, then, must turn its attention from addressing the problems of responding to poverty to addressing the problem of wealth and privilege. In doing this, social work will be returning to its 4th-century roots, where it was not poverty that was theologised as a problem but rather wealth. It was only after the Reformation that wealth was re-theologised as a sign of divine favour and therefore no longer a problem.

Social work as a discipline and occupation has now encountered cultures, worldviews, and epistemologies quite different from its Western origins. Liberal humanism is alien to Islamic philosophy and theology; Islam dominates in some 45 countries in the world and has a significant presence in many others. Social work educators and field supervisors in North Atlantic and post-colonial states cannot continue to teach social work values, ethics, and methods as they always have, and expect Muslim students to 'catch up', or to abandon deeply held personal worldviews, values, and beliefs in order to join a liberal humanist social work endeavour. Likewise, in nations and cultures where Confucian, Hindu, Buddhist, African, or indigenous epistemologies dominate, social work must be prepared not merely to be respectful of diversity, or even to find common ground, but be willing to transform so that as a discipline we do not simply reproduce North Atlantic and liberal humanist values. Western social work actively encourages the transformation of our curricula, values, ethics, and methods. That will take work. Deeply held traditions and beliefs must be unearthed, examined, critiqued, and reformed. If we expect social work to be a truly global discipline and profession, that is the way forward. Otherwise, social work will simply continue to reproduce ancient Judaeo-Christian religious values and liberal humanist worldviews. Maintaining those values is, of course, an option, and one about which the international associations of practitioners and educators will need to make decisions, but if we wish to create a meaningful international discipline, then we must change our ways of thinking and our practice. We cannot change our past, but we can create the future. That decision is the challenge I will explore in the final chapter.

What qualifies me to undertake this project? That's a fair question. In short, my interest in developing this book comes from my own background and professional experiences. My first profession was as an Episcopal (Anglican) priest. When my then-bishop was quite clear that I would never work in the church as an openly gay man, I searched for a future I had not anticipated. Early in the HIV epidemic in the northeast US, I began to work as an HIV counsellor and soon found myself developing a prevention and education programme for which nothing could have prepared me. Most of the people who were affected by HIV in the city where I lived were poor; many were also injection drug users who had tried drug treatment (most many times), but it had failed them. I looked for a comprehensive discipline that could help me theorise and develop interventions for these communities and I discovered social work. It was love at first sight, and I pursued academic degrees and a career in social work for the next 35 years. After I left HIV work in the early 2000s, I began working as a university lecturer in Aotearoa New Zealand, where both my parents were born and where I had roots reaching back 150 years. As an academic, I had an opportunity to participate in national, Asia-Pacific regional and international social work organisations. I was impressed by the many different ways social work was taught and practised around the world. I was privileged to participate in the task forces that revised the joint *Global Definition of Social Work* in 2014, and the 2018 *Global Social Work Statement of Ethical Principles*. In helping to create these two documents, I engaged with extraordinarily talented colleagues from a wide array of languages, religions, and cultures around the world. My theological background in this context provided me with a unique lens to try to understand and reconcile the many differences, perspectives, and challenges we faced. In my academic role, I also have had the opportunity to supervise research students from a wide array of cultures and countries, including Buddhist and Muslim social work research students trying to make sense out of Western social work. I am grateful to them for teaching me. All of those experiences together have led me to try to make sense out of what I have seen and lived in order to contribute to a global future for a discipline I love.

Legitimate criticism of this study may well be to ask, why, if I am advocating a decolonised, internationalised, and global approach to social work, I have chosen to focus so much on the evolution of the discipline and profession in Britain and the North Atlantic. The reason is found in Younghusband: social work did first emerge as a distinct occupation in the slums of East London – that is where the term was first used. For better or for worse the religious, political, and philosophical contexts that created British social work as a way of addressing the excruciating poverty exacerbated by the 1834 Poor Law were exported throughout the world by British colonialism, missionisation, mercantilism, and slave trading. Love it or hate it, British social work history is what most social work in the world has adopted, evolved from, or is reacting against. If we understand the implicit values, philosophies, and theologies that created that occupation, then we will be in a far better position to reassess those implicit drivers and make decisions about whether we need to retain or reform them. This book does not attempt to be comprehensive but to set out a critical model, and I hope there will be other work and theorising that grow out of responses to it. By engaging in a radical – that is, from the roots – critique, I hope it will encourage such future work.

The scope set out in this book is nothing less than how human beings have addressed inequalities and vulnerabilised persons throughout human history, and as such is, as a colleague phrased it, like writing the history of the universe. As you read, you may find yourself agreeing with Hamlet that there are more things in heaven and earth than are dreamt of by our philosophy. That is one of the exciting things about social work as a discipline. By focusing on my argument – that 21st-century social work remains significantly informed by its religious history, and that in order to create a truly global discipline in the future we must be aware of and critique that history – I hope to be able to maintain the boundaries of this exploration. As we critically consider where social work has come from we can ponder, choose, and create a global future.

2

A royal responsibility

A central contention of this book is that the foundational philosophy and practice of social work as we currently know it has been highly influenced by the history, theology, and epistemology of the Christian West, and more specifically of the North Atlantic axis. The profound influence of Christianity in the West and on secular humanism is explored more broadly in Tom Holland's 2019 work *Dominion: How the Christian revolution remade the world*. Holland writes that even the notion of *secular* which first appeared in the English press in 1846 (or the French notion of *laïcité*, which predated the use of secular by four years), is an attempt to be *not religious* and therefore neutral, but which instead, Holland writes, trailed 'incense clouds of meaning that were irrevocably and venerably Christian' (p 427). The notion of secularity (or *laïcité*) is not, therefore, neutral or value-free, he argues; it presupposes religion in order to define itself.

In order to explore this argument in the areas of social work and social justice, we will need to begin with some understanding of the key texts which shaped Christian religious responses to the poor, and the contexts in which those texts were developed. There is a saying among theological students that 'text without context is pretext', meaning that it is necessary to understand the historical, social, and political context of the writing before we can really understand what the authors intended to say. Disagreements about that principle have led to the remarkable diversity of interpretations of biblical texts throughout history. The approach I take here is that we do not take biblical texts literally, but we do take them seriously. The language of metaphor and legend is powerful and need not, and perhaps should not be taken literally to understand meanings. Taking texts seriously means understanding as well as we can from this distance the many influences, documented and undocumented values, and expectations that shaped oral traditions, which became written traditions, which in turn were selected, compiled, and edited over many centuries to create a significant and influential body of texts now called the Bible.

Biblical texts are not always consistent with each other. The selection of traditions and texts and calling them the 'word of God' was itself a political and social process, a product of moments of time, what Whitehead might call the concrescence of occasions, over many centuries. One obvious example of this is the biblical stories about creation in the book of Genesis. (I'm not going to specify which version of the Bible you should use if you choose to follow along, as long as the version you use is from the last 100 years or so. That means the King James version, dating from 1611, is out. God does not write or speak in 17th century English any more than we write or speak today in the English of Shakespeare.) In Genesis 1:1–2:4a, God, called Elohim, creates the world in six days, then rests on the seventh. In Genesis 2:2b–24 God, called YHWH, creates the world and humanity in just a couple of days. These two traditions came from different ancient Near Eastern sources, and it is very difficult to reconcile them with each other; but the point, the meaning, for both creation stories that appear in Genesis is that the world owes its existence to a single creator. This idea will recur in other stories in Genesis (such as the Flood), and, as we shall see, throughout much of the First Testament.

Identifying and exegeting all the texts that are relevant to our story in their ancient languages and understanding their contexts would be a massive task, one which would require an introduction to the history and cultures of the ancient Near East, hermeneutics, biblical criticism, and the peripatetic history of the ancient people known as the Hebrews. We would then need to trace the development of Israelite philosophy and theology known as the First or Old Testament over two millennia through the development of the collection of codification of Christian scriptures, or the New Testament. This work has already been done by biblical scholars of many different persuasions. Reproducing that work in detail here might try your patience and would delay us from getting on with the present task. I also write with the awareness that the history of social welfare has been extensively set out by Day and Schiele (2013) and by others, and these well-researched histories are most useful. What I will do here is to identify the key features and examples which illustrate the case I am making, and encourage you to explore on your own.

Ancient Near Eastern texts

Our story begins, then, many thousands of years ago in the ancient Near East, in Mesopotamia (literally, the 'land between the two rivers', the Tigris and Euphrates) in what has been called the cradle of civilisation,[1] or the Fertile Crescent. Civilisations, empires, and dynasties in this region began to emerge and consolidate about 6,500 years ago, beginning in the 4th

---

[1] The notion of the Near East, of course, implies that it is east of some basic reference point; the term seems to have emerged in Europe to locate the Ottoman Empire in the 19th century and describe that part of Asia closest to Europe. I will use the terms Near East and Ancient Near East reluctantly, aware of their Eurocentric orientation but because it is likely that they will be familiar to the most readers.

millennium (4500–4000 BCE). These empires emerged, conquered, and were in turn conquered during what we now call the Copper, Bronze, Iron, and Classical Ages. The great empires such as the Phoenician, Sumerian, Akkadian, Assyrian, Babylonian, Hittite, Persian, the Seleucid and Macedonian, and finally the Roman and Ottoman helped to shape what we know today as the modern Middle East, and by extension Egypt and northern Africa, western Asia, and eastern Europe. The influences of the cultures, customs, traditions, and laws of these ancient peoples live on today not only in our history books but in our literature, laws, and, sadly, in modern border disputes. In order to think about these ancient civilisations, we need to put aside contemporary notions of what we think is appropriate social equality, gender rights, slavery, and social class. In pre-modern times, power belonged to the strong. The elites (nobles and warriors) who had power ate, flourished, and conquered others; those who did not have power (such as slaves) fed the powerful, sometimes fed themselves, and relied on the powerful to protect (and feed) them.

In a life that often depended on sheer muscle power for farming, trades, or warfare, orphan children who had no family to care for them and solo widows were the most vulnerable in their societies. Girls and women were protected (or controlled) by their fathers until they married, at which time they were put under the protection (or control) of their husbands; widows lost the protection of their husbands' families. Widows had the right to inherit in some but not all of these cultures, and some widows, of course, didn't have much to inherit. A widow could remarry, at which point, of course, she ceased being a widow and entered the protection of her new husband. Polygamy and concubinage were common in the region, although some ancient Near Eastern cultures, like Babylon, as we know from the Code of Hammurabi (ca. 1754 BCE), were primarily monogamous (Mendelsohn, 1948). In order to protect widows, some cultures had a custom of levirate marriage or the (re)marriage of widows to the husband's brother. In some cultures, levirate marriage was expected; in some cultures it was optional; others, like the Sumerians, prohibited it. (Levirate marriage of widows became obligatory for brothers-in-law and childless widows in Hebrew culture, as we read in Deuteronomy 25:5–10, and later became an issue of law for the Sadducee sect of Judaism in Jesus as we read in Matthew 22: 23–33, paralleled in Luke 20:27–40). There was also something called a sororate marriage, where a widower was expected to marry his deceased wife's sister, of which there is evidence from the Persian era (Stol, 2016). The apparent purpose behind levirate marriage was not (necessarily) to oppress and control women (although their property and dowry might well pass into the new husband's control) but to ensure that they were protected. Both levirate and sororate marriages would have ensured that the husband's name and property were passed down to his children, but they seem to be a part of codified social protection.

What the orphan, the widow, and other poor (slaves were property and had no rights) had in common was their precarious social status and their impotence to maintain their rights. It became possible for others to oppress them – by taking them into slavery to pay off debts, for instance – or to take advantage of them, for example, by insisting on exorbitant interest on loans (Gowan, 1987). Furthermore, becoming an orphan or widow was an involuntary status: it was something over which they had no control. A family which comprised a widow and her children, or an orphan with no family, would find it difficult or impossible to survive independently. The problem, of course, was power – or the lack of power.

> The worst problem, that which these groups have in common, is powerlessness and its consequences: lack of status, lack of respect, making one an easy mark for the powerful and unscrupulous, so that those who are not poor are likely to become poor and those who are poor are going to get poorer. (Gowan, 1987, p 344)

And if you were poor you didn't eat; perhaps you sold yourself into slavery in order to survive.

Protection of the orphan, the widow, and the poor came to be seen as a desirable virtue of gods, kings, and judges – in other words, it was a virtue of elites who were powerful enough to ensure that protection was offered. Protection of these vulnerable groups was an apodictic policy of ancient Near Eastern cultures (Fensham, 1962); the idea was so commonplace that it was unwritten but understood by everyone, although it had no specific enforcement attached to it. It became a virtue of which the powerful could boast. Over time in the literature, laws and customs of some of these ancient Near Eastern civilisations (perhaps most of them – we can't really know) the obligation to care for the orphan, the widow, and the poor was codified, and the key person responsible was the most powerful: the king (and they appear mostly to have been kings). Whether or not this principle was meant to be a kind of check on royal power (so that the king did not take advantage of the powerless) or a moral obligation (that the powerful protect the powerless) is not clear. Kings boasted of their virtue in protecting the powerless, perhaps because it demonstrated how powerful they were, or it demonstrated their righteousness before the gods. There were indeed divine consequences for a king who neglected this virtue.

> Great Mesopotamian kings like Urukagina, Ur-Nammu and Hammurapi [Hammurabi] boast in their legal inscriptions that they have accomplished this principle. Success was not possible if this

principle was not carried through. In bad times, in times of decay, the protection of widow, orphan, and the poor was neglected. Widows, orphans, and the poor were sold as credit-slaves and kept in a state of slavery for a lifetime. To obliterate this abuse, laws and also religious pressure were used as compulsory methods to protect the rights of this group. (Fensham, 1962, p 129)

Protecting the most vulnerable people was a royal responsibility, and it was to the gods, represented by religious authorities, that the royal was responsible. The principle was eventually quite literally carved in stone. The oldest written representations of the obligation to protect the orphan, the widow, and the poor appears to be from the law codes of Urukagina of Lagash (in modern-day Iraq), dating from about 2400 BCE, and of Ur-Nammu in the 21st century BCE (Patterson, 1973). In the Ur-Nammu code, we find praise for justice: 'The orphan was not delivered up to the rich man, the widow was not delivered up to the mighty man; the man of one shekel was not delivered up to the man of one mina' (Pritchard, cited in Lohfink, 1991, p 35).

The later but better-known Code of Hammurabi, King of Babylon (ca. 1754 BCE), which seems very similar to Sumerian codes of 200 years earlier, also makes it clear that the king was responsible for ensuring that the strong did not oppress the weak. The Code of Hammurabi states that the king shares that responsibility with the sun-god Shamash. From at least the 2nd millennium BCE, then, the protection of the orphan, widow, and poor belonged to the realms of the state (in the person of the king) and of the divine. In the Prologue to the Code, Hammurabi states his purpose:

> To make justice appear/in the land
> > To destroy the evil and wicked
> (and so that)/The strong might not oppress the weak

And in the Epilogue the Code recapitulates,

> So that the strong might not oppress/The weak (and so as)
> > To give justice to the orphaned/(homeless girl) and to
> the widow.
> > > (Patterson, 1973; see also Lohfink, 1991, p 36)

However, there is a notable omission in the Code: while the Prologue and Epilogue to the Code of Hammurabi seem committed to preventing the oppression of the poor, there are no laws within the Code itself that protect the oppressed (Lohfink, 1991); there appears to be a discrepancy or a hole within the Code itself. This suggests one of several possibilities: that the Code was strong on theory but not so much on practice; that there was no need to specify the practices since they were familiar; that the practices were too varied to be specified; or that protection was a right reserved for the king.

The obligation to protect the orphan, the widow, and the poor are echoed in other ancient Near Eastern civilisations. In Egypt during Dynasty XII (generally combined with Dynasties XI to XV and is considered to extend from 1991 to 1802 BCE) it was the pharaoh and (again) the sun-god who were responsible for protecting the orphan, widow, and poor; the good pharaoh boasted of being a good protector; indeed, an Egyptian tomb inscription reads 'I gave bread to the hungry, water to the thirsty, clothing to the naked, and a passage to those who had no ship' (cited in Lohfink, 1991, p 34). In the Canaanite Tale of Aqhat, there is a passing mention of Daniel, a Rapha-man (possibly a giant) who is 'upright, sitting before the gate beneath a mighty tree on the threshing floor, judging the cause of the widow, adjudicating the case of the fatherless' (Pritchard, 1969, p 151). The tale was dictated by Attani-puruleni, one of the chief priests in Ugarit in the second quarter of the 14th century BCE, suggesting that the story was current among the class or people responsible for maintaining good relationships with the gods.

All of these ancient Near Eastern texts attest that the justice for the orphan, the widow, and the poor – that is, the most vulnerable and powerless in their cultures – was the specific responsibility of the ruler and the gods and that this responsibility extends back at least to the 4th millennium BCE, in many, if not most, of these cultures. Using today's language, we can conclude that there was something like an ethos of social protection throughout much of the ancient Near East, at least for the involuntary poor, although since we have only one side of the story we do not know how this ethos was actually put into practice. I don't want to get too far ahead of ourselves, but isn't it interesting that most of contemporary social work still attends to fatherless children, women (particularly solo women), and the poor? As much as we would like to think about how far we have come in 6,500 years, we still seem to be working with the same problems.

Hebrew scriptures

The Israelite kingdoms of Judah and Israel were not included in the list of civilisations identified earlier because they form something of a special case in our story, although it may seem as though there is very little on the topic of the orphan, the widow, and the poor that is not found in other ancient Near Eastern sources. These kingdoms were relatively minor ones in the complex history of the ancient Near East, but they turned out to be possibly the most enduring because the inhabitants of these kingdoms – including their prophets, priests, poets, and kings – produced literature that continues to influence many cultures today. The literature of ancient Israel, its Law (Torah), Prophets (Nevi'im) and Writings (Ketuvim), known collectively as the Tanakh, or to Christians as the Old or First Testament, has had an extraordinary influence on Western culture, religious and secular traditions, and values. Jews, Christians, and Muslims all trace at least their spiritual history to the patriarch Abram, later known as Abraham (Gen. 17:5) and are therefore known as the Abrahamic religions. In the Qur'an, Abraham (whose name appears as Ibrahim, PBOH) is recognised as a prophet and messenger of God in Islam (Sura 87:19), and parts of his story appear throughout the Qur'an.

The Hebrews (the origin of the name עברים *'apiru* is contested and may be related to a similar word for former slaves or freebooters; it is now generally agreed that this is a social rather than an ethnic designation) were a nomadic people of the ancient Near East who according to the book of Genesis (11:28, 31) originated in the wealthy Chaldean city of Ur (modern-day Tell el-Muqayyar, not far from Nasiriyah in Iraq). If you cannot locate Ur in your mind, that's fine – go Google it now. I'll wait. It is impossible to date the Hebrew origin story, or the events, stories, and legends described within it, with any accuracy, but although the events it describes are ancient, the biblical narrative that tells that story was likely composed much later, sometime during the 6th century BCE, a critical time in the history of the Hebrews when they were exiled in Babylon from their adopted homeland in Canaan. In Genesis, Abram is described as a nomad who was called by his God to journey from Ur through Canaan, then down through the Negev to Egypt, back to the Negev, and eventually settling as a sojourner in Canaan. Canaan, roughly contiguous with modern-day Palestine and Israel, was located at the southern edge of the territory ruled by the Hittites and happened to be already occupied by the Canaanites, Perizzites, and some other tribes. In Genesis 17 we read that when Abram was 99 years old, his God (named El Shaddai, the One of the Mountains) made a covenant with him that he would be the father of many nations, and changed Abram's name to Abraham. The key feature here is that Abraham was a stranger, a sojourner, a temporary dweller, a guest, or an alien (Brown et al, 1976); translations vary, so we'll use the Hebrew, גר, *ger*, from now on, with the intention that it includes all of those meanings) with no inherited rights wherever he went. Abraham was even a *ger* in the land where he finally settled in Canaan, with permission of the inhabitants, a point which becomes important. Abraham had a complex history of marriages and concubines, a son Ishmael from his slave-girl Hagar (who played a key part in the history of Islam, as we read in the *Hadith*), and a son Isaac from his wife Sarah (who was also his stepsister). He also had six more children from his later wife Keturah, and there seem to have been other concubines (Gen. 25:1–6). We are told that Abraham died at the ripe old age of 175 (Gen. 25:7), having become a father of many long past an age when most people would be looking for a quiet retirement.

The story of the Hebrews is that of a people who sojourn often, usually at the call or direction of their God who is known by various names, depending on the source of the story. (The name Israel comes from Jacob's encounter with God in Genesis 32:28, where Jacob is renamed Israel, meaning 'One who strives with God'; Israelites are the descendants of Jacob/Israel's 12 children by various mothers.) At one point, because of a famine in Canaan (where Abraham had settled), the central characters of the Genesis story find themselves in Egypt (Gen. 47:27ff) and are permitted to settle there, in Goshen, by the pharaoh. However, they did so well in Egypt that the Egyptians became resentful. The new pharaoh was fearful that the Hebrews would join with Egypt's enemies and fight against Egypt, so he sent them to work as forced labourers and eventually as slaves (Exod. 1:8). A leader named Moses emerged to lead the Hebrews out of slavery into a land that would be their own. However, the Hebrews ended up wandering around the desert for 40 years (during which time God, named in this story as YHWH, made a new covenant with Moses, and the Ten Commandments were a seal of that covenant). Finally, around 1250 BCE, the peripatetic people arriving at the Jordan River (Josh. 1) took over the land of Canaan and settled in it for the next 500 years or so. Various forms of government and structures of faith developed. The Hebrews, who divided into two kingdoms, Israel in the north and Judah in the south, were eventually conquered by the powerful empires that surrounded them, first the Assyrians in 721 BCE, who took the citizens of the northern kingdom away into exile; then the Babylonians, who removed the Judeans into exile beginning in 597 BCE. It is thought that much of the First Testament that we have received was written in Babylon so that the people would not forget where they had come from or how to worship their God. After 70 years or so, Babylon itself was conquered by Cyrus the Great of Persia. Cyrus, perceived and portrayed in the prophetic literature as a messianic figure, allowed the Judeans to return to Judah under Persian supervision. The prediction of the falls of Israel and Judah, the exile and return of the Israelites are the focus of the prophetic writings (particularly Isaiah and Jeremiah) in the First Testament. The minor prophets address the later history of the Israelites: Palestine was conquered by Alexander (the Great) in 332 BCE, then in 198 BCE by the Greek Seleucids and, finally, by Rome starting in 63 BCE until 324 CE when Rome fell to Byzantium. (I have tried to summarise a very complex story in a few sentences. You can read the full story by searching the history of Palestine online or, of course, reading about it from the Hebrew point of view in the First Testament.)

Although biblical scholars and historians of the ancient Near East will no doubt be horrified to see the history of Israel reduced to a single paragraph, the point here is that the Hebrews, later Israelites, were a nomadic people, and their nomadic history shaped how they saw and understood the world. Like the patriarch Abraham, whose wanderings very much parallel those of the whole Hebrew people up until the Babylonian exile, the Hebrews were *ger*, rarely in one place for very long, and were accustomed to living as strangers on foreign lands. Even after their return from exile, the people had to cope with living under foreign hegemony, laws, and customs for the next two millennia. In their travels, in their trade, and as conquered people they were exposed, for better or worse, to a wide array of ancient Near Eastern customs, laws, myths, and stories, and ways of telling those stories. They adopted and adapted these foreign customs, laws myths, and stories: as one scholar wrote, 'The Old Testament can now be seen as part of a broader and intricately interrelated cultural milieu whose customs, institutions, and linguistic and literary patterns were shared in large measure throughout the Fertile Crescent' (Patterson, 1973).

However, the Israelites made one major and critical change to these Near Eastern stories: they were monotheistic, and instead of a range or council of local gods and deities, they had only one supreme God, a God who was unattached to place or phenomenon (like the sun or moon). The Israelites believed that they had a unique and particular covenanted relationship with one single God, and that covenant and its obligations shaped the theology and policies of Israel and its relationships with the nations and that surrounded it, and with its poor. While the Hebrew authors of law, prophecy, and writings seem to have adopted the general ancient Near Eastern protections for the orphan, the widow, and the poor (Lohfink, 1991, proposes that Israel inherited the word pair 'widow and orphan' as a symbolic name for all those in need of help), their particular sympathy for the *ger* means that the *ger* was added to the groups who were entitled to special protections.

Despite their prominence and perhaps familiarity, then, Hebrew texts were not the first literature to require justice for the orphan, widow, or the poor. In fact, it is quite likely that the authors and editors of these Hebrew texts were aware of many of the stories, laws, and customs that circulated around the ancient Near East and adapted them for their own use. What they added to the list of the vulnerable was the *ger*, the non-Israelite who had found a home in Israel. These sojourners were dependent on the goodwill of their Israelite hosts because they had no natural ties to the social structure or the land and may have been easily identified because of the customs, manner of dress, and accent. Throughout the Tanakh, the Hebrew scriptures that included law, prophets, and writings, we see reference to protections for the orphan, the widow, the *ger*, and the poor. The following are some key examples from these three sets of writings.

Law

The first five books of the First Testament are known as the Torah, the Law, which set out the origin stories and particular cultic responsibilities that were incumbent on the Hebrews as a people with a covenant relationship with God. In the Torah, we find the story of Abraham, of course, and much of the received history of Israel, as told by at least four sources. Torah (also known as the Pentateuch, the first five books of the First Testament: Genesis, Exodus, Leviticus, Deuteronomy, and Numbers) specifically set out laws, statutes, and ordinances by which the covenant people were meant to live their identity.

The Book of Exodus describes events that probably took place between 1350 and 1200 BCE, although it too was probably written during the Babylonia exile nearly 750 years later. Exodus tells the story of the Hebrews' legendary escape from slavery in Egypt and their 40 years in the desert wilderness. During this journey, they were led by Moses, who received the Ten Commandments on Mount Sinai. In addition to the Ten, there were many additional ordinances (it is generally accepted that there are some 613 which govern almost every aspect of personal and community life), which were a part of the Covenant (in Exodus) and Holiness (in Leviticus) Codes. The words in Exodus are placed in the mouth of YHWH: 'You shall not wrong or oppress a resident alien, for you were aliens in the land of Egypt. You shall not abuse any widow or orphan. If you do abuse them, when they cry out to me I will surely hear their cry' (Exod. 22:21–2).[2]

Caring for the *ger* (here, 'resident alien') would have been important for the Hebrews when they were in Egypt, Hebrews who were settling the already inhabited promised land of Canaan, and as exiled captives in Babylon.

The Book of Leviticus is a kind of priestly guide to worship that sets out the responsibilities of living a holy and obedient life in great detail. Leviticus too was probably developed over a long period and achieved the form with which we are familiar during or shortly after the exile in Babylon. The writers are not merely concerned with the absence of oppression but also of caring for the poor and the *ger*:

> When you reap the harvest of your land you shall not reap to the very edges of your field, or gather the gleanings of your harvest. You shall not strip your vineyard bare, or gather the fallen grapes of your vineyard; you shall leave them for the poor and the alien. (Lev. 19:9–10; see also Deut. 24:19–22)

---

[2] All biblical texts cited are from the New Revised Standard Version (NRSV) unless noted otherwise.

> When an alien resides with you in your land you shall not oppress the alien. The alien who resides with you shall be to you as the citizen among you; you shall love the alien as yourself, for you were aliens in the land of Egypt. (Lev. 19:33–4)

The people are expected to leave part of the harvest for the poor who would follow the harvesters and pick up the gleanings, the remains, of the harvest. This notion of charity was institutionalised in the annual harvest cycle: every seventh year (or the year of remission, or sabbatical year) there was to be no planting; the people were expected to live on the harvest of the sixth year, and the poor and the *ger* would gather what grew wild among the untended fields (see Exod. 23:10–11; Lev. 25:1–7; Deut. 31:10–13). During a sabbatical year, all debts were also remitted. While there is scholarly debate about the details of how this year of remission was calculated and how it worked, or even about whether it was ever put into practice, it seems clear that the purpose was to ensure that debt was not overly burdensome on the poor and to remind the wealthy that the powerless were worthy of the same respect as they were (Gowan, 1987). The Covenant and Holiness Codes comprised the social welfare system of ancient Israel (Kaufman, 1984). Since the stories of the poor rarely survive, it is impossible to say to what extent these cultic instructions were actually carried out.[3]

The Book of Deuteronomy (or 'Second Law') is a reiteration and reinterpretation of the first giving of the Law in Exodus and is set during the reconstruction of the Temple (the Second Temple) in Jerusalem after the return from the Babylonian exile. The theme of caring for the powerless is emphasised several times throughout Deuteronomy:

> For the Lord your God is God of gods and Lord of lords, the great God, mighty and awesome, who is not partial and takes no bribe, who executes justice for the orphan and the widow, and who loves the strangers, providing them food and clothing. You shall also love the stranger, for you were strangers in the land of Egypt. (Deut. 10:17–19; see also 14:28–9; 16:13–14)

---

[3] There is a school of thought which proposes that the First Testament as we have received it only reflects the values of the elites of Hebrew society, and the formulaic inclusion of the widow, the orphan, and the *ger* merely served to further the class interests of a post-exilic hierocratic, hegemonic elite by appearing to include these vulnerabilised groups without actually doing anything for them; see, for instance, Sneed, 1999. Interesting as it is, that discussion is beyond our present scope.

The God of the Hebrews was incorruptible and, as such, impartial and just in caring for the orphan, the widow, and the *ger*. Perhaps this insistence on being incorruptible was intended as a counterpoint to wealthy Israelites who did not care so much about being righteous in the eyes of YHWH and therefore continued to oppress the poor and powerless. Clearly, however, placing the care of the poor into the hands of the mighty and awesome God involved the divine directly in their care in the same way that Shamash, the sun god of Babylon, was involved. To tend to the poor was to honour divine will.

Prophets

The prophets of Israel spoke on behalf of the God of Israel. They were not prophets in the sense that they foresaw the future, although they did warn of consequences if the people or their leaders did not conform to the Law. Under the monarchy (in the books of 1 and 2 Samuel and 1 and 2 Kings), some prophets were part of the of the royal court and provided counsel to the king; however, true prophets who spoke only in the name of God ('Thus says the Lord …') challenged these court prophets (who were aware that their income and perhaps lives depended on the goodwill of the king) and the behaviours of the sitting king, usually for failing to be obedient to the Covenant Code, and often for failing to care for the weak; even the great King David was severely reprimanded by the prophet Nathan for sending Uriah, the husband of Bathsheeba, into battle to be killed merely in order to satisfy his lust for Bathsheeba (2 Sam. 11–12).

Perhaps the best known of all the prophets is Isaiah, who was active in the late 8th and early 7th century BCE. He repeatedly warned the Israelites that if they did not return to the way of God they would be taken into captivity. The Book of Isaiah is traditionally divided into three parts: the first, chapters 1–39, was written before the exile and warned the kings and the people that if they didn't observe covenant law dire things would happen. The second and third parts, chapters 40–55 and 56–66 were written while the people were in exile, offering words of comfort and hope to a people separated from their heritage, their land, their Temple, and even, it seemed, their god. The second and third parts were likely written by someone or a group writing in Isaiah's name, a common practice at the time. In the first chapter of Isaiah, the prophet frames his warning as a vision:

> [Hear the word of the Lord] … Learn to do good;
> seek justice, rescue the oppressed,
> defend the orphan, plead for the widow. (Isa. 1:17; see also 10:1–2)

Fasting and animal sacrifice were part of the usual cultic rituals required by the Law, but in the last part of Isaiah, the notion of fasting is reinterpreted. Isaiah writes that when people fast they served their own interests and (perhaps because fasting made them ill-tempered) they quarrelled and fought and oppressed their workers. Instead, he writes, speaking on behalf of God,

> Is this the fast that I choose:
> > to loose the bonds of injustice,
> > to undo the thongs of the yoke,
> To let the oppressed go free,
> > and to break every yoke? (Isa. 58:6–8)

Isaiah's calls for justice for the oppressed (and specifically for the poor, the orphan, the widow, and the *ger*) were echoed in the so-called minor prophets who were writing around the same time: Micah 6:8 (active around 730 BCE); Amos 5:24 (760–50 BCE); Hosea 2:19–20 (720 BCE); and Zechariah 7 (518 BCE). Zechariah's post-exilic description of how a healthy community should fast could have been written at any point in Israelite history: 'Thus says the Lord of Hosts: Render true judgments, show kindness and mercy to one another; do not oppress the widow, the orphan, the alien, or the poor; and do not devise evil in your hearts against one another' (Zech. 7:9–10).

Where the Law set out the expectation of justice and care for the orphan, the widow, the poor, and the *ger* as a feature of the people's covenant relationship with God, the prophets consistently reminded (or pestered) the people and the leaders to keep that covenant.

Writings

The third major section of the Tanakh is the poetic books (Psalms, Proverbs, and Job), the five 'Megillot' or instructive books (Song of Songs, Ruth, Lamentation, Ecclesiastes, and Esther), and three other books (Daniel, Ezra-Nehemiah, and Chronicles). These books include poetry and hero stories and are considered less authoritative than the Law and the Prophets. However, they serve to show us what ideas were circulating among the writers and poets of the time. They reflect, rather than shape, the lives of the people of the covenant. The Book of Psalms, often called Israel's hymnbook, was composed over a period of perhaps 500 years. In it we find clear evidence that caring for the poor was part of the discourse of worship:

> For [God] delivers the needy when they call
> > the poor and those who have no helper.
> He has pity on the weak and needy
> And saves the lives of the needy;

> From oppression and violence he redeems their life
> and precious is their blood in his eyes. (Psalm 72:12–14)
> Give justice to the weak and the orphan;
>> maintain the right of the lowly and the destitute. (Psalm 82:3)
>
> [The wicked] kill the widow and the stranger,
>> they murder the orphan,
>> and they say "The Lord does not see,
>> the God of Jacob does not perceive".
>
> (Psalm 94:6–7; see also Wisdom of Solomon 2:10)
> The Lord watches over the strangers;
>> he upholds the orphan and the widow,
>> but the way of the wicked he brings to ruin. (Psalm 146:9)

Similar themes and language appear in Job 22, Proverbs 14, Proverbs 22, and in other psalms. Psalm 72 is particularly interesting because it appears to be a royal psalm, used on occasions of the coronation or enthronement of the Israelite king (Dahood, 1979). Addressing God, the psalm expresses the hope that the king would 'govern your people with justice/and your oppressed with judgment … defend the oppressed of the people/save the children of the needy, and crush the extortioner'[4] (Ps. 72:2, 4, trans. Dahood, p 178). Once again, we see that protecting the poor was the responsibility and expectation of the king. Nevertheless, the admonition to care for the orphan, the widow, the poor, and the *ger* is a clear and explicit part of all three aspects of the First Testament, law, prophets, and writings. What began in the second millennium as an apodictic responsibility of royalty in most if not all of the ancient Near East became an explicit, written responsibility of all righteous people of Israel, a responsibility of which they were frequently and forcefully reminded by the prophets.

All this is modestly interesting, you may be thinking, but what does this have to do with our story? Firstly, the story of Abraham (Ibrahim PBOH) is shared by 3.8 billion people on earth, roughly half the total population of the planet, so it is worth knowing about. Secondly, the First Testament forms the theological and cultural background to the New Testament, which we will get to in just a moment. Thirdly, if we consider the central focus of contemporary social work and social policy, it is pretty obvious that the poor, the orphan, solo women, and the *ger* (in the form of migrants and refugees) continue to be a major focus. How we got from Lagash, Ur, and the Code of Hammurabi to today will form the rest of the story.

---

[4] This translation emphasises not that God oppresses the people but rather that oppressed people belong to God.

Christian scriptures

Early in the first century of the common era (CE), a child was born in Bethlehem, nearly 9 kilometres from Jerusalem, and was named Jesus. According to accounts written many decades later, the birth was attended by all the portents and signs one would expect of a royal birth: astronomical phenomena (a star), singing angels or divine messengers, and μάγοι (*magoi*, or 'wise men from the east') bringing royal gifts of gold, frankincense, and myrrh. However, this birth was anything but royal: we read that it took place in a stable, and the child was laid in an animal feeding trough. According to one account (Matthew 2:7–15), Jesus and his parents followed the now well-worn path to Egypt to escape the wrath of the Roman client-king Herod I (the Great) who saw him as a threat to his power before they returned to Nazareth several years later.

What was important about this birth was not so much who this Jesus was or what he said but rather who people believed him to be and what they remembered. These beliefs emerged from a First Testament context. Some of the people who followed him – and there appear to have been many besides a chosen core group of 12 – believed that Jesus was the fulfilment of First Testament prophecies of a messiah, a deliverer from foreign oppression. Some people believed he was a teacher, others, a prophet; still, others proclaimed that he was the son of God. That Jesus challenged the religious authorities of the time seems quite clear, and the stories we have tell us that Jesus was eventually arrested by Roman authorities at the behest of the Jewish leaders, convicted of a capital offence against Roman order, and put to death by crucifixion, an excruciating but not unusual method of execution at the time.[5] Holland writes that crucifixion was not merely a punishment, but a means to achieving dominance meant to be felt as a dread in the guts of the subdued (Holland, 2019). In case any of the people believed that Jesus was going to overthrow Roman hegemony or upset the delicate balance that the Jewish leaders had forged with the Romans, the Roman authorities were determined to exterminate that hope.

Unless, that is, you believe that the death of the crucified Jesus was not the end of the story. Three days after his death, we read, some of his followers saw Jesus again, and those stories became the core of a faith that proclaimed that the story of Jesus was far from over.

Christian scriptures, or what forms the New Testament, were written in a kind of Greek (*koine* Greek), which was the common language during the Hellenistic, Roman, and Byzantine periods, and are divided into two main

---

[5] 'The death of Jesus of Nazareth on the cross is an established fact, arguably the only established fact about him' (Vermes, cited in Holland, p 4).

groups: the first group is the gospels Matthew, Mark, Luke, and John, the first three forming the so-called synoptic gospels that tell a story about Jesus' life, and the fourth offering more of a theological interpretation of that life. The second group is the epistles, or letters, written by key believers in Jesus (notably, but not only, Paul) to other followers who were attempting to make sense out of the life of Jesus and to put it into practice. The Book of Acts is a kind of second act to Luke's gospel and describes the development of the early community of believers. These gospels and epistles emerged out of the context of the Hebrew Tanakh, attend to the texts of the First Testament (sometimes citing them directly, although often out of context), and form the foundation for what was to become a new religion that spread throughout the known world. The 27 books that we now find in the New Testament, including four gospels, 21 letters, the Books of Acts, and Revelation, were not the only ones of their kind that were written, but they were the ones selected by Christian leaders and codified in 382 CE for the Roman or Western Church (and in 692 CE for the Orthodox or Eastern branch).

No one was documenting the events of the time in the way we now understand historical records, so much of what we know about the early followers of Jesus Christ, who came to be known as Christians, must be inferred from these gospels or epistles, which are themselves based on retrospectively recalled events. The occupying Romans always understood this group to be a Jewish sect. The tolerance of the Roman emperor Titus with turbulent Palestine and its ongoing insurrections ran out, and the first Jewish-Roman war (66–73 CE) resulted in the Roman sack of Jerusalem and the destruction of the Second Temple in 70 CE. Tradition holds that Jerusalemite Christians fled Jerusalem to the city of Pella across the Jordan River. The biblical scholar C.S. Mann (1979) and others propose an important alternative scenario. Mann proposes that (at least some) early Jewish Christians fled Jerusalem and arrived at the settlement of Qumran, on the north-western shore of the Dead Sea. You may have heard of Qumran because of the discovery of the Dead Sea Scrolls in the 1950s, but Mann proposes that ancient Qumran was occupied by a group of strictly observant Persian Jews known as the Essenes (who flourished between the 2nd century BCE to the 1st century CE), whose origins are obscure but may have been among a community that fled to Judea after the Parthian invasion of Persia about 140 BCE. Josephus reports that there were thousands of Essenes throughout Roman Judea so that identifying a specific location or community for them is problematic. The Essene Jews had a very complex initiation structure and a highly developed community life: for instance, the Roman historian Philo tells us that they bathed daily (not usual for the time), ate meals in common, and held all property in common. Mann argues that when the Jerusalemite Christians encountered the Essenes they saw how consistent the common life of the Essenes was with recorded sayings and the traditions about Jesus, and began to adopt some of their practices to include Essene practices.[6] Mann writes, 'only by a perversity of scholarship is it possible to deny that the Jerusalem Church (and the Corinthian Church, at last, too) received its structure from Essene models' (p 280). The Essene scholar S.J. Joseph (2018) is a little more cautious:

> [I]t is not always entirely clear where the boundaries between [the Jesus Movement and the Essenes] should be drawn, especially given the internal diversity of both movements … The geographical and chronological overlapping and thematic similarities between the two movements makes it virtually inconceivable that Jesus and his followers never encountered – let alone learned from, interacted with, or were 'influenced' by – the four thousand Essenes reported to have been living in Judea at the same time. (pp 8, 9)

Nevertheless, Joseph writes that the 'ethnic, social, cultural and geographical proximity in first-century Palestinian Judea inevitably lent itself' (p 102) to the mutual interaction and influence between the Jesus Movement and the Essenes; he proposes even that the historical Jesus was influenced by the Essenes and that this mutual relationship gave rise to some of the literary and theological features of the earliest Jesus tradition. In Qumran scroll 4Q521, for instance, we read that,

> 7. [The Lord] will honor the pious on a throne of an eternal kingdom,
> 8. Liberating the captives, giving sight to the blind, straightening the bent …
> 11. And glorious deeds that never were the Lord will be perform as he said
> 12. For he will heal the wounded, revive the dead, and proclaim good news to the poor. (Joseph, 2018, p 86)

This is the Essene vision of the messiah who was to come; the similarities with Jesus Movement language are striking. While the contemporary historians Josephus, Philo, and Pliny claim that the Essenes were celibate,

---

[6] This interpretation has been indirectly disputed by scholars who say that Qumran was a Roman military outpost, and for a community of highly observant Persian Jews to establish a community there would have been highly improbable. For a full exploration of the historical and contemporary scholarly arguments about the Essenes and their relationship to early Christianity see Joseph's masterful summary in his 2018 book *Jesus, the Essenes, and Christian Origins*.

Joseph writes that several Qumran texts presuppose women and children among their communities. The Jesus Movement practice of sharing all things in common (Act 2:42, 46; 4:32–5; 6:1), later caring for poor congregations, widows, and the needy may well have been borrowed from Essene practice.

Whether the Jerusalemite Christians encountered Essenes at Qumran or somewhere else, or developed these practices independently, is less important (for our purposes) than the reality that early Christians held all things in common, esteemed and performed charity and good works, and, in particular, cared for the widows and orphans in their community.[7]

The early Christian church developed throughout the Roman and Greek worlds and was influenced by the thought and cultural norms of those worlds. Its earliest advocates, notably the apostle Paul (Acts 9:1–19 is the story of Saul's conversion and renaming as Paul), communicated through letters. Some of those letters were collected and accepted as scripture, and those epistles have become our earliest record of early Christian community life and thinking. Letters from Paul, or believers writing in his name, to Christian communities in Rome, Corinth, Galatia, Ephesus, Philippi, Colossae, and Thessalonica, as well as letters to or from other leaders to Christian communities provide the first glimpses into the life of those communities. Within a decade or so after the death of Jesus, some believers began to write down stories about the life of Jesus and included some of the sayings attributed to Jesus.[8] Those gospel writers – who we know as Mark, Matthew, Luke (and his companion story Acts), and later John – put the life of Jesus into a narrative context, each of whom had a slightly different story to tell, although each was probably aware of similar sources. The epistles and the gospels that we now have were selected, standardised, codified, and finally adopted by the early church several hundred years later as the core documents that shape Christian theology, values, and ethics.

The gospels and Acts

In the gospels, the sayings of Jesus about the poor are very clear. The Beatitudes – 'Blessed are the poor for theirs is the kingdom of heaven …' (Matt. 5:3–10, paralleled in Luke 6:17, 20–3) – the expectation that giving

---

[7] The notion of the גר, *ger*, the sojourner or alien, does not appear so much in the New Testament as it does in the First Testament (Easton, 2020). This is partly, of course, because the New Testament was written in Greek; it may also be because the Roman occupiers were strangers of a sort, and the New Testament faithful would hardly be expected to show hospitality to brutal oppressors who used crucifixion to send their message of social, political, and religious control.

[8] The common source of these sayings is known as 'Q', after the German word *Quelle* or source document.

alms is an expression of piety (Matt. 6:1–4), Jesus' condemnation of the wealthy and self-righteous and the commendation of the poor widow (Mark 12:38–44, paralleled in Luke 21:1–4) are all ways in which Jesus recognises that the poor are especially worthy of respect and love (and the rich and powerful worthy of condemnation). In fact, in Matthew 25, Jesus makes it clear that caring for the poor is the same as caring for Jesus himself:

> Then the king will say to those at his right hand, "Come, you that are blessed by my Father, inherit the kingdom prepared for you from the foundation of the world; for I was hungry and you gave me food, I was thirsty and you gave me something to drink, I was a stranger and you welcomed me, I was naked and you gave me clothing, I was sick and you took care of me, I was in prison and you visited me". Then the righteous will answer him, "Lord, when was it that we saw you hungry and gave you food, or thirsty and gave you something to drink? And when was it that we saw you a stranger and welcomed you, or naked and gave you clothing? And when was it that we saw you sick or in prison and visited you?" And the king will answer them, "Truly I tell you, just as you did it to one of the least of these who are members of my family you did it to me". (Matt. 25:34–40)

The king in this passage, of course, is Jesus himself, and he is instructing believers how to live until his return brings in the final kingdom. This eschatological ethic is one that specifically instructs his followers to take care of the hungry, the poor, the stranger, the sick, and the prisoner. The revolutionary nature of this saying may have been lost over the millennia. It is not the rich and the wealthy who are beloved of God and blessed with health and wealth but rather the poor. The new kingdom upends the First Testament expectations of a good life and a good end for the wealthy and satisfied and continues the ethic of the blessed poor found in the Beatitudes.

The Gospel of Luke has been called the Gospel of the Outcast because throughout Luke (and particularly in Luke 15) Jesus recognises the poor, the sick, and the outcast as being particularly worthy of inclusion and God's love. This messianic sympathy for the poor begins even before Jesus' birth, in his mother Mary's song (recalling the First Testament song of Hannah in I Samuel 2:1–10), which has been sung in Christian liturgies over the centuries as the *Magnificat*:

> My soul magnifies the Lord and my spirit rejoices in God my Savior,
> For he has looked with favour on the lowliness of his servant …
> He has shown strength with his arm; he has scattered the proud in the thoughts of their hearts.

> He has brought down the powerful from their thrones, and lifted up the lowly;
> He has filled the hungry with good things, and sent the rich away empty. (Luke 1:46–7, 51–3)

In his first adult public appearance, Jesus confirms that he has come to fulfil the promise of justice for the poor. He reads from the third section of the prophet Isaiah,

> "The Spirit of the Lord is upon me,
>   because he has anointed me to bring good news to the poor.
> He has sent me to proclaim release to the captives
> and recovery of sight to the blind, to let the oppressed go free,
> to proclaim the year of the Lord's favour".
> And he rolled up the scroll, gave it back to the attendant, and sat down. The eyes of all in the synagogue were fixed on him. Then he began to say to them, "Today this scripture has been fulfilled in your hearing". (Luke 4:18–21, and citing Isa. 61:1–2, 58:6)

This public declaration (which also clearly echoes the language of the Qumran scroll 4Q521) sets the tone for the rest of Luke. There are many references to widows, the sick, and demon-possessed in Luke, all of whose suffering is addressed or healed by Jesus. Luke continues this theme in Acts, which describes the development of the early church. The followers of Jesus 'devoted themselves to the apostles' teaching and fellowship, to the breaking of bread and in the prayers ... All who believed were together and had all things in common; they would sell their possessions and goods and distribute the proceeds to all, as any had need' (Acts 2:42, 44–5).

These verses may be where we see crucial aspects of Essene influence. Just as important, in Acts 6 we read,

> Now during those days when the disciples were increasing in number, the Hellenists[9] complained against the Hebrews because their widows were being neglected in the daily distribution of food. And the twelve called together the whole community of the disciples and said "It is not right that we should neglect the word of God in order to wait on tables. Therefore friends, select from among yourselves seven men of good standing full of the Spirit and of wisdom, who we may appoint to this task, while we for our part will devote ourselves to prayer and to

---

[9] Greek-speaking Jews or Jews who had adopted Greek customs, or less likely, Greek Gentiles. (See Macgregor, p 88).

serving the word". What they said pleased the whole community, and they chose Stephen, a man full of faith and the Holy Spirit, together with Philip, Prochorus, Nicanor, Timon, Parmenas, and Nicolaus, a proselyte of Antioch. They had these men stand before the apostles, who prayed and laid their hands on them. (Acts 6:1–6)

These seven people (and the Greek does say ἄνδρας *andras*, 'men', I'm afraid, but we'll need to leave that discussion for others) became the first deacons, whose specific responsibility was to care for the widows of the early church. Making the needs of the world known to the church remains a chief responsibility for the order of deacons in Christian denominations to this day.

We must remember that the life of Jesus and the development of the early church all took place under Roman hegemony. In the Roman Empire,

> The large majority of poor survived through labour, scavenging, begging, theft, and even by selling themselves or their children into slavery. Until the third century CE the accepted stance among most of the Roman elite was that people begging, who were invariably viewed with disgust and contempt, should be ignored. (Walker, 2014, p 9)

It is hardly surprising, then, that this new Christian community took it upon itself to look after its own widows and poor, and it did so by designating a specific group of people to do it.

The epistles

The letters provide what is probably the earliest insight into how early Christian communities managed to care for their widows, orphans, and poor. Like the Jerusalemite Christians, the early believers scattered throughout the Roman Empire appeared to be quite insular; they were more concerned about the poor within their communities of faith than in their wider communities. There are not many specific references to responding to the poor in the epistles. Three are relevant to our discussion.

Firstly, 1 Timothy is a letter intended to provide guidance about the administration of the early church and to oppose false teachings. Scholars vary widely on the authorship and date of the letter: while it is written in the name of Paul, there are key features of the letter that bring that attribution into doubt. Further, the date of the letter could be any time between 60 and 180 CE. 1 Timothy 5:3–16 sets out for the first time categories of widows: *real widows* are older women who depended on the church for support (cf Act 6:1); *list widows* (if we may call them such) are women who do good works, show hospitality, help the afflicted, and do good in every way (v.10); and *young widows*. Real widows should be supported by the community, as should list widows. Young widows should remarry. At least there is some attention to the needs of widows in this letter.

The letter of James (again, authorship and the date are disputed, but it may date between 50 and 70 CE and may be attributable to a brother of Jesus) is addressed to the 'twelve tribes in the Dispersion' (that is, the Jewish diaspora outside of Palestine). It is more of a treatise in the style of the Jewish Wisdom tradition than a letter. James writes that 'Religion that is pure and undefiled before God the Father is this: to care for orphans and widows in their distress, and to keep oneself unstained by the world' (Jas. 1:27). Since the writer is clearly from the Jewish tradition, mentioning orphans and widows is to be expected. But James challenges traditional notions of favouring the wealthy and segregating the poor:

> My brothers and sisters do you really with your acts of favouritism really believe in our glorious Lord Jesus Christ? For if a person with gold rings and in fine clothes comes into your assembly, and if a poor person in dirty clothes also comes in, and if you take notice of the one wearing the fine clothes and say "Have a seat here, please" while to the one who is poor you say "Stand there", or "Sit at my feet", have you not make distinctions among yourselves and become judges with evil thoughts? ... Has not God chosen the poor in the world to be rich in faith and to be heirs of the kingdom that he has promised to those who love him? But you have dishonoured the poor. Is it not the rich who oppress you? (Jas. 2:1–6a)

James is clear about the equality of believers. But he goes further,

> What good is it, my brothers and sisters, if you say you have faith but do not have works? Can faith save you? If a brother or sister is naked and lacks daily food and one of you says to them, "Go in peace, keep warm and eat your fill" and yet you do not supply their bodily needs, what is the good of that? So faith by itself, if it has no works, is dead. (Jas. 2:14–17)

James, like Luke's gospel, is explicit about God's preference for the poor, the outcast and the marginalised, and set out the expectation of a specific and practical response to the needs of the poor.

Finally, for our purposes, there is the second letter to the Thessalonians. This letter could have been written by Paul in the early 50s CE, or by someone else between 80 and 115 CE. If the former, then it and the first letter to the Thessalonians are among the earliest New Testament writings we have, only a couple of decades after Jesus' death. In these letters, Paul addresses the expectations of early believers that Jesus would return again immanently, and he instructs them on how to act in the meantime, that is, while they are waiting. In 2 Thessalonians he instructs believers to continue living their lives in a regular and orderly way. He chastised idlers:

> Now we command you, beloved, in the name of our Lord Jesus Christ, to keep away from believers who are living in idleness and not according to the tradition that they received from us. For you yourselves know how you ought to imitate us: we were not idle when we were with you, and we did not eat anyone's bread without paying for it; but with toil and labour we worked night and day so that we might not burden any of you ... For even when we were with you we gave you this command: Anyone unwilling to work should not eat. (2 Thess. 3:6–8, 10)

As we will see later, 2 Thessalonians 3:10 created a foundation for the requirement to work in order to receive assistance that appears in medieval Catholicism and later Protestant theologians such as Calvin. This ecclesiastical expectation in turn became a foundation for later statutory requirements (such as the Elizabethan Poor Laws) that anyone seeking public assistance must work in order to receive that assistance. However, if we look at the larger context, Paul is instructing early believers on how to live their lives *while they waited for the return of Jesus*: they were not to give up on life, sit around, and gawp at the heavens. Instead, Paul instructs them to continue to live their lives as they always had, because the return of Jesus was completely unpredictable.[10]

While many social workers have been taught that the roots of social work are found in the slums of East London in the late 19th century, notions of caring for the poor, the widow, the orphan, and the stranger are ancient, and roots may be found in the ancient Near East and recorded in Judaeo-Christian scripture. My purpose is to lay a foundation for the argument that Judaeo-Christian religions form the foundation of contemporary liberal humanist and therefore social work responses to the poor.

By focusing the discussion so far on Judaeo-Christian texts we cannot ignore significant texts and traditions that address the issue of poverty and the poor in cultures around the world. We shall return to these traditions and the contexts in which they flourished – particularly in South and East Asia – in a later chapter.

---

[10] The problem of the delayed *Parousia*, or the delay of the return of Jesus, continues to be a problem for many Christian sects and cults, and is addressed throughout the later New Testament writings.

Summary

While there is no unitary or even consistent understanding of poverty and the poor, or wealth and reward throughout all of the Hebrew and Christian scriptures, there is a reasonably consistent message that the widow, the orphan, the *ger*, and the poor should be protected from abuse by the wealthy and the powerful. In Christian texts, this message was refined to ensure that the community of believers should pay specific attention to caring for widows, orphans, and the poor within their own communities as they waited for the imminent return of their Christ. Various scriptural text passages have been used selectively by theologians and policymakers throughout Christendom and continue to influence social welfare and social work; that is where we shall turn our attention next.

3

Inventing the poor

The early Christian Church and the state

What happened in the early years of the relatively minor Jewish sect called Christianity[1] has been explored extensively by historians and theologians, and, as we have seen, also in the letters of the New Testament. It is not my intention here to duplicate the research done by historians of social welfare such as Tierney (1959), Handel (2009), or Brown (2012), or theological historians such as Holman (2009) or Holland (2019), and I encourage serious students of this history to explore their work. My purpose here is to gather key narrative themes that support the argument of the first part of this book, that for better or worse, it is Christianity and Christian theology that has largely shaped the contemporary structure and values of social welfare and social work.

In its earliest years, most Christians (as adherents called themselves, Acts 11:26) expected to live to see the Second Coming, or imminent return of the risen Christ, and the end of the age in which they lived. Texts such as Matthew 24:34 ('Truly I tell you this generation will not pass away until all these things have taken place'; parallels Mark 13:30 and Luke 21:32), and Matthew 16:28 ('Truly I tell you, there are some standing here who will not taste death before they see the Son of Man coming in his kingdom') certainly implied that the return of Jesus was not far away. The letters and other writings of the early church also reflected this eschatological theme (see, for instance, 1 Thess. 4:15–18; Jas. 5:7; Rev. 1:7) where it was held that those who were alive at that time would see the Second Coming in their lifetimes. That return did not happen as expected. Followers of Jesus were left with the problem of what to do in the meantime. It was the meantime that presented practical problems of how to believe in a Jesus who was not present, and these problems became more urgent. Early believers were faced with questions of not only what to believe and how to express that belief but how to live their lives and how to live in and get along with a community of other believers. These meantime challenges are the focus of much of the early writing of Paul (e.g., 1 Thess. 4:13–5:11).

---

[1] The term *Christianismos* appears first to have been used by Ignatius of Antioch, early in the 2nd century (Holland, 2019, p 120).

The Roman Empire, which reached its peak in the early 2nd century CE, included all the regions where followers of Jesus lived; it comprised the entire Mediterranean region and extended from modern Britain in the northwest to northern Africa and Egypt in the south and southeast, and in the east, of course, Palestine and Syria. Indeed, it was the existence of the Roman Empire and its trade and transport systems, which allowed Christianity to disseminate so widely. Roman power experienced something of a rebirth under the rule of Augustus Caesar (63 BCE–14 CE), the adopted son of Julius Caesar; Augustus claimed the title *Divi Filius*, 'Son of God' (Holland, 2019). He imposed Roman peace throughout its provinces by the sword and capital punishment for any group or individual who resisted Rome's power or who failed to acknowledge him as a god. Various regional religions and philosophies reached accommodation of sorts with Rome's power, and they were tolerated as long as they acknowledged the supreme authority of the Roman emperor and were willing, at least publicly, to acknowledge his divinity. Jews and Christians could not do that (since they believed in only one God), and they had to be – and were – dealt with harshly.

In the eastern part of the empire, Greek language and thought dominated, and indeed, there were more Greek-speaking than Hebrew-speaking Jews. Due in part to strong imperial leadership, the peace of Rome was firmly established, and it was this peace that was proclaimed as ευαγγέλιον (*evangelion*): good news. Early Jewish-Christian apostles and missionaries such as Paul could move more or less freely throughout the far reaches of the Roman Empire to tell the story of Jesus who was crucified and resurrected; it has been estimated that Paul travelled some 10,000 miles (16,000 km) in his life (Holland, 2019).

Paul's proclamation of a Jewish messiah was shaped in response to other philosophies and religions he encountered in his travels. One of the first controversies that arose in the early church was whether non-Jews, or Gentiles, could become Christians. Apostles and elders met at the Council of Jerusalem (ca. 50 CE) to debate this urgent question. Was adherence to the Law of Moses, which governed many aspects of daily life, including circumcision of males, a prerequisite to becoming a follower of Jesus? While circumcision was repellent to Greeks, it was mandated by Hebrew custom. Acts 15 contains a summary of the deliberations and outcomes of the Council: 'For it has seemed good to the Holy Spirit and to us to impose on you [Gentiles] no further burden than these essentials: That you abstain from what has been sacrificed to idols, and from blood and from what is strangled, and from fornication' (Acts 15:28–9). This decision was disseminated throughout the reach of the early church. With this point settled it became possible for anyone to become a follower of Jesus with no greater barrier than a confession of faith and baptism with water, as long as they followed the three essential stipulations. This early apostolic council is the point at which Christianity became severed from its Jewish roots and its rigid adherence to the Law of Moses in the First Testament. It was also the point when Christianity became more available to many more people throughout the Roman Empire. However, Paul found that this liberalising of entry requirements to the new church had its limits when he discovered the libertine habits of some of the faithful, particularly in Corinth ('It is actually reported that there is sexual immorality among you, and of a kind that is not found even among pagans; for a man is living with his father's wife'; 1 Cor. 5:1). The Law of Moses that governed the daily life of Jews was replaced by a new law, which said that 'All things are lawful, but not all things are beneficial' (1 Cor. 6:12) to the building up of the community. 'Commandments were just ... because they worked for the common good' (Holland, 2019, p 93). Paul's response to the imperial *evangelion* was to co-opt it and replace it with the *evangelion* (or in English, gospel) of Jesus Christ. For this, he was imprisoned three times and eventually beheaded in Rome (sometime between 64 and 68 CE).

The early church's solution to living in the meantime was to develop communities of faithful people and to instruct them how to live together. What was essential was to live in harmony, or *caritas* (after the Latin word *caritas*, to be costly, to esteem, and later, to love all): that is, benevolence and mutual affection. We have already seen in Acts how early Christian believers constructed communities of faith and took up collections and distributed the excess to the poor, the widow, and the orphan that lived among them, and appointed specific ministers to carry out the distribution. This practice of almsgiving soon extended beyond their immediate communities of Christians to include 'aged household slaves, shipwrecked persons, and persons imprisoned, exiled or working in mines as punishment for their Christian beliefs' (Handel, 2009, p 48). This practice of collecting and distributing contributions paralleled the existing Roman practice where trades were organised into associations (*collegia*) where members made contributions into a common fund to support other members. Initially, Christian charity was limited to Christians but was later extended to the poor regardless of religion (Day and Schiele, 2013).

A significant centre of gravity in the Roman Empire was Byzantium (now known as Istanbul). Byzantium provided a cultural, linguistic, and philosophical Eastern counterbalance to Rome in the West. Traditionally said to be founded in 667 BCE, Byzantium sat at the mouth of the Black Sea, on the boundary of the Asian and European continents. Its location made it an inviting military target, and Byzantium was taken over by a succession of empires throughout its history. It became an ally of Rome after the fall of the Seleucid Empire and the appropriation of its eastern provinces by the Roman general Pompey. In 272 CE Flavius Valerius Aurelius Constantinus (Constantine to you and me) was born in Dacia (now Serbia) and raised in York (now England), where his father (who may have been married to Constantine's mother, Helena) was deputy emperor of Britannia. Constantine had a brilliant and clever military career and was himself acclaimed deputy emperor in 306. After a brief civil war, he eventually became the sole emperor of the Roman Empire in 324. Constantine decided in 330 that Byzantium would be his imperial residence. The city was renamed Constantinople, or City of Constantine, after his death in 337.

There is no denying that Constantine was a pivotal figure in the history of Christianity, and, as we shall see, in the Christian response to the poor. The refusal of Christians to acknowledge the divinity of the Roman emperor had made them a frequent target of Roman persecution. Whatever his motivation (tradition tells us that he saw a heavenly vision which said 'In this sign, conquer' at the Battle of the Milvian Bridge in 312), Constantine set upon a path to his own conversion to Christianity. In 313, while still emperor in the West, Constantine met with his Balkan counterpart Licinius in Mediolanum (now Milan) and they jointly agreed to issue an edict that directed that Christians be tolerated throughout the Roman Empire. Property that had been confiscated from Christians during the Diocletian Persecution (a severe persecution of Christians that began in 303) was returned, and the edict also directed individual reparations by individual Roman citizens to Christians. The Edict of Milan effectively legalised Christianity in the Roman Empire, although possibly following a custom that baptism only washed away sins that had been committed in the past, or possibly for political reasons, Constantine himself seems not to have been baptised until his deathbed in 337. This reversal of fortunes allowed Christianity to emerge and eventually to flourish throughout the Roman Empire.[2] Christianity was declared the state religion in 380 by the Edict of Thessalonica by Emperors Theodosius I, Gratian, and Valentinian II, which established a catholic (universal) and orthodox (correct) faith. The Edict of Thessalonica also condemned various heterodoxies (heresies) which threatened the catholicity of the faith and therefore the unity of the empire. The environment for Christians and Christianity throughout the Roman Empire had changed completely in a lifetime.

Roman persecution notwithstanding, many different kinds and features of Christian belief had evolved over the nearly 300 years since the death of Jesus. In Constantine's time, there was great confusion and controversy about

---

[2] Brown (1993) cautions that it is misleading to speak of a single comprehensive explanation of the Christianisation of the Roman Empire; the complexities of the 'triumph' of Christianity over Greco-Roman paganism are beyond our scope here. Here we are concerned with how Christian theology and thought developed and eventually came to dominate imperial thinking and its management of the poor, the widow, and the orphan.

what was orthodox, or right belief, and what was heterodox, or heretical. In 325 Constantine called together an ecumenical council of bishops of all Roman provinces at Nicaea (modern Iznik, in north-west Anatolia, Turkey) to resolve key theological issues, establish orthodox doctrine, and bring order, peace, and unity to Christianity within the Roman Empire. Attendees at the month-long meeting included between 250 and 318 bishops, along with their theologians and retainers. Among the theological issues was whether Jesus was begotten of God the Father and therefore was uncreated, or created from nothing and therefore was created (this latter position was known as Arianism and was condemned as heresy), when to celebrate Easter Day,[3] and various other matters of liturgical practice.[4] The Nicene Creed, which Holland (2019) observes was a fusion of Christian theology and Roman bureaucracy, established a standardised, basic, orthodox Christian doctrine that proclaimed itself universal. While histories of Christianity and theology focus on the theological outcome of the Council of Nicaea, the establishment of a standard of orthodoxy became a lodestone in the response of the Christian Church to the poor.

Charity also became a political tool to manage heresy: in one fact-finding mission, Constantine sent two officials, Paulus and Macarius, to Carthage in North Africa with alms to relieve the poor (Holland, 2019), although this relief may have provided cover for them to investigate social unrest which was traced to the Donatist heresy.

Philanthropy and wealth

It will hardly be surprising to learn that Christians were not the originators of the idea of eleemosynary[5] aid. The Greeks and Romans had philanthropic systems in place for hundreds of years before Christianity emerged (Constantelos, 1968; Handel, 2009; Brown, 2012). Plato (d. ?348 BCE) had defined *philanthropia* as the love of the divine for humanity (Constantelos, p 4), and was demonstrated by the various gifts of the gods – the moon and stars, seasons, water, fire, the arts – to humans. *Philanthropia* also means politeness, courtesy, kindness, generosity, and simply being a civilised human being (Martin, in Constantelos), and was reflected in a society's concern for the orphan, the aged, the sick, and the stranger. Illustrations

---

[3] Easter is the first Sunday following the first full moon after 21 March, the vernal equinox in the Northern Hemisphere, or autumnal equinox in the Southern, in case you were wondering. One popular alternative was Quartodecimanism, the custom of celebrating Easter to coincide with the date of 14 Nisan of the Hebrew calendar, the beginning of Passover.

[4] Such as banning the practice of kneeling during the Great Fifty Days of Easter.

[5] An under-utilised word which means, simply, charitable giving, or alms-based assistance.

of *philanthropia* are found in Homer's *Iliad* and *Odyssey* (8th century BCE), where the stranger was considered as a dear brother, and orphans were viewed with compassion. Aristotle and Thucydides confirm that care for orphans of citizens who died in battle was maintained at public expense. Temples had hospices (καταγώγια, *katagogia* attached to them) to serve as shelters and even clinics, and healers attended to those who rested there without requiring payment. Means-tested public relief was also available in Athens, and Xenophon notes a similar generosity to prisoners of war, the aged, and orphans in Sparta. However, writes Constantelos, 'What was current could not be compared to what we encounter in the Graeco-Christian civilization of the Byzantine world – love and compassion, church- or privately- or state-organized institutions' (p 11).

In the Greek provinces of the Roman Empire, the Greek word *philanthropia* became the prevailing term for Christianity's greatest virtue of ἀγάπη, *agape*, love because, *philanthropia* resonated better with the ideas of the pre-Christian world (Miller, 2016), although Constantelos cautions against a direct parallel. It was expected that rulers, wealthy elites, and later, citizens, in general, would make material philanthropic gifts to the city-state, or associations within the state; these gifts would mirror the gods' generosity to humanity, This civic generosity (known as εὐεργεσία[6] *euergesia*, or euergetism, the practice of doing good) was understood as a kind of investment in the common life of the community and was recognised by assemblies by bestowing honours (plaques, statues, titles, and the like) on the benefactor in proportion to the donation; whether these honours were foremost in the minds of donors is speculation I will leave to others. Greater wealth allowed greater donations and came with greater expectations that the wealthy donate. Donations by the wealthy were distributed to members of the designated association (or city) regardless of need. Handel notes that there is evidence that the ancient Greeks distinguished between worthy poor – the educated and formerly wealthy who had fallen on hard times – and unworthy poor – the uneducated and permanently poor. They had little sympathy for the unworthy poor. 'Greek philanthropy was prompted by love of honor and by fear and not by concern for the weak and helpless' (Handel, p 45). As we shall see, this distinction between the worthy and unworthy poor was adopted by some bishops and Christian church leaders when they became overwhelmed by the rising tide of apparent need by mendicants and professional beggars and was later encoded in the Elizabethan Poor Laws.

Since Greek and Roman civilisations were so closely aligned, Roman attitudes to wealth and poverty were quite similar to the Greeks, although there is evidence that concern for the poor, at least among individuals,

---

[6] Also attested in the New Testament, in Acts 4:9 and 1 Tim. 6:2.

had begun to emerge in Rome, even if only motivated by a desire to keep the streets free of beggars. Euergetism, however, remained limited by citizenship: non-citizens were not considered recipients because they simply did not count. In Rome, for instance, this distinction became acutely obvious: by the first and succeeding centuries, in a city of some half a million residents, most suffered disease and malnourishment; yet only some 200,000 citizens (the so-called *plebs frumentaria*) were eligible for free grain (or bread) handed out by the state, and to purchase other foodstuffs at discounted prices (Frumetariae leges, 1875). Nevertheless, such distributions of benefits were one way of avoiding civic unrest and keeping the peace. Poor people, however, were simply expected to work harder or to migrate to outlying colonies where economic opportunities were greater. In fact, Brown (2012) writes that civic euergetism was opposed by the church because it did not contain an element of compassion for the poor.

After the legitimation of the church by Constantine in Byzantium, the church was granted certain privileges and rights, notably the right to collect donations, to own property, and, to a certain degree, to be financially independent of the state. The church was also given the responsibility to provide assistance to the poor. It seems that in delegating that responsibility to the church, Constantine had in mind the idea of euergetism, and in doing good, the church would be acting as a good civic leader. (Constantine may have had the intention of co-opting Christian networks of giving for his own purposes.) In return for the privileges granted to them by Constantine, bishops and church leaders were required to provide evidence that they were using these privileges responsibly. Despite Jesus' admonition to provide charity quietly ('But when you give alms, do not let your left hand know what your right hand is doing, so that your alms may be done in secret; and your Father who sees in secret will reward you', Matt. 6:3–4), it would have been of little advantage to the church if its bishops gave to the poor in secret: it was important to let the emperor know what good they were doing. However,

> The bishops and their helpers – lay and clerical alike – are more than symptoms. They were, themselves, agents of change. To put it bluntly: in a sense, it was the Christian bishops who invented the poor. They rose to leadership in late Roman society by bringing the poor into ever sharper focus. They presented their actions as a response to the needs of an entire category of persons (the poor) on whose behalf they claimed to speak. (Brown, 2002, pp 8–9)

In other words, the Christian church leadership did not merely respond to the needs of the poor: they *created a category* of 'the poor' which had not existed before as a social class. Certainly, there were poor people; in fact, most people were poor. Increasing urbanisation (as poorer farmers were dispossessed of their land by wealthier landowners) also meant that the poor were both increasing and more visible in the cities. Certainly, some people had received assistance, the citizen-*plebs frumentaria*. But now the church became responsible for providing aid to poor people whom the state declined to aid, and in doing so created a new social (and theological) class. The poor became big business for the church, and a way for the church to secure its place in Roman society and imperial polity. In Byzantium we see the founding of hospitals (ξένον, *xenon*, a house for strangers) in 370 (these were known as πτωχοτροφεῖον, *ptochotropheion*, poor houses, in Constantinople), which provided shelter for the poor (πτώχοι, *ptochoi*), lepers, and travellers. We also see the founding of the *Orphanotropheion*, the Imperial (or Great) Orphanage, by Zotikos (apparently a moderate adherent of Arianism) in the middle of the 4th century; notably the *Orphanotropheion* was open to non-Christian children (Miller, 2016), although it may have been used to convert these children to Christianity. These institutions were adapted from long-established Hellenic practices (Constantelos, 1968) and were made possible – even necessary – by Constantine's recognition of the Christian Church, the granting of privileges to the church, the evolving theology of the church, and its struggle to solidify its place in Byzantine society.

The Cappadocians

The Christian Church's preference for the poor was not merely a matter of expediency; care for the poor was also shaped by an evolving theology which linked the poor with the person of the Incarnate Christ himself. Key figures in developing this new theology of the poor were Macrina (327–379) and her brothers Basil, who became Bishop of Caesarea (later called 'the Great', 330–379), Gregory, Bishop of Nyssa (330–395), and Gregory of Nazianzus (329–389), a friend of the family, at least until Basil made him Bishop of Sasima, 'a detestable little place without water or grass or any mark of civilization' (Payne, 1957, p 181).[7] Perhaps best known, however, was John (347–407), Bishop of Constantinople, who was given the appellation 'Chrysostom', meaning 'golden mouth', for his gift of preaching. All of these church leaders lived or flourished in Cappadocia, a region in central Turkey. Although they did not create a systematic theology, together this tremendously influential group developed a theology that reimagined the suffering of the poor, and through their writing located the suffering of the

---

[7] It is unlikely that Gregory ever visited his diocese, and apparently fled into the mountains and became a monk rather than live in Sasima. Basil seems to have ordained and appointed Gregory against his will, for strategic reasons (Fortescue, 2015).

poor in the body of Christ himself. Since the church was the body of Christ, then the Cappadocians firmly and specifically theologised the poor into the church. (It should also be noted that these figures are not uncontroversial today, particularly in the ways they spoke of Jews; see Nixey, 2018.)

It was Macrina who convinced her brother Basil to abandon his career in law to embrace Christianity; after some searching, Basil became a Christian monastic. His idea of monasticism, however, was not simply one of isolation and asceticism. Following the example of the monastic Eustathios, Basil founded a monastery on the outskirts of Caesarea. Attached to this monastic community he built the *Basileias*, an institution for the care of the sick, the leper (the 'dead before death', as his brother Gregory described lepers), and the *ptochoi*, the poor. In effect, the *Basileias* became the first hospital (Miller, 2011).[8] The *Basileias*, a kind of multiservice agency, appears to have become a model for the notion of indoor relief in later centuries. Not only were the *ptochoi* welcomed into the protection of the church, but the poor now became a focus and purpose of the church.

Deuteronomic tradition held that wealth and health were divine rewards for obedience, and poverty and illness punishments for sin. From there it was a short but not sound theological leap to understand the wealthy and healthy as divinely blessed, and the poor and ailing as sinful (Henrickson and Fouché, 2017). In a theological reversal of this First Testament construction of poverty and illness, Basil instead challenged the wealthy: 'The bread in your board belongs to the hungry; the cloak in your wardrobe to the naked; the shoes you let rot to the barefoot; the money in your vaults to the destitute' (Homily 6, cited in Holland, 2019, p 142).

This admonition was consistent with gospel portrayals of the ways Jesus had spoken about the poor, and indeed Christianity had always been popular (but not popular exclusively) among the poor. Yet we moderns can barely begin to imagine how challenging this representation of the poor as a category was to the wealthy and privileged of the Roman Empire, for they simply did not acknowledge the poor. In Cappadocian Christian theology, the poor were identified with God-made-human, the Second Person of the Trinity (Holman, 2009), Jesus himself. That Jesus had become human flesh theologically raised the standing of all of humanity – and particularly the poor – to an association with the divine; if Jesus Christ was the human incarnation, the en-flesh-ment of the Divine, then the poor were the embodiment of Christ. The often-cited text from Matt. 25:31–46 was a foundation of this theology, the salient and most familiar portion we saw

---

[8] So successful was this concept that five centuries later, Charlemagne, King of the Franks and crowned by Pope Leo III as emperor of what would later become known as the Holy Roman Empire, required every cathedral in his empire to have a hospital attached to it.

previously, 'Truly I tell you just as you did it to one of the least of these who are members of my family, you did it to me' (v. 40) ... '[A]s you did not do it to one of the least of these you did not do it to me' (v. 45).

This passage from Matthew clearly, and in no uncertain terms, identifies Jesus with the poor and the poor with Jesus. This was the scriptural foundation for this innovative Cappadocian theology. John Chrysostom explicated this text from Matthew and asserted that the poor who walked along the streets of the city were the contemporary incarnations of Jesus. Indeed, it was Jesus himself who walked the streets, he said. By assisting the poor, Christians were assisting Christ himself. Gregory of Nazianzus wrote:

> Let us minister to Christ's needs, let us give Christ nourishment, let us clothe Christ, let us gather Christ in, let us show Christ honor ... through the needy who today are cast down on the ground, so that when we all are released from this place, they may receive us into the eternal tabernacle in Christ himself. (Oration 14, 'On the love of the poor', in Holman, 2009, p 299)

This is an extraordinary reversal of the way the poor had been conceived by Hebrews, Greeks, and Romans. Both the Jewish concept of poverty as a punishment for sin and the Graeco-Roman notion of the poor as disgusting and contemptible had been replaced by the Christian notion that it was the poor who would precede the wealthy into the kingdom of God. By reinterpreting the First Testament prophet Isaiah's Suffering Servant as an allegory of the connections that the poor and the leper shared with the able-bodied, Gregory transformed the leper into both a mirror of the universal human condition and a sign of hope of ultimate transformation (Wessel, 2016). Perhaps just as importantly, this sermon sought to push Christians towards caring not only for Christian widows, orphans, and the sick, but to address social problems more generally, looking beyond their brothers and sisters in faith. Holman (2016, p 28) compares this larger understanding of care to the Hebrew ideal of צדקה, *tzedakah*, meaning an act of justice, generosity, or charity. *Tzedakah* has Syriac and Arabic cognates, which means the notion informs Jewish, Christian, and (as we shall see later) Islamic concepts of social justice for all: 'The highest degree of *tzekadah* seeks to eliminate social injustices rather than simply alleviate symptoms' (Keidan, cited in Holman, 2016, p 28).

At the first Council of Constantinople in 381, Gregory of Nyssa, Basil's brother, declared that all humanity had a common nature and that the poor and marginalised were equals to the wealthy and privileged. In fact, he claimed, the poor bear the very image of God. Gregory emphasised this theme in his preaching: 'Do not despise those who are stretched out on the ground as if they merit no respect. Consider who they are ... they bear the countenance (πρόσωπον) of our Saviour'. (*De pauperibus amandis* [On the love of the poor], in Holland, 2019, p 313). Orthodox theology shifted from a sacrificial theology that understood Jesus' offering of himself on the cross as an atonement sacrifice for the sins of the world to an incarnational theology of Christ as God-made-flesh who at the same time identified completely with the poor. No longer did the faithful have to appease an angry and jealous god through ritual animal sacrifice: God had become human and bridged the gap between the created and uncreated orders. The voluntary impoverishment of God meant that God had embraced humanity and particularly the poor. Furthermore, to love the poor was to offer a service to God (Holman, 2009). That this theological shift spread throughout the empire is evidenced by the emergence of holy figures who embraced the poor, such as Martin of Tours (336?–397) in the Loire Valley of Roman Gaul – who as a wealthy soldier had famously divided his cloak[9] with a beggar – renounced worldly goods, and began himself to live as a beggar monk. Martin captured the popular imagination, was unexpectedly elected Bishop of Tours in 371 and became one of the most beloved saints in Christian history.

It should then be no surprise that the 4th-century church promoted a charitable theology in which to provide assistance to the poor through the giving of alms was also to provide a benefit to the donor. Donations to the church benefitted the poor, the donor, and, not incidentally, the church. Now, however, the inscribed tablets honouring the donor would not be placed merely in the urban streets but in the streets of heaven itself.

This theological and humanitarian approach of the church to the poor, the assertion that all persons were equal, and all were worthy of assistance simply by virtue of their humanity rather than their citizenship, was not without controversy, however. Such an approach risked destabilising the social balance of the empire.

> To present poverty as the sole requirement for generosity from the rich devalued the status of thousands of persons who thought of themselves as citizens first and only then as poor. It treated them as part of the same miasma of misery as the beggars, the homeless, and the immigrants who crowded into every city. So wide and so indiscriminate a vision undermined the delicate balance of institutionalized groups – benefactors, town councillors, and populus – on which the life of the cities of the Roman Empire had depended for centuries. (Brown, 2012, p 70)

---

[9] In the 5th century, this cloak, or *capella*, was recovered; it became an object of veneration and was guarded by the *capellini*, from which the English word 'chaplain' derives (Holland, 2019, p 158).

This problem could only be resolved by challenging and ultimately changing the entire worldview of the Roman Empire – and eventually Western societies – towards wealth and poverty, and indeed the very meaning of citizenship. This is, of course, what eventually happened.

A second key biblical text which informed the Cappadocian theology of the poor, and particularly the theology of John Chrysostom, was Luke 16:19–31, the story that Jesus tells of a rich man and Lazarus, a homeless beggar covered with sores. Lazarus died and was 'carried away by the angels to be with Abraham' (v. 22). When the rich man (who did not even merit a name in the story,[10] although tradition has called him Dives) died, he appeared in Hades, looked up and saw Lazarus in the arms of Abraham. He begs for mercy from Abraham, who answered him, 'Child, remember that during your lifetime you received your good things; and Lazarus in like manner evil things; but now he is comforted here, and you are in agony' (v.25). John Chrysostom wrote:

> Not to share our own wealth with the poor is theft from the poor … If we have this attitude we will certainly offer our money; and by nourishing Christ in poverty here and laying up great profit hereafter we will be able to attain the good things which are to come, by the grace and kindness of our Lord, Jesus Christ. ('Second sermon on Lazarus and the rich man' (trans. Roth), in Holland, 2019, p 301)

Poverty and suffering were no longer the theological problems; rather it was wealth, or at least how the wealthy used their resources, that became the focus of theological attention in the latter part of the 4th century. As a result, the pauper became a person with a claim upon the great (Brueggemann, 2003), and the great responded as to the face of Christ himself. It was not necessary to assess the claims of the poor upon the church to see if they were worthy of assistance. John inveighed against the notion of the examination of the poor to see whether they merited assistance: 'Let us have no more of this ridiculous, diabolical, peremptory prying' (cited in Tierney, 1959, p 55) he wrote. Notably, it was only those requesting aid who claimed to be priests who should be examined to determine the veracity of their claim on the church, but otherwise the poor should be helped without further inquisition.

---

[10] Naming in Judaeo-Christian scripture is very important: names reflected one's identity and position in the society, and to know someone's name conferred a kind of power; in these scriptures when God gave someone a new commission that commission was frequently signified with a new name. In this case, not to have a name is a signal of the rich man's ultimate unimportance.

John's generous position was later to be disputed by Gratian, a 12th century monk in Bologna, in his immensely important work the *Decretum Gratiani* (1140), which attempted for the first time to synthesise the many canons and practices of the church, Roman law, the Bible, the writings of church theologians, papal decrees, and the acts of church councils and synods from throughout the church and its history – many of which contradicted each other – into unified canon law, and which was taught in all the law schools of Christendom. We will consider the *Decretum* more in the next chapter, but the authorities on which Gratian bases his arguments wrote and preached during this earlier period. Gratian advanced the earlier Greek notions of deserving and undeserving poor. While a bishop was to be generous, Gratian wrote, 'In this generosity, due measure is to be applied both of things and of persons: of things, that not everything is to be bestowed on one but on various individuals' (in Tierney, 1959, pp 55–56). He cited two theological giants as his authorities for this position. The first was Ambrose, Bishop of Milan, who was considered one of the greatest practical poor relief administrators of all time. Ambrose's work *De Officiis*, Ambrose (2002), written in the late 380s, sought to replace Cicero's Roman secular understanding of moral standards with a bolder, superior Christian moral vision. In *De Officiis*, Ambrose set out how clergy should discriminate among different classes of poor who sought assistance from the church and provided an order of preference for providing assistance: firstly, faithful Christians, who would be an embarrassment to the church if they were seen as unassisted; then the old and sick; those who had fallen from riches into want and who would thereby feel shame, especially if it was through no fault of their own; and finally their own parents since the faithful were commanded to honour their parents in the First Testament. Ambrose did not intend to exclude anyone from assistance but rather to establish an order of claims on the alms of the church.[11]

Gratian's second authority was the early 5th century African Bishop of Hippo (in modern-day Algeria), Augustine. Augustine had studied rhetoric in Milan, and through his mother Monica's influence, was baptised by Ambrose in 387. Augustine wrote that resources should not be wasted on followers of reprehensible professions such as fortune-tellers, gladiators, actors and actresses, and prostitutes (Tierney, 1959, p 56). 'It is better to love with severity than to deceive with lenience', he wrote. 'The Church ought not

---

[11] It is worth noting that Ambrose and the citizens of Milan surrounded their cathedral in 386 to resist a demand from the Empress Justina that it be made available to the imperial family (Ambrose, trans. Liebescheutz, 2010). In a sense, this act established the independence of the church from the state. However, part of the present inquiry is to consider whether the state can be independent of the church.

to provide for a man who is able to work ... for strong men, sure of their food without work, often do neglect justice' (Tierney, 1959, p 58). While Augustine was focused more on combatting heresy and promoting justice than on establishing an ethic of poor relief, his words took on a life of their own in the developing theology of the church. Denying food to a person who was likely to be unjust if their source of food were secure became an important point to theologians of poor relief.

Despite the orderliness of Ambrose and the misgivings of Augustine, several decades later Pope Leo the Great (r. 440–461) still maintained, 'Let all those who come to the aid of the poor realize that they are actually spending this donation on God' (in Holland, 2019, p 308); this giving should be done without thought of reward on the part of the wealthy, although the 'alms themselves will pray for you' (Holland, 2019, p 309). As the bishops of the church developed ways to publicise the face of the poor to secure the political and social situation of the church, a passion for the poor was transferred from the churches and hospitals in Byzantium and Rome throughout the whole of the Roman Empire. The church's theology of poverty and the obligations of the wealthy and powerful to care for the poor and the powerless reshaped social and political relationships throughout the empire.

Monasticism, mendicants, and voluntary poverty

Two additional threads shaped the reconceptualisation of the new class of poor: the first, monks and mendicants; and the second, the rise of feudalism after the fall of the Roman Empire. If the poor were so closely identified with Jesus, then obviously the way to identify closely with Jesus was to become poor. A number of faithful individuals emerged in the 2nd and 3rd centuries who committed themselves to living holy and solitary lives of voluntary poverty. In the first decade of the 4th century, these hermits and ascetics were organised by early monastics such as Antony of Egypt ('the Great', 251?–356) into communities of hermits,[12] who lived a common rule, or way of life, forming the basis for monks who lived in what became religious orders.[13] It was these orders which ministered at the shelters, hospitals such as the *Basileias*, and orphanages, and which were to become central to the Christian response to the poor over the next thousand years. Monastics committed themselves to lives of chastity and self-sacrifice, although if they had private means they often turned their sources of income over to the monastery. The beggar life of Martin of Tours whom we considered

---

[12] I acknowledge the apparent oxymoron of living alone together; these hermits were known as κοινόβιον (*koinobion*, cenobites, those who lived a common life) and lived under an abbot.

[13] The term 'monk' comes from μοναχός, *monachos*, meaning 'one who lives alone'.

previously won him both the hearts of the people and the suspicions of his episcopal colleagues: his way of life served as a reproach to those abbots and bishops who valued comfort and status in this world. The escalation of poverty to the office of a bishop, although unusual, spoke to the redemptive power of poverty in Christian theology of the time.

Monastic orders began to proliferate, including those who followed the Rule (or *Asketikon*) of St Basil (356 CE), still followed today by Eastern Orthodox monks; the Rule of St Augustine (ca. 400), the oldest Western monastic rule; or the Rule of St Benedict (516), which has formed the foundation of the contemplative discipline of many Western monastic communities. Six hundred years later monasticism saw a revival in the Cistercian Order of St Bernard of Clairvaux, who revived the Benedictine rule in the 12th century at Cistercium (Citeaux) in France. However, St Francis, who founded the Italian order named after him (1209), and Dominic, who founded his eponymous order in Spain (1216) both disdained elaborate monastic buildings and created mendicant (begging) orders that relied on alms to survive. Monks of all of these orders renounced worldly goods in order to live a life of voluntary poverty. However, the very idea of voluntary poverty was theologically problematic for many, although Tierney (1959) writes, 'Medieval men were quite capable of distinguishing between holy poverty and idle parasitism' (p 11). The Scholastic theologian Thomas Aquinas (1224–74)[14] held that under the notion of natural law all things should be held in common in order to meet the basic necessities of life, for it was only human laws that create possessions; the danger for Aquinas was in voluntary poverty when religious in orders with no common possessions 'deprive themselves of the means of subsistence, they expose themselves to mendicancy' and other theological and practical dangers (Jones, 1995, p 424). Aquinas' position was challenged by later Protestant reformers, and their opposition became a theological framework for distinguishing between the 'deserving' (truly) poor versus the 'undeserving' (voluntary) poor reflected in later secular poor laws (Tierney, 1959). There was no reason that the church should offer charity or alms to someone who had voluntarily renounced their wealth and income and begged rather than worked. Such a person could only be understood as a burden on the church and its donor resources, despite their holy intentions.

In the West: feudalism and the rise of the church

In 476, the Roman Empire fell. Much has been written about this pivotal event in Western history, and it is not central to this story to elaborate all the

---

[14] Canonized as St Thomas Aquinas in 1323.

possible reasons for the decline of Rome: there is little doubt that the rise of the Huns (from 370) under Attila (fl. 444–453) in Central Asia and their regular invasions of the Eastern Roman Empire, and Gaul; the increasing power of the Goths, Visigoths, and Vandals in the north, the Berbers in the south, and Angles and Saxons in the northwest, all of whom invaded parts of the empire; civil wars and rebellions throughout the empire; corruption, internecine rivalry, and incompetent leadership in Rome; disease; and even climate change all contributed in some measure to the collapse of this vast empire. The Visigoths led by Alaric besieged and plundered Rome in 410, leaving the city and its population destitute and starving. Regular and further barbarian invasions followed, leading to internal political strife and political manoeuvring. The last emperor, the 16-year-old Romulus Augustulus, was forced to abdicate by Odoacer in 476, who was himself cut in half by Theodoric in 493. Although the Roman Senate continue to exist in name until sometime in the 7th century under the Ostrogothic Kingdom (now reduced to the Italian peninsula and the north-eastern Adriatic) and later Byzantine Empire (which ended a thousand years later in 1453), the Roman Empire in the European West was gone.

After the fall of Rome, there was no clear central authority or military to offer protection to the population during the many armed conflicts of this period.

> [T]he Western world endured a long age of chaos. It was a bleak and brutal time. There was no security or stability for peaceful folk; men [sic] willingly bargained away freedom for the protection of a lord; the sharpest argument was the edge of the sword. The Church shared in the general degradation. Nearly all ecclesiastical appointments and ecclesiastical revenues fell under the control of lay lords who commonly exploited them for their own economic advantage. (Tierney, 1959, p 6)

This period gave rise to hierarchical societies and feudalism. Feudalism has traditionally been understood as an exploitative economic relationship between lord and peasant. However, Fukuyama (citing Bloch) proposes that feudalism was more of a contractual arrangement between lord and vassal by which the latter was given protection and land in return for offering military service to the lord (Fukuyama, 2011); the dependent relationship was on both sides and needed to be renewed annually. The monarch granted land, or a fief, to vassals, who in turn allowed lords to build on and maintain land, and so forth down the ranks; peasant-serfs worked the land, all in exchange for protection and the right to earn a livelihood from the land (Handel, 2009). The monarch was in turn, of course, a vassal of God, and this hierarchy of protective relationships influenced the worldview and theology of the age. Fiefs could be inherited, and thus feudalism limited the mobility of the serfs (although not absolutely); this restriction on movement will reappear in the labour ordinances and poor law requirements towards the end of this period. Western Europe entered what we have come to know as the Dark Ages (generally accepted as 400–1000 CE). However, the importance of feudalism, writes Fukuyama, was not the economic relationship between lord and vassal, but the decentralisation of power it implied. After the fall of Rome, when its capitals were the centres of power, feudalism was a recognition that traditional centres of power and protection had become widely diversified, and allowed for the possibility – if not inevitability – of localised practices.

As the central authority of imperial Rome declined, the power of the Roman Church increased. The church took on what centralised authority there was during this period, although with many local adaptations and variations in practice. A church hierarchy developed, and the administration of poor relief was taken on by the bishop of each diocese (or region); bishops effectively became governors of their territories (Thompson, 1928/1959).

> Power and wealth gravitated to the church and its bishops, who not only accepted gifts and donations – from which they were expected to give freely to the poor – but also solicited them. Even the most sympathetic writers about the early and medieval church acknowledge that not all bishops lived up to their charitable obligations. (Handel, 2009, p 50)

The church attracted the brightest and best minds and administrators of the age. It became the repository and protector of culture and knowledge and earned the respect, however grudging, of barbarian and pagan tribal leaders and lords. Many of these tribal lords were baptised, along with their tribes. Some of these conversions, of course, may have been driven by pragmatism rather than a genuine conversion of the heart, a wish to avoid conflict as *Pax Romana* devolved and fragmented. This is the era when the church sent missionaries throughout Europe and the Slavic kingdoms in an attempt to draw and convert rulers and their peoples. This missionisation may have been driven by the motivation to win souls; it may have been driven by a wish to keep the peace; it may have been a desire to extend the influence of the church, or a combination of all three. This is the period of such names as Patrick of Ireland (386–461), Columba of Ireland and Scotland (521–597), and David of Wales (520–601). Gregory I ('the Great') sent Augustine (of Canterbury, d. 604) to convert the tribes of Britain; Columbanus (540–615) went to the Frankish kingdoms; Willibrord (658–739) went to Frisia (in modern-day Netherlands); Boniface (675–754) went to the Germanic tribes; Anskar (801–865) went to Denmark and Sweden. Cyril (826–869) and his brother Methodius (815–885) went to convert the Slavs. Unnamed missionaries were sent out to Iceland (740), Moravia (822),

Slovakia (828), Bulgaria (864), and Serbia (867). The Norman peoples converted to Christianity in 912, the Magyars in 948, the Danes in 965, the Poles in 966, and the Russians in 1015. In its own pragmatic way, the church had converted and legitimated the rulers of the various regions of Europe, who, in turn, legitimated the appointments and role of the church. Soon all of Europe was united not by an emperor or an army but by the church. Whereas before the fall of Rome the church had been a creature of the state, 'now many states owed the Church fealty and its spiritual bond held the Western world together' (Day and Schiele, 2013). What is also important for us is that the church disseminated its theology, or perhaps more appropriately its theologies, of the poor along with the gospel. Theology and the practical distribution of alms and assistance were very much coloured by local circumstances and the personalities of local church leaders. Quite widely divergent practices developed; not until Gratian in the 12th century, almost 800 years after the fall of Rome, was an effort made to align and codify these practices.

What we know about this period is filtered through the writings of historians and canonists such as Bede (of England) and Gratian. While missionaries carried with them the history and diverse theological positions and practices of the church, during this period, church and secular authorities maintained separate governance, one over the spiritual realm (which was broad indeed, and included marriage, inheritance, wills and estates, and social and moral concerns, as well as care for the poor), and the other over political concerns. These two areas frequently overlapped, and it was in the interest of the temporal lords to exercise as much influence as possible over the appointments of spiritual authorities up to and including the election of the Bishop of Rome (the Pope) himself. Care of the poor was the unchallenged domain of the church, which generally understood that church property was public property to be used for the common welfare, and especially for the sustenance of the poor (Tierney, 1959). Here we may find the roots of later administration of poor relief through the parish.

Emergence of Islam

Rome and Byzantium of course were only two of many powerful empires in this region of the world, although they were certainly the most influential in the development of a Western theology of social welfare and the poor. It is nevertheless important to be aware of one of the other major world religions that emerged during this period: Islam.

Proto-Arabic peoples were first identified (by their written language) in 853 BCE,[15] where they are thought to have been vassals of the Assyrian

---

[15] In the record of Gindibu the Arab, who despite his enormous force of infantry, cavalry, chariots, and camels, was defeated by Shalmaneser, King of Assyria.

Empire. The ancient Arabs (which root word is probably related to nomad, wilderness, or desert) were tribal societies and occupied territories from the ancient Near East and the Arabian Peninsula in the east, across Mediterranean Africa to modern-day Mauritania in the west. Arabs are mentioned sporadically in Hebrew scripture (for example, 2 Chron. 17:11), and Genesis 10 includes a list of the descendants of the common Semitic ancestor Shem, son of Noah, of Ark fame. Over time, a number of Arab tribes and kingdoms established themselves throughout the region. The vastness of their territory and influence meant that many Arabs could be successful traders: the incense trade route (which traded much more than incense and also dealt spices, precious stones and metals, perfumes, woods, and textiles) was a network of land and sea routes that stretched east from the Arabian peninsula to India and southern Asia, south to the Horn of Africa, and north to the Levant (contemporary Syria, Jordan, Lebanon, and Palestine). The incense trade route flourished for 800 years until the 2nd century CE and produced great wealth for Arabic empires. Just as, or more, important was the Silk Road trading route, which extended from East, Central, and South Asia, through to southern Europe, and flourished for the better part of 2000 years from the 2nd century BCE to the 18th century CE. Many empires and kingdoms took advantage of the Silk Road trade route, which brought not only goods and wealth but also ideas and religions. Pre-Islamic Arabic religions were a conglomerate of traditional polytheism, Christianity, Judaism, and other regional religions. While (as we saw previously) there were individual acts of *tzedakah* (or ص د ق, *ṣadaqa*), there was no core text to establish shared values about how to understand or respond to the poor. Tribal Arabic society was highly relational (or collectivist), which meant that each tribal group looked after its own members.

Mecca was located near the junctions of several important trade routes in western Arabia; it was also the site of the venerated Kaaba, the holy site and object of pilgrimage during the sacred months. Ibrahim (1982) writes that during the 6th century CE pre-Islamic Mecca came under the control of the Quraish[16] tribe. The growing importance of Mecca as a trading, negotiating, and regulatory centre meant that many wealthy Arab traders came to Mecca to invest their surplus wealth; likewise, many poor also moved to Mecca either because they were indebted to a Meccan merchant or they did not want to be a burden on their tribe's collective wealth. The movement to the city accelerated the fragmentation of tribal and clan social relations and itself created problems, such as how to feed the large influx of dependant poor. One way for an individual to address the problem of becoming a

---

[16] Transliterations vary, and I will take the English rendering of the author in question, while also attempting to be clear. This will mean some variations.

burden on clan or tribe was to commit *itiftād*, or ritual suicide, either by starving to death (Ibrahim, 1982, p 344) or drinking alcohol (Dabbagh, 2005); this was an admittedly drastic way to solve the problem of poverty, and merchants created syndicates modelled on the mutual assistance of tribes as a kind of collaborative business insurance (Ibrahim, 1982). Mecca became a highly polarised society based on wealth or the lack of it. A complex social hierarchy developed in Mecca[17] ranging from the very wealthy to the very poor. When contemplating this pre-Islamic period, one is reminded of contemporary hypercapitalist societies today and can understand why it is called the *jahiliyyah* (the time of ignorance) by Muslims (Armstrong, 1993).

One successful trader, a member of the Qurayash tribe, was Muhammad Ibn Abdallah (PBOH). He was a devout follower of the old religions and felt acutely the dramatic disparity between rich and poor in Mecca. Old tribal values of mutual care had been replaced by a 'rampant and ruthless capitalism' (Armstrong, 1993, p 132) where the new religion was money. Muhammad was concerned that the new cult of wealthy individualism would mean the disintegration of the tribal structures and the fragmentation of traditional Arabic mutual care. In 610 CE, Muhammad began receiving a series of visions which ordered him to recite (*Iqra!*), and during the next 23 years, he received revelations that were recited, recorded, and ordered, and became the holy book the Qur'an. The Qur'an did not claim to teach anything new but to remind the hearer of things they knew already. It proclaimed clearly that there was one God, al-Lah, not a profusion of territorial gods and religions. It adopted habits and rituals already in practice, such as the *hajj*. While not all Arabs initially welcomed the new religion, many were immediately struck by the beauty and power of the Qur'an (whose beauty does not come across as well in English), and the religion quickly unified believers across Arabian territories.

Muhammad is considered both a great religious teacher and a social reformer. In contrast to the great inequalities which Muhammad had witnessed in Mecca in 610, the Qur'an presents a vision of a just society:

> In practical terms, islām mean that Muslims had a duty to create a just, equitable society, where the poor and vulnerable are treated decently. The early moral message of the [Qur'an] is simple: It is wrong to stockpile wealth and to build a private fortune, and good to share the wealth of society fairly by giving a regular proportion of one's wealth to the poor. Almsgiving (zakat) accompanied by prayer

---

[17] *Sayyids* or chiefs, free clan members, *halīf* or allies, *mawālī* or clients – who could be manumitted slaves – *qinn*, slaves, who were property, and the *muwalladūn*, or children of *qinn*, who were at the very bottom.

(salat) represented two of the five essential 'pillars' (rukn) or practices of Islam. (Armstrong, 1993, pp 142–3)

Muhammad's message was rejected by some powerful compatriots, and in 622 he was forced to flee to Yathrib (later renamed Medina) in what became known as the *Hegira*. It is from the *Hegira* that Islam is dated. Muhammad originally intended his prophecy to be consistent with the People of the Book (the Jews), but they ultimately rejected his overtures. Followers were then directed to pray facing the direction (*qibla*) of Mecca rather than Jerusalem as they did at first. In Medina, Muhammad developed Islam from a religious prophecy into a political reality. In Islam, all religious people have a duty to work for a just and equal society, including regular giving to support the poor, the emancipation and protection of women through the granting of legal rights of inheritance and divorce (this anticipated the rights enjoyed by women in so-called developed nations by 1,300 years), education, and the moral and spiritual equality of the sexes (Armstrong, 1993, p 158).

> Surely the men who submit and the women who submit, and the believing men and the believing women, and the obeying men and the obeying women, and the truthful men and the truthful women, and the patient men and the patient women, and the humble men and the humble women, and the almsgiving men and the almsgiving women, and the fasting men and the fasting women, and the men who guard their private parts and the women who guard, and the men who remember Allah much and the women who remember – Allah has prepared for them forgiveness and a mighty reward. (Surah Al-Ahzab [33]:35)

Here the poor are not theologised (or philosophised) as a class of persons but as individuals who naturally exist in any society and who need to be cared for by the entire society.

Muhammad's great recital recreated *ummah* (community, or unity) among Arabs. In social and geo-political terms, 'Arab tribes were turned from their raiding of one another to a great raid on the lands without. Thenceforth there were to be no more Arab tribes, but only Arabs, Moslems arrayed against non-Moslems' (Thompson, 1928/1959). The *ummah* of Arab Muslims was formidable and resulted in the fall of the Sasanid Persian Empire in 651 CE; the conquest of Syria, Palestine, Egypt, and Mediterranean Africa soon followed, as well as several assaults on Constantinople (in 654–668, 667, and 672–73). By 750 the Caliphate extended from Iberia in the west, across Mediterranean Africa and the Mediterranean islands, encompassing the former Persian and Sind territories in the east, the Byzantine Empire, and north through the Slavic regions. Islam did not spread only through military conquest: Arab traders spread the religion in their work and by intermarrying with local peoples, particularly in South Asia (modern India, Pakistan, Bangladesh, and Afghanistan) and Central Asia along the Silk Road. Now that there was a single text to unify them, Muslims were a formidable force not only militarily but also morally. And there was, at least in theory, a unified response to the poor.

In the East

Since in many ways, the poor (as a class) and the early Christian Church's response to them were created in Byzantium and the East it is well worth following through – at least briefly – what occurred in the thousand years between the Cappadocians and the final fall of Constantinople. While a great deal occurred politically, intellectually, and militarily in Byzantium during this millennium (the Muslim conquest during the 7th century and the loss of Egypt and Syria to the Arabs; the arrival of the Turks in Anatolia in the 11th century; the sack of Constantinople during the Fourth Crusade, 1202–04; the re-establishment of the empire in 1261; and the gradual erosion and fall of the Byzantine Empire to the Ottomans in 1453), nevertheless it would seem that little changed in respect of the way the church theologised and cared for the poor. This may be because the church in the East remained more centralised than in the West, and perhaps because Byzantium was preoccupied with defending itself against the threat of conquest. The increasing tensions between Rome and Constantinople meant that the church in the eastern part of the Roman Empire became increasingly independent. The Ecumenical Patriarch of Constantinople (also now styled as New Rome) became the effective leader of the Christian Church in the East and finally separated from Rome in the so-called Great Schism of 1054. This split gave rise to what we now know as the Catholic Church in the West and the Orthodox Church in the East. While the theological differences between the two branches of Christianity may seem today like so much hair-splitting,[18] these differences were the overlay of fundamental cultural, political, and theological differences which had accumulated over many centuries,

---

[18] Does the Holy Spirit proceed from the Father and the Son or directly from God the Father (the *Filioque* controversy)? Should only unleavened bread be used at the Eucharist? Is hesychasm [contemplative prayer] a heresy or an intimate way to experience the divine? These were not, of course, trivial questions at the time, nor is what they represent trivial even now. However, to non-believers looking in at the controversies, they may not arouse much passion.

particularly since the fall of Rome in 476. The German Pope Leo IX's (r. 1049–54) claim to Rome's universal jurisdiction over all of Christendom by divine appointment was for the Ecumenical Patriarch no doubt the most grievous and most unacceptable of the differences. The Great Schism[19] divided what is now Eastern Europe (include the regions of the Middle East, East Africa, south-eastern and Mediterranean Europe, Russia, and the Caucasus) from Western Latinate Europe (excluding, of course, Iberia) and Scandinavia. This schism inevitably meant that there were different theologies and practices in caring for the poor in the East and the West.

What is important for our purposes is to consider what happened to the poor in the East. Orthodox theology was quite different from Western theology, and while it drew on the same scriptural sources, the cultural hermeneutic – the way scripture was interpreted – was significantly different. The theological roots of caring for the poor were in the East, of course, and those roots continued to nourish the theology of the Orthodox response to the poor. The incarnational theology of the Cappadocians evolved into the concept of *theosis*, 'becoming God', or union with God; *theosis* is 'the profound communion that exists between God and humanity/world with the birth of Jesus Christ. St Athanasius summarises this theological tenet when he says "God became man so that man can become like God"' (Prodromou and Symeonides, 2016, p 8 n5). The theological implications of this statement are that each person not only has divine value but has the potential to become like God. This theological framing requires not only that the wealthy value the poor and care for them but that the wealthy treat their wealth in the same way that they would expect God to treat them: with generosity. The parable of the rich man and Lazarus remains constantly in the background. An 'impressive range of hospitals, shelters for orphans, widows, and widowers; hospices for the terminally ill with contagious diseases; and schools and libraries' continued in the East through medieval times (Prodromou and Symeonides, p 2). It seems, then, that the practical needs of the poor were cared for in the Orthodox East at least until the fall of Constantinople. Orthodox theologians continued to address issues such as poverty, environmental stewardship, and charitable and philanthropic action. This is of course exactly what we would expect to see growing out of the incarnational foundations established by the Cappadocians.

---

[19] The Schism was actually carried out by mutual and retaliatory acts of excommunication and condemnation between Pope Leo IX and the Ecumenical Patriarch Michael Cerularius. Since Leo had died by the time his notification of excommunication was delivered, it was no longer considered valid. Church history can be quite complex.

Summary

In this chapter, we have seen the development of what I argue is the seminal period of the religious response to the poor, which in turn was responsible for the foundations of both religious and secular responses to the poor in the West for the next two millennia. Early Christian believers lived between the Ascension of Jesus and his expected return. The delay of Jesus' return meant that these believers had to figure out how to live in the meantime. Communities of believers developed, and specific people were appointed to care for the widows and orphans in their midst. As this Jewish sect expanded throughout the Roman Empire it encountered, then adapted, the language and metaphor of the Roman state. Christians developed an *evangelion*, a proclamation of good news, at first for its own (Jewish) adherents, and then for all people (Gentiles). After he became emperor and moved the capital of the empire to Byzantium, Constantine laid the collegial practice of caring for members on the early church; he expected church leaders to enact both philanthropy and euergetism, the practices of giving and doing good for the benefit of the widow, orphan, and sick in order to maintain order within the state. The church effectively created the poor as a class of people because in one sense the church needed the poor to ensure its social and political role and relative independence. The Cappadocians developed and promoted an incarnational theology of the poor – that is, that the poor were the contemporary embodiment of Jesus – and preached that caring for the poor was caring for Jesus. The Cappadocians developed specific institutional responses to the poor: hospitals and leprosaria, orphanages, and monasteries with facilities to care for the poor as part of their structures. They rejected traditional Greek notions of worthy and unworthy poor (although these concepts will re-emerge in later theological formulations) and abandoned Roman notions that assistance should be available only to citizens. The Cappadocians so identified the poor with the person of Jesus that they theologised wealth and private property as the problem rather than poverty, and introduced a notion of social justice into the theology of the early church. Early church theologians finally decided that wealth was acceptable because it allowed the wealthy to do good works; merit would be achieved because grateful recipients would pray for the almsgiver. This was a radical reversal of previous conceptualisations of poverty and sickness as divine punishments. This retheologising also worked to enhance the social and material wellbeing of the church, as the wealthy gave to the church to care for the poor on their behalf. So identified did the poor become with Jesus that in order to be more like Jesus some believers became poor voluntarily and became mendicants. Voluntary poverty became theologically problematic for some church leaders, and the idea of the worthy (non-voluntary) and unworthy (voluntary) poor re-emerged. Diverting the resources of the church from the truly poor when one could have fed oneself was burdensome to the church, as was distracting the resources of the wealthy away from the church.

As the Roman Empire declined, the power of the Roman Church increased. The Western church gradually spread throughout much of western and northern Europe and adopted divergent practices and theologies in caring for the poor as it encountered local tribes and leaders. These diverse practices were not aligned and codified until the 12th century. In the East (which included the Middle East, East Africa, south-eastern and Mediterranean Europe, Russia, and the Caucasus), however, the Byzantine Empire remained largely centralised in Constantinople and continued to address poverty, through philanthropy and charity.

Meanwhile, in 622 Islam was born and unified and spread rapidly throughout the Arab nations to create one of the largest empires the world had seen. A unified Islam meant a consistent response to the Muslim poor, and almsgiving became one of the central pillars of faith for all Muslims. And in the East, the incarnational understanding of Christ in the poor continued to inform the church's response.

4

Reforming the poor

Since Constantine had committed the poor (as a designated class of persons) to the care of the church, it is now to the church that we must look for the way the poor (and the wealthy) were theologised and managed during the Middle Ages. The purview of the church was of course shaped by many secular political and social forces and contexts during this period, and not every legal principle that was approved in theory was effectively enforced in practice (Tierney, 1959). We saw in the previous chapter that diverse local practices in caring for the poor (and theologies about wealth) emerged throughout the church in the 700 years from the fall of Rome to the *Decretum* of Gratian about 1140. The point of Gratian's work was to bring order and consistency to the miscellany of practices in the church.

During the Middle Ages, some of the greatest thinkers of the church appeared, and the theological attention of the church's scholars (the so-called Scholastics, Anselm, Abelard, and Hildegard, and High Scholastics, Aquinas, Scotus, and Ockham) was focused on developing a more systematic, consistent approach to the church's theology, and on navigating the increasingly turbulent space between the church and the emerging secular powers. Monarchs drew on ancient and developing church theologies that they had a right to rule because they had been granted that right by God – this notion of divine right seems to be an obvious development of the Deuteronomic idea that if you were successful you had been divinely blessed and therefore could claim divine authority and answer only to God. In 1173, Hildegard, a polymath abbess and counsellor to many, wrote that hierarchical society may have been accepted as 'necessary', but, she continued, the poor still bore 'the image and likeness of the Lord' (Hildegard of Bingen, 2004, Letter 378). Likewise, Francis of Assisi (d. 1226), the founder of the Franciscan Order, 'found in the poor, in their wretchedness, their powerlessness, their dependency, the poverty Christ had preached' and dignity and the promise of divine love (Wandel, 1990). For St Francis, the physical conditions of poverty reflected humanity's spiritual condition. As in 4th century Byzantium, Western theological attention remained largely focused on how the wealthy used their wealth, rather than on the poor, and it was common for wealthy landowners to feed the local involuntary poor regularly. However, the voluntary and absolute poverty practised by some religious orders was not uncontroversial. Pope John XXII deplored this kind of poverty, and in 1318 he burned at the stake four Spiritual Franciscans for heresy. In 1323, Pope John denounced as heresy the teaching that Christ and his apostles did not own any property – and he thus attempted to sever the spiritual foundations of voluntary poverty. He was unsuccessful in suppressing this form of piety, and later in that century popes came to support it.

As we shall see, events – notably the Great Famine and the Great Plague of the 14th century, the fall of Constantinople, and the flight of its scholars and artists – and the emergence of church reformers in the 15th and 16th centuries contributed to the decline of the power, influence, and centralised authority of the church. These also contributed ultimately to the transfer of the church's authority and responsibility to care for the poor to secular and civic authorities. The Reformation resulted in a complete reversal of the church's theology of wealth and poverty in Protestant regions. It also established the foundation for the fundamental tension between caring for the poor from a position of compassion ('the image and likeness of the Lord') and a position that prioritised maintaining social order and the preservation of class privilege.

The misconception that the so-called Dark Ages was a period of intellectual and technological dormancy has led many people to assume that nothing much happened during the thousand years between the fall of Rome and the Reformation other than periodic wars, invasions, and crusades.[1] On the contrary, technologies such as the spinning wheel, watermill, windmill, crank, cam, flywheel, rudder, compass, stirrup, horse collar, and nailed horseshoe made a peasant's life a little easier and more productive, and the long bow and cross bow made making war more efficient for knights and their lords (Day and Schiele, 2013). This is not to suggest that a peasant's life was easy. Even when they were not being overrun by invaders, the life of a peasant-serf was affected by wars and political strife. Even in secure areas, resources (such as food, horses, and other supplies) could be appropriated to areas of direct conflict and combat. More efficient agricultural technologies increased the wealth of landowners and increased the burden to produce on both vassal and the land. Although peasants worked the land of their lords, each was usually given a small plot on common land on which to produce food for themselves and their households. However, this system came under threat by increasingly powerful landholders. In England, for instance, the Statute of Merton (in 1235, 20 years after *Magna Carta*) allowed lords to enclose or wall-off common land for private use for the first time. This

---

[1] The period of the so-called Crusades, the Reconquista and other religious wars began in 1096 and lasted until 1492. Although they were of great political and military significance in these centuries, and in the contemporary relationship between Christians and Muslims, they did not directly impact the Christian Church's theology or treatment of the poor (except those who were in the way of the invader armies), and we will not consider them here.

statute provided the legal foundation of the Enclosure Movement, which in turn formed the legal basis for individuals to create and hold private property. Although it was intended to limit the power of the king, this seminal statute[2] had the effect of defining ownership of land so that the owner was entitled (quite literally, since they now had the title to the land) to use the resources of the land (such as wood for heating or shipbuilding, or grazing lands for stock or deer) for themselves rather than for the common good. This also meant that tenants and their households could be pushed off land by wealthy lords because the tenants could not afford the costs of 'enclosing' it. (Enclosures were amplified in England under the Statute of Mortmain in 1279 and by similar statutes in continental Europe, which also severely curtailed the granting of lands to ecclesiastical institutions.) In short, the management of wealth and poverty was dynamic and rarely under the control of the poor and less powerful. The independent wealth of landowners increased. Church institutions – monasteries, abbeys, cathedrals, and some larger parishes – were often among these wealthy landowners.

Caring for the poor, managing wealth

The poor of medieval and late medieval Europe were not only the obvious and usual involuntary poor – widows and orphans, the disabled and disfigured – but also included what we would now call the working poor, including temporarily unemployed artisans, day labourers between harvests, urban wage earners, rural peasants whose lands and harvests had been devastated by natural disaster or war, and those who worked in so-called dishonourable professions[3] (Wandel, 1990). In addition, the so-called unworthy poor also begged in the urban streets, and rural poor came into the towns. By the late 15th century, the magistrates of Basel listed 25 different categories of so-called phony beggars (Davis, 1968), or unworthy poor. Guilds protected their members from the extremes of poverty in bad times, but membership was not available to all. Marginal workers were increasing along with the poor and could include journeymen, householders, and artisans 'heavily burdened with children' (Davis, p 223); the burden threshold was set (in Lyons at least) at three children or more. Tax records show that in some Swiss towns, for instance, between a half and two thirds of the population was considered poor by 1460, and up to a fifth did not receive regular nourishment (Wandel, p 11). The poor

---

[2] The Statute of Merton is considered the first statute passed by the English Parliament.
[3] These included sex workers, executioners, and gravediggers, people who worked in prisons, tower guards, and itinerate professions such as troubadours, mimes, and jugglers, and so-called dishonourable people such as Jews, gypsies, bastards, and moral deviants (Wandel, 1990, p 9).

were not quietly poor: they were considered a 'disruptive and periodically violent presence – as a source of social unrest and consequently a focus for social control' (Mollat, cited in Wandel, p 12), and also a threat to public health (Davis, p 228). This unruliness was of obvious concern to the civic authorities.

Although wealthy individuals often routinely fed and clothed the poor, care for the poor remained largely the responsibility of the church through its clergy or designated almoners. Almost a century after the publication of Gratian's *Decretum*, new law was developed by the papacy, including the five-volume *Decretals* of Gregory IX (published in 1234), the *Liber Sextus* (the 'Sixth Book') of Boniface VIII (1298), and the *Clementines* (1317), named after Clement V (who had died in 1314). These four works, published over 150 years, formed the *Corpus Iuris Canonici* ('The body of canon law'), around which grew many glosses, commentaries, and interpretations. The *Decretum* dealt with a wide array of theological as well as legal and philosophical issues. On the contested issue of the possession of property, Gratian proposed that so-called natural law required that property be held in common. It was only human law that established ownership, he wrote, and since natural law superseded human law, individual claims to property were invalid. By this reasoning, special provisions for the poor would never be required since anyone and everyone had a right to whatever they needed. Commentators first addressed this uncomfortable notion of biblically-based communalism by amending the understanding of 'natural' to 'primitive', in a kind of prelapsarian understanding of the human condition: there was no want in the Garden of Eden because everything was available, and no one owned anything. A commentary on the *Decretum* by Teutonicus (d. 1245) threaded a pragmatic way through the problem by asserting that natural law stated that all things were common, and although private ownership could not be denied, excess resources were to be shared in time of necessity. Teutonicus made connections between natural law and the obligations of charity, and between the right to own property and the right to use of excess property. Citing the theological writings of Basil and Ambrose, Teutonicus inveighed,

> You own property you say? What? From what stores did you bring it into this world? When you came into the light, when you came forth from your mother's womb, with what resources, with what reserves did you come endowed? No one may call his own what is common, of which, if a man takes more than he needs it is obtained by violence ... Who is more is more unjust, more avaricious, more greedy than a man who takes the food of the multitude not for his use but for his abundance and luxuries? (cited in Tierney, 1959, p 34)

The *Decretum* and its commentators established the moral (but not statutory) right of the poor to be supported by the excess wealth of a community. This principle was also applied to church property. Providing for the poor from the resources of the church – whether a great cathedral or a tiny chantry – was not charity but simply providing to the poor what was already theirs, held in trust by the church for the common welfare. Theologically, the church was neither a charitable institution nor a dispenser of charity but a public institution redistributing the community's wealth back to members of the community as they required.

The 12th-century *Decretum* drew on documents as old as the 5th century. Its theological focus remained on the wealthy donor, the right use of wealth, and the appropriate administration of assistance. Gratian set out a fourfold division of church property: one part for the bishop; one part to be distributed by the bishop among his clergy; one part for the building and repair of churches; and one part for the relief of the poor (these were not necessarily, nor intended to be, equal parts since situations would vary throughout Christendom).[4] This allocation worked at a time when the church's organisation was highly centralised into dioceses, and the bishop was the key figure responsible for its administration. During the church's period of expansion after 476 and into the high Middle Ages, however, diocesan organisation throughout Christendom had devolved into parishes, smaller units of a diocese, and each parish was a separate (although not independent) unit. Parishes introduced complexity into the centralised system imagined by the *Decretum*. The priest who served a parish may or may not have had direct control of the income of the parish;[5] that income might go to a local lord, a local monastery, or in some other way be diverted. It was not possible to apply the 5th-century allocation standard set out by the *Decretum* to the 12th- and 13th-century church, although the expectation of the right use of wealth, hospitality, and care for the poor continued.

Huguccio's commentary on the *Decretum* (published 18 years after the publication of the *Decretum*) was one of the first commentaries that focused on the characteristics of those who received aid. In his commentary, Huguccio divided the poor into three categories: people who were born poor and willingly endured their poverty for the love of God; those who had possessions but voluntarily gave them up in order to more closely identify with Christ (like monks, mendicants, Beguines, and Beghards[6]); and those

---

[4] In 1014, King Ethelred in England reduced this four-part division to three parts: one for the clergy, one for church buildings, and one part for the poor.

[5] Derived from income from the land, the offerings of the people including fees for baptisms, marriages, and funerals, and a tithe, or tax, of 10 per cent on each parishioner.

[6] Beguines and Beghards were groups of faithful laypeople (that is, they did not take religious vows), mostly women, in Europe (particularly northern Europe) who believed that a truly

who were so-called necessarily or involuntarily poor. The poor in this third sort of poverty, he thought, were 'filled with the voracity of cupidity' (Tierney, 1959, p 11), or, put more simply, greedy. Huguccio's words suggest that the church did not consistently consider the state of being poor one of Christ-like holiness, although poverty itself was not considered a vice that should be punished. This attitude, however, was controversial: while one commentator on the *Liber Sextus* stated explicitly, 'Poverty is not a crime' (cited in Tierney, 1959, p 12), Joannes Teutonicus Zemeke in his commentary on the *Decretum* cited the Roman law that 'a man able to work, who accepted public relief, was to be treated as a criminal and condemned to slavery' (cited in Tierney, 1959, p 58).

The poor had legal rights, including the right to sue in court; they were even exempted from paying court fees and had the right to free legal counsel provided by a (church) court. Tierney (1959) suggests that the generous treatment of the poor by church courts may be motivated by a conviction that the order and harmony of the church would be furthered by maximising the influence of church courts:[7]

> There was a general agreement among the canonists that the Church had a special duty to protect the class of people they called miserabiles personae, 'wretched persons' – 'poor wretches',' we might say. The term was used of widows and orphans in particular, and of all the poor and oppressed in general. As Gratian himself put it 'The bishop ought to be solicitous and vigilant concerning the defense of the poor and the relief of the oppressed'. (Tierney, 1959, p 15)

In addition to parishes and monasteries, hospitals continued to be built at the behest of wealthy benefactors. Benefactors came from all sectors: kings, bishops, lords, merchants, guilds, and municipalities. Hospitals, as always, were more than places for the sick but also included orphanages and lying-in hospitals for pregnant women; they also looked after the aged and the poor. In fact, notes Tierney (1959), these hospitals were more like what we would later come to know as almshouses or workhouses where indoor relief was provided. So popular were these institutions throughout Christendom (and also in the Islamic world, where hospitals were supported by *waqfs*, dedicated

---

religious life required extreme poverty and asceticism. They lived in communities but were not convents or monasteries. Remnants of the Beguines endured until the late 20th century. Beghards were a similar northern European group of men which endured until the mid-19th century.

[7] This again suggests that the church used its treatment of the poor to further its own standing, as it had when it encouraged almsgiving through the church in 4th century Byzantium.

charitable foundations), that Charlemagne[8] decreed that every cathedral and monastery should have a hospital attached to it. Hospitals, infirmaries and *xenones* (hospices), *gerocomeia* (homes for the aged), and orphanages continued to be endowed and built throughout the Byzantine Empire through the 11th and 12th centuries (Constantelos, 1968). The 13th century saw an explosion of newly built hospitals in the West, led by Italy; the states of the German Kingdom saw 150 hospitals built between the 13th and 16th centuries; in England, there were over 600 hospitals by the middle of the 14th century. Often these hospitals took the name of the local church that was associated with it. There was no test associated with receiving aid from these hospitals; sometimes the poor were fed daily by the hospital although they did not live in it. Hospitality in its broadest interpretation seems to have been the guiding principle of these institutions.

The schools of the church were also open to the poor as well as the wealthy. It could be said that education for all was one of the only things the church did at a structural level to prevent poverty; its other ministrations responded to existing poverty. The church as an institution was very much a creature of its time, and had no thought of social reform (at least publicly) or doing anything that might disturb the divinely installed hierarchy or its own privileged position in that hierarchy. In preserving feudal structures, the church was looking after its own interests as a landowner, which were often on the scale of a great feudal lord, or more. Preserving these structures also ensured an income for the church, which it could then distribute or use itself. A key aim and task of the church was, as we have seen, to promote and maintain social stability – or social control, if you will – and this made it a creature of the secular authority. Stability meant ensuring that the wealthy were reasonably content with the church so that the income streams of the church were not disrupted. Stability also meant that the poor were sufficiently cared for so that they did not become unruly and cause ructions for their lords, threaten public safety or health, or embarrass the church. However, in their later history of poor relief, the Webbs (Webb and Webb, 1927) – no allies of the powerful – believed that in practice there was very little parochial relief in England available from the 12th century onward because funds were diverted for other purposes.[9]

---

[8] King of the Lombards from 774, of the Franks from 786, and first Holy Roman Emperor, 800–14.

[9] 'Already by the twelfth century, it seems, the tithe had ceased to supply any appreciable sum toward the relief of the poor. The high dignitaries of the Church, the alien priories, the various conventual or collegiate bodies in England itself, and lay impropriators gradually got into their hands most of the well-endowed benefices, or the greater part of their tithes: and in spite of repeated injunctions, and even statutory provisions, it seems clear that, by the end of the fifteenth century at any rate, these absentee proprietors made no regular

The social imaginary

Regardless of how we understand the institution of the Christian Church, the compromises it made to preserve itself, or the ways it administered relief to the poor, there can be little doubt that – at least in Eastern and Western Christendom – there was a shared social imaginary about life, the universe, and everything. We have been talking about the ways church thinkers theologised the poor, but of course, in theologising about the poor they also created comprehensive theologies about how the world works, how the Christian God works, and how the divine and earthly realms interact with one another. Taylor (2007) writes that social imaginaries often begin among a small group of elites, and then filter through an entire society. This, I think, is what happened beginning with the Cappadocians and continued through the Middle Ages. It was the church that not only created but sustained that shared social imaginary by being the primary provider of education and through its ecclesiastical courts throughout greater Europe. It is not surprising that it was a Christian imaginary (of a sort) that came to dominate throughout this period. It was the Christian imaginary that allowed Christian monarchs to claim their thrones and their right to rule; it was the Christian imaginary that justified the Crusades and the appropriation of the lands and wealth of non-Christians; it was the Christian imaginary that supported hierarchical social structures and allowed the wealthy to remain wealthy and the poor to remain in thrall to them; and it was the Christian social imaginary that required the wealthy (including the church) to use a portion of their wealth justly to feed the poor in order to maintain social order.

The writings of Gratian and the commentators on his work had an effect far beyond the institutional church: the practices and theologies set out in these works shaped the way entire societies understood and lived in the world. It is here that we see the foundations of what we would now call 'the West', even when those societies and states expressly understand themselves to be secular, or non-religious. Taylor notes that the notion of secularity requires a notion of sacred against which to establish itself. The theological elites of the Middle Ages imagined a divinely established, hierarchical, and therefore divinely ordered and stable society, where divine justice looked after the good and punished the guilty, either in this world or the next. We shall see that it was when stability was disrupted and ill befell the good

---

subventions for the poor of the parishes whence their revenues were derived' (Webb and Webb, 1927, p 3). Tierney (1959, p 116) supports this point: 'Altogether the complaints about the neglect of parish poor relief, which bec[a]me loud, frequent and bitter at the end of the fourteenth century, were, from one point of view, only a minor symptom of a general decay in standards of ecclesiastical administration in the later Middle Ages.'

as well as the guilty, and perhaps in the rise of humanism, that the social imaginary was forced to evolve.

Part of maintaining social order and a consistent social imaginary was ensuring that there was a shared understanding of what that social order should be: this meant ensuring a clear understanding of the authority of the church to decide what was orthodox in order to maintain the purity of the church. This was an age when it was part of the social imaginary that divine wrath was manifested in the form of disasters and catastrophes on disobedient humans and that the deviance or heresy of even one person could result in divine punishment being visited on entire communities and nations. The authority to determine and enforce truth and orthodoxy was, therefore, essential. Gregory VII (r. 1073–85) began papal reforms to correct secular influences over the church and laid the foundation for what became an inquisitorial approach to the theologies and practices of the church.

This approach included increasing hostility toward women (Deane, 2011) as seductive temptresses unable to resist the temptations of this world, and who would tempt men to abandon right living.[10] In the 14th century, during the height of the anti-witchcraft craze, it is estimated that as many as nine million women in Europe may have been killed (Day and Schiele, 2013). Many of these were independent women who supported themselves as healers, guild workers, or businesswomen; some were sex workers but others were women who had simply outlived their husbands and had become economic burdens on society.

> The religious legitimation for gynocide allowed men to reaffirm religious and political power over women. In a social sense, the witchcraze rid society of an unwanted, perhaps threatening population: independent women. In the economic sphere, society no longer had to support excess women and their never-to-be born children who might have added to unemployment and dependency. (Day and Schiele, 2013, p 97)

Since these women and marginalised persons were tried in inquisitorial courts there can be no doubt about the church's complicity in these mass persecutions and executions, although Klaits (1985) argues that later Protestants were equally active in the prosecution of witches, and in fact, most witch trials took place during and after the Renaissance and Reformation.

---

[10] This same accusation was laid on same-sex attracted men (who we may anachronistically call 'homosexuals', a word first coined by Kertbeny in 1869 (Crompton, 2003); apparently the commitment of men to live rightly ordered lives that conformed to the social imaginary was fragile and quite easily swayed.

Both Protestants and Catholics were conscious of the ability of witches to create profound disruption in societies. Most 'witches' in Europe were poor beggar women, and Klaits (1985) proposes that poverty and social reactions to them were fundamental to the prosecution of witches, born of resentment about the expectation of charity. Without a doubt, the churches had a significant role in maintaining a kind of social order and a consistent, if brutal, social imaginary.

Despite this, there is little doubt that the church and its bishops continued to understand that caring for the poor was part of their canonical obligation, even when such care grew beyond its capacity. In 1250, Bishop Grosseteste of Lincoln proclaimed to the papal Curia,

> Moreover, the work of pastoral care consists not only in the administration of Sacraments and the saying of canonical hours and the celebration of masses ... It consists in the feeding of the hungry, in giving drink to the thirsty, in clothing the naked, in receiving guests, in visitation of the sick and prisoners, especially of one's own parishioners, to whom the temporal goods of the churches belong. (Tierney, 1959, p 101)

At the Council of Lambeth in 1281, the church affirmed that rectors of churches 'should exercise the grace of hospitality through their agents,[11] according as the resources of their churches suffice and so that at least the extreme need of the poor parishioners is relieved' (Tierney, 1959, p 100). There is no doubt that at least from the 4th until the 14th centuries the church at least tried to maintain its obligation and prerogative to care for the poor.

Disasters strike

Two great catastrophes impacted Europe and Asia in the 14th century, disrupted the social imaginary, and are generally considered to mark the end (or at least the beginning of the end) of the Middle Ages. Together with the rise of secular monarchical states and what we would recognise today as national boundaries, they also mark the beginning of the ebb of the mostly unquestioned authority of the church. The first catastrophe was the Great Famine (1315–17), which resulted in the deaths of millions in northern and central Europe, reduced human life expectancy by 15 per cent, and reduced the number of stock (and therefore wealth and food) by up to 80 per cent. There were a number of contributing factors to the Great Famine. These included an unsustainable population increase over

---

[11] Almoners, distributors of alms, latterly called wardens.

the preceding century;[12] excessive rain and cold over several years, and the consequent failure of the harvest throughout Europe (especially in 1316); high food prices generally, together with an increase in the cost of living; and the diversion of resources of the wealthy nobles from providing for increasingly indebted and impoverished monasteries (where they could have been used to support the poor) to war-making. Naturally, the church blamed heretics for the famine:

> Of course, heresy in this period in the north seemed more than merely irrational. It smacked of revolution. To be sure, not every heterodoxy that found expression in famine-stricken areas owed its origin to the famine conditions. But the social and economic tensions that accompanied the harvest shortfalls, high prices, and violence of war sharpened authorities' perceptions of heterodox believers as threats to the political and social order, both secular and ecclesiastical. Sectarians who had been suffered to exist, if not quite tolerated, for thirty years or more came to be tarred by those in power as diabolical and ripe for extirpation in the charged atmosphere of 1315–1322. (Jordan, 1998, p 164)

At the time of the Great Famine, 85–90 per cent of the population was rural, but because of the famine, the rural indigent and starving began to migrate and massed near towns seeking food. In some parts of Europe, up to a third of rural homesteads and land were abandoned. Villages were turned into towns where waves of beggars threatened violence, and there was an increase in lawlessness in places like the lower Rhine, France, and England. Starvation led to increased vulnerability to other diseases such as typhus: up to 10 per cent of the malnourished population may have perished from disease. Famine strained the ability of ecclesiastical institutions to respond to the needs of the poor and starving, although many appear to have tried to do so. Some churches and monasteries were forced to declare themselves bankrupt.[13] Municipalities, however, were able to procure and negotiate the price of grains and other foodstuffs: 'As the cost-of-living squeeze began to affect many of the well-to-do, both lay and ecclesiastical, there was a retreat from private almsgiving, and it became increasingly common for municipal governments to act in the name of the general welfare' (Jordan, 1998, p 158).

It was at the beginning of the Great Famine that we see the beginning of the shift of the provision of public assistance from the church to

---

[12] Deane (2011) notes that the population of Europe doubled between the 12th and early 14th centuries, in part due to advancing agricultural practices.

[13] Jordan notes, for example, that the Bolton Priory, which was ultimately bankrupted, was forced to cut its charity by 90 per cent in the second year of the Famine (Jordan, 1998, p 109).

secular authorities, although this shift was less likely to be from charitable motivation than an interest in maintaining social order and civic authorities' unwillingness to tolerate the social, reputational, and public health risks from piles of emaciated corpses. Nonetheless, the social imaginary required those with resources – even corporate secular entities such as cities and states – to care for the starving poor who bore the imprint of Christ.

The second disaster was the Great Plague,[14] the bubonic plague, which peaked between 1347 and 1353 (although there were periodic outbreaks over the next several centuries). Estimates of plague-related deaths range from 25–200 million, that is, between 25 and 50 per cent of Europe, and the impact continued over many decades. Tierney (1959) estimates that in England, for example, by 1400 the population was little more than half the pre-plague number. It took nearly two centuries for Europe to return to its pre-plague population level. Modern theory attributes the plague to fleas on rodents migrating from the desiccated grasslands of central Asia. The prevailing contemporary theory was that the Great Plague was the punishment of God for some awful infraction. It was tempting to blame vulnerable and heterodox populations for the catastrophe:

> When the Great Mortality – the bubonic plague – arrived in Europe in 1348, sweeping away up to a third of the population, conspiracy theories about Jews poisoning water supplies spread like wildfire. Although some contemporaries pointed out that Jews were also dying of the plague and therefore were probably innocent of the crime, entire Jewish communities were slaughtered by enraged mobs. (Deane, 2011, p 20)

The ineffectiveness of the church's prayers to ease the sufferings associated with both the Great Famine and the Great Plague meant that popular trust in the church as a conduit to appease an angry God and a source of divine power and favour greatly waned. As the church also suffered the effects of famine and pestilence, its own numbers and resources were greatly impaired. The plague overwhelmed the resources of the church, which meant that the care of the poor was increasingly and inevitably secularised. Villages, towns, and cities found they could barely cope with caring for their own inhabitants, and as a result of the population movements associated with these twin disasters, population stability – social stability – became an urgent matter.

---

[14] Believed to be caused by the bacterium later identified as *Yersenia pestis*, and known by many names, but we will use the contemporaneous names, the (Great) Plague or Pestilence. The appellation 'Black Death' was not applied until several centuries later and sits uncomfortably on modern ears.

The most immediate and obvious effect of the Great Plague was to create a massive labour shortage. With as much work to be done and fewer people to do it, surviving workers could demand higher wages and improved working conditions. Serfs bound to the land demanded to be freed to move about so they could sell their services to the highest payer. Landowners (and governments) sought to limit the movement of workers, and this exacerbated class tensions between wealthy and poor. This tension in turn generated an outcry for law and order.

> There was never a time when so many men had such strong incentives to wander away from their towns and villages to try to better their condition, and the roads became filled with vagrants looking for work or for loot or lured by promises of fabulously high wages in the depopulated parts of the country. (Tierney, 1959, p 112)

Ironically, although the plague killed people of all ages across two continents, this may have resulted in a kind of horrible natural selection that created stronger and more resilient survivors and their descendants (DeWitte, 2014).

With all the concern expressed by wealthy landowners about the availability of affordable labour and social stability, it is not surprising that we see legislative and civic responses. In England, the 1349 Ordinance of Labourers (23 Ed. 3 ; Ordinance of Labourers, 1349) was issued by Edward III (and confirmed by Parliament as the Statute of Labourers in 1351):

> Because a great part of the people, and especially of workmen and servants, late died of the pestilence, many seeing the necessity of masters, and great scarcity of servants, will not serve unless they may receive excessive wages, and some rather willing to beg in idleness, than by labour to get their living.

The Statute set out several things:

- Every man and woman, free or bond, under the age of 60 was required to work.
- Employers could not hire excess workers (this restriction would increase the availability of the workforce).
- Wages, liveries, meed,[15] and salary were set at pre-plague levels (that is, in the 20th year of the reign of Edward).
- Workers could not leave their work before the agreed term of service was completed.

---

[15] A share, reward, or compensation.

- Victuals (food) were to be sold at a reasonable price.
- Almsgiving directly to 'valiant beggars' was banned because it encouraged idleness.

Those found in violation of the Statute could be whipped, branded (with the letter 'F' for Fugitive) on their foreheads, put in stocks, or put to work for royal households or for anyone who claimed them. It is worth noting that part of the Statute directed William of Wyckeham, Bishop of Winchester, the richest estate in medieval England (Hare, 2006), to promulgate it throughout the churches. The Statute also regulated the salaries of stipendiary chaplains so that clerical salaries would not be excessive (the numbers of clergy, too, were devastated by the Great Plague, but mass still had to be said, baptisms administered, confessions heard, marriages recorded, and the dead buried). Simon Islip, Archbishop of Canterbury, also supported the Statute. Although it was poorly enforced, the Statute of Labourers proved to be the foundation of a series of English Poor Laws over the next three centuries: it classified the poor as worthy or unworthy and began the shift in the secular mindset that individual failure was responsible for economic hardship. The church collaborated fully in this shift.

A similar ordinance was published in France in 1351, where King Jean II proclaimed an *Ordonnance sur la métier de la ville de Paris* [Ordinance on the trades of the city of Paris] (Vivier, 1921). This ordinance compelled able-bodied men and women to accept any work, banned begging and giving alms to those who could work; wage rises could not exceed one third of their pre-plague levels, prices were fixed, and profits were regulated.[16]

The Statue of Labourers effectively brought an end to feudalism in England. The effects of the Statute paralleled trends in continental Europe where feudalism came to an end everywhere except France and Russia, where it continued for several more centuries. Popular responses to these (and similar) interventions by wealthy elites were neither welcoming nor passive. There were uprisings throughout Europe, including the 1358 Jacquerie (in the Oise Valley north of Paris); the 1382 Harelle (in Rouen); the 1378–82 labourers' Revolt of the Ciopmi in Florence, Italy; and the short-lived Peasant's Revolt in England in 1381, which resulted in the deaths of 1,500 people. There can be no doubt that secular and civic responses to the poor and those who laboured were seen for what they were: social control.

---

[16] Vivier (1921) attributes the similarity of the ordinances in the two kingdoms to the fact that they occurred from the same cause, the plague ('en Angleterre les mêmes ravages qu'en France') and the same 'misère générale' (general misery).

British Poor Laws

Social mobility in England and Wales had become a problem that required secular intervention on a national scale. The Great Plague, combined with the consequences of increased enclosures, resulted in a great increase in the number of vagrants roaming the countryside looking for well-paying work and preying on the traveller. These vagrants included not only displaced villeins or manorial tenants but also soldiers returning from the Hundred Years' War (1337–1453), skilled in the use of arms, and reluctant to return to quiet village life. 'From the mid-fourteenth century on, the problem of relieving poverty became inextricably intertwined with the problem of suppressing vagrancy' (Tierney, 1959, p 113). The social order had been seriously disrupted by the disasters of the famine and pestilence, as had the social imaginary: no longer could the church be counted on to care for the poor, to placate an angry God, or to satisfy the hungry. It did not have the theology, authority, or ability to address social mobility. Poverty relief, therefore, became increasingly secularised and intertwined with the suppression of vagrancy for the next 500 years (Ambrosino et al, 2008). The diversion of manorial income from dioceses and parishes to royal war-making and the support of the lesser nobility meant that the church had to find alternative ways to keep itself fed and flourishing, as well as to meet its canonical and historical obligation to care for the poor. Yet it still maintained its traditional medieval theology, canons, and practices towards the poor, using old wineskins to attempt to contain the new wine of new social challenges; and the old wineskins were not up to the job.

The ability of the church to respond to the needs of the poor had been eroded, and in England and Wales secular intervention was required to address the problem of the poor. The Statute of Labourers was only the first British secular legislation that began to bring pressure on the church to fulfil its obligation to the poor. The Statute also signalled that the attitude of the secular authorities and the church towards the poor had shifted from a more or less benevolent one to a less tolerant, more controlling, and even punitive, one. Parliament had shifted the theological gaze of the church from the problem of wealth to the problem of the poor. It was no longer enough to divide beggars into the able-bodied and the 'impotent' (or disabled) poor, but that

> [T]he real problem that was emerging was to distinguish among the able-bodied themselves. There were those who were downright idle, those who were eager and willing to work but could find no work, those who would not work on the old terms and had left their villages looking for better conditions of casual labor; and for each

category there were subsidiary question to be considered regarding the eligibility for help of their wives and children. (Tierney, 1959, p 119)

The Statute of Artificers of September 1388 (under Richard II) fixed labourers in their places of work, punished able-bodied beggars, and required impotent (that is, disabled) beggars to remain in the town where they were living. Three years later, another Act (15 Ric. 2, c6; Oosterhoff, 1977) obligated diocesan bishops to ensure that a sum of money from their benefices was set aside to be given to vicars and poor parishioners (rather than keeping it to themselves, as apparently had become a practice). In this 1391 Act, Parliament reaffirmed that the poor needed to be cared for and required in the statute that the church meet its own existing canonical obligation to care for the poor. In these two acts we see the threads of the future British Poor Laws beginning to come together: they both problematised poverty and the poor, yet still required that the worthy poor be looked after.

In various minor acts the British Parliament continued to strengthen its anti-vagrancy stance and the expectation that the church would care for the poor. However, 140 years after the Act of 1391, in 1531, Parliament passed an Act which further penalised vagrants (by various means including branding) and required justices of the peace to licence beggars. In 1536 (under Henry VIII) Parliament required a designated collection on behalf of the poor to be taken in churches. In 1552 (under Edward VI), an Act provided that the giving of alms could be enforced by denouncing to the bishop any person who refused to give. In 1563 (under Elizabeth I), almsgiving was made compulsory and was enforceable by law by the threat of imprisonment, and in 1572 a poor rates assessment was enacted. The well-known Elizabethan Poor Law with its anti-vagrancy requirements and three classes of poor (impotent, abled-bodied, and idle) was, of course, enacted in 1601 as any student of the history of social work knows. But rather than being an innovation to provide care for the poor, as the Poor Law is often constructed, it is really situated firmly in the heritage of the 1351 Statute of Labourers (all people were expected to work; people were classified by their ability or willingness to work) and the 1388 Statue of Artificers contributed to control of social mobility. All of these various modifications, including the 1601 Poor Law, maintained the system of poor relief through the churches and were designed to compel either the churches or parishioners of churches to provide alms – but only to the worthy poor. Each Act of Parliament gradually eroded the authority and independence of the English Church but retained the essential structure of existing canon law and the church's responsibility to care for the poor, and added the notion of the able-bodied poor from 1536 onward. It was in the 1601 Act that Parliament and the Queen almost completely eclipsed the authority of the church,[17] although the infrastructure of the delivery of assistance continued to be administered through the parishes of the church (and poor recipients had to be known to the almoner of the parish). All of these acts were intended to restrict the movement of the poor and maintain social order. Klaits (1985) writes that the poor laws increasingly bureaucratised charity, so that charity became depersonalised, less the responsibility of the individual, and more the responsibility of formal institutions. The 1601 Act was hardly the benevolent response of a benign monarch to her hungry people: it was, rather, another step in a centuries'-long effort to maintain social order, one which required the church's complicity in its implementation. And again the church complied.

As the centralised authority of the church began to fragment, poor laws also evolved in other regions and cities, particularly in Christian northern Europe, as secular authorities took up the slack of a church no longer capable or competent to carry out its canonical responsibilities. We shall return to this shortly.

Reform

Our focus on the evolution of the church's theology of the poor has meant that we have bypassed some critical world events. As we turn our attention to the Reformation we must also acknowledge that the unity of Christendom – and thus its relatively consistent theological foundations – had long been under threat. These threats include the so-called Great Schism between the Western (Roman Catholic) Church and the Eastern (Orthodox) Church in 1054, and the final fall of Byzantium in 1453 as the Ottoman Muslims finally succeeded in conquering Constantinople and embellishing the Ottoman Empire. But these were only the beginning. The schism between East and West was the culmination of hundreds of years of theological and political tension between Constantinople and Rome, and in 1054, Christendom gave up even the appearance of being unified. Nevertheless, the theology and treatment of the poor appear to have remained largely consistent in both branches of Christendom, which is not surprising since they both largely drew on the theological work of the Cappadocians of the 4th century and the canonical compilation of Gratian's *Decretum* (until the Mamluk Sultanate of Egypt and northern Africa were conquered by Selim in 1516 Christians formed a significant part of the Ottoman Empire; see Mikhail, 2020).

Because of its significant future implications, it should be noted that in 1452, the papal bull *Dum Diversas* [Until Different], issued by Pope Nicholas V,

---

[17] Acknowledging, of course, that since 1527 the monarch had also become the head of the Church of England.

authorised Alfonso V of Portugal to enslave Muslims of West Africa. This bull created the theological justification for slavery for the next four centuries. Alfonso brought Muslim slaves to Iberia for re-education and conversion to Christianity before they were then exported to the Americas. The bull was renewed by popes Callixtus III in 1456, Sixtus IV in 1481, and by Leo X in 1514. The trade route to India that Christopher Columbus was seeking was for European traders to avoid the Ottomans and Mamluks, which lay between Europe and South Asia; in his discovery of what would become the Americas, Columbus found something ultimately much more lucrative – and unimaginably horrific. With, of course, the full support of the popes.

The capture of Constantinople by Mehmed II in 1453, which marked the end of both the Byzantine and the rump Roman Empires, was of unique importance in global and military history and serves as a convenient marker to the end of the Medieval Age. Constantinople was informally renamed İstanbul[18] and served as a gateway for the Ottoman Muslims to influence and enter Central and Eastern Europe. The three-day plunder and slaughter of Christians in the city after its fall resulted in an exodus of surviving scholars and artists to Western Europe, and these scholar-refugees contributed to what was becoming a robust European Renaissance through the influence of Greek and Islamic philosophy, arts, and science. This secular learning also gave rise to what we now call humanism, in turn to the Reformation, and eventually to the Enlightenment. These three movements had profound impacts not only on Christian theology and its understanding of the place of humans in relation to the Divine but also on economic systems and the treatment of the poor in Western societies. 'With the Reformation came the dissolution of the Catholic welfare organization ... and the state assumed the burden of welfare. As for the poor, in this capitalistic world they were losers, to whom the winners no longer feel any special obligation' (Klaits, 1985).

The 'discovery' of the so-called New World and its indigenous peoples by European explorers also presented significant challenges to the theological orthodoxy of the (now) Roman Catholic Church (and from now I will use 'Church' with a capital C to refer to this institution). The inquisitors were strongly motivated to maintain the boundaries of the Church's tolerance. In 1506, Pope Julius II began plans for a massive structure on the Tomb of St Peter, envisioning the largest church building in the world (it was eventually completed in 1626, 120 years later). This building was to be a symbol of the enduring permanence and magisterium of the Church, a statement

---

[18] The re-naming was not formalised until the Ottoman Constitution of 1876, and only confirmed as the globally standard name in 1930.

project to oppose the Ottoman threat to Europe and the West,[19] a physical manifestation of Augustine's City of God. This new St Peter's Basilica in the Vatican would also sponsor some of the greatest art in the Western world; it attracted such Renaissance architects and artists as Bramante, Rafael, Michelangelo, della Porta, Moderno, and Bernini, and would ultimately house one of the greatest libraries and art collections of its time.

To support the building of the Basilica and other major projects, Julius and his immediate successor Leo X[20] needed vast sums of money, and so the Roman Catholic Church set about raising those funds, mostly from the sale of indulgences.[21] The claims of these indulgences, and the corruption that inevitably accompanied them, were challenged in 1517 by a German Augustinian monk and professor of biblical studies at the University of Wittenberg named Martin Luther (1483–1546). Luther's protest of the corruption of the Church, whose protest extended to the authority of the papacy itself, took the form of his Ninety-Five Theses, or propositions. For authoring this document Luther was ultimately found guilty of heresy but his protector Friedrich III, Elector of Saxony,[22] ensured that Luther remained safe and alive. Following his conviction, Luther was released from his monastic vows. His earthy style of speech and his challenge to the Church's authority and corruption made him very popular with the peasant class, although it seems reasonably clear that Luther's writing and theology include much that is both misogynist and anti-Semitic[23] by 21st century standards.

---

[19] The 25 million Ottomans (ruled from 1520–66 by Sulaimon I, the Magnificent) were recognised by the popes and Christian monarchs of Western Europe as a significant military threat.

[20] Followed by Adrian VI (1522–23), the only Dutch pope, and Clement VII (1523–34), who like Leo, was a de'Medici.

[21] Indulgences date from the 3rd century of the church as a way to ease the temporal penance of a Christian awaiting martyrdom. The practice evolved over the centuries, and became subject to abuse as professional 'pardoners' sold indulgences to support specific projects. While outrageous examples of this practice (sometimes making extraordinary promises of hundreds and even thousands of years of remission for both living and dead for significant contributions) went beyond the scope of church doctrine, it continued until it was challenged by Martin Luther.

[22] An Elector had considerable power and influence because these seven princes had the authority to elect the Holy Roman Emperor, emperor of the German nations, and most of Europe, who would be crowned by the pope himself.

[23] Luther wrote, 'The word and work of God is quite clear, that women were made either to be wives or prostitutes', although the apparent meaning of this epithet requires more exploration (Swan, 2011); as distasteful as it is on modern ears, it is unlikely to have been inconsistent with the theology and sentiment of his time; some scholars attribute Luther's anti-Jewishness to his extreme disappointment in later life that Jews did not convert to Christianity in the numbers he expected, despite his efforts at reform.

Luther lived in a time when the new learning of Renaissance humanism in the Italian centres and the Dutch Catholic priest Desiderius Erasmus Roterodamus (1466–1536), known as Erasmus, was disseminating throughout northern Europe. Humanism was a new philosophy (derived from the ancient Greeks and brought to Europe by Ottoman refugee-scholars) that held that individual human beings each had value, and each had the right and responsibility to determine the course and meaning of their own lives. In the West, humanism relocated the divine spark from 'heaven' above, to within each individual, and the individual was therefore sacred. This relocation marks a turning point in the anthropology of the West and became a fundamental difference between European-influenced worldviews and that of relational or collectivist cultures. There can be little doubt that both in his student and teaching days Luther would have encountered, and indeed been surrounded by, humanism (Wright, 2017). Humanism was also a major shift from feudal hierarchical understandings of society where the class of people above told the class below what to do and how to think, and where the church held authority and responsibility for the lives of all Christians.

Luther's theological humanism (although he did not call his theology humanistic) held that each individual Christian was responsible for their own lives and their own salvation. No longer was the Church required or wanted to mediate between the individual and God. Luther's theology placed the primary authority in the Bible, as interpreted by an individual's conscience, and he produced the first German vernacular translation of the New Testament from the Greek in order to make it available to the common person (it had previously only been available to the educated elite in Latin). He held that the rituals and sacraments (and indulgences) of the Church were unable to redeem men and women from hell: such redemption was available only by the grace of God. That grace could not be earned (or paid for) but understood only as a gift. His challenge to the papacy also fell on the sympathetic ears of secular princes who wished to be more independent of papal authority. However, despite its popularity, Luther's theology was not particularly amenable to the poor and peasant. Luther pragmatically recognised that his protection (from being burned as a heretic) and the future of church reform lay with the nobility. He repudiated the German Peasant's War (1524–25), an uprising against the nobility that resulted in the slaughter of at least 100,000 poorly armed rebels (Holland, 2019). Although his work was its theological inspiration, he feared that the peasants might ultimately rebel against the newly reformed church.

Luther's theology of the poor appears to have gone through at least four periods of evolution (Brummel, 1980). In the first period (1513–16), he identified the poor with the faithful, but his theology spiritualised poverty: the poor and the exploited could not be oppressed by the powerful and rich, since authority and wealth are 'in a plane removed from the spirit' (Brummel, 1980, p 42), and therefore are unable to exercise power over the poor in spirit; the poor aspire to eternal realities, while the rich aspire to accumulate temporal wealth in the world. The only true enemy of the poor, Luther held, is the heretic. In the second period (1516–19), he began to understand poverty in a more traditional way as a socio-political and economic reality, and argued that both the Church and the state must take responsibility for the prevention and amelioration of poverty and social injustices. He wrote that 'Christians must be taught that giving to the poor or lending to the needy is a better work than buying indulgences' (cited in Brummel, 1980, p 47) because everyone accepted that Christians have a clear obligation to respond to the needs of the poor. This giving, however, should not be done directly, but through a common fund. Toward the end of this period, he began his third and most developed theology of poverty, which has been called 'Christians under the Cross' (1519–30), in which he refuted any interpretation of biblical language as having to do with the economically poor, and instead theologised economic poverty as spiritual poverty. The recipients of Christian love were no longer the poor; they were replaced with 'the neighbour', and the neighbour's needs were spiritual. The suffering incurred by poverty was equated with the suffering of the cross, and therefore redemptive. Luther held that the revelation of God is understood only in the suffering of Christ's Passion on the cross; the pathway to knowing and understanding God, therefore, requires participation in that suffering and excludes any effort to relieve suffering. Being Christians under the cross meant sharing in the suffering of Christ, and is, therefore, necessary and precious, because God accepts only those who are lowly and despised. While this may have been modest spiritual comfort to the economically poor, it neither put food on their tables nor relieved the oppression imposed on them by their overlords.

During this, his most influential period, Luther's theology of the poor was drawn from the Passion (that is, the suffering of Jesus) and the cross, rather than that of the Incarnation – that the poor bore the imprint of Christ – which is how the Church had understood poverty since the 4th century. It was in the fully human form of the person Jesus that God could relate to the sufferings of the poor. For Luther and his followers, the sufferings of the poor were the pathway to understanding God. Poverty was no longer a problem because Luther spiritualised it: poverty was about the *poor in spirit* who would receive an eternal reward, the love of God, for their worldly suffering. For Luther, no longer did biblical language about the poor refer to economic poverty and hunger. Wealth – before now, the main focus of theological attention – was a problem only if it was used to build up worldly treasure, and drew attention from God. Spiritual poverty (which was available to all, regardless of economic status) was a desirable state because only by being aware of one's misery could one count on being fully open to and embraced by God. None of this could be achieved by works or merit. It was only through faith – *sola fide*, the heart of Luther's theology – that one could count on being justified and acceptable to God.

Not surprisingly, Luther held that secular governments were licit and instituted by God in order to restrain those who violate secular laws; the task of secular government was to maintain social order. Both spiritual governance – which produces true justice before God – and secular governance was necessary for a just and orderly world. Luther condemned the Peasants' War because it appealed to natural law, a law shared by non-Christians as well as Christians: 'We have all we need in our Lord who will not leave us, as he has promised. Suffering! Suffering! Cross! Cross! This and nothing else is the Christian law' (cited in Brummel, 1980, p 55). Thus, Luther began the reformed church's withdrawal from secular cares and occupations.

In Luther's fourth and final period (1530–46) he was mostly concerned with creating an enduring alternative to Roman Catholicism. The theology of the cross disappears, and he advances his case with the secular rulers of his era in order to embed what (in 1529) became called Protestantism. The most effective and preventive solution to poverty was for princes and lords – that is, secular powers – to prevent oppression. However, the way princes and lords of the Reformation chose to govern their subjects was to appropriate large portions of existing Roman Catholic Church canon law and make it their own (Holland, 2019, p 324). This meant that rather than looking to Rome for governance, Church canon – now secular law – was enacted by secular authorities within their own principalities. Kahl (2009) argues that Christian social doctrines of this period became embedded in the secular institutions of poor relief and reinforced those doctrines as secular values and norms and that in turn, these social doctrines affected the way the churches related to state involvement in poor relief. However, the state response to poor relief was built with the collaboration and within the framework of existing church institutions, and parochial priests 'became the local representatives of the rulers' (Kahl, 2009, p 272). Lutheran countries balanced feeding the poor with a strong socialised obligation to work. Denmark-Norway (which included Iceland) became Lutheran[24] in 1537; the religion of Sweden(-Finland) officially became Lutheran in 1593 (although King Gustav was made head of the national church in 1527), and

---

[24] Luther preferred the term 'Evangelical', which was used by like-minded reformers who rejected the authority of Rome. The word 'Protestant' itself referred to those German Lutheran princes who opposed the Holy Roman Emperor Charles V, and therefore at least between 1529 and 1549 a Protestant was by definition, a German.

the Luther-inspired movement then spread throughout the Baltic region. Most, but not all, German principalities separated from Rome and became Lutheran. Poor laws were enacted throughout the region (for instance, Wittenberg in 1520, Nuremberg in 1522, Denmark in 1708) to build civic responses to the poor. Throughout the Prussian region, municipalities were required to develop community authorities to administer poor relief uniformly. A secularised Lutheran approach to poverty remains part of the national approaches to social assistance in these countries.

Luther's theology and popularity were pivotal in the evolution of a theology of poverty and a pragmatic theology of social order, but he was not the only reformer of his day. Ulrich (Huldrych) Zwingli (1484–1531) began his career as a Roman Catholic priest in the Swiss canton of Zürich, and in fact, was rewarded for his early support of the Church by Pope Julius II. Gradually, however, humanism (he studied with Erasmus) and the centrality of scripture played an increasingly larger part in Zwingli's theology, and he ended up challenging many practices of the church, including fasting during Lent,[25] images in churches, infant baptism, frequent celebrations of the mass (he advocated only four times per year), liturgical ceremony, indulgencies, pilgrimages, and priestly celibacy (he had secretly married in 1522, affirmed by a public wedding in 1524, and became a father three months later). These objections he presented at a public Disputation in January 1523 in the form of 67 Conclusions, which went unchallenged when the bishop's representative withdrew. Zwingli placed scripture at the heart of his reforms and received support from the local governing council keen to be independent of the influence of Rome. He attacked the voluntary poverty taken up by mendicants, and insisted that monasteries be converted to hospitals and other welfare institutions; the local council did so in the Poor Law of 1525, secularising church properties, pensioning the monks and nuns, and establishing new welfare funds and programmes for the poor[26] (Wandel, 1990). Key to Zwingli's plan to preventing poverty was the education of children. This was an ancient church strategy and entirely consistent with his own humanist education. Zwingli died in the Second

---

[25] The 'Affair of the Sausages' is considered the beginning of the Reformation in Switzerland. Zwingli's close friend Christoph Forschauer publicly ate wurst during Lent, breaking the prescribed fast, because, he said 'a Christian life rests not in food, nor in drink, indeed in no outward works, but alone in a right belief, trust and love, by which we live with one another truthfully, rightly, in friendship and simply; in Scripture I believe' (Wandel, 1990, p 33).

[26] So impressed was Henry VIII by this move that he adopted the same strategy in England with the Dissolution of the Monasteries in 1536. After his break with Rome, Henry was designated head of the Church of England, the Anglican Church. He confiscated the wealth of the monasteries into the royal exchequer; in doing so, however, he unleashed thousands of poor and newly homeless monastics onto the countryside.

Kappel War between Roman Catholic Swiss cantons and reformed Zürich. His direct influence is limited to Switzerland, although he is considered the theological forerunner of the Reformed Church movement in Europe and throughout the world. Zwingli's reforms came to the attention of Luther, but although they met once in 1529 they were not able to come to full agreement on key points of doctrine and did not further their alliance.

Zwingli's doctrinal heir on the continent was Jehan (Jean, or anglicised as John) Calvin (or Cauvin) (1509–64). Born in Catholic France, Calvin received a theological education at the University of Paris but later studied law in Orléans and Bourges. He was exposed to humanism (Bouwsma, 2020) and the Greek and Latin classics, and studied Greek and Hebrew to aid his biblical studies. Because the French government had become increasingly less tolerant of religious reform movements such as the Huguenots (France was not much tolerant of Protestants of any stripe), Calvin left France for Switzerland. In Switzerland, he published his major work *Institutes of the Christian Religion* in 1536, which he continued to revise up until the final four-book version of 1559. Ultimately settling in Geneva in 1541, Calvin and the town council set about establishing his vision of church order that would ensure that the city's residents conformed to God's law. He saw himself as a biblical humanist who derived his theological vision *scriptura sola*, solely from scripture. His best-known theological principle is probably his theology of predestination: that the ultimate salvation of human beings is predetermined by God before they are even born (a notion he largely shared with Luther, and for that matter with Augustine of Hippo and Aquinas), although this idea was not a central one for him.

Even more important for Calvin was his theology of work: the purpose of all human activity is to glorify God, and the best way to glorify God is to work. Work and service are the means through which the faithful express their gratitude to God for their redemption, and are a sign that they are among the predestined elect. Idleness and begging were banned in Calvin's Geneva, although Calvin had an otherwise quite generous view of charity. Nevertheless, Calvinism gave life to the Apostle Paul's command 'Anyone not willing to work should not eat' (2 Thess. 3:10). Hard work, frugality, and thrift were the marks of the truly faithful Christian, and Calvin understood wealth as a signal of divine favour on the hard-working believer. Although wealth-as-divine-favour was a relatively minor aspect of his own theology,[27] it was a point of view that was adopted and expanded by the newly wealthy merchant classes to justify their own wealth and their exploitation of labourers. Here we see an upending of the millennium of

---

[27] But it achieved a kind of notoriety after Max Weber highlighted it as the foundational theology of capitalism in his crucial 1905 work *The Protestant ethic and the spirit of capitalism*.

theology that problematised wealth, not poverty. But Calvin's understanding of work helped to bolster the foundations of mercantilism and emerging capitalists: wealth justified faith. Calvinism provided the moral energy of the capitalist entrepreneur (Giddens, in Weber, 1930/2001, p xiii). His reforms revived the Deuteronomic Principle that if you are obedient to God and do good (that is, work hard) you will be rewarded, and if you are disobedient (that is, if you are idle) you will be punished. Reward was temporal wealth, and wealth indicated God's favour; God helped those who helped themselves. It was a short leap for the wealthy and powerful to assume that poverty was punishment and that therefore those who were poor had sinned, and had incurred God's disfavour. Secular Calvinism (if we may call it such) was the final reform of the poor: that poverty was a punishment from God, and that the poor were poor because they were sinful, flawed, or idle. Beggars were 'as rotten legs and arms that drop from the body' (Perkins, cited in Taylor, 2007, p 109). For the heirs to capitalism, the real moral object to wealth, writes Weber in his analysis of Protestantism, is 'relaxation in the security of possession, the enjoyment of wealth with the consequence of idleness and the temptations of the flesh, above all of distraction from the pursuit of a righteous life' (Weber, 1930/2001, p 104).

Calvin's legacy can be found in Reformed churches around the world, on the European continent, in Switzerland, France, and the Netherlands, but also in Scotland (in the preaching of John Knox), and in Great Britain by the Puritans who felt that the English Church needed even more fundamental reform than had already occurred. The Puritans migrated from England to Massachusetts in the American colonies in the 17th century, to establish their idealised Calvinist world, which was intolerant of other religions (and arguably of each other). The New World colonial population was overwhelmingly British and Calvinist/Reformed Protestant (Kahl, 2009), and poor relief followed the English and Dutch workhouse (indoor relief) model. Presbyterian, Congregational, Unitarian, and some Baptist churches trace their theological heritage to Calvin, and evangelical colonialism ensured that the reformed ethos was conveyed around the world.

Jacobus Arminius (or Jakob Hermanszoon, 1560–1609) was a Dutch Reformed theologian who led the next generation of reformers in a response to Calvin. Arminius studied a variety of reformed theologies and developed views that differed from Calvin on grace, predestination (or election), and free will. Key to his theology was God's prevenient (or 'going before') grace: that is, through the Holy Spirit, God's grace is available to all people despite corrupt human nature, and therefore through that grace, all people may achieve salvation if they take advantage of it. Grace, therefore, comes from the effort of God, not humans, and is available to all, not only the elect. Later, Calvinists condemned Arminianism and the Remonstrants (as they were also known) and persecuted them in the Netherlands, but John

Wesley, the founder of what became Methodism, became the best-known exponent of Arminianism. As we shall see, Arminianism (or some aspects of it, particularly the notion of prevenient grace) also made its way into Anglican, Baptist, Adventist, Pentecostalist, and other Evangelical theologies.

Secularising relief

There has been some scholarly debate about whether during this period the dominant religious orientation (Roman Catholic or Protestant) of a country or region influenced whether the response to the poor remained in the religious or secular domain. The pervasive influence of humanism makes this debate somewhat moot since both faithful Roman Catholics and Protestants alike were influenced by humanism and its belief in the innate value of the individual (although it looked different in each faith tradition). The twin disasters of the famine and plague both created overwhelming need and devastated the church's ability to respond to the need and meant that the church's response – both temporal and spiritual – was inadequate. The Roman Catholic Church affirmed its traditional principles of poor relief at the Council of Trent (1545–63) and opposed the secularisation of poor relief because such a secular system would 'erase the divine benevolence of the giver' (Kahl, 2009), by now a very familiar notion to us. Roman Catholic doctrine was criticised by Protestants and elites for not dealing with the undeserving poor, including the 'sturdy beggars', who could and should go to work. Roman Catholic Spain resisted the reforms and maintained the traditional medieval responses to the poor. In France, a country that remained aligned with Rome, civic authorities took up where the Church could not respond, although religious charities persisted, and as a result, poor relief became largely uncoordinated and often duplicated. In northern Europe, reformers collaborated with civic authorities to promulgate a mostly traditional Christian but secularised response to the poor that included almsgiving, collections (taxes) for the poor, and discriminating between the worthy and unworthy poor. In Amsterdam, the idle poor were put in cells where the water slowly rose as long as they remained inactive (Taylor, 2007, p 109). The boundary between sacred and civic was blurred by theocratic Protestant reformers. Davis (1968), in her case study of Lyons, and Wandel (1990), in her study of Zürich, argue that the divide was not between Catholic and Protestant but between humanist and civic: 'the reform of poor relief took place at the local, for the most part, civic level' (Wandel, 1990, p 15). The major European exception to this was England where reform of poor relief was undertaken at a national level, by the ruler of the day.[28]

---

[28] For a more detailed analysis of how the different theologies of poor relief became embedded

Summary

Constantine charged the 4th-century church with the responsibility of caring for the poor in order both to stabilise the place of the Christian church in formerly pagan Constantinople and also to maintain social order by requiring the church to provide for the poor. Basil, the two Gregories, and John Chrysostom advocated an incarnational theology of compassion that rationalised this responsibility and problematised wealth; the poor bore the countenance of Christ. That theology dominated for nearly 1,500 years. The reformers retheologised poverty: it was no longer compassion for the image and likeness of Christ, but Suffering! Suffering! Cross! Cross! – living or recreating the suffering of Jesus in their own day – that motivated them. (It is worth pointing out that none of these reformers themselves appear to have been at risk of hunger or involuntary destitution.) Civic authorities increasingly took up the responsibility of managing the increasing number and demands of the poor, and a key goal of their response was to maintain social order through social control. This tension between compassion and social control also sets out the foundations for the tension implicit in contemporary social care: eligibility workers, child protection workers, forensic and probation workers seek to protect society and its resources by managing the poor on behalf of the state; and non-governmental (NGO) services that include clinical, health and mental health workers, and other social care workers who seek to maximise the potential and freedoms of the individual. This separation also goes some way to explaining how what is called social work today can look so different in different national and cultural settings. Our task in the latter part of this book will be to consider how to set about reconciling those global divides.

---

in different national secular responses to the poor in Europe and colonial America, see Kahl's 'Religious doctrines and poor relief: A different causal pathway' (in van Kersbergen and Marrow, 2009).

5

Capitalising the poor

In the previous chapter, we began to consider how the theologies of the Protestant Reformation reconceptualised poverty and the poor. The Reformation highlighted the historic tensions between care and social control in church and state responses to the poor. The reformers generally took a much sterner position towards the poor and their responsibility for their impoverishment than had the church until that time. The influence of Paul's admonition in 2 Thessalonians, 'Anyone who is not willing to work, let them not eat' (2 Thess. 3:10) and the Augustinian approach that 'It is better to love with severity than to deceive with lenience' prevailed. It is in the Reformers that we encounter the many lifestyle prohibitions that exert social control, including dancing, alcohol, festivals, shameful language, excesses of any kind, and, of course, idleness. The religious attitudes of the Reformers morphed into a kind of civic theology and were reflected in civic law and regulations in Europe and eventually in the colonies of the European powers. They also created an environment for the development of a new economic system: capitalism.

Luther's later theology transformed the 4th-century patristic incarnational theology of poverty – seeing Christ in the face of the poor – to a theology that prioritised personal identification with the Passion and suffering of Jesus. Voluntary poverty, of the kind adopted by ascetics and other religions during the Middle Ages, was still esteemed as godly in much of Europe, and by extension, other kinds of poverty were prized as a kind of virtue. At the very least, they provided occasions for the faithful to be virtuous by their donations. In Lutheran regions, the worthy or righteous poor were cared for by donations (or levies) paid to a common fund and administered by civic authorities, almoners, or a combination of the two. In the reformed regions of northern Europe, extreme poverty became a problem when it led to social unrest during times of plague, famine, and natural disaster, which rendered the self-sufficient poor, and the poor extremely poor; these extreme times led to the promulgation of civic poor laws (as opposed to the church's traditional canonical practices), which provided a kind of social safety net to the morally sound, while also ensuring a relatively reliable workforce. Theologically, disasters such as plague or famine were interpreted as an angry God's punishment on entire societies that were apparently disobedient or sinful, but civil authorities still required stability, especially in times of disaster. In this sense, then, the Protestant movement reaffirmed the Constantinian contract – that the church would be granted legitimacy by the local secular authority as long as it ensured social stability. In most places, including, and perhaps especially England, even after the secular authority assumed responsibility for allocating resources to the poor through poor laws, civic authorities still delegated the authority for the administration of those laws through local parishes.[1] The local almoner, overseer, or church warden and his (and surely it was always a 'his') oversight committee determined both the worthiness and neediness of the applicant for assistance.

Calvin, on the other hand, believed that the universal human condition was an abyss in which all humans have lost their way and that the only way out was through a personal conversion of the heart: to accept the love and utter reliability of God.[2] Although highly influenced by Renaissance humanism, extremely well-educated, and a prolific writer, Calvin appealed to the heart rather than the head of the believer. If the believer truly accepted the grace of God their life could be transformed; they could experience rebirth or *regeneratio*. This experience would motivate them to participate fully in society through work, which was the glory of God. Certainly, these reformed societies did not have a monopoly on encouraging hard work (for instance, a traditional New Zealand Māori whakataukī, *Tama tū, tama ora; tama noho, tama mate*, which can be roughly rendered, *The one who stands and works will flourish; the one who only sits will perish*; many cultures will have similar proverbs), but the reborn believer constructed work as an expression of devotion.

If work was the glory of God, wealth was evidence that the individual had been sufficiently transformed and blessed by God. The church's historic doctrine of salvation by good works held that a believer could obtain sufficient merit by doing good works, which included the purchase of indulgences from the church (one of the reformers' chief complaints against Rome), was replaced with a doctrine of salvation by faith (*sola fide*). Good works were different from work done for one's own benefit or sustenance, but contributed to, or were evidence of, the likelihood of one's entry into heaven. Calvin's reformed theology – shared in this respect by most Protestants – held that only certain persons have been elected or destined by God before the foundation of the world to eternal life. In this

---

[1] Remember that all persons were expected to be members in good standing of their local parish church, and known to their clergy and wardens, the lay leaders. Poor laws delegated to wardens the authority to impose a poor tax on church members, which would sustain a common fund to support the worthy poor.

[2] 'Chapter IX (of Free Will), No. 3. Man, by his fall into a state of sin, hath wholly lost all ability of will to any spiritual good accompanying salvation. So that a natural man, being altogether averse from that Good, and dead in sin, is not able, by his own strength, to convert himself, or to prepare himself thereunto' (Weber, 1930/2001, p 57).

sense, even the poor could achieve salvation in the next life, which solved one future problem for them; but the problem of providing food for one's children in this life had to be faced daily. Not every citizen was expected to live a saintly life, but the godly elect could bring about a rightly ordered society by controlling the unruly, which, of course, would have included most of the hungry and poor. To manage the unruly, a more robust – one might say intrusive – civic authority was required to define and maintain order. Civic authority regulated the poor, but since civic authority was made up of the godly, it was the moral standards of the godly that were codified and enforced. Thus, the church's doctrines and responses to the poor translated readily to civic codes and eventually to missionary activity around the world.

Weber has proposed that Calvin's doctrine of predestination and election, which Calvin himself felt was relatively unimportant, was central to Calvin's entire theology, because *regeneratio*, or a kind of genuine conversion, led to good works; good works were a sign of the believer's authentic *regeneratio*:

> Thus, however useless good works might be as a means of attaining salvation, for even the elect remain beings of the flesh, and everything they do falls infinitely short of divine standards, nevertheless they are indispensable as a sign of election. (Weber, 1930/2001, p 69)

The accumulation of wealth through work became a sign of divine favour among the northern reformed believers. Eventually, the accumulation of wealth itself was the only sign that was required. Weber proposes that it is in Calvin that we find the roots of the theological justification both for Western liberal humanism,[3] or individualism (since the individual alone was responsible for their conversion, not priests, sacraments, or church), and capitalism, the accumulation of individual wealth through private trade and profit. Weber traces this theology through its later manifestations Pietism (a Lutheran movement), Methodism, and the various Baptist sects; we might add to Weber's list the so-called prosperity theology of the late 20th- and 21st-century Evangelical Churches (Goodstein, 2009).

The key influences that informed Reformed theologies of poverty emerged during the 16th to 18th centuries: labour and capitalism; exploration and exploitation; and the influence of Enlightenment liberalism. These influences formed what we may call the long tail of the Protestant Reformation. Firstly,

---

[3] This may well have been borrowed, or at least influenced, by Erasmus, so-called Prince of Humanists, although Erasmus himself distanced himself from the Protestant Reformers.

we need to consider how the theology of Calvin crossed into England and informed the legal and social responses to poverty and the poor. It is in the English version of Calvinism (which also gave birth to Puritanism and later modern Evangelicalism) and responses to it that we find the theological wellspring of what became social work in the late 19th century. This is a rich and turbulent area of theological and social awakening, and the theologies of the Reformation (and the Counter-Reformation, which emerged in Roman Catholic-dominated regions) were dynamic. For some of this period, city squares in Europe and the British Isles were lit by the flaming bodies of accused heretics and heterodox theologians, and rivers were saturated with the bodies of accused witches (many of whom, as we saw earlier, were poor women who had earned the resentment of their communities). In order to contain this discussion, our focus must remain on church and civic theologies of poverty and the poor, and many key developments will not be included. Nonetheless, theologies were often stretched to accommodate the political, economic, and social realities of the day.

Protestantism in England

Some political background is valuable to understand how Protestantism took root in England and how Protestant theologies informed attitudes towards the poor. 'The Reformation in England was not the smooth uninterrupted outworking of a coherent plan … It was a complex contingent contradictory concatenation of incidents' (Avis, 2002, p 4). Whether Protestantism was welcome in England, or a 'political imposition by a ruthless minority against the cherished traditions of a pious people of England' (Avis, 2002, p 5) remains debated among scholars. The Reformation was the first time Western Christendom had to deal with differences within itself, and the results were often unfortunate, and occasionally deadly. The word 'Protestant', or someone who protests, was coined in Germany in 1529 (two years after Henry VIII of England disestablished the English Church from Rome) and referred to princes who protested at the Diet of Speyer (which was intended to heal the divide created by the condemnation of Luther at the Diet of Worms); early use of Protestant in English referred exclusively to the alliance of Lutheran states against the (Roman Catholic) Holy Roman Emperor Charles V. At least at first, then, a Protestant was a German (Marshall and Ryrie, 2002).

If you are confident in your knowledge of the Tudors then you may wish to skip ahead a couple of paragraphs. This summary is intended for people who are not so familiar with the background of the Reformation and the Elizabethan Poor Law. The struggles of Henry VIII to produce a male heir, his matrimonial dramas, his break with Pope Clement VII in Rome (1527), the Act of Supremacy which made him head of the Church in England, the dissolution of the monasteries in England, Wales, and Ireland

(1536–41), and the royal appropriation of their wealth are well known;[4] these dramas arguably led to the establishment of Protestantism in England. Henry's only living male son, Edward VI (r. 1547–53)[5] was the first English monarch to be raised Protestant, and although he was crowned when he was only nine years old (and died of tuberculosis when he was just 15), he was surrounded at court by Protestant reformers active in his father's court. These included Thomas Cranmer, Archbishop of Canterbury, who had ensured the annulment of Henry's first marriage, and who authored the first English *Book of Common Prayer* (1549, revised further in 1552[6]). This prayer book formed the foundation of Anglican theology and liturgy and ensured that these were held in common throughout the realm. Cranmer was influenced by Protestant theologians such as Martin Bucer in England (Bucer was a proponent of public relief for the poor) and Luther, Zwingli, and Calvin on the continent. The influence of Calvin was very strong, that of Luther less so. There is correspondence that documents the warm relationship between Calvin and Cranmer (Toplady, 1774).

During the brief but bloody reign of Roman Catholic Mary I (r. 1553–58),[7] the word Protestant achieved currency in England as an epithet for any reformer.[8] However, in the 16th century, Protestants referred to themselves as brethren, gospellers, or evangelicals to demonstrate how their faith was founded in the New Testament gospels rather than in the historic church and its institutional structures. However, both Roman Catholics and Reformers claimed to be both Catholic and Evangelical, and the division between the two affiliations was very flexible. Protestantism was seen to be 'a European phenomenon with local manifestations' (Marshall and Ryrie, 2002, pp 9–10). During Mary's reign, many English Protestants became exiles and, effectively, Puritans in the making (Tyacke, 2010). They returned to England after Mary's death to demand a purer, more Bible-based church and a Bible-based government. This meant that a government should conform

---

[4] Perhaps not so well known is that an estimated 12,000 people in religious orders were rendered homeless and destitute by the dissolution of the monasteries (Bernard, 2011), although some received a pension.

[5] Son of Henry VIII by his Protestant mother Jane Seymour (Henry's third wife), who died of post-natal complications two weeks after Edward's birth.

[6] Both were supported by Parliamentary Acts of Uniformity, which required the use of these prayer books throughout the kingdom under penalty of imprisonment, or worse; unsurprisingly these acts were repealed by Mary I in 1553.

[7] Daughter of Henry VIII by her Spanish Roman Catholic mother Catherine of Aragon (Henry's first wife).

[8] It is worth noting that after Cranmer and his allies Hugh Latimer and Nicholas Ridley were found guilty of heresy, Mary ensured that Cranmer was burned at the stake in Oxford in March 1556.

to God's word which teaches that 'all membres of the body must seek "the prosperitie and wealthe one of another"' (John Ponet, Bishop of Winchester and intimate of Archbishop Cranmer, cited in Tyacke, 2010, p 530). It would seem that these early Puritans were more concerned with church polity, liturgy, and government generally than with the poor specifically. They were also concerned that there should be very little space between government values and Reformed religious values. Puritans remained strong advocates of godly government that saw to the welfare of all citizens, and this influence continued through at least the English Civil War (1642–51) and the Restoration.

On the accession of the more religiously tolerant and practical Elizabeth I[9] (r. 1558–1603), the English Reformation became embedded in England in the Religious Settlement of 1559, which structured the Church of England (or so-called Anglican Church) but made some allowances for the beliefs of evangelicals, Lutherans, and Roman Catholics (by accommodating more flexibility in the doctrine of the Eucharist and the use of vestments in worship). The Puritans remained within the Church of England and pressed hard for more radical theological, liturgical, and governance reforms within Anglicanism, including increasing poor relief (although with this increased relief also came increased social regulation of the poor, including enforcing residency requirements and moral behaviour). The Puritans strongly associated poverty with immoral behaviour: 'the effect of much Puritan rhetoric was to associate the poor with social threats of all kinds' (Slack, 1984). After the Restoration of the monarchy in 1660, the Puritans were forced out of the Church of England because of what was perceived as their extremist theological views, including the rejection of the authority of bishops and the prayer book. Many fled to the Netherlands where Calvinism prevailed and finally to the American colonies where they put their reformist ideals into practice.

Nevertheless, more moderate evangelicals remained in England, and some even remained affiliated with the Anglican Church. Perhaps best known of these were John Wesley (1703–91) and his brother Charles (1707–88), both Anglican priests. The Wesleys' brand of circuit-riding evangelicalism became known as Methodism. Methodism rejected Calvin's notion of pre-election in favour of Arminianism's prevenient grace. The Wesley brothers remained within the Anglican Church during their lifetimes, although their followers

---

[9] Daughter of Henry VIII by her mother Ann Boleyn (Henry's second wife, whose marriage was annulled, and Ann was later beheaded for treason; Elizabeth was declared illegitimate by Pope Pius V in 1570, cementing the division between Rome and England). Elizabeth had to denounce the Pope's authority in England in order to establish the legitimacy of her reign.

separated from the Anglicans[10] shortly after John Wesley's death. John, a high churchman educated at Oxford, had been impressed by a group of evangelical Moravian Brethren[11] and had a kind of personal conversion experience while at evensong one evening (where his heart was 'strangely warmed'). He then ventured to preach outside of formal church settings and established a system of smaller chapel societies of believers that he regularly visited. John was an outspoken social critic and abolitionist (Keefer, 1990), and, among other things, supported women preachers. Wesley's earnest preaching found a home among the working classes of England. He preached active philanthropy as a religious duty (Richter, 1964) and advocated sharing property. This compassion for the poor created a sharp divide between him and other Evangelicals such as the Puritans: 'Thus he preached three precepts: Gain all you can; Save all you can; and Give all you can. The first two can be justified only by the third' (Richter, 1964, p 21). Bowpitt (2007) makes the point that the impulses underpinning the Evangelical Christian entrepreneurial endeavours were both missionary and philanthropic. The Wesley 'method' served as a foundation for the Primitive Methodists (founded ca. 1810 and led by Hugh Bourne and William Clowes), the Nazarenes, and the Salvation Army (founded in 1865 in London by Methodist circuit preacher William Booth), as well as other Evangelical movements. Methodism (along with John Howard, 1726–90 and Elizabeth Fry, 1780–1845, a devoted Quaker) engaged particularly with prison reform. The circuit-riding organisation of the Methodist movement also suited the times and context of the American frontier very well, and Methodism became well established in America. As the poor became wealthier, and Methodism became more established in the lower-middle and middle classes, the Social Gospel theology was dropped from Methodism, and poverty again became associated with sin. In Britain, some Methodists returned to the Established (Anglican) Church: 'Lack of charity and profound individualism are the attitudes of a rising middle class' (Richter, 1964, p 23).

A core precept of English Evangelicalism, as we saw earlier, is the notion that an individual must have a personal experience of rebirth in order to claim the saving power of the Gospel (the Evangel) for one's own. Conversion was a familiar idea to both Protestants and Roman Catholics,[12] and practically synonymous with the concept of repentance,

---

[10] The Wesleyan Church (and variants) also owes its origins to the Wesleys; however, the Wesleyan Church did not become a separate denomination until the mid-19th century.

[11] This was the earliest group of Protestants, founded on the reformed theology of Jan Hus (?1372–1415) in Bohemia in 1457 but popularised from 1722 in Moravia.

[12] 'Early evangelicals were late medieval Christians' (Gregory, 1999, cited in Marshall and Ryrie, p 28).

that is, acknowledging one's sinfulness (being lost in the abyss) and separation from the divine. Conversion occurred in distinction to the ordinary social experience of belonging to a church because one's parents belonged, as did their parents (and so forth), or because the law required regular church attendance on Sundays and holy days. The emphasis on the personal and transforming experience of the divine in one's life was the essence of the Evangelical experience. By personally experiencing divine grace a person could transform their lives. The most prominent biblical model for such an experience is the Jewish Pharisee Saul, persecutor of Christians, who experienced a conversion on the road to Damascus; he was struck blind for three days, healed, converted, and renamed Paul (Acts 9:1–18). Paul became the foremost evangelical and author of many of the letters of the New Testament that encouraged new Christians and churches throughout the Mediterranean. For Evangelicals, the reward for a conversion experience, of course, was increased divine favour, generally in the familiar forms of health, wealth, and happiness. How one could evoke such a transformation – through divine grace, faith (as the English Evangelicals believed), or works, and so forth – are theological points[13] that need not concern us here. What is important is that by personally turning to the divine an individual could transform their life and demonstrate that transformation by working hard and living a godly life, filled with all good things. Even when the converted were persecuted for their faith, their fortitude, or martyrdom was seen as an opportunity for divine grace, for the power of their faith would inspire others. As we have seen repeatedly, the poor, whose lives were decidedly not filled with good things, and constituted at times up to 30 per cent and never less than 10 per cent of the population of England during the Tudor period, were evidence that they had not had such transformational experiences. Stigmatising the poor – by requiring, for instance, that licensed beggars wear badges, as Mary Tudor's 1555 poor law reform required, or by locking away the undeserving poor in prison – was a way to encourage such divine fervour in them and provoke in them a more socially acceptable life as evidence of divine reward, or at least forcing them to work.

One consequence of conversion was the urge to share that experience and to encourage others to their own personal conversions. Another consequence was that Protestant converts returned to the Bible in order

---

[13] The notions of justification and sanctification were essential to Evangelicals: justification was unmerited 'acquittal' of one's guilt or sin, available by grace, and sanctification was the complementary process whereby 'the Holy Spirit brought about the regeneration of the elect, and a visible and outward holiness which was the consequence not the cause of salvation' (Marshall, in Marshall and Ryrie, 2002, p 23).

to understand and interpret the word of God for themselves rather than relying on church-authorised priests and preachers to do it for them. This, of course, required that people could read, and so Evangelicals undertook to educate those people who could not read and write. Some of this pedagogy was formal – in schools – and some informal and even underground, so to avoid detection by the Established Church authorities who strongly discouraged individual study of scriptures lest it lead to error, dissent, or heresy. For Evangelicals, charity was an instrument of spiritual revival; 'charity was not only a feature of the redeemed life, but an instrument in the redemption of others' (Bowpitt, 1998, p 679). It also had the added benefit of improving the income of the poor.

Davis (1968) argues that while attitudes towards poverty were changing prior to the 16th century, poor relief measures were not limited to Protestant influences but can be attributed to the influence of Christian humanism (such as propounded by Erasmus and the Spanish humanist Juan Luis Vives) on both reformers and Roman Catholics. In 17th century Roman Catholic France, for instance, confraternities, or mutual aid societies, clearly associated the poor with sin: they saw in the poor 'not Christ, but the Devil himself' (Norberg, 1985, p 34). The poor were confined in hospitals and workhouses so that they could be better controlled or at least isolated, lest their idleness infect the rest of the community. Humanist approaches to the reform of the poor were not limited to moral reform. In Lyon, for instance, the Aumône-Générale (General Almoner), who attended to both Roman Catholics and Protestants, combined reformist views with humanist views on education and training to create an extensive education, training, and apprenticeship programme that ensured that orphaned children were better positioned than their parents (Davis, 1968). Davis attributes the problem of poverty in this era to the increasing urbanisation of the poor in times of crisis:

> Trouble was caused by country-dwellers and others from outside the city who poured in at times of famine or war … but also by the men, women and children who lived in the city all the time. Protestant cities and Catholic cities, and cities of mixed religious composition initiated rather similar reforms usually learning from each other's efforts. (p 267)

Whether Reformed or Roman Catholic, each society found its own theological justification to eliminate begging and poverty. The basic structure of approaches to the poor looked the same – contain, control, reform, and put to work – and these rationales informed civic and secular approaches to the poor.

Labour and capitalism

I have argued that the primary purpose of civic and national poor laws throughout Europe and what became Great Britain was not in the first instance charity, compassion, or relief of poverty but maintenance of social order and ensuring a reliable and stable labour force. Even in the religious turbulence resulting from the royal reversals in the leadership and lawful religion of England, the poor laws and their administration by parishes remained reasonably consistent, subject to only minor amendments (for instance, the addition of badging, branding, flogging, or imprisoning beggars, or further restricting their movements). This suggests that the church's theology of the poor, adopted as a civic theology by the state after the Great Plague and shaped by the reformers, remained embedded in the sequence of poor law reforms. In the late 1590s, an economic crisis in England resulted in bread riots throughout the country. These riots resulted in an increase in royal and Parliamentary focus on the management of the poor. Civic (rather than religious) almshouses for the 'impotent' (disabled) poor and workhouses for the able-bodied poor were authorised for the first time by Parliament in the Poor Law reform of 1597, although their theological foundations remained unchanged and were usually administered by the local parish on behalf of the state. Older family members were required by law to support younger family members, and younger family members were required to support older ones. This residualist reform was an important acknowledgement that the old feudal structures, where the land-owning lord supported all dependents, was no longer viable; the village manor was being replaced by individual households (Handel, 2009).

The Elizabethan Poor Law was another waystation in over a century of increasingly repressive attempts to regulate the poor in England, standardise the public response to the poor, and manage an economy still suffering the aftershocks of the Great Plague.[14] Responsibility for social welfare was placed under the authority of the Privy Council. The Poor Law allowed for marriages later in life and working for wages, both of which contributed to economic reform and nascent English capitalism.[15] While individual charity to beggars was restricted, as it had been under previous poor laws, in absolute terms, philanthropy increased under the 1601 reform (Krausman

---

[14] There were waves of plague in Great Britain in 1563, 1603, 1625, and 1665 in which about a fifth of the population of London died due to plague; in 1665 of the 80,000 people who died of plague, at least 45,000 were under the age of 15 (Payne, n.d.).

[15] 'Never has the connection of social welfare to labor maintenance been so clear, setting the patters of public assistance not only for England but also for the United States' (Day and Schiele, 2013, p 104).

Ben-Amos, 2008). What the Poor Law of 1601 did was standardise, stabilise, and centralise poor relief throughout England, more so than any other European country (van Nederveen Meerkerk and Teeuwen, 2013). Perhaps only early modern Netherlands, with its equally high rate of urbanisation, developed a similarly strong wage labour and capitalist economy, and although the structure of poor relief administration was very different, the amount of relief distributed appears relatively similar in both countries. In England, institutionalisation (so-called indoor relief) of the poor became the preferred option particularly in urban areas, rather than assistance in the community (so-called outdoor relief) because costs could be contained, behaviour closely monitored, and the poor removed from the public gaze. Orphanages, almshouses, workhouses, and prisons were indistinguishable from one another and were often little more than sheds with rooms (Day and Schiele, 2013). Sanitation was minimal, food inadequate, and the mentally unwell were often chained in place.[16] House overseers were given a fee to support their facilities, and what was unspent could be retained by the overseer; this provided the incentive to provide the absolute minimum required to inmates. Work done by workhouse inmates, often with materials supplied by the government, was sold, and the profits went to the overseer, not the inmates. The corruption of these overseers was so flagrant it was brought to the attention of Parliament by Lord Lyttleton in 1775 (Hansard and Cobbet, cited by Cribelar, 2001).

Where the poor were not stigmatised, they were punished, and where they were not punished, they starved. Under the growing Calvinist influence in Great Britain, work was considered essential to give meaning to life and glory to God, even if the work itself was not particularly meaningful. Outdoor relief was mostly available to the impotent poor (the aged, ill, or disabled), but such relief was controversial because it was thought to encourage idleness and mendicancy. Dependent children were placed in foster care, sold, or placed in state orphanages where they were very likely to die within their first year.[17] Anyone seeking public relief who could work had to leave their families and accept this indoor relief. In a later reform in 1722, the Workhouse Act made workhouses available to both men and women, together with their children. One of the evangelical Anglican societies, the Society for the Promotion of Christian Knowledge (founded in 1698) advocated for an increase in the availability of relief through parish workhouses: by 1776 there were nearly

---

[16] The English word 'bedlam' derives from a contraction of the name St Mary of Bethlehem Hospital in London, an asylum for the management of the 'insane', and appears to have come into usage to mean utter chaos or pandemonium during this period.

[17] The social reformer Jonas Hathaway estimated that 82 per cent of children in orphanages died in their first year (Day and Schiele, 2013).

2000 of them in England. One view of these workhouses is that they were designed to demean and exhaust the able-bodied poor with the assumption that only the truly desperate would accept such conditions. If people did not accept these conditions, relief was refused.[18] It was not until 1795 that policy reform made outdoor relief possible for the destitute so that the poor could receive assistance while living in their own homes.

And if all else failed, there were always the prisons. Wacquant writes that 'in historical reality penal institutions and policies ... simultaneously act to enforce hierarchy and control contentious categories, at one level, and to communicate norms and shape collective representations and subjectivities, at another' (Wacquant, 2004/2009, p xvi). This was certainly true under the 1601 Poor Law. Prisons were a clear assertion of the state's power over the poor, and imprisonment was liberally used to punish the poor for minor and desperate offences like stealing bread or for failing to pay even small debts. The criminalisation of poverty was in a sense the inevitable outcome of a social imaginary informed by a Calvinist theology of the value of work, which informed English polity: anyone not willing to work should not eat. Prisoners were forced to pay their jailers for their daily upkeep and were not released until their full debt was paid. This incurred an inevitable cycle of poverty that trapped the poor in poverty and maintained the magisterial authority of the state. Conditions in prisons were deliberately appalling even by standards of the day, and disease, brutality, and violence were common, all at the whim of jailers. It was not until 1877 that prison administration became centralised and more standardised, and the prisons themselves became slightly more humane.

These institutions were a far cry from the relative benevolence of the *ptochotropheion* and the *Orphanotropheion* of 4th-century Constantinople, even if the implicit goals of both – social stability through social control – were similar. The difference was a significant shift in the religious and civic theology, which understood poverty, its causes, and solutions in very different ways. In 1690, Sir Josiah Child, governor of the British East India Company, wrote a tract advocating for what we would recognise as a universal basic income for the poor. His justification for this was, in part,

> That the Children of our Poor bred up in Beggery and Laziness, do by that means become not only of unhealthy Bodies, and more then [sic] Ordinary subject to many loathsome Diseases, whereof very many die in their tender Age, and if any of them do arrive to years and strength, they are, by their idle habits contracted in their Youth rendered for

---

[18] We shall see in the next chapter that Higgenbotham (2014) has a more sympathetic view of workhouses following the 1834 reform of the Poor Law.

ever after indisposed to Labour, and serve only to stock the Kingdom with Thieves and Beggars. (Child, 1690)

The root cause of this 'beggery', said Child, was the 'decease of charity' following the Elizabethan and later Stuart poor law reforms. The face of Christ was no longer seen in the poor, but the economic challenges of the time, together with the need to ensure a stable workforce and to control the poor in order to maintain social order, culminated in the gruesome realities of poor relief in the 17th and 18th centuries. Although many people did work from home at the beginning of the transition from the manorial system, increasing industrialisation and the mechanisation of traditional processes of production meant that wage labour became dominant, and capitalism effectively became the emerging theology (Day and Schiele, 2013). Calvinism, particularly in its Puritan expression, and capitalism became the foundational theology in the American colonies.[19] Weber, however, proposes that Puritanism simply reinforced the individualist tendencies that were emerging as the result of the end of feudalism and the collapse of the manorial system.

To support capitalism, which brought with it relatively stable if poorly waged employment and tax revenue, British government policies allowed employers to do as much as they wished with workers. The primary motivation of capitalism, of course, is profit for the owner class, and if a capitalist enterprise does not succeed, another will take its place in the market. In such a competitive system, all decisions are made on the basis of increasing profits for company owners, which means keeping wages low, because keeping wages low – effectively maintaining a poor and dependent class – meant ensuring a ready and desperate workforce. Capitalism meant profits for the wealthy but increased poverty for the poor because wages were kept low, or work did not exist. The Scottish economist Adam Smith wrote in *Wealth of Nations*,

> What are the common wages of labour, depends every where upon the contract usually made between those two parties, whose interests are by no means the same. The workmen desire to get as much, the masters to give as little as possible. The former are disposed to combine in order to raise, the latter in order to lower the wages of labour. It is not, however, difficult to foresee which of the two parties must, upon all ordinary occasions, have the advantage in the dispute, and force the

---

[19] Not all the colonies were Puritan, or Protestant, of course; Maryland, for instance, was founded as a Roman Catholic colony. A consideration of how a Calvinist theology of work permeated each of the American colonies is beyond the scope of this project.

> other into a compliance with their terms. The masters, being fewer in number, can combine much more easily; and the law, besides, authorises or at least does not prohibit their combinations, while it prohibits those of the workmen. We have no acts of parliament against combining to lower the price of work; but many against combining to raise it. In all such disputes the masters can hold out much longer. (Smith, 1776, Ch. VIII, Sec. I, Of the Wages of Labour, pp 33–4)

In other words, underpaid workers remained at the mercy of wealthy masters. The result of this economically stratified society was social unrest, which in turn meant that the state collaborated with economic elites to put in place increasingly restrictive social assistance policies, laws that allowed penurious wages and poor laws to control the poor. While all this was unlikely to be what Calvin had in mind in his theological reform, Calvinist and Evangelical theology had laid the foundation for this outcome.

Capitalism and control of the poor were reflected in the philosophy and ethics of the day. In his *Second Treatise on Government* published in 1690, the English philosopher John Locke said that the most important human right was the right to appropriate and exercise control over property and other resources, which occurred when the individual contributed labour and extracted value from the resource (Swan and Vargas, n.d.).[20] Jeremy Bentham (1748–1832), founder of Utilitarianism, whose Panopticon became a symbol of efficient state control over the poor in prison, and later John Stuart Mill (1806–73)[21] – who was for 35 years an administrator for the British East India Company – advocated an ethic that proposed that right actions were those that produced the greatest pleasure for the greatest number of people. Both Bentham and Mill held that wealth was the primary source of pleasure or economic advantage. Mill advocated for the violent suppression of 'mutinous' Indians who disrupted the kind of social order imposed by English imperialism and the extraction of wealth in South Asia (Klausen, 2016). In 1798, the demographer and economist Thomas Malthus (1766–1834), in 'An Essay on the Principle of Population', supported the elimination of poor relief and protection of wealth because if the poor were supported, while their suffering would be temporarily eased, they would then have more children, and eventually, the population of the world would outstrip the world's ability to feed it. Malthus was later used

---

[20] It should be noted that Locke's views differed from other philosophers of his day: Hobbes held that the right to ownership could only be bestowed by the relevant political authority, and Hume held that property should be apportioned by consensus. We will return to the implications of Locke's views in the discussion of slavery in Chapter 6.

[21] His father James was a colleague of Locke's.

by Social Darwinists to call for the elimination of assistance and poor relief. A lower birth rate (in the lower classes, naturally) brought about by hunger, disease, war, birth control, and celibacy was the way to restrain population growth and reduce human misery.

Exploration and exploitation

In Europe, this was an era of increasing technologies of transportation, exploration, and exploitation. (In other parts of the world, these technologies were well established, although they looked quite different to the ones found in Europe.) Earlier land trading along the Silk Roads (Frankopan, 2016) opened the possibilities of trade with Asia. Building on their post-Ottoman successes, the Portuguese and Spanish sailed along the Africa coast and the Indian Ocean and established European settlements as they went. They then sailed across the Atlantic to the so-called New World in search of even greater wealth. British and Dutch entrepreneurs were inspired to search for profit around the globe. The East India Companies of both nations (the British EIC founded in 1600, the Dutch Vereenigde Oostindische Compagnie (VOC) two years later) launched two centuries of global trade, colonisation, and missionisation for these two nations. Both private corporations were state-sponsored and acted effectively as government agents. The British dominated in South Asia (the original charter in 1600 granted a trade monopoly between the Cape of Good Hope to the Straits of Magellan), and the Dutch established themselves in Southeast Asia and the West and East Indies (the Caribbean and modern Indonesia). The VOC was permitted to wage war, imprison, and execute prisoners, coin money, negotiate treaties, and establish colonies on behalf of the Dutch government. The EIC enjoyed much the same status, as well as the military support of the British government. British colonies were established in the Americas and the Caribbean, of course (where they had to divide up the islands with the Dutch, France, and Denmark), and although slavery and slave-raiding had disappeared in Britain and Ireland from about 1200 CE (Gillingham, 2014), overseas trade in slaves remained legal and profitable – however horrific the consequences. Still, both nations seemed surprised when their hegemony was not welcomed.

What the British and Dutch did not acknowledge was that there were existing civilisations and societies in the areas they sought to colonise, and the existing civilisations in Asia and the Pacific had well-established empires linked by the Pacific and Indian Oceans, including more than 500 islands. These islands themselves had been settled and cultivated for some 65,000 years (Sivasundaram, 2020). In the Pacific, the triangle settled by Polynesians and Micronesians, which stretches from modern-day Hawai'i, Rapa Nui (Easter Island), and Aotearoa (New Zealand), is the size of the

Asian and European landmass combined. Highly refined technologies were developed by ocean-going peoples that relied on navigation by stars, wind, and ocean currents, and they had sailing vessels that could cope with long ocean voyages. That the Europeans did not recognise the sophistication of these technologies says more about the European frame of reference than it does about the peoples and empires they encountered.[22] In the Indian Ocean, cultures and trade from the Red Sea to the Malay Peninsula were well established by 2000 BCE. Sivasundaram writes that Islam, as a relative latecomer, 'should not be seen as the only factor which wove the ocean together from the seventh century; for the spread of Buddhist and Hindu doctrines to Southeast Asia occurred in the first five centuries of the common era' (2020, p 10). Globalisation and international commerce in the Pacific and Indian Oceans existed long before the arrival of the Europeans. Nonetheless, the military strength of the *arrivistes* and their economic and tax structures meant that European trade and control were imposed on a large scale and, writes Sivasundaram, this makes it difficult at times 'to differentiate what already existed from what had newly arrived' (2020, p 11). In 1793, for instance, two Māori men, Tuki and Huru, were kidnapped from Aotearoa and taken to Australia to teach newly arrived convicts how to work flax;[23] Tuki drew the first European-style map of Aotearoa, showing Te Ahi No Maui (North Island) and Te Wai Pounamu (South Island) and other key details, for the commandant of the convict settlement of Port Jackson. Technologies and the ability to convey those technologies to alien cultures were well in place long before the Europeans arrived in the neighbourhood. Despite ongoing resistance, both peaceful and violent, by colonised peoples (culminating in South Asia most notably in the sepoy 'Mutiny' or Indian Uprising of 1857–58, which ended the rule of the EIC in the region), in 1824 the Whig politician Thomas Macaulay said of the British Empire, 'It is to her peculiar glory not that she has ruled so widely – not that she has conquered so splendidly – but that she has ruled only to bless, and conquered only to spare' (cited in Gopal, 2019, p 11). We shall return to this critically important issue in the next chapter.

For the Europeans, global trade offered not only business but also missionary opportunities,[24] albeit with limited success. Christian missionaries had travelled to China, Japan, and Korea over the centuries but failed to achieve much, largely because Christianity was considered too disruptive

---

[22] The first use of firearms in Europe was in the late 14th century, a development that conferred a significant advantage to the Europeans.

[23] Ironic, because working harakeke is work performed by wāhine (women).

[24] Kollman (2011) argues that the there was no Christian mission *per se* before the 16th century because the language to describe such work did not appear until that century.

to social harmony. The EIC put obstacles in the path of British Evangelical missionary societies, but Carson (2012) argues that these societies and the general public put pressure on Parliament to require the EIC to be responsible for the moral and religious improvement of Indians. This responsibility was reflected in the 1813 EIC charter, and Carson (2012) attributes the 1857 uprising to the implementation of this expectation. During the age of European exploration, missionaries had powerful economic or political allies to encourage their evangelical message. The Spanish and Portuguese *conquistadores* brought their Roman Catholic priests to Latin and Central America, and parts of Africa, the Caribbean, India, and China. The French took priests to North America, and later to Indochina and Africa. The Dutch brought their preachers to the East and West Indies, and southern Africa. In England, Thomas Bray founded the Society for the Promotion of Christian Knowledge (SPCK), and, soon after, also the Society for the Propagation of the Gospel in Foreign Parts (SPG) in 1701. These societies, together with Evangelical missionary societies, exported the gospel and British values to British colonies. However, Taylor (2007) writes that the missionary and business objectives were conflated:

> Missionaries brought Christianity to the non-Western world, often with the sense that they were also bringing the bases of future prosperity, progress, order and (sometimes also) democracy and freedom. It became hard for many to answer the question, what is Christian faith about? The salvation of humankind, or the progress wrought by capitalism, technology democracy? The two tended to blend into one. (p 736)

The conflation of Christian mission with prosperity and order is telling, and by now is familiar. In an interesting statistical analysis, Woodberry (2012) argues that conversionary Protestant missionaries were crucial catalysts in the development and spread of religious liberty, mass education and literacy, mass printing, newspapers, voluntary and political organisations, and colonial reforms, and created conditions that made stable democracies more likely. Where Roman Catholic missionaries were in competition with conversionary Protestants, they were also likely to establish mass education and literacy. But, he finds in countries where Roman Catholic missionaries were not in competition with Protestants they did not undertake these activities and autocracies were more likely. The assumption that underpins this analysis is that mass education, literacy, and democracy are valued within a country and that education and knowledge are passed in written formats. As we shall see shortly, interventions promoted by the conversionary Protestants were very much aligned with Enlightenment values. Abuses by British colonisers and missionaries perhaps reached their nadir in the slave trade and the 19th-century practice of 'blackbirding': kidnapping indigenous peoples and forcing them to work as slaves and labourers in places far away from their homes.[25]

The contemporary literature about European colonialism (see for instance Aldrich, 2003; Ames, 2008), post-decolonisation, and resistance is extensive and growing (Denzin and Giardina, 2007; Huygens, 2011; Richardson, 2012; Greensmith and Giwa, 2013; Zufferey, 2013; Chilisa et al, 2017; Gone, 2017). What is important for our purposes is to understand that European ideas, religions, and values were carried with these corporations, colonisers, and missionaries, and imposed for decades, or even centuries, on local and indigenous peoples and civilisations for whom European values would have been truly alien. Even at the time of writing this book, the British monarch remains head of state in 15 countries, and there are 54 countries in the British Commonwealth (where the British monarch has been head of state at some time), constituting nearly a quarter of the global population. Today over 90 per cent of the Commonwealth population is found in Africa and Asia. The British did not leave South Asia (the 'Jewel in the Crown') until 1948. The Dutch Empire did not recognise the independence of Indonesia until 1949. To be sure, this was not the first era in which Europeans had attempted to export their religion and values. But as the Portuguese Ferdinand Magellan (1480–1521), the Dutch Abel Tasman (1603–59), and the English James Cook (1728–79), as well as many other European explorers, conquerors, and *conquistadores*, sailed further around the globe, they discovered, claimed, and impacted the lives of more and more indigenous peoples, and claimed more and more territory and resources for their European masters. The era of colonisation and its consequences of territorial acquisition, harvesting global wealth, Christian mission, diseases, and the global slave trade had begun.

Enlightenment and liberalism

While this chapter has so far focused primarily on the main *dramatis personae* and the complex theological, social, and political reforms that played out on centre stage during the 16th and 17th centuries, in preparation for the next and final stage of our historical overview, we cannot ignore the major philosophical movement in the 17th and 18th centuries that was retrospectively called the Enlightenment. Immanuel Kant wrote that the Enlightenment was humankind's emergence from its self-incurred 'immaturity', its 'lazy and cowardly submission to the dogmas and formulas'

---

[25] Some scholars argue that African slaves were considered more desirable than any other because the presence of the trait HbAS in some of the population confers resistance to malaria, an important trait when colonising places where malaria is endemic (Depetris-Chauvin and Weil, 2018; Esposito, 2019).

of religious or political authority (cited in Pinker, 2018, p 7). Keane (2016, 9 April) writes that the season of the Enlightenment was a messy affair, more like multiple enlightenments than a single, cohesive movement. Even the beginning and the ending dates of the movement are fungible: some historians date its origins from 1650 through 1750, others in the latter two thirds of the 18th century. Major figures of the Enlightenment were educated European elites (including, among others, Diderot, Hume, Kant, Leibniz, Locke, Rousseau, Smith, Spinoza, Voltaire, and Wollstonecraft) who prized reason above, or in place of, religious belief. Today we think of the Enlightenment as the period that saw the emergence of modern positivist, empirical science: for Enlightenment thinkers, science replaced what they deemed superstition (that is, religion), and indeed most philosophers and thinkers associated with the movement professed themselves as non-religious, or at best, deists. Thomas Paine (1737–1809), one of the founders of the American nation, condemned organised religion as 'nothing other than human inventions set up to terrify and enslave mankind, and monopolize power and profit' (cited by Keane, 2016, p 2).

Just as important were the values that emerged from the Enlightenment: progress, democracy, and liberalism, that is, the intrinsic value of the individual, together with individual rights and human liberty. Enlightenment thinkers with their idea of a discoverable universal human nature and humanist notions of human agency were instrumental in moving the social imaginary from a vertical (feudal) to a more accessible horizontal (democratic) perspective (Taylor, 2007). Liberal humanism gradually transformed the social imaginary of the time (and notably provided the theoretical justification for the French and American Revolutions which toppled their overlords and promoted individual liberty) and the centuries that followed. In Europe and North America, Enlightenment philosopher-politicians advocated for more equal and democratic societies, although to be sure, some people – white, male landowners – remained more equal than others, notably women, the landless and poor, and slaves. Liberal humanism, that is, individualism, is one of the defining characteristics of the West, particularly when compared with Confucian, Buddhist, Islamic, or most indigenous cultures, which remain more relational, or tribal, in outlook. Although liberal humanism claims to be non-theistic, we can only wonder if its emergence would have been possible without the reformed theologies that preceded it, and their emphases on individual *reformatio*. In retrospect, the Enlightenment seems a natural development from the Protestant reformers' focus on the individual: the secular view simply removed the divine from the experience of the individual or confined such belief to the individual's private sphere.

Of course, removing God from the popular imagination and the social fabric was not at all simple. Charles Taylor (2007) devotes considerable attention to the question of why it was virtually impossible not to believe in God in 1500 in Western society, while today such non-belief is not only easy but inescapable. The extent to which the Christian deity was integrated into every aspect of European existence up until the Enlightenment is almost unimaginable to us in the 21st century: as a part and cause of the natural order, including the movement of the sun and stars across the sky, as well as storms and drought, plagues and healing, harvest and famine; as part of the vertical structure of society, from monarchs and lords down to the peasants and serf that worked the land; and what Taylor calls the enchanted world (spirits, demons, and other moral forces) which inhabited and controlled the world in which people lived. This way of understanding and interpreting the world formed the social imaginary of the times. Even in the 21st century, the seven-day week, weekends, and the statutory holidays of many nations are based on Christian rhythms and seasons (the Republican government instituted after the French Revolution recognised this in its experiment with calendar reform from 1793–1805, which used ten-day weeks). The Enlightenment, beginning with the Reformation, challenged these fundamental notions and ultimately changed the social imaginary.[26]

An exhaustive or even extensive consideration of the Enlightenment, and the less organised response to it, the Counter-Enlightenment, is far beyond our present scope, of course, and would lead us far afield; such explorations are readily available (see, for instance, Israel, 2001, and his recommendations in Gottlieb, n.d.), and I am aware of the perils of oversimplifying a very complex and sprawling intellectual movement in the present context. Still, there are some contributions of this movement that are important to identify for our present discussion. Pinker (2018) writes that four key themes emerged from the Enlightenment: reason, science, humanism, and progress. Reason, of course, is first on this list. The Enlightenment demanded that individuals make their beliefs available for rational scrutiny in order to understand and make meaning of the world, rather than rely on religious doctrine, dogma, or authority. What constitutes reason, of course, is shaped by particular worldviews. It was reason that required an explanation of the world beyond that of a divine creator and invited empirical exploration of that world. The endorsement of reason did not assume that all humans are perfectly rational agents but rather held that through reason we can overcome human folly and irrational passions. War would no longer be necessary as long as nations or people with differences were willing to reason out their differences. This would be welcome news indeed in an era that was emerging

---

[26] Taylor's answer to his question goes far beyond the Enlightenment as he considers at length the origins and implications of disenchantment for the social imaginary of the contemporary world.

from devastating conflicts, many of which were religious in origins, and the ensuing disease and famine. Enlightenment thinkers promoted a reasonable way to understand the world, empiricism, which required evidence based on observations and measurements in order to make claims about the world. Empirical science avoided the need for any kind of deity to make sense of the perceivable world.

Enlightened thinkers recognised that we humans can never really understand the world apart from ourselves, however, and that we mediate our understanding of the world through our own experiences. Adam Smith, for example, wrote in *The Theory of Moral Sentiments*,

> As we have no immediate experience of what other men feel, we can form no idea of the manner in which they are affected, but by conceiving what we ourselves should feel in the like situation. Though our brother is upon the rack, as long as we ourselves are at our ease, our senses will never inform us of what he suffers. (Smith, 1759/2002, Part 1, Sec 1, Para 2)

Objective empiricism offered a solution to this. Recognising that humans are subject to their own biases in their observations, an objective science of humanity attempted to counter these biases that are found in all humans. Pinker compares these various areas of enquiry to the contemporary fields of cognitive neuroscience, evolutionary psychology, social psychology, and cultural anthropology. These proto-disciplines provided lenses to inspect the individual person. Empirical notions of knowledge formed a platform for the emergence of independent academic disciplines, which in turn gave rise to experts with expert knowledge in these fields, and to a modern idea of profession to which we will return in a later chapter.

Humanism, writes Pinker, 'privileges the well-being of individual men, women and children over the glory of the tribe, race, nation or religion' (2018, p 10). Because of this humanist understanding of the value of the individual, Enlightenment thinkers were acutely aware of and mindful of both the religious violence and secular cruelties of their age, 'including slavery, despotism, executions for frivolous offences such as shoplifting and poaching, and sadistic punishments such as flogging, amputation, impalement, disembowelment, breaking on the wheel and burning at the stake' (p 11). This condemnation of human misery as inhumane gave rise to Enlightenment notions of civil rights, social justice, and democracy, even if only a minority of Enlightenment thinkers advocated these notions (Israel, 2001). Thomas Paine, for instance, held that it was 'the duty of citizens everywhere to take an interest in the misfortunes of others' (Keane, 2016, p 3), and while he supported private property and free markets, he also supported what we would now call a universal basic income to prevent societies from dividing into rich and poor. Social and economic inequalities were deemed shameful, and poverty was recognised not as part of the divine order but of human origin.

Contemporary post-colonial scholars have challenged the values of the Enlightenment in its European context, critiquing its ideals such as universalism and social emancipation for having established the foundations for colonialism. They argue for instance, that 'liberal philosophy, culture, economics and government have been commensurate with, and deeply implicated in, colonialism, slavery, capitalism and empire' (Lowe, cited in Gopal, 2019, p 15). In his detailed historiography of resistance to British imperialism in the Caribbean, Egypt, Africa, and South Asia, Gopal acknowledges these abuses, but he also cautions against an uncritical embrace or dismissal of Enlightenment values as only European. He proposes that so-called Enlightenment values such as universal rights and social justice had been theorised in many global cultures, and he writes that there is a 'global history of human resistance to tyranny and exploitation' (Gopal, 2019, p 14). Critics of European hegemony may be replicating the same paternalism, which suggests that colonised and occupied people did not resist colonialism, or were incapable of doing so, when, in fact, there were mutinies and rebellions aplenty, some successful and transformative, others brutally put down. In fact, Gopal suggests,

> The making of an empire that was forced over time to make concessions, offer reforms, attend to human rights (if only notionally), embrace 'humane' considerations and even regard itself as an emancipator in the first instance, must be read as a response to resistance. (p 27)

In other words, resistance to colonial hegemony reshaped Europe as much as European colonisers reshaped the cultures, politics, and religions of their colonial vassals. This may be small comfort to post-colonial cultures and nations still recovering from the imprint of European powers, but it does allow an alternative perspective to Macaulay's arrogant assumptions of benevolence.

While the Enlightenment had a major impact on the politics of its day, and especially on the decline of monarchies and the birth of modern European-style democracies, its immediate impact on existing poor laws was modest. In England, for instance, all ensuing amendments were relatively minor revisions to the Poor Law of 1601. These amendments included the Poor Relief Act 1662, which ensured that poor relief was made available only to residents of a parish (which had the effect of reducing the mobility of labourers). In 1685, the period of residence was further defined, and in 1691, parishioners who received poor relief had to be registered. In 1697, beggars were required to wear approved badges. In 1722, the Workhouse

Act encouraged greater use of parish and shared workhouses by parishes that were administering poor relief. In 1773, an Act for the Better Regulation of Lying-in Hospitals, and in 1782 an Act for the Amendment of the Laws Relating to the Settlement, Employment and Relief of the Poor ('Gilbert's Act') unsuccessfully encouraged established larger parish workhouses or so-called outdoor relief; and as noted previously, in 1795, a Poor Law Act authorised outdoor relief to be provided in recipients' own homes rather than requiring them to live in workhouses.[27]

The situation in post-revolutionary Roman Catholic France was a little different. The French Revolution was in some ways the most tangible expression of the optimism and liberal and democratic ideals of the Enlightenment. However, 'the First Republic's hopes for a new system of poor relief met almost complete frustration' (Weiss, 1983, p 47). The transition from traditional church charity to a centralised state-directed and egalitarian *bienfaisance*, although well intended, was unsuccessful because of the gulf between the administrative centre of Paris and the provinces where the need was most urgent (Forrest, 1981), and because of the distraction of continuing war which absorbed necessary resources. Weiss writes that 'legislating in Paris surrendered the effectiveness of local flexibility for the ideological purity of uniformity' (Weiss, 1983, p 47). This is no idle concern because in 18th-century France, it has been calculated that the poorest 30 per cent of the population subsisted on around 1,574 calories per day (today's recommendations are between 2,000–2,500; Fogel, 1993, cited in Griffin, 2010, p 2), barely enough to be able to do a few hours work in a day. However, he continues, by the time of the Third Republic (1871–1914), nearly 80 years later, the bureaucratic, social, and political infrastructure had sufficiently matured to allow improvement in the distribution of outdoor relief to the French poor through community welfare bureaux. Still, these bureaux looked and functioned remarkably like the assistance groups found in both Calvin's Geneva and English parishes; and half the hospitals[28] were operated by Roman Catholic nuns. Assistance varied considerably among jurisdictions.

In the Netherlands, there was no central legislation to define or administer poor relief. The Dutch Republic, with its federalised structure of the 16th and 17th centuries, relied on local districts to raise funds and distribute

---

[27] Interestingly, actors were classified as 'rogues and vagabonds' until 1788 and were restricted from assistance; however, the Theatrical Representations Act of 1788 appears to have condoned prostitution in theatres, which catered not only to sailors but also to the 'irregularities of the higher classes' (Burwick, 2015, pp 4–5).

[28] Criticised as "magnificent dormitories for pauperism" by Paul Cère (cited by Weiss, 1983, p 55).

them as required. Reflecting its Reformed roots, funds were raised through charitable donations and church collections (which was seen as a civic duty toward the poor), interest from real estate and capital investments, and various other sources, including public funds and subsidies; in Delft, deacons were permitted to go door-to-door, and in both Delft and Utrecht, lotteries were held to raise funds for poor relief. Capitalism thrived in this highly urbanised society, and wage labour markets and industries were developed early (van Nederveen Meerkerk and Teeuwen, 2013). Still, in some towns, outdoor assistance was the shared responsibility of public, religious, and private institutions, and charities to provide to the deserving poor. In others, public relief was provided by the Reformed diaconate, almoners, or both, to Reformed, Roman Catholic, and Jewish communities alike. As funds became less available in hard times, however, non-Reformed religions were required to take care of their own in a process called the confessionalisation of poor relief. As economic crises impacted local charitable giving and increased demand, assistance was more tightly controlled, and administrators began to put residential requirements in place[29] or to demand guarantees from new migrants that they would not require assistance for a given period. Occasionally, as we saw earlier, good behaviour was enforced by physical threats. Though the relief system in the Dutch Republic was not centralised, and in some ways was more ad hoc than the English system, the practices of relief in both systems were not so very divergent (van Nederveen Meerkerk and Teeuwen, 2013); the flexibility offered by the Dutch system allowed each town to decide how to raise funds and how to administer them. On the other hand, the Dutch system also meant that each town had to find its own funds, mostly through charitable giving, and put an administrative system in place to manage them.

In other words, there is little legislative or historical evidence that the reason, science, humanism, or progress advocated by Enlightenment thinkers had much if any impact on the actual assistance to the poor through the end of the 18th century in either Reformed or Roman Catholic countries. Statutes and regulations that were essentially Calvinist in nature continued to contain and control the poor.[30] When resources were scarce, access to

---

[29] In Amsterdam, the residency requirement was two years in 1620, which increased to seven years by the end of that century.

[30] One of the ways this was done was with the so-called Bloody Code in Britain (the Waltham Black Act of 1723; see also (Wallis, 2018). In 1688, the death penalty was applicable to 50 crimes; by 1800 it was mandated to apply to 220 offences, including ones as involving small theft, and could be applied to children as well as adults. Transportation to British colonies was introduced as an alternative, which ensured that the individual was cut off from their families and society in general. Criminalising behaviours and execution was a way the state exercised its power to control and maintain order. Life could indeed be nasty, brutish, and short.

assistance was made more difficult. The last decades of the 18th century were an assertion of Calvinist reform in poor relief.

> Motivated by religious zeal, the humanitarians sought to remove all those obstacles, ignorance, sloth, intemperance, and prodigality, which hindered the individual's salvation. They were alike in their desire to convert the lower classes to a new life of industry, frugality, honesty, and temperance, and to bring to the upper classes a new sense of social responsibility, commensurate with their wealth and privilege. (Cowherd, 1960, p 329)

Some of these reforms were humanitarian. Gilbert's Act of 1782,[31] for instance, separated the workhouses from the houses of correction, thereby segregating criminals from the rest of the poor; the Act also barred the able-bodied poor from the workhouses and encouraged greater use of outdoor relief. This left the workhouses for the aged, sick, and infirm. Gilbert had in mind the ending of the American Revolutionary War and was concerned about what would happen to returning soldiers demobilised from that conflict. Cowherd's detailed account sets out the complexities of successful and unsuccessful efforts to reform the poor laws at the end of the 18th century. Even where Enlightenment values were radically adopted, assistance to the poor remained well entrenched in statute, and administration largely fell to church and local civic authorities until well into the 19th century.

The claim has been made that 'Social Work [sic] is deeply rooted in the eighteenth-century Enlightenment with its dream of a world constantly improving' (Moffatt and Irving, 2002). Although it is premature to consider this issue in depth at this point, it is useful to pause a moment to reflect on this claim. Certainly, as we will see, Enlightenment values such as progress, rationalism, and liberalism are embedded in what we know as modern social work in liberal humanist nations. We have seen, however, that the roots of contemporary care for the poor are far older, and the agenda for such care is more complicated. The Enlightenment in Europe certainly created a shift in knowledge from the enchanted imaginary to a more rigorous empirical and positivist approach: 'the modern profession of social work is taken up by those who believe that reality is made up of deep structures that are knowable through the proper application of empirical investigation and

---

[31] This is named for its sponsor Thomas Gilbert (1720–98), a long-time member of Parliament. It should be pointed out that the 1782 Act was brought about at the behest in wealthy landowners in response to an increase in unemployment and the poor throughout Britain (see Shave, 2017).

measurement' (Moffat and Irving, 2002, pp 415–16). Nevertheless, civic responses to the poor (and thus, in this period, parochial administrative responses) remained largely shaped by the need for social stability and social control, and resourcing these responses took their place in a long queue of needs.

Summary

Social work as a way of responding to and caring for the poor as a method of social stability, social harmony, social control, and even state care and protection, has a lengthy history arguably dating back to the ancient Near East, and certainly to Constantine. It would be nice to add compassion to this list, but individuals, not states or religions, experience compassion (and as Adam Smith reminded us, we really only feel compassion for another mediated by our own experiences). As a consequence of Enlightenment values – liberty, democracy, progress, individual rights and freedoms, and a basis in empirical research – 18th century Enlightenment thought may be said to have significantly influenced the emergence of what we know as contemporary social work. Western social work ethics that hold that individuals should be autonomous, independent, and self-determining and that human dignity, human rights, and social justice are core ethical values, are clearly rooted in the Enlightenment. Enlightenment liberal humanist values do not sit easily – in fact, they make no sense – in autocratic, theocratic, or highly relational (collectivist) societies that prioritise the welfare of the many over the individual.

During the 16th to 18th centuries, a variety of responses to the poor continued, including the highly centralised system established by the English Poor Laws and administered by local parishes, the fragmented system of the Dutch Republic that was highly locally responsive, and the highly centralised system of post-Revolutionary France that was impractical to administer in the provinces. Meanwhile, post-Enlightenment liberal humanist states encouraged the development of private capital, colonisation, global exploitation, and alongside these, Christian missionisation.

Liberal humanist states and their colonial and post-colonial offspring in general retained the Constantinian measures that promote social stability and harmony, social control, and state care and protection of the powerless (such as children and the very old), although they have also done this in brutal ways (through, for instance, the Bloody Code). The social welfare policies of liberal humanist states also retained the Reformed Church's understanding that anyone who does not work should not eat, and that every person must conform to state-prescribed values (which are largely the values of the Reformed Church) in order to receive assistance. We will see that relational cultures and societies maintain very different structures and values. If social work aspires to be a truly global profession how then can it reconcile or synthesise these very different values systems? This question will guide the second part of this enquiry. First, however, we need to consider the next period of our historical enquiry, the 19th century, which saw the emergence of something we would recognise as contemporary social work.

6

Industrialising the poor

Europe at the beginning of the 19th century was a tumultuous place. The French Revolution had occurred in 1789, threatening the stability of governments throughout Europe. In 1799, Napoleon had seized the leadership of France ending the (First) Republic, and from 1803 to 1815 he led a series of wars that not only destabilised much of Europe but drained national resources, particularly in Britain as they opposed Napoleon. In addition, the rise of capitalism, European mercantile expansionism, and superior weapons (Diamond, 1999) ensured that European values, science, religions, and arms were imposed widely throughout the world, as resources, including human beings, were extracted and traded for profit. During this period, economies became increasingly industrialised, and competition and capitalism flourished. Industrialisation began in Britain and peaked between 1820 and 1850.[1] Great factories replaced farms, and workers moved from the countryside to towns and villages as economies continued to convert to waged labour. The Enclosure Movement was by this point complete: anyone who did not own land was excluded from common land, pastures, and water, making farming and husbandry all but impossible for anyone but the wealthy. Agricultural workers were forced to work for wages for tenant farmers, and wages declined through the early 1830s as tenant farmer-employers relied on the Speenhamland System[2] to make up the difference between what they paid and what was considered subsistence for labourers. In England, the so-called Captain Swing Riots of 1830 protested against relatively wealthy tenant farmers who did not pay a fair wage to labourers, mechanisation

---

[1] The term 'Industrial Revolution' appears to have originated in France, with an attempt to draw parallels with the then-recent French Revolution. Whether the period was a revolution or an evolution remains debated by historians. The term is firmly established in English by the early 1880s as attested by the lectures of Arnold Toynbee, published in 1884, as *Lectures on the Industrial Revolution in England: Popular Addresses, Notes and Other Fragments.*

[2] The Speenhamland System was devised in Berkshire in 1795, where the wages of labourers were topped up by the local council to ensure that families were fed adequately; the system also included a child allowance. While the system seems humane, the burden fell on landowners to make up the difference with their rates between actual wages paid and the threshold deemed necessary to live, and it was widely felt that the system incentivised employers to pay low wages since they knew that the council would top up wages. See the extensive economic analysis by (Blaug, 1963, Blaug, 1964).

which reduced the demand for those labourers, and the church tithe. The tithe was levied on everyone, whether a member of the Anglican Church or not; it supported both the church and the poor in the parish, and the demand was often more than labourers could afford. The post-war financial stresses, the increase in the numbers of the poor, and the social disorder attributed to the poor laid the foundations for the 1834 reform of the Poor Law in Britain. Reforms did not arrive in continental Europe or America until the latter part of the 19th century.

The Industrial Revolution

The Industrial Revolution and its reliance on coal and steam (and people employed to mine coal and create steam) resulted in improved incomes, literacy, and lives for many in the working class (Griffin, 2010). Paradoxically, increased production lowered the value of individual labour, resulting in widespread unemployment (Burwick, 2015). By using new technologies such as the spinning jenny, the steam engine, and the power loom (to use Toynbee's examples[3]), fewer people could produce more goods, which was a great economic advantage for the industrial owners. However, by the early 1860s, Toynbee labelled the Industrial Revolution a social catastrophe, which had 'torn up the population by the roots … The effects … prove that free competition may produce wealth without producing well-being' (cited in Griffin, 2010, p 145); this impression was confirmed later by Toynbee's brief first-hand experience working in the settlement house in the East End of London later named in his honour. Workers accepted longer hours, and entire families, including children, worked at the local mill or factory. The Combination Act of 1799,[4] foreshadowed by Adam Smith, prohibited collective bargaining and trade unions, forcing workers to organise in secret. 'Within the crowded metropolitan enclaves of the labouring class, suffering gave rise to malcontent and anger, which were easily ignited into rage and riot' (Burwick, p 2). There were 617 riots reported in the 20 years between 1790 and 1810, at least half of which were related to food, or the lack of it. Some occupations created mutual aid or friendly societies, but there had

---

[3] Toynbee's, 1884 *Lectures*, cited in Wilson (2014).
[4] This was repealed in 1824 and re-enacted in 1825 with a provision permitting labour unions. This Act was passed in conjunction with the Corresponding Societies Act, which outlawed all national associations with local branches of labour unions as seditious (Burwick, 2015, p 76). Local attempts to organise were put down by force; in 1797 in Tranent, East Lothian, Scotland, a petition by local weavers and colliers against forced conscription was met by troops who fired on the protesters. Between 12 and 20 men, women, and children were killed. The troops went on to rape the wives and daughters of the petitioners. Other anti-labour massacres occurred at Peterloo and Nore.

to be something with which to provide aid, and the destitute pauper had nothing. Nevertheless, it appears that overall real wages rose modestly (by at most 15 per cent) during the 19th century, although the extent to which they rose is still debated by historians (Griffin, 2015).

As a result of (and in reaction to) the New Poor Law in 1834, which we will explore further in a moment, there were calls both for harsher treatment of the poor and for more thoroughgoing and compassionate social reform. The Industrial Revolution and its smaller revolts created an environment of increasing repression of the working classes and especially the poor, and there was increasingly restrictive regulation of the poor. Marx and Engels published their well-known critiques of capitalism and its exploitation of the poor to the benefit of elites. Marx, of course, held that when governments align with economic elites a workers' revolution would eventually overthrow those governments and elites. Although such a revolution did not happen in the North Atlantic, there was a strong movement in the churches towards what became known as Christian Socialism. Throughout the century, more compassionate (if paternalistic) responses to the poor by churches and charities emerged in an effort to compensate for the harshness of the 1834 reform. In the later part of the century, led largely out of the churches by activist women as well as clergy and academics, we see the birth of what we would now consider modern social work.

Slavery

Although our focus is on how theology shaped responses to the poor, we cannot pass through the 19th century without acknowledging slavery and the slave trade. In doing so, we may acknowledge the efforts of Evangelical Christians and Quakers, Africans such as Olaudah Equiano, and former and current slaves such as the 1763 rebellion in Berbice in then-Dutch Guiana (modern Guyana) (Kars, 2020), the landmark Haitian Revolution of 1791 led by Toussaint Louverture and Jean-Jacques Dessalines, and the 1831–32 Christmas Rebellion in Jamaica led by Black Baptist Deacon Sam Sharpe to abolish the slave trade and slavery itself in England. In the US, of course, despite the efforts of the Quakers and other abolitionists (such as Richard Allen, Absalom Jones, John Brown, Lewis Hayden, Harriet Jacobs, Harriet Beecher Stowe, Henry Ward Beecher, Harriet Tubman, and many others) slavery continued until the American Civil War.

The tragic history of slavery has been well documented, although much of that history has been suppressed and omitted from textbooks. Slavery and slave trading were widespread throughout most tribes and peoples in Europe (as indeed in many early civilisations around the world), beginning at least with the Roman Empire, who exported Britons as slaves to Rome. Dublin was a major trading port for the Viking slave trade from the 8th to 11th centuries, and Bristol also became a major slave export centre. According to *Domesday Book*, in 1086 at least 10 per cent of the population of England were slaves (Davis, 1988). After the Norman conquest of England (in 1066), slavery began to decline and was relatively unknown by the 13th century. The slave trade was never formally outlawed in Britain, however, and during the late 17th and 18th centuries, Bristol, Glasgow, and Liverpool became major ports in the 'Triangular Trade' of human beings from Africa via Britain to the Americas and the Caribbean. While other European countries (including Portugal – recall the 1452 bull *Dum Diversas* in which Pope Nicholas V gave the Portuguese the right to enslave Muslims in West African – , France,[5] and the Dutch VOC[6], which operated ten slave ports in what is now modern Ghana) had laws in place that regulated (and even encouraged) slavery, there were no such laws in Britain.[7] The Church of England was deeply implicated in slavery, including, and perhaps especially, through its colonial missionary society the SPG. In Barbados, for instance, at the SPG-owned Codrington Plantation, slaves had the word 'SOCIETY' branded on their backs (BBC News, 2006). Some contemporary historians have proposed that these missionary societies encouraged slavery in order to encourage slave conversion (Gerbner, 2018).

Christian views of slavery have varied through the centuries. In the New Testament, Paul's letter to Philemon appears to endorse benevolent slavery; other New Testament texts from Paul (e.g., Eph. 6:5) also appear to support slavery, even though God made no distinction between Jew nor Greek, slave nor free, male nor female, 'for all of you are one in Christ Jesus' (Gal. 3:28). In I Corinthians 7:21, Paul wrote 'Were you a slave when called? Do not be concerned about it. Even if you can gain your freedom, make use of your present condition now more than ever'; Paul expected Christ's return immanently, and so was not much concerned with a believer's existing social status. Nevertheless, these verses have been used for millennia to defend the right to own and trade slaves. John Chrysostom opposed unjust slavery but appears to have accepted slavery as a social and economic reality. However, other theologians and bishops opposed slavery (including John's contemporary Gregory of Nyssa, who we met in Chapter 3, and Patrick of Ireland who witnessed the Viking slave trade in Dublin) and advocated for

---

[5] See the *Code Noir* of Louis XIV.

[6] The Dutch operated at least ten slave ports in what is modern Ghana, and more information about Amsterdam's role as a slave trade port over 200 years is emerging (Boffey, 2020); Dutch abolition was announced in July, 1863.

[7] In 1772, the Somerset Ruling (named for the slave in question), also known as the Mansfield Ruling (after the Lord Chief Justice), ruled that no slave could be forcibly removed in Britain and sold into slavery (National Archives, n.d.); it did not emancipate slaves or outlaw slavery in Britain.

emancipation, or at least manumission, through baptism. Through baptism, former slaves could be incorporated into (Christian) civil societies in the West. As we have seen, a number of popes tolerated or encouraged slavery, particular of non-Christians. However, in 1537 Pope Paul III revoked the authority of colonisers to enslave indigenous peoples of the Americas and declared that they were human: the papal bulls *Sublimus Dei* and *Altituda Divini Consolii* proclaimed that indigenous peoples were not to be robbed of their freedom or their possessions (Howard, 2011).[8]

The Atlantic trade in Black African humans made many white slave traders in Europe and the Americas extremely wealthy. It is estimated that at least 12 million West Africans were enslaved and transported to the Americas by the 'Middle Passage', of whom two million died en route, and another 50 per cent died in camps shortly after arrival. About 55 per cent of slaves were taken to South America, 35 per cent to the British and French West Indies, and 5 per cent to North America; a small number were taken to continental Europe (notably to Portugal and Spain). John Locke, the champion of Enlightenment individualism, condoned the slave trade and was an investor, although Adam Smith opposed slavery on economic grounds.[9] Inikori (1987) is among those who have proposed that the slave trade allowed the Industrial Revolution to happen in Britain by creating profits for investment in British industry. He holds that because of the slave trade, the entire Atlantic region must be treated as a single interdependent economic region, and draws parallels with the 21st-century relationship between developed and developing nations.

Slavery was not limited to the Atlantic. Traders engaged in 'blackbirding' in the Pacific, where 62,000 people from over 80 islands were transported to Australia to work the cotton and sugar cane fields in Queensland, Australia; of these, about a quarter died in captivity.[10] Blackbirding continued until the New Zealand government banned the practice in 1898;[11] the Australian Parliament passed the Pacific Island Labourers Act of 1901, which banned further recruitment and mandated a mass deportation of slaves in Australia

---

[8] These bulls left intact the provision of the 1493 bull *Inter Caetera* (which granted the Spanish monarchs Ferdinand and Isabella the right to a substantial portion of the so-called New World), which said that colonists had a duty to convert to Christianity the native people they encountered.

[9] Smith noted that there were no incentives for slaves to work hard since their housing and food were provided and incurred costs to the owner.

[10] Smaller numbers were transported to Samoa, Tahiti, and New Zealand.

[11] After the murder of Bishop Coley Patterson and two missionary colleagues in the Solomon Islands in 1871, where they may have been mistaken for blackbirders, the British Parliament passed the Pacific Islanders Protection Act, which increased regulation but did not ban the practice of blackbirding by British vessels and captains.

back to their islands.[12] The British also transported an estimated 61,000 indentured workers from India to Fiji between 1879 and 1916 to work the sugar cane fields.

It would seem that slavery and the slave trade have been an integral part of human history for millennia, but it is only since the Enlightenment with its democratic understanding of all humans that most people have come to view it with horror. Still, when there is profit to be made, it seems that human rights take a distant back seat, and even slavery can be justified. Anstey (1979) proposes that there are five threads that were woven together to form anti-slavery religious attitudes in the late 18th century: these include Arminianism, redemption, sanctification, post-millennialism, and denominationalism. What these principles meant is that all persons, including slaves, have an opportunity to take hold of the grace of God for themselves; that every person, including a slave, has an opportunity to be redeemed, or saved, by the grace of God; that believers are living in a time when Christians have an opportunity to bring about good (the Kingdom of God) and defeat evil (the forces of Satan that oppose God), and that Christ will return when that is accomplished. Denominationalism recognises that some Christian denominations chose to take up different charitable causes (Prochaska, 2006). In this worldview, slaves are full human beings (not three fifths, as in the American Constitution), and the grace of God is available to slaves as well as free. These egalitarian beliefs became characteristics of Evangelical and Protestant Churches.[13] It is not surprising, then, that in Britain and the US, it was largely Evangelical religions and sects, and particularly the Quakers on both sides of the Atlantic, who advocated strongly for abolition. After reading a work by Quaker author Anthony Benezet, John Wesley was moved to write in his diary about 'that execrable sum of all villainies, commonly called the Slave-trade' (Rogal, 1988, p 39), but since abolition remained a Quaker project, 'this meant that Wesley – through his journals, sermons and tracts – could only inform and educate his Methodist followers rather than actually mobilize them toward a specific action' (Rogal, 1988, p 40), although it is not entirely clear why. Equally, it is unsurprising that the landed or business classes – and their Established Church (Anglicanism) – that

---

[12] Although the motivation in Australia appears to have been to 'protect' white Australians from cheap labour.

[13] This is not to suggest that racism was not pervasive or enduring: we need only remember the story of Absalom Jones and Richard Allen at St George's Methodist Episcopal Church in Philadelphia, US. They were former slaves who ministered to Black worshippers at the church, but one Sunday in 1787 they were confined without notice to the balcony of the church by the white congregation. The Black congregation walked out of the church. Later Jones became the first Black priest of the American Episcopal Church; Allen went on to found the African Methodist Episcopal (AME) denomination.

benefitted directly or indirectly from slavery were at best ambivalent about abolition. Since in England non-conformists like the Quakers could not stand for Parliament, in 1787 they began to recruit establishment politicians and, in particular, William Wilberforce (1759–1833), an Anglican layman who had converted to Evangelicalism,[14] to work for the abolition of slavery and the slave trade. The passage of the Slavery Trade Act of 1807 which abolished slave trade by British ships (and was enforced by the Royal Navy), and the Slavery Abolition Act which banned slavery in the British Empire from 1834 (with the notable exception of territories held by the EIC), can be largely attributed to Evangelicals[15] and their egalitarian values.

Poor Law Reform 1834

In the financially straitened period after the Napoleonic wars, there was widespread social unrest in Britain. The scarcity of affordable food was exacerbated by the Corn Laws, which imposed tariffs on grain imports between 1815 and 1846, ostensibly to favour British food production; but if British harvests failed then food was not only scarce, it was very expensive. For the working classes and poor, capitalism and industrialisation, together with the Corn Laws, brought about increasing class distinctions, hunger, and poverty. Per capita expenditures under the Poor Law were consequently at their highest in the post-war years of 1817–18. Since political elites (who were largely landowners whose income depended on rents from tenant farmers) had no interest in restricting profit by controlling prices, they decided to do something about the disorder.[16] The benignly-named Act for the Regulation of Parish Vestries (also called the Sturges Bourne Act) of 1818 established a hierarchy in parish vestries, or the councils of each church, which allocated votes to each member by the value of the property they owned,[17] clearly allowing the interests of wealthier landowners to dominate. An 1819 amendment to this Act mandated that vestries make the (by now very familiar) distinction between deserving and undeserving poor; it also allowed vestries to hire salaried overseers to help them administer assistance, keep accounts, and manage the local workhouse for indoor relief. These reforms were not directed at improving state responses to the poor but rather

---

[14] He was a member of the Clapham Sect, a pious Evangelical sect of Anglicanism which flourished between 1780s to 1840s.

[15] The Slavery Abolition Act mandated that compensation be paid to the owners for the loss of their slaves but not to the slaves themselves.

[16] The Metropolitan Police Act, which established a police force in London, was enacted in 1829.

[17] This scale system was later carried over to elect guardians under the 1834 Poor Law.

in managing the demand for assistance by increasing restrictions on eligibility, excluding as many people as possible from access to relief, reducing costs by creating efficiencies within the system of relief, and expanding indoor relief.

The Swing Riots following the failed harvests of 1828 and 1829 became the proximate cause for the establishment of the Royal Commission into the Operation of the Poor Laws in 1832 (hereafter, the Royal Commission). The Whig-led government, looking over their collective shoulder at the French Revolution, was deeply concerned about social stability, social order, and the drain on the public post-war purse created by poor relief. Some estimates suggested that as many as 30 per cent of Britons received some form of assistance around that time. Despite the nascent humanitarian reforms at the end of the 18th century, British philosophers, notably Jeremy Bentham, Thomas Malthus, and the political economist Nassau William Senior (1790–1864),[18] a devotee of Adam Smith, were increasingly vocal about their opposition to the existing Poor Law because they believed it rewarded idleness among the poor and resulted in permanent paupery – or, in modern terms, it created a culture of poverty. The labouring poor and the paupers were increasingly conspicuous (although Himmelfarb, 1984, argues they were not more numerous) because they had moved from the countryside into the towns and cities; there they were collectively more visible, and there were more people to see them.[19] Malthus in particular believed that poor laws should be abolished entirely because they created an unsustainable and growing class of poor. Advocates for poor law reform criticised the Speenhamland System for undermining the moral character of agricultural workers by levelling all wages (Dunkley, 1981) even though the Speenhamland System had generally disappeared by 1832 (Blaug, 1964). Guided by Thomas Hyde Villiers,[20] Parliament established the Royal Commission to investigate the effects of the existing Poor Law and to '[root] out the allowance [Speenhamland] system "at whatever hazard"' (Dunkley, 1981, p 127). To populate the Royal Commission, Villiers and Senior drew from a group called the Oriel Noetics[21] who believed that

---

[18] Bentham, who we met in Chapter 5, was the son of an attorney; Malthus, who we also met in Chapter 5, was an Anglican cleric; Senior was the son of an Anglican cleric.

[19] One could argue that the case for sentencing more than 160,000 convicts to be transported to Australia between 1788 and 1868 (many for relatively minor offences of poverty, such as stealing food or prostitution) was one effective way of making sure they were never seen in the byways of Great Britain again.

[20] Villers (1801–32) was a Cambridge man but nevertheless a Benthamite and associate of John Stuart Mill; at the time of the appointment of the Commission he was Secretary to the Board of Control, which was responsible for overseeing the British East India Company.

[21] Noetic is derived from a Greek word meaning 'reasoner', and Oriel is the Oxford College with which most of the group were associated.

public allowances drove down wages, spurred population growth, and contributed to the disruption of the labour market and social disorder. The Noetics were firmly situated within the Enlightenment Movement and its liberal individualist and free-market orientation. Their contribution to Enlightenment philosophy (particularly that of Bentham) was to include natural theology (which proposed that humans have certain God-given rights), the new science of political economy, and to employ evidence of scripture and inference drawn by human moral reasoning (Mandler, 1990). For the Noetics, human improvement consisted not in greater material comfort but in striving for higher levels of virtue; wealth was a visible token of virtue and 'the gateway to new levels of moral achievement, for only the rich can exercise the higher virtues, such as benevolence, which are motivated by duty alone' (Sumner, 1816, cited in Mandler, 1990, p 87). Although Bentham detested the notions of natural law and natural theology, his influence can be discerned in the Noetic utilitarian demand to strive for the greatest good (or virtue) for the greatest number. Bentham's influence can also be seen in the liberal Enlightenment notions of the separation of church and state, rights for women, the abolition of slavery, and individual economic freedoms.[22]

The 1832–34 Royal Commission consisted of clergy, lawyers, and Senior as the political economist. The Commission included:

- the Rt Revd Charles James Blomfield (Bishop of London) – Chairman;
- the Revd Henry Bishop (Fellow of Oriel College);
- Walter Coulson (barrister and newspaper editor, associate of Jeremy Bentham);
- Henry Gawler (barrister);
- Nassau William Senior (political economist);
- the Rt Revd John Bird Sumner (Anglican Bishop of Chester);
- William Sturges Bourne (chairman of the 1817 Parliamentary Commission); and
- James Traill (barrister; but ultimately he was too ill to serve).

Edwin Chadwick, a barrister and former secretary to Bentham, was at first employed as staff by the Royal Commission, then made a full member in 1833. After the Poor Law Reform Act in 1834, he was made secretary of the Poor Law Commission from 1834 to its dissolution in 1847. George Taylor, also an advocate of Noetic views, was brought out of his retirement and made Secretary of the Royal Commission. Of the members of the

---

[22] In a posthumously published paper, Bentham also called for the decriminalisation of homosexual acts (Campos Boralevi, 1984).

Royal Commission, Bishop, Blomfield, Senior, Sturges Bourne, and Sumner were all directly connected to the Noetics, and Gawler's and Taylor's views aligned closely with the Noetics; Walter Coulson was a former pupil of Senior (Mandler, 1990). In short, the Royal Commission was made up of men who were closely philosophically aligned. Chadwick and Senior had 'a powerful and principled hostility to the practice of paternalism and an optimism about the ability of a free economy to secure the social order of the countryside in its stead' (Mandler, 1990, p 82). There is a strong historical opinion – beginning with Sydney (1848–1943) and Beatrice Webb (1859–1943)[23] – that the report of the Royal Commission was largely written by Senior and Chadwick in advance of its investigations and collection of evidence, and that the evidence was presented selectively to support those predetermined conclusions (Blaug, 1964). If this was the case (as seems quite likely) it may go some way to explain why scholars have found the data collection instruments employed by the Royal Commission deeply flawed.

The Royal Commission concluded that poor relief, and particularly the Speenhamland System, was responsible for permanent paupery and that poor taxes were used as subsidies for profit-making by employers; the Poor Law sapped 'both the wages and the virtue funds: "Skill and capital are all wasting away", and that the poor must be thrown back upon their own devices and paid only for their independent labour' (Mandler, 1990, p 100). The Royal Commission proposed that a nationally uniform and economically orthodox policy must be imposed. This much was agreed upon within the first few months of the Royal Commission. There was considerable disagreement about how to achieve those ends, but it was clear that poor relief would be both standardised and significantly reduced throughout the country. Parliament received the report, and the Act for the Amendment and Better Administration of the Laws Relating to the Poor in England (better known as the New Poor Law) received Royal Assent in August 1834.

The New Poor Law declared that the poor were responsible for their poverty and that public assistance was no longer a right. The new law established:

- separate workhouses for different types of paupers including aged, children, able-bodied males and able-bodied females;

---

[23] They were early members of the Fabian Society, co-founders of the London School of Economics. Beatrice was a member of the Poor Law Commission 1905–09, and together they authored the *Minority Report of the Royal Commission on the Poor Laws and Relief of Distress 1905–09*.

- the grouping of parishes into Poor Law Unions to provide workhouses (to improve efficiencies and consistency);[24]
- the banning of outdoor relief (except for the impotent poor and widows with children) so that the poor had to enter workhouses in order to claim relief; and
- a central authority to implement these policies and prevent the variation in practice that occurred under the Old Poor Law.

Benjamin Disraeli, future twice prime minister of Britain, but at the time an early-career Tory politician, decried the New Poor Law by stating that it 'announces to the world that in England, poverty is a crime', although Himmelfarb (1984) writes that 'The reformers had not, in fact, said or meant that; it was pauperism, not poverty, that they saw as the problem, and they saw it as a disease rather than a crime':

> The 'stigma' of pauperism, which was meant to differentiate the pauper from the poor, had the perverse effect of stigmatising the entire body of the poor, thus reinforcing the very ambiguity the reformers had so strenuously tried to remove. The new ambiguity, however, was different from the old in one important respect. Where the old had assimilated the pauper into the body of the poor, the new unwittingly assimilated the poor into the class of the pauper. (p 2)

In other words, argues Himmelfarb, the New Poor Law was premised on a conflation of meanings between the *labouring poor* and the *class of pauperism*, that is, collectively those people who were trapped in a chronic culture of poverty. Pauperism was a moral problem, both for the society and for the individual: the New Poor Law was intended to re-moralise the poor by helping them to avoid pauperism. The Calvinist foundations for such a view are obvious: both the poor and the pauper had a moral obligation – and an opportunity – to better themselves through *reformatio* and hard work. The means lay in Smith's laissez-faire economic approach, which would allow – or require – the poor and the pauper to be free agents in a free market capitalist system. The assumption that underpinned the New Poor Law was that opportunities, like God's grace, were equally available to all people.

---

[24] Higginbotham (2014) has a more generous view of these workhouses in contrast to the more popular Dickensian caricatures of how they worked. Applicants for assistance were 'offered' a place at a workhouse which they were free to take up or not, and residents were free to leave more or less at will; some stays were quite short. Health care was offered at the infirmary, which over time, came to offer care to the local community as well.

One of the problems with the Royal Commission was that it was constituted of privileged, educated, like-minded men. They were all social, political, or religious elites who had no idea what it was like to live without those privileges. That they came to agreements relatively quickly, and before the data were even amassed, suggests that there was not much room for disagreements, even if there had been any. The Royal Commission showed little awareness that meaningful work and opportunities were not equally available to all people. Despite their claims to enlightened reasonableness, the Noetics were heirs of Calvinism, not the Cappadocians. Their goal was to maintain social order and the resources of the Crown, and they believed that unfettered capitalism provided an opportunity for economic wellbeing to anyone who worked hard (and would therefore choose not to have too many children). They were apparently unable, or unwilling, to see the structural fetters that kept the poor in poverty: a lack of education, a system of class structures that allowed only the meanest kinds of employment to the poor; poor nutrition, poor sanitation, and poor health that were the inevitable consequences of poverty.[25] Further, the Royal Commission consisted mostly of political or ecclesiastical elites who were reliant on the rents of the labouring classes: they were faced with striking a balance between ensuring that there was a working class to support them but that the labouring poor did not slip into actual paupery that would be a bad look for the Crown and a drain on its resources. The New Poor Law, therefore, had to make the consequences of paupery so unbearable that the working poor continued to work.

A Poor Law Commission (1834–47) and then a Poor Law Board (1847–71) were established to oversee the implementation of the New Poor Law. Both were considered ineffective in addressing paupery and providing assistance to the working poor, in part because it was ignored in some parts of the country. By the 1850s, public assistance to the unemployed or their families had 'all but ceased in England and did not re-emerge until the early twentieth century' (Thomson, 1998, p 11), although as we shall see, private charity flourished. Public pensions for the aged and poor came under attack because it was felt that individuals and families should bear the costs for their own old age, although the restrictions of the New Poor Law were not meant to apply to the aged. By the 1880s, old age pensions had fallen to half of the numbers of the 1850s. The proportion of the elderly in workhouses doubled from

---

[25] Diseases of poor sanitation such as typhoid, dysentery, and cholera were all spread through raw sewage that flowed through the streets; tuberculosis flourished in poorly ventilated accommodations that kept windows shut against the cold; as a consequence, even poor families spent between 8–11 per cent on (legal) opioids including laudanum, which eased diarrhoea and coughs (Davenport-Hines, 2001).

1851 to 1901. Between 1815 and 1914 nearly 10 million people emigrated from Britain: about half went to the US, and most of the rest to Australia and Canada, with smaller numbers to New Zealand and South Africa (Lloyd, 2007). In Australasia (where assisted migrants were carefully vetted by colonial officials for their health and ability to work) colonists from all social strata were so averse to the British Poor Laws and their consequences that they determined not to reproduce it in any way. They envisioned a 'world without welfare' (Thomson, 1998), where everyone would pay their own way, or, as would be the case in New Zealand, be required to call upon the support of relatives (a law which continued until 1968).[26]

Theological and social responses to the New Poor Law

That the New Poor Law failed to address both paupery and the needs of the working poor was almost immediately obvious. Writers like Charles Dickens who, although highly critical of churches, held Christian views (Slater, 2009; Colledge, 2012). He created the iconic stories and characters of *Oliver Twist*, *Nicholas Nickleby*, *David Copperfield*, Little Nell, and of course Tiny Tim in *A Christmas Carol*, from the late 1830s to 1870, making the struggles of the poor and the orphan widely available to sympathetic readers in magazines and books. After the New Poor Law was enacted, members of the rising middle class were confronted daily by the increasingly visible beggars and orphans on the streets and were moved to give private alms directly to them. Christians of all kinds were particularly moved to respond. This direct almsgiving was condemned as ineffective and an act that promoted paupery. F.D. Maurice (1805–72), the Anglican priest who is widely considered the founding father of Anglican social theology[27] (Morris, 2017) believed that the real social problem was not wealth or poverty but rather social inequalities and the 'lack of "connection" between the rich and poor, the "feeling of alienation"' (Himmelfarb, 1984, p 4). Maurice, a graduate of Exeter College, Oxford, and his colleagues are remembered for, among other achievements, founding the Working Men's College (1854), the earliest adult education centre in Europe, in order to provide an alternative for education for those for whom

---

[26] In New Zealand, the Destitute Persons Act 1846 placed responsibility for care of the indigent with the near relatives of the person in question, modelled after the 1601 Poor Law, but unlike the Old Poor Law there was no right to parish assistance or from any other entity in colonial New Zealand (Thomson, 1998, pp 23–4) until 1885, which allowed for but did not specify charitable aid. Nevertheless, from the enactment of the Hospitals and Charitable Institutions Act of 1885, charitable aid boards did provide (if somewhat grudgingly, according to Tennant (1989)).

[27] Maurice, with his colleagues Charles Kingsley (Anglican priest, and novelist) and John Ludlow (a barrister and journalist), eventually accepted the label of Christian Socialist.

the elite universities, Oxford and Cambridge, were not an option. Maurice supported Chartism (extending the vote to working men), but he also realised that uninformed voters were dangerous. (He later worked with Elizabeth Malleson to establish the College for Working Women in 1874.) Maurice vehemently condemned both the Evangelicals and the Tractarians (who we will consider in a moment) as representing 'excessively individualized forms of faith, holding out the prospect of rewards and punishments as motives for faith, and differentiating sharply between people by dividing them into the saved and the damned' (Morris, 2017, p 9). The solution, he felt, lay in creating opportunities to make connections between people and classes, particularly through the church and its sacraments (Gray, 1986) where all people truly were equals.

> The Church is ... human society in its normal state: the World, that same society irregular and abnormal. The world is the Church without God; the Church is the world restored to its relations with God, taken back by Him into the state for which He created it. (Maurice, 1881, cited by Morris, 2017 p 9)

Maurice was not especially politically active, nor did he ever develop a systematic theology or even a 'blueprint for Christian social ethics' (Morris, 2017, p 18). Rather, what he did was lay a kind of rough theological foundation for a socially conscious faith and groups such as the Fabian Society (which advocated incremental but continuing social reform) formed in 1884, and later the Christian Social Union (with its so-called 'muscular Christianity' which advocated putting faith into action). Maurice introduced a kind of Trinitarian theology as a model for living his faith: the theology of the Trinity holds that God is one God and at the same time three persons: Creator, Christ, and Holy Spirit, each an aspect of one God, united yet distinct and always in a relationship (or *perichoresis*) with each other. It is this relational aspect of God that appealed to Maurice. Millbank (2017) writes that 'Maurice's recovery of a dynamic and relational doctrine of the Trinity, wholly biblical in emphasis and offering a mode of communion with others through our mutual life in God is surely the beginning of a true social theology' (p 27).

Maurice was a favourite and mentor of Octavia Hill (1838–1912). In a letter to her sister in 1854, a 16-year-old Octavia wrote of Maurice that 'It was he who had led me to the Church, who had shown me a life in the creeds, the services and the Bible; who had interpreted for me much that was dark and puzzling in life' (Maurice, 1913, cited by Ryan, 2017, pp 42–3). Even though Hill felt that her work was motivated by her faith, 'strongly felt but dimly articulated' (Boyd, 1982, in Ryan, 2017 p 48), she disliked 'those who try to *force* their notions, their *faith* on everyone; who decidedly set to work to convert people' (Boyd, 1982, cited in Ryan, 2017, p 48; italics in original). The Maurice and Hill families were closely united when Octavia's sister Emily married Maurice's son Frederick. Octavia herself had a 'passionate intimacy' with Sophia Jex-Blake, the first woman physician in Scotland, and among the first in Great Britain; Octavia's long-time companion was Harriot Yorke who lived and worked with her for 30 years, and they are buried together (Historic England, n.d.).

Florence Nightingale (1820–1910)[28] demonstrated statistically how malnutrition and poor sanitation were to blame for widespread disease in urban areas of Britain and among British soldiers in the Crimea and India. While in the post-Poor Law reform era of the 1840s the heightened social consciousness of the middle classes was channelled into legislative reforms, in the 1880s what emerged were private philanthropies, institutions, and charities (Himmelfarb, 1984). By the latter part of the 19th century – because of the egregious and manifest failure of the New Poor Law as an Enlightenment experiment to eliminate pauperism, and the renewed attention of Evangelical, Tractarian, and Broad Church Christians to the issue of pauperism – public faith in public solutions to pauperism was at a very low ebb. In this context, we might also suggest that public faith in what were perceived as punitive and dehumanising Calvinist responses to pauperism were being replaced by other kinds of responses: direct charitable aid and the Settlement House Movement.

The Tractarians

The Evangelical faction of the Church of England continued to be a powerful force in Britain during the early 19th century. Their successes in the Act for the Abolition of the Slave Trade in 1807 and the Slavery Abolition Act in 1833 demonstrated their engagement with Enlightenment values such as social justice and human rights. Also in 1833, John Keble (1792–1866), an Anglican priest, preached what became the founding declaration of the Oxford Movement (so-named for the university). Adherents were also known as Tractarians (for the *Tracts for the Times* the group published), or more pejoratively 'Newmanites' or 'Puseyites' after two other leaders of the movement, John Henry Newman and Edward Bouverie Pusey. Tractarians were 'High Church' – that is, their ecclesiastical theology put great value on the sacraments (particularly baptism and the centrality of Eucharist, or Holy

---

[28] Florence Nightingale reformed nursing and health care for soldiers and the poor in England (and established the first secular school of nursing in London in 1860); her work strengthened the Public Health Acts of 1874 and 1875. Her story is for nursing to tell, but the religious motivation for her work is certainly consistent with the times we are considering here.

Communion in worship, beliefs with which Maurice had great sympathy), ordained ministers, and more formal ceremonial in worship services. During the 1830s and 1840s, the Tractarians called for the revival of early church theology, teaching, and practices in the Anglican Church. Members of the Oxford Movement also encouraged a revival of the monastic tradition for men and women (which had never recovered from the dissolution of the monasteries under Henry VIII), and several religious orders were founded during this period.

The liturgical ambitions of this group need not concern us here, except to note that the liturgical reforms reflected the revival of interest in the teachings of the early church – an era we explored in Chapter 3. Unsurprisingly perhaps, the Tractarians were criticised by Evangelicals[29] for what were perceived as Roman Catholic beliefs and practices (and, in fact, Newman did leave the Anglican Church for the Roman Catholic Church in 1845). What is important is that because of their High Church tendencies, Anglican clergy sympathetic to the Oxford Movement were denied livings[30] by their usually Evangelical or Broad Church bishops; many of these priests ended up being employed in what were considered undesirable (and less remunerative) positions in the slums of the cities, particularly in London. While employed in these poor areas, Tractarian clergy were exposed to the extreme poverty of their parishioners and saw social injustices created by the Poor Law of 1834. While there was no doubt some ecclesiastical snobbery among these clergy, there appears to have been no class snobbery. Tractarian anthropology was level: all Christians were equal in the eyes of God and the church. Tractarian clergy turned their parishes into centres for social justice (Skinner, 2004). They rejected the notion of civic assistance and recovered the 4th-century notion that it was the duty of the wealthy to provide for the poor directly through the alms they gave to the church. Tractarians strongly encouraged personal charity and also reinvigorated the idea that paupery was not a problem of the poor but of the wealthy, exacerbated by social injustices (such as substandard housing and sanitation) and inequitable public laws such as the New Poor Law. Referencing the work of the British historian Boyd Hilton, Skinner (2004) suggests that between 1850 and 1870, an Age of Atonement (which stressed the essential sinfulness of humanity, and which required the Crucifixion as a redemptive act of sacrifice to appease an angry God, advocated by Evangelicals) was replaced by an Age of Incarnation, with a renewed emphasis on Jesus as God-become-human

---

[29] One such person included Anthony Ashley-Cooper, Earl of Shaftsbury, an evangelical Anglican, who worked assiduously for justice and reform of lunacy laws and laws regarding child labour, child miners, and child chimney-sweeps.

[30] Stipended, or paid, positions.

(which stressed the love of God for humanity) rather than as sacrificial lamb. However, this was not an entirely new idea: we have seen this incarnational theology before in the 4th-century sermons of John Chrysostom who urged believers to see the face of Christ in the poor. Set against the Calvinist and even Arminian theology of the Evangelicals, however, it was a radical notion indeed. Tractarians were largely responsible for Christian Socialism, which arose in the 1850s, and after a series of short-lived societies resulted in the founding of the Christian Social Union in 1889, initially with branches in Oxford and London.[31] Tractarianism also found its way to America in the missionary work of James Lloyd Breck (1818–76) and others throughout what was then the American western wilderness.

Charity Organisation Society

Following the New Poor Law, there were five independent sectors contributing to the relief of the poor: the Poor Law Guardians, administering state relief; the magistrate, who was able to offer casual help to those who came before the court; ecclesiastical bodies distributing charity according to their denominations; benevolent institutions, which were the multiplicity of charitable aid societies; and private aid by individuals. The Charity Organisation Society (or COS as it quickly became known; see Barnett, 1918, p 28) was founded largely to address the lack of coordination between the many charitable aid societies that had sprung up to address what they saw as the shortcomings of the New Poor Law and the incompetence demonstrated by the Guardians charged with administering it. To answer the question of why yet another society was needed, Helen Bosanquet (1914) wrote in her history of the COS:

> And first, we may mention those which, in the attempt to mitigate the evil, were undoubtedly aggravating it. In the front rank of these we may place the frivolous public, which, whether moved by fear or pity or sheer carelessness, supported the great army of beggars, and made laziness and imposture more profitable than work. (p 6)

> The Poor Law itself was perhaps the arch offender in the matter of giving indiscriminate and inadequate relief. The Guardians and the charities were engaged in running after each other in a vicious circle. The Guardians made their relief inadequate because they were sure it was being supplemented by charity; the charities gave because the Guardians' relief was so inadequate. (p 8)

---

[31] It later expanded to 27 branches by 1895 and eventually had branches in Anglophone nations around the world.

The New Poor Law was so bad, and the effects of it so unjust, that the general public could see the effects and was moved to direct charitable giving to beggars they encountered on the street. Bosanquet and the founders of the COS were clear that such uncoordinated individual philanthropy was not only ineffective but harmful. Her condemnation may also be a not very subtle dig at some of the well-intended efforts of Tractarian and other clergy in the slums of London who were encouraging parishioners to give alms through the churches:

> The greater number of the East End clergy have converted themselves into relieving officers. Sums of enormous magnitude are annually collected and dispensed by them either personally or through district visitors, nine-tenths of whom are women, and the bulk silly and ignorant women. A hundred different agencies for the relief of distress are at work over the same ground, without concert or co-operation, or the slightest information as to each other's exertions, and the result is an unparalleled growth of imposition, mendicancy, and sheer shameless pauperism. (Bosanquet, 1914, p 12)

Bosanquet's impatience with the ineffectiveness, inefficiency, and redundancy of private and parish efforts comes through very clearly. Indeed, the COS was not universally welcomed by urban clergy in part because they perceived a lack of inefficiency in the Society but also because COS members 'had on public platforms often pointed a moral or adorned a tale by instances of clerical ignorance, imbecility, pig-headedness or even dishonesty' (Bosanquet, 1914, p 67). However, the COS modelled itself after a system apparently developed by an Anglican clergyman that involved the entire community:

> In December 1868 the Rev Martyn Hart started his system of free mendicity tickets in Blackheath.[32] Every householder was supplied with tickets with which to refer beggars to a central office. Cases were enquired into by an experienced officer; if hungry they were fed, and if capable of being permanently assisted they were helped from funds raised in the district. (Bosanquet, 1940, p 11)

---

[32] Hart was the incumbent of St Germain's (Anglican) Chapel. He later emigrated to Denver, Colorado in the US (Linscome, 1972) and became Dean of the Episcopal Cathedral in Denver. Hart took his charitable inclinations and organisational skills with him. He was one of the four interfaith cofounders of the Charity Organisation Society in Denver in 1887, which became the seed of the United Way Campaign in 1888, which eventually spread throughout the US.

Octavia Hill, who we met previously, was essentially a philanthropic property developer,[33] and the committee of which she was a part clearly saw their role as coordinating the efforts of the many different charitable societies and thereby increasing overall effectiveness. They began to organise in June 1868, after a talk[34] by the Rev Henry Solly (1813–1903), a Unitarian minister.[35] However (and here Bosanquet barely disguises her impatience with the men who were the financial backers of the Society), there were a number of false starts, and it was not until April 1870 that the COS was formalised and its work began. This was a high-profile undertaking with a very well-connected governing council: the patron of the COS was Queen Victoria, and the president was the (Anglican) Bishop of London, John Jackson (who had been appointed by Disraeli).

Hill and her committee understood that their work with an individual necessarily included a visit to that individual's home environment and an assessment of that environment.

> From its earliest days the Society has endeavoured to enlist the services of voluntary workers in visiting the homes of those in need of assistance. That any material assistance given should always be accompanied by such friendly visitation is one of its first principles. (Bosanquet, 1914, p 53)

In an age where sanitation was rudimentary at best, where raw sewage flowed in the streets, water was hardly drinkable, and where most homes were heated with coal, which produced both particulates and carbon monoxide in rooms closed against the cold, assessing the environment

---

[33] In 1864, Hill had, with John Ruskin as a major investor, begun to rebuild slums in London and founded the Commons Society to restore access to parks, gardens, and recreational facilities for the poor.

[34] 'How to deal with the Unemployed Poor of London and with its "Roughs" and Criminal Classes.'

[35] The roots of Unitarianism are found in roughly 2,000 Protestants who left the Anglican Church (the so-called Great Ejection) after the Restoration and the Act of Uniformity in 1662 which established The Anglican Book of Common Prayer of 1662 as the compulsory form of worship in Britain, and required an oath of clergy to that effect. The Act of Toleration of 1689 (supported by the new coregents, William III and Mary II, Protestants of the Dutch House of Orange) permitted 'non-conforming' ministers to preach in non-conforming congregations. Unitarianism rejects the doctrine of the Trinity (God in three Persons, Creator, Christ, and Spirit) in favour of the singularity of God, were largely anti-clerical authority, and believed in the importance of Bible study by individuals. However, Unitarians rejected Calvinist doctrine of predestination and election. In this sense, the Unitarians were aligned with the Baptists, Congregationalists, Quakers, and similar dissenting groups.

of the poor was no trivial matter. A home visit should not be done by 'silly and ignorant' persons. There was a recommended reading list of books, pamphlets, reports, speeches, and papers for these visitors, which formed a kind of curriculum. Titles included (among others) *Chalmers' Christian and Civic Economy of Large Towns*;[36] *London Pauperism among Jews and Christians* (Stallard); *London: Its Growth, Charitable Agencies, and Wants* (C.P.B. Bosanquet); *Pauperism and the Poor Laws*; *Suggestions to Charity Agents*; *Guide to Workhouse Management* (E. Smith); *The Systematic Visitation of the Poor in their Own Homes* (C. Trevelyan); *Speech of the Bishop of London on the Organisation of Charity*; and so forth. The list was revised and updated regularly, and by 1875 there was a list of 23 special publications of the COS. Visitors were not merely being trained to visit the poor, they were being educated to see how their work fit into a larger sociopolitical and religious context. Visits should not be intrusive; they should have a definite errand or purpose, and the granting of relief should not be directly connected with the visit.[37] The visits should also be done by someone within the neighbourhood, who had some sympathy for the context and challenges with which an individual who sought relief was confronted daily. By the time she reaches the year 1877 in her history of the COS, Bosanquet is using the words 'social work' and 'case work': this is quite probably the earliest use of these words, and she uses what modern social workers would recognise as case studies to convey her points. By 1883 the Society recognised that relying on volunteers was not working as well as it might, that while the case work was being done well, the volunteers were overstretched, and carrying out what was 'scarcely more than Investigation and Relief Societies' (Bosanquet, 1914, p 69). The proposed solution was to appoint five paid officers, men or women, 'to give up their whole time to perfecting the local work and organising charity' (Bosanquet, 1914, p 70). This is the first recorded instance of paid social workers.

Despite the annoyance of the members of the COS with the methods and inefficiencies of some parochial clergy, it is clear that there was a very close relationship between the urban churches and the COS. Indeed, by 1898–9 the St Marylebone Charity Organisation Committee (of which Octavia Hill was a member at the parish where Samuel Barnett had worked before he moved to Whitechapel) was represented on the parochial relief

---

[36] Chalmers was a Glaswegian political economist, moral philosopher and Evangelical churchman who promoted the idea of private, voluntary charity provided through churches in an organised way, and believed that the poor should be enabled to help themselves.

[37] 'Mr A.H. Hill feared the injury which the invasion of these lady-brigades from the West End would do to the East; it should be left to neighbours to help each other' (Bosanquet, 1914, p 55).

committees of five different churches in an effort to ensure that 'a higher standard of work' should be adopted by them (Bosanquet, 1914, p 81). In contemporary language, this may make her the first consulting social worker, or even professional supervisor.

Settlement House Movement

The intellectual atmosphere at Oxford was rich with the Tractarian theological legacy and the radical implications of Maurice and Christian Socialism. Among the students and clergy influenced by these ideas was Samuel Barnett (Harris, 2002), cofounder (with Henrietta, his wife) of Toynbee Hall[38] in November 1883, part of what became the Settlement House Movement. Barnett was educated at Wadham College, Oxford, a choice made by his father 'to mitigate the horrors of free-thinking ... [and] because its warden, Dr Simmonds was an unbending Tory and a rigid evangelical' (Barnett, 1918, p 10). Apparently quite a reserved man, Samuel 'greatly dislike the undergraduates' prayer-meetings, feeling it was neither healthy nor modest to examine other people's souls nor to expose his own' (Barnett, 1918, p 12). At Oxford, despite his Evangelical warden, Samuel appears to have been a Broad Churchman (someone who accommodated both Evangelicalism and High Church theology); he was doubtless exposed to the legacy of Oxford Movement thinkers, and certainly to the discourse of social reform.

At Oxford, Samuel Barnett encountered Benjamin Jowett (1817–93), classist, Anglican priest, and severe critic of the New Poor Law, Thomas Hill (T.H.) Green (1836–82), whose Idealism succeeded Utilitarianism as the dominant philosophical school in British universities, and which became a programme for left-wing reformers (Richter, 1964, p 13), and of course the economic historian Arnold Toynbee. Jowett (whom Henrietta Barnett would later call 'the great Mr Jowett', p 304) was a Broad Churchman who argued that while the broad truths of Christianity are valid for all time, it must adapt itself to the best knowledge of the age (Richter, 1964, p 27). He proposed that the metaphysics of Idealism allowed a resolution of the apparent conflict between science and religion since both relied on human perception. The question with which his student and later colleague T.H. Green wrestled was how a thinking person and scientist could subscribe to an Evangelical inheritance which (at the time) held that scriptures are the unmediated and literal revelation of God's word. Building on Jowett, Green

---

[38] This was named for Arnold Toynbee (1852–83), the Oxford economic historian and social reformer, and a friend of the Barnetts, who had died in March 1883 at the age of 30.

sought to replace fundamentalist Evangelicalism by a metaphysical system that would transform Christianity from a historical religion into an undogmatic theology. This would turn the attention of those disciplined in Evangelical families away from the means of personal salvation in the next world to improving the conditions of this one. (Richter, 1964, p 19)

In this way, he sought to transform faith into a thoughtful and engaging experience rather than simply an emotional one. The claims of Evangelicals were based on scripture and individualism; those of the Tractarians were based on the authority of church tradition; those of the Broad Church were based on reason, avoiding the extremes of the other two.[39] Green's theology proposed that religion must be fully engaged with the world. In an 1866 letter to Henry Scott Holland on the occasion of Gerard Manley Hopkins' conversion to Roman Catholicism, Green wrote,

> Does it not appear that mere religious agency does but touch the surface of our modern rottenness: that the people who cry 'Lord, Lord' do no wonderful works and never get nearer to any organisation of life; that the only hope lies in such 'secular' agency and 'human' philosophy as requires a religious zeal, not less self-denying and much more laboriously thoughtful than that of the monk, to bring into action? ... Whether the outcome will be new forms of religious society or a gradual absorption of all such forms in simple religious citizenship, I do not predict: but I have faith that the new Christianity, because not claiming to be special or exceptional or miraculous, will do more for mankind than its 'Catholic' form hampered by false antagonisms it has ever been able to do. (cited by Richter, 1964, pp 31–2)

Green advocated for a new kind of Christianity that was fully engaged with the world, and that addressed 'modern rottenness', tended to no extremes, and did not overclaim. While this may seem an unextraordinary vision from a 21st-century perspective, in the context of the heated religious factionalism of the latter part of the 19th century and the wreckage created by the New Poor Law, this was a significant departure. Green created a theological foundation for the full engagement of Christians

---

[39] Scripture, reason and tradition are the three sources of authority set out for Anglicans by Reformation theologian Richard Hooker (1554–1600) in his work *Of the Lawes of Ecclesiasticall Politie* (1593–97), which was intended to defend the Anglican Church of Elizabeth I against both Roman Catholics and Puritans.

with the world without straining at the gnats of scriptural hermeneutic or liturgical form.

Toynbee, as we have seen, was deeply concerned with the dehumanisation of the worker brought about by the Industrial Revolution, and was opposed to notions of unrestrained free-market capitalism that would result in a kind of social Darwinism: that is, only the economically fit would, or should, survive. Toynbee was an intimate of the Barnetts; he engaged in education for workers in Whitechapel (in the East End of London, where the Barnetts would later establish the settlement house), encouraged his students to do the same, and established libraries for workers. It was these several generations of thinkers at Oxford[40] that fomented the dynamic atmosphere of both critically engaging with theological and religious traditions advocated for moving beyond the factionalism that prevailed, and for applying that religious energy into practical engagement with the 'rottenness' of the world.

In 1867, after his graduation, Barnett visited post-Civil War America for several months (New York, Boston, Philadelphia, Washington, Baltimore, Richmond, Charleston, Georgia, and New Orleans). On his return to England, he was ordained deacon and began as curate (assistant) of St Mary's Bryaston Square (Marylebone), London, and ordained priest a year later. St Mary's is a so-called 'Commissioners' Church', built by funds provided by Parliament (under an 1818 Act) as a kind of thanksgiving for Britain's victory over Napoleon at Waterloo. These state-funded churches were intended for poor urban areas that were underserved by Anglican churches. By ensuring access to Anglican churches, the government hoped to maintain social stability and prevent uprisings, particularly among the lower classes (Anglicanism was the state Church of England, after all). Church designs had to be approved by the High Church faction, which required that altars and baptismal fonts be given prominence over pulpits (large pulpits emphasising preaching over sacraments were an Evangelical legacy). While it does not automatically follow that Commissioners' Churches were High Church or Tractarian, it was in this building and its accompanying architectural theology and history as a socially-aware parish, that Barnett took up his first position.

Henrietta Rowland was a friend and protégée of Octavia Hill who had sat on the COS Committee from its inception. So too did Helen Bosanquet[41]

---

[40] One of whom, it is worth pointing out, was the mathematician Alfred North Whitehead, founder of process philosophy, and who was on the governing board of Toynbee Hall for a period.

[41] Bosanquet later chronicled the history of the COS in her book *Social Work in London, 1869–1912: A history of the Charity Organisation Society* (1914).

(1860–1925), who was the author of the history of the COS, and whose husband, Bernard Bosanquet, was a philosopher and social reformer. Samuel Barnett knew Octavia Hill through St Mary's Church from her charitable work.[42] At Hill's birthday party in 1870, Henrietta met Samuel Barnett, and in January 1873 became his devoted wife[43] and partner in the Settlement House Movement. If you read those four sentences again you will come to realise that there were not independent strands for social reform floating about London, but the key movers and shakers of the COS, the Settlement House Movement, and other key social reformers knew each other well and regularly met with each other in the various committees responding to the holes in the social safety net left by the New Poor Law. Further, they met with each other (at first) in the context of St Mary's Anglican Church, Marylebone, London. In 1873, Samuel and Henrietta Barnett settled across town in the parish of St Jude's, Whitechapel, in the impoverished 'slums' of the East End of London, where 11 years later they founded the Toynbee Hall settlement house. Here is the rationale for Younghusband's claim that social work began in the slums of London.

In 1874, Samuel Barnett wrote:

> The relief of the poor is a matter which I hold to be of the greatest importance. Indiscriminate charity is among the curses of London. To put the result of our observation in the strongest form, I would say that 'the poor starve because of the alms they receive …' Alms are given them – a shilling by one, a sixpence by another, a dinner here and some clothing there; the gift is not sufficient if they are really struggling, the care is not sufficient if they are thriftless or wicked. (Barnett, 1918, p 83)

Samuel was not opposed to poor relief, of course, but he was quite opposed to piecemeal charity, given impulsively by private individuals without assessing and responding to the needs of the whole person, and in this, he was entirely aligned with Bosanquet, Hill, and the COS. Responding to the whole person was the goal of the settlement houses. The settlement house was a place where 'University men bec[a]me the neighbours of the working poor, sharing their life, thinking out their problems, learning from them

---

[42] According to his biographer, Henrietta, Samuel 'took a most active part in this reform [the COS], and it was in connection with it that his friendship with Miss Octavia hill began' (Barnett, 1918, p 28).

[43] This is Henrietta's expression; I know nothing of their relationship, of course, but the fact that she published an extensive and exhaustive biography of her husband after his death certainly speaks to a measure of devotion.

the lessons of patience, fellowship, self-friendship'. This would 'alleviate the sorrow and misery born of class division and indifference. It will bring classes into relation ...' (Barnett, 1918, p 310). In 1883, Samuel wrote, 'Inquiries into social conditions lead generally to one conclusion. They show that little can be done *for*, which is not done *with* the people ... Such poverty of life can best be removed by contact with those who possess the means of higher life' (Barnett, 1918, p 307). This notion of a level society where people of all classes encounter and learn from each other in neighbourhood settings has clear resonance with the theological foundations set out by Maurice and the Christian Socialists, the Tractarians, Jowett, and Green, and is reflected in the short career of Toynbee.

The Barnetts did not open the Whitechapel settlement house on their own, of course; they were actively supported by a committee with a formal structure at Oxford University, and they visited regularly there. Toynbee Hall was named after Arnold Toynbee's early support and untimely death (it was said to be of exhaustion) in 1883 at the age of only 30. It was only the first settlement: Oxford House, founded by the Tractarians, opened in Bethnal Green three months after Toynbee Hall; and in 1890, Congregationalists from Oxford opened Mansfield House in Canning Town (Palmer, 2014). By 1914, Helen Bosanquet writes, there were over 20 settlement houses in London, as well as school and college missions. The first Women's University Settlement (renamed the Blackfriars Settlement in 1961) was founded in 1887 by Alice Grüner,[44] a teacher and a mature student at Newnham College, after a talk by Henrietta Barnett to the Cambridge Ladies' Discussion Society; Octavia Hill was also involved in Women's University Settlement Committee. The Women's Settlement was the first to provide 'whole time service' and regular training for residents (Bosanquet, 1914, p 76).

The COS and the Settlement House Movement (including the university settlements) were not wholly independent groups working for different purposes. Rather, there was a great deal of integration of the two movements; their committee memberships, aims, values, philosophies, and theologies were aligned. Only their approaches were different – the COS worked with poor individuals and the settlement houses sought to create connections between poor communities and educated elites – and not at all at odds with each other. Each method understood and witnessed the failures of the punitive Calvinist-informed poor laws (both Old and New), believed firmly in the importance of connections between classes and that members of all social classes could learn from each other.

---

[44] In her obituary, the *Times* of London names her as Alice Gruner (1846–1930), born in Estonia, a teacher and suffragist (1930).

Across the Atlantic

As complex as this 19th-century story is in Great Britain, across the Atlantic there were developments. You will recall that the foundational religious theology in the US came from the Calvinist Puritans, who created a kind of theocratic structure in some of the early colonies. Governance of the individual colonies was relatively independent of each other until the American Revolutionary War (1775–83). The Declaration of Independence established the new nation in 1776, and the new Constitution, ratified in 1787, allocated specific powers to the federal government, and others were left to the states. Poor relief was left to the states and local authorities. Nevertheless, until the late 19th century, the response to the poor in America was largely consistent with the Elizabethan Poor Law and the residual Calvinist influences which motivated the Puritans to leave England in the first place.

> Without historical traditions of care for the poor, cut off from pre-Protestant Christian traditions, influenced at a vulnerable state of development by a strict capitalist political economic, social welfare in the United State became 'stuck' in its harsh antipoor, worker-exploitative past. (Day and Schiele, 2013, p 114)

Early colonial legislatures and later state governments required residence to receive relief; contracting (similar to the English system where individuals were put in the care of a tenant farmer who would care for them, and presumably get work from them, for a given sum of money) and auctioning (where a family was placed with another couple or family who would bid for then care for them for a small amount of public funding) were common in rural areas. Indoor relief and limited outdoor relief were also available (Hansan, 2011). Because the conditions and reputation of the poorhouses had deteriorated by the middle of the 19th century, including mismanagement and rising costs, outdoor relief came to be seen as the more desirable option. However, 'The concept of public assistance conflicted with Calvinist values and was sometimes viewed as impinging on the personal gratification derived from private works of charity' (Hansan, 2011). Protests against penurious aid, and occasionally unrest and riots, resulted in the development of private charities in American municipalities in much the same way as we saw in response to the New Poor Law in Great Britain. Both public and private charities emerged to address the lacuna between the needs of the poor and the limited public assistance that was available.

At the same time, events in Europe began to influence the American social and economic scene in important ways: Scandinavian migration to America began in 1840; the Great Famine in Ireland (1845–49) resulted in the addition of an estimated 1.5 million desperate and poor Irish to American cities. The American Civil War (1861–65) resulted in widespread movements of people, including the movement of troops in both the North and the South, and ultimately the emancipation of an estimated 3.9 million slaves, some of whom moved north to find paid work. Freedom was a mixed blessing for many ex-slaves as many newly freed slaves suffered from disease, including smallpox and cholera (Downs, 2012), or starved; as many as one million freed ex-slaves may have died between 1862 and 1870. Italian immigration peaked between 1880 and 1924 as they sought relief from poverty and hunger on their peninsula. All of these groups stressed already challenged poor relief systems, particularly in urban areas such as Boston, New York, and Chicago. In short, there were mass migrations of very poor, hungry, undereducated, and often sick people throughout the troubled American states between 1840 and 1920, and social care systems were hard pressed to keep up with the demand.

Into this complex scene emerged Jane Addams (1860–1935) and Ellen Gates Starr. They opened Hull House, a settlement house in Chicago, in September 1889. Addams was born to a wealthy Evangelical Protestant family (her father was a 'perfectionist' Quaker), and in her early life, she had experienced great sympathy for people in social distress. During a European tour in 1883–85, she was 'irresistibly drawn to the poorer quarters of each city' (Addams, 1910/2011). In 1886, at the age of 25, and influenced by her reading of Tolstoy (referred to extensively throughout her memoir *Twenty Years at Hull House*), she converted to Christianity and was baptised in the Presbyterian Church. For Addams, Christianity was an institution that stood for universal fellowship and gave practical expression to the 'ideals of democracy' (Addams, 1910/2011, p 24). In 1887, she read a magazine article about Toynbee Hall which inspired her to make another European trip that specifically included a visit to Toynbee Hall in June 1988, where she met the Barnetts, Octavia Hill, and the Webbs; she particularly commented that she was pleased that Oxford House, the Tractarian settlement house in Bethnal Green, was 'carried on by a churchman' (Addams, 1910/2011, p 79). It is worthwhile quoting her views on Christianity and the Settlement House Movement at length:

> Other motives which I believe make toward the Settlement are the result of a certain renaissance going forward in Christianity ... That Christianity has to be revealed and embodied in the line of social progress is a corollary to the simple proposition, that man's action is found in his social relationships in the way in which he connects with his fellows; that his motives for action are the zeal and affection with which he regards his fellows ... It was a new treasure which the early Christians added to the sum of all treasurers, a joy hitherto unknown

in the world – the joy of finding the Christ which lieth in each man, but which no man can unfold save in fellowships ... The Settlement movement is only one manifestation of that wider humanitarian movement which throughout Christendom, but pre-eminently in England, is endeavoring to embody itself, not in a sect, but in society itself ... I believe that this turning, this renaissance of the early Christian humanitarianism, is going on in America, in Chicago, if you please, without leaders who write or philosophize, without much speaking, but with a bent to express in social service and in terms of action the spirit of Christ. Certain it is that spiritual force is found in the Settlement movement, and it is also true that this force must be evoked and must be called into play before the success of any Settlement is assured. (Addams, 1910/2011, pp 36–7)

In her undogmatic way, Addams expresses the democratic values of the Christian Socialists and Tractarians, advocates for connections among different kinds of people, and also evokes a kind of incarnational theology which both sees the Christ in every person and motivates those who can to act.

On her return to the US in the first part of 1889, Addams and Starr searched for an appropriate facility in Chicago, the destination hub for many migrant communities. With her inheritance, she renovated and leased a house that had been owned by Charles Hull, a Chicago real estate magnate and philanthropist who had recently died (Knight, 2010). Their purpose was 'To provide a center for higher civic and social life; to institute and maintain educational and philanthropic enterprises, and to investigate and improve the conditions in the industrial districts of Chicago' (Addams, 1910/2011, p 33). Addams was proud that Hull House was distinctly Christian, following the model of Toynbee Hall (this perhaps in response to Coit's Neighborhood Guilds, which I will describe shortly). It is interesting to note in passing that the Barnetts visited Hull House in 1891, so communication among the settlement houses was active; she writes that the Barnetts 'were much shocked that, in a new country with conditions still plastic and hopeful, so little attention had been paid to experiments and methods of amelioration [of poverty] which had already been tried' (Addams, 1910/2011, p 88). After Starr and Addams separated, Addams and her life companion of 30 years Mary Rozet Smith (1868–1934) continued to operate Hull House. By 1893, there were 19 settlement houses in the US, all operating in the university settlement model. For this and her later work,[45] Jane Addams was awarded the Nobel Peace Prize in 1931, the second woman, and the first American woman to be awarded the prize.

---

[45] This included founding the Women's International League for Peace and Freedom in 1919, her outspoken opposition to the lynching of Black men in the American South, her

Hull House may be the best-known and most enduring settlement house in the US,[46] but it was not the first. The first (also inspired by Toynbee Hall) was the Neighborhood Guild (later known as the University Settlement House) on the Lower East Side of New York City, founded in 1886. Stanton George Coit (1857–1944) was a follower of Felix Adler and the Society for Ethical Culture. The Ethical Movement believed that morality is independent of theology, that philanthropy is a duty, and that social improvement should accompany self-improvement. Coit had visited Toynbee Hall for three months in 1885 after completing his doctoral degree in Berlin, and on returning to New York he bought a building and established himself in a poor, largely Jewish section of the city. In 1887, he returned to London to take up a ministry in the Ethical Movement and established a similar guild in Kentish Town. When he left for London, the New York guild 'nearly collapsed' (Social Welfare History Project, 2011) but was revived and reorganised as University Settlement in 1891 by Charles Stover and Edward King, although Coit seems to have returned periodically until 1893. Coit was aware of Octavia Hill's 'system of rent collectors' (as he called it) and served for two years on the COS committee. He wrote,

> But in this matter the Guild does not set itself up as a competing system, but rather as a larger plan, comprehending the special methods which Miss Hill has developed ... Miss Hill's method becomes infinitely more powerful for good when joined to the hundred other forces of the Guild which make for social regeneration. (Coit, 1892)

Coit was quite explicit that the Neighbourhood Guilds should be free from 'the ulterior motive of religious propaganda' (Coit, 1892, p 36) and seems to have been explicitly setting them against existing models such as the Salvation Army, Toynbee Hall, and other churches:

> And still the difference between [Toynbee Hall] and [the Guilds] is fundamental. The men at Toynbee Hall believe in having no method or system, but simply in watching their opportunity to do anything good that turns up, and in learning the condition and mental habits of the people. Now to begin without preconceived plan is the only

---

support for the foundation of what became the National Association for the Advancement of Colored People, and her international work for pacificism.

[46] Thanks largely to the Congress of Social Settlements that Addams organised in association with a Chicago World's Fair ('World's Columbian Exposition') in 1893, which brought a stream of visitors to Hull House.

> scientific attitude toward social problems; but on that principle one should continue, after years of practical work and observation, to have no formulated methods and principles, is itself a dogma. (p 86)

> The main difference between the Guild and the clubs in connection with religious societies is the same as that between it an almost all other clubs as now conducted. These latter are inspired by no far reaching and definite purpose of social reconstruction. Accordingly they are aimless and confined to details, they have no further object than to keep boys off the street, or men out of public houses, and to teach chess, draughts, or reading. (p 89)

Coit resided in England for the rest of his life. Despite their putative scientific method, neighbourhood guilds do not appear to have outlasted Coit in their original form, although some of them became known as settlement houses. In New York, from the 1920s, settlement house activists turned their attention from neighbourhood organising towards policy reform (Activist New York, 2016).

The same challenges in addressing the needs of the poor in the US emerged as occurred in Britain in the mid-late 19th century, and the public response was largely the same. Although there were some private charities, there was little organised relief in the US until 1863. State boards began to develop and consult with each other. The National Conference of Charities and Correction was organised in 1879, but its attention was limited to 'defectives, delinquents, and paupers who filled institutions of confinement' (Schlabach, 1969). Frustrated by the disorganisation of American charitable aid, the Rev. Stephen Humphreys Gurteen (1836–98), an Episcopal priest who had been put in charge of relief work in Buffalo, New York during the depression of 1873–78, founded the first COS in America in 1877 in that city. Gurteen was born in England and had visited England in 1877 to observe efforts to assist the poor. He identified the processes that were important for 'scientific charity' in his 1877 book *Phases of Charity* (Garvin et al, 2020). He later developed these concepts in his book *A Handbook of Charity Organization* in 1882.

> The major purpose of the COS, toward which cooperation and all other COS techniques pointed, was a frontal attack on indiscriminate almsgiving. On the one hand, wrote Gurteen, 'we find a vast band, composed of organized societies and noble-hearted individuals', promoting their particular (often sectarian) hobbies and flooding the field of charity with a plethora of ill-conceived schemes and institutions. On the other hand was the relief that public officials dispensed under the ancient poor laws, which too often relieved 'the idleness of the community at the expense of its struggling industry, fostering habits

of dependence, destroying manliness and self-respect, and tending to render pauperism a permanent institution'. The hand of the public official moved 'while the heart is untouched', Gurteen charged, since the officials took 'note of naught save the bare fact of destitution'. (Garvin et al, 2020)

Within ten years, there were COSs in 52 American cities, although these varied in effectiveness.

After becoming involved with a Unitarian Church in Baltimore, Maryland, Mary Richmond (1861–1928) applied to work at the local COS. She later took up the role of head administrator at the Philadelphia COS, and finally became director of the Charity Organizational Department at the Russell Sage Foundation in New York City in 1909 (Virginia Commonwealth University Libraries, n.d.). There she applied her skills to codifying the work of the American COSs. Her best-known work today, *Social Diagnosis*, provided the framework for a scientific method of social casework, and she was perhaps the first person clearly to identify the importance of the relationship between the individual and their environment.

> Though the social worker has won a degree of recognition as being engaged in an occupation useful to the community, he is handicapped by the fact that his public is not alive to the difference between going through the motions of doing things and actually getting them done. 'Doing good' was the old phrase for social service. It begged the question, as do also the newer terms, 'social services' and 'social work' – unless society is really serviced ... The social workers of the United States form a large occupational group.[47] A majority of them are engaged in case work – in work, that is, which has for its immediate aim the betterment of individuals or families, one by one, as distinguished from their betterment in the mass. Mass betterment and individual betterment are interdependent, however, social reform and social case work of necessity progressing together. (Richmond, 1917, p 25)

Richmond addressed the relationship between a person and their environment in both a theoretical and practical way in *Social Diagnosis* and her subsequent publications and many presentations. She was a powerful advocate for professionalising the role of a social worker.

---

[47] She notes that there were 3,968 social workers in New York City in 1915 (in a population of about 5.5 million).

Summary

The Industrial Revolution and its promulgation of capitalism, profit, and wage labour had far-reaching direct and indirect effects throughout Britain, Europe, and America. The Old Poor Law and its amendments were perceived as inadequate either to respond to the different needs of the labouring poor and the pauper, or to protect scarce state resources, and the New Poor Law, informed by the Royal Commission's report, which drew heavily on Calvinist assumptions and theology, was enacted in 1834. The New Poor Law standardised poor relief but remained premised on the Calvinist assumption that the poor and the pauper were responsible for their own poverty and for being able to work their way out of it. The New Poor Law was even more restrictive and punitive than the Old Poor Law.

Bowpitt (1998, p 679) asks how far social work was a distinctively Christian concept and practice. He responds that Christian charity consists of three parts: compassion, testimony, and personal regeneration, and that Christian charity emerged when social action was dominated by Evangelical charity. While I concur with his response that what we know as social work clearly has Christian roots, we have seen both that Christian charity antedates Evangelicalism, and that there were many theological influences in play in the 19th century that shaped the COS and settlement house responses to the New Poor Law. Those influences are not merely Evangelical and its emphasis on personal regeneration but come from the Christian Socialists, Tractarians, and Broad Church factions (and even, briefly, the Ethical Movement), and the British Idealists through Jowett and Green. These multifarious religious influences emphasise active compassion – the sentiment (perhaps along with outrage) that Dickens sought to evoke in his readers, and which motivated those connected with both the COS and the Settlement House movements on both sides of the Atlantic. Evangelicals (mostly of the Arminian persuasion) were certainly prominent in many key issues of social reform including the abolition of the slave trade, the improvement of working conditions, and prison reform. However, Tractarian ecclesiology and theology sought to counter the individualistic Evangelical focus on personal *reformatio*, and recovered the incarnational theology of the 4th century. Because Tractarianism and its liturgical appurtenances were in disfavour with Evangelical bishops, Tractarian and other High Church clergy were often relegated to living in very poor urban areas. Exposure to the extreme poverty of these areas encouraged many of these clergy to respond to poverty in their parishioners, and eventually to the establishment of the Christian Social Union. Christian Socialists took up a number of social policy reforms including just wages, infant mortality, and industrial working conditions. Broad Church women and clergy were deeply critical of the punitive and inadequate New Poor Law, the atomised efforts of

Evangelicals and Tractarians, as well as the private charity of individuals, and they developed community-level interventions that systematised poor relief. On both sides of the Atlantic, COSs and settlement houses attempted to fill in the gaps left by Calvinist public policies of poor relief and their failed attempts to prevent pauperism. The next chapter, the last of this historical survey, will consider how social work became a formal occupation, codified and internationalised.

7

Liberalising the poor

The responses to British Poor Law reforms resulted in fundamental changes to both public and voluntary charitable responses to the poor on both sides of the Atlantic. While the significant developments of 20th-century social work and social policy in the North Atlantic have been well-explored in detail elsewhere,[1] we can broadly discern three major periods: the movement from Calvinist-informed classical liberalism augmented by free-market capitalism to social liberalism (roughly 1898–1928); the emergence of public welfare, social insurance, and the welfare state (1929–79); and the rise of neoliberalism, the resurgence of a Calvinist social imaginary, and a return to privatisation of government services and the expectation of individual responsibility (1979–present). Global events – including the first World War, the Great Depression, the Second World War, global pandemics, an integrated global economy, and the rise of accessible global and social media – greatly influenced the social imaginary about poverty, disability, and disease. It is difficult, for instance, to make a case against government assistance for returning soldiers who had lost limbs fighting for those governments, or against highly interventionist public programmes when the unemployment rate is nearly a quarter of the potential workforce, or against rebuilding a post-war or post-pandemic society where infrastructure is severely damaged, or large portions of the population who are not permitted to work. Such events were social catastrophes entirely out of control of the people most affected, and even the most hardened residualist could understand that. At the same time, governments understood that those social catastrophes could pose a significant risk to social order – and thus to themselves – and social welfare policy played an increasingly important role in government programmes and budget priorities.

Global events also meant that novel funding arrangements were developed to respond to various crises. In the UK, for instance, private charities such as the National Relief Fund and the Women's Institute received funding from the government during the first World War (Prochaska, 2006). The German bombardment of Britain during the Second World War devastated the religious and charitable sectors, which meant that instead of charities filling

---

[1] See, for instance, Trattner (1999), Tannenbaum and Reich (2001), Prochaska (2006), Davis (2008), Jennissen and Lundy (2011), Day and Schiele (2013), and Armfield (2014).

in the gap between state assistance and the need for poor relief following the 1834 Poor Law reform, the state now stepped in to fill the gap in charitable services on which it had come to rely. In post-war Britain, the state became the primary provider of social welfare assistance and relief. This support ensured that some charitable services continued, but 'partnerships between charities and government departments increasingly enmeshed volunteers in bureaucratic regulation' (Prochaska, 2006, pp 92–3). In the US, advocacy for more generous public interventions and social protections reached sympathetic political ears, such as the 1909 White House Conference on Children, which ultimately resulted in the establishment of the first national Children's Bureau five years later. This is not to suggest that advocates for reform did not meet robust opposition reciting familiar arguments against poor relief or that attitudes that created the restrictive poor laws had vanished. Rather, advocates for the poor were increasingly able to make their cases to policymakers who were willing and able to enact reforms. However, all of that changed in the last decades of the century with the rise of neoliberalism in Thatcher's Britain and Reagan's America.

Classical to social liberalism

Calvinism's continuing influence on British Poor Law reform at the beginning of the 20th century can be seen in two areas: increasing the requirement that the poor and the pauper take responsibility for their own lives, which minimised the demand on public assistance (and maximised demand on non-governmental charities); and maintaining social order through increasingly restrictive or punitive measures associated with poor relief (for example, offering relief only through workhouses). Maintaining social order in these ways ensured that dominant social values and expectations were promoted and enforced. The Calvinist emphasis on personal *reformatio* and productive work[2] as an expression of that transformation served the purposes of policymakers in Britain, its colonies, former colonies, and dominions (including those in North America) very well. Individuals were expected to work themselves out of poverty or to avoid pauperism by working. While in Britain parish churches remained the primary places where poor relief was assessed and delivered and where applicants were allocated to workhouses, the formulary for relief after the reform was centralised and standardised.

---

[2] Later, work will be expanded to include education by Bourdieu (Fowler, 2020), who constructed education as cultural capital (which is typical converted into economic capital) and proposed that education served as a way symbolically for dominant classes to intimidate subordinate classes.

In the same period in the US and Canada, responsibility for poor relief was held by state, provincial, or local civic authorities who distributed limited assistance through guardians (or what amounted to eligibility assessors). Public authorities maintained social order by preventing or minimising paupery and hunger, which could lead to rioting and social disorder (as they had in much of the first two decades of the 20th century in Britain and France; Bohstedt, 2015). The social situations on both sides of the Atlantic were made more complex by great movements of people emigrating from Europe and the UK to the US, and within the US following the Civil War. Pauperism was still constructed by both public guardians and non-government charity workers as a moral as well as an economic and social failure by the individual (Hall and Howes, 1965). Trattner (1999) writes that in the US, charity workers 'did not really consider their clients as equals, or even potential equals, but as objects of character reformation whose lowly condition resulted from ignorance or other deviations from middle-class norms – intemperance, indolence, improvidence, or whatnot' (p 99). Nevertheless, by 1907 the general secretary of the New York COS, Edward Devine, commented 'We may quite safely throw overboard, once and for all, the idea that the dependent poor are our moral inferiors, that there is any necessary connection between wealth and virtue, or between poverty and guilt' (Trattner, 1999, p 102). COSs evolved from relying on voluntary charitable workers to hiring trained caseworkers who could assess individual situations according to established protocols, such as those proposed by Richmond; voluntary workers were eased to the margins.

In the exhaustive analysis of the English Poor Law policy that they submitted to the Royal Commission on Poor Laws and Relief of Distress (1905–09),[3] Sydney and Beatrice Webb found that 'at least nine-tenths of all the paupers arrive at pauperism along *one or other of three roads* – the Road of Neglected Childhood, the Road of Sickness and Feeble-mindedness, and the Road of Unemployment (including "Under-employment")' (Webb and Webb, 1910, p 305; italics in the original). Two reports were issued from the Royal Commission itself, the Majority and Minority Reports. The Majority Report (supported by the COS and local government board members) used the word 'prevention' to refer to the prevention of pauperism generally, and, presumably, its consequences for social order. The Report

---

[3] See Woodroofe (1977) for a description of the Royal Commission and of the conditions in which the poor lived at the time. Of the 20 commissioners, six were from the COS, including Octavia Hill and Helen Bosanquet; there were five Guardians, three representatives of local government boards, two political economists, and representatives of the Church of England and the Roman Catholic Church in Ireland in addition to researchers Charles Booth and Beatrice Webb.

proposed dividing people into two classes: those who could be helped by private charity and those for whom public assistance was most appropriate. The Minority Report, led by Beatrice Webb (supported by the Labour Party appointees to the Royal Commission), used the word 'prevention' to mean prevention of individual or family destitution. The Minority Report argued that pauperism was caused by, or at least accompanied by, social factors and that addressing these factors would go far to prevent pauperism.[4] Acknowledging social factors as contributors to pauperism was a significant step beyond understanding the individual as primarily responsible for their own poverty, and a giant leap beyond the Calvinist assumptions that lay behind the existing poor laws. In their analysis, the Webbs claimed that 'All experience shows that it is impossible even to begin to deal successfully with personal character until we dismiss the idea of relieving destitution as such and go boldly for a definite policy of preventing or arresting the operation of each separate cause of destitution' (p 305).

While the Majority and Minority Reports appeared to differ widely, Woodroofe (1977) argues that the two reports were not as far apart as the Webbs portrayed them in their later (1927) history and analysis. The Majority Report for instance no longer blamed individuals alone for their poverty but acknowledged 'modifications and developments in our industrial system which cannot be ignored' (Woodroofe, 1977, p 151) as contributors to paupery. The Majority Report moved away from the Poor Law's punitive position of deterrence and encouraged a system of careful and varied assistance, of which financial assistance would be only one part. However, because of the Royal Commission's apparent lack of agreement on a way forward, the Liberal government of the day was safely able to finesse both reports and moved its policy towards poor relief from the existing classically liberal laissez-faire economic approach to its preferred position of social liberalism and increased government intervention. For instance, the Children and Young Persons Act in the UK was introduced by the Liberal government in 1908, which increased protections for children, introduced juvenile courts and borstals – separate detention centres for children – and regulated foster carers for the first time. The old-age pension, which the Royal Commission's Majority Report had opposed, saying that it was the responsibility of individuals to plan for their own support in old age, was also introduced the same year.

---

[4] It is certainly worth pointing out that the Webbs described these challenges as 'outward and visible signs of the inward and spiritual shortcomings'; the Anglican Book of Common Prayer described sacraments as 'outward and visible signs of inward and spiritual grace'. Whatever their private beliefs, the Webbs certainly were familiar with prayer book language and indeed sprinkled religious and biblical language throughout their report.

Charity and social workers were beginning to understand that poverty and dependence were not the results of individual moral failures but rather that the poor were at the convergence of forces and larger structural failures outside their control, including accidents, poor health, low wages, economic trends that created widespread unemployment, and profit-motivated capitalists and landlords with little regard for the workers and tenants who produced their profit. Even the Royal Commission's Majority Report had acknowledged that. In addition, while infant mortality varied considerably among nations in the 19th century, by the mid-20th century, considerably more people survived infancy and lived longer[5] thanks to innovations in infant and child nutrition and feeding patterns, public health (including sewage disposal and access to clean water), and similar lifestyle and environmental changes (Corsini and Viazzo, 1993). This meant there was an increased need to support older persons. Indeed, New Zealand, that 'world without welfare', was the first Anglophone nation to introduce an Old Age Pension Act (1898) to support (white European) settlers who had arrived young and healthy in previous decades but were no longer able to do the heavy lifting. Other Anglophone nations followed; national old-age pension schemes were introduced in Australia in 1906 (there were schemes in some states before this), the UK in 1908, Canada in 1927 (although there were provincial acts prior), and the US in 1935 (although some individual states had support in place prior). These acts represented a marked shift from a perspective that it was the responsibility of the individual to save for their old age or to be supported by their families. Alternative approaches gradually emerged in Calvinist-informed Anglophone public welfare policy as the social imaginary evolved and more empirically-based government policy prevailed.

Maintaining social order has been a key motivator for civic social welfare policy and practice for nearly two millennia. In the 20th century, two kinds of methods were used by governments to attain that goal. Macro-level methods include the prevention or amelioration of poverty (basic financial assistance, including old age pensions); protection of children; school social work; and police, justice, and corrections.[6] Micro-level methods include ways to help individuals and families to overcome difficulties: health, mental health, and counselling; child guidance; and similar. The Webbs, of course, added in

---

[5] The divergence between nations reduced from of hundreds of deaths per 1,000 to between 25 and 50 per 1,000.

[6] By including corrections here I do not mean to imply endorsement of so-called corrections programmes in the ways they may be currently configured, but only that protecting societies from violence and crime is a state function. Supporting individuals to live lives that are not violent or criminal is one way to protect societies, and that work may involve non-state interventions.

structural and policy contributors to poverty, but these can be constructed at either the macro or micro levels. Various occupations within each of these fields of practice operated separate systems of education and training. Richmond's 1917 *Social Diagnosis* was seminal in establishing a common theoretical foundation and taxonomy for what we now know generally as social work, in an environment where many different practice contexts were emerging.

While many, if not most, settlement and COS workers appear to have been motivated by their personal religious beliefs, in non-Roman Catholic countries they also increasingly disconnected relief from religious institutions and began to establish a theoretical, or scientific foundation for the practice of what we can now call social work. COSs in the US began to focus on specialist fields of practice – hospitals, schools, prisons, and so forth. Casework, as it became called, focused on individuals. The first training programme for social workers was established at Columbia University in 1898 in New York City, followed in 1901 by what became the University of Chicago's School of Social Service Administration (originally the School of Civics and Philanthropy). By 1917, there were 17 schools of social work in the US.[7] In Britain, the University of Birmingham was the first university to give aspiring social workers full status as students in 1908 (Davis, 2008, p 3), and settlement houses around the country linked with higher education institutions (Manthorpe et al, 2005) to research poverty and its causes. Gradually social work became an occupation and transitioned from volunteer visitors to paid social workers who were expected to undertake formal training. With a recognition of the structural causes of poverty and an increasingly secular (sometimes called scientific) approach to individual pauperism, the transition from a theological, church, or parish-based social assistance model to a notionally secularised social work was in full sway.

In the US during the 1920s and 1930s there was a 'Freudian deluge', where, following the 1930 publication of Virginia Robinson's *A Changing Psychology in Social Case Work*, casework was placed 'squarely in the camp of the psychiatrists and psychologists' (Trattner, 1999, p 266n). Robinson was a strong advocate of the Freudian psychoanalytic school[8] of the newly

---

[7] Despite this scientific emphasis, Abraham Flexner, a leading authority on professional education, made a now-infamous speech in 1915 saying that social work could not be considered a profession because it lacked specificity, technical skills, or specialised knowledge. We shall return to Flexner and the question of whether social work is a profession in a later chapter.

[8] Founded, of course, by the Viennese physician and former mesmerist Sigmund Freud (1856–1939).

emerging discipline of psychology after the first World War. She felt that a new group of clients, the families of the soldiers and sailors,

> not previously known to any social agency, not accustomed to asking or receiving assistance; the large group of Red Cross workers, recruited some from the ranks of trained Charity Organization Society workers, others untrained and inexperienced – these raised new problems of approach, of contact, of training. (Robinson, 1930, p 53)

Robinson believed that psychology was the answer to these new problems. She critiqued Richmond's *Social Diagnosis* for its lack of knowledge of psychology and therefore its presumed inability to meet the post-war needs of this new client population. She felt that understanding and treating individuals must rest upon a 'substantial genetic and social psychology' (Robinson, 1930, p 81), enlarged by contributions from psychology and psychiatry. Robinson noted that psychiatric social work had become so much in demand in the US that by 1919 it commanded the centre of attention of the national conference of social work and found that the 'swing of opinion was in favour of accepting the psychiatric point of view as the basis of all social case work' (pp 54–5). She quoted Mary Jarrett,

> The special function of social case work is the adjustment of individuals with social difficulties. It is the art of bringing an individual who is in a condition of social disorder into the best possible relation with all parts of his environment. It is the special skill of the social case worker to study the complex of relationships that constitute the life of an individual and to construct as sound a life as possible out of the elements found both in the individual and in his environment. Our relations to our environment are caused by mental, physical, and economic factors existing in our own experience and in the experience of other persons. It is no matter which of these three classes of factors is considered of primary importance since they are all of fundamental importance in dealing with a case of social disorder. (Jarrett, cited in Robinson, 1930, p 55)

It is this last sentence that allowed Robinson to claim that the psychiatric approach was not essentially different from Richmond's generalist person-in-environment approach to social work, while in practice Robinson proposed to redirect the focus of attention of the social worker (and mental health clinician more generally) to the individual. In contemporary terms, we would say that Robinson proposed to relocate problems from the person's transactional relationships with their environment to the person. 'Men out of work were no longer regarded as able, healthy people willing to work if given a chance; rather they were viewed as abnormal or maladjusted individuals whose mental or emotional deficiencies were the causes of their unemployment' (Trattner, 1984, p 240). Robinson's psychiatric approach differs only in language from the theological approach that says that the individual is responsible for their own salvation. Calvin's preaching-gown of the pulpit was exchanged for the white lab coat of science. Once again, the poor were problematised because they had difficulties, although now the difficulties were constructed as mental.

American social workers as a group became besotted by Freudianism and the psychoanalytic school for the next several decades; this orientation also gave them a readily understood professional identity as psychiatric social workers. Social workers continue to work as mental health workers (for a fee, both independently and as part of larger medical and private practices, using an array of job titles) to this day in the US. Here is the era where Atlantic social work diverges. Robinson and the psychiatric school had an indelible long-term impact on the understanding of casework in the US: social work in the US was refocused from the generalist person-in-environment and poor relief approach favoured by COSs on both sides of the Atlantic to the more individualist approach that continues to dominate social work in the US. The psychiatric social work movement problematised individuals, not policy environments, and like any problematising assessment, it perceived and focused on problems. It was arguably in response to this problematising approach that brief treatment, solution-focused, strengths-based, and task-centred models were developed beginning in the mid-1970s.

The emergence of the welfare state

Meanwhile, in the nations of northern Europe, countries informed by a Lutheran social imaginary focused on environmental and structural factors to prevent pauperism. These nations moved forward to become social welfare states considerably earlier than the Atlantic nations. In Prussia, the Roman Catholic Church retained a leading role in preventing pauperism in the rump Holy Roman Empire[9] by continuing to provide relief through its churches and associations (known as Kopling Houses, after the priest who established them) that effectively functioned as settlement houses. By the outbreak of the First World War, there were 400 such houses throughout Germany (McMillan, 2013). Yet although the state continued to recognise its responsibility to the poor through local poor relief boards, widespread poverty before the failed *Märzrevolution* in 1848 was a contributing factor

---

[9] The Holy Roman Empire had been dissolved by Napoleon in 1806.

to that revolt. Otto von Bismarck (1815–98), the first chancellor of a unified Germany, introduced a workers' compensation scheme and health insurance in 1883, and an old-age social insurance programme in 1884. These programmes ensured that all German workers were covered by social insurance (International Labour Organization, 2009), and arguably served as the model for British social welfare reform after the Second World War. Even though Bismarck himself was no supporter of social welfare, these social insurance schemes created a foundation for a German welfare state (with the social control that accompanies such a state). A Scandinavian-style welfare state (which emerged in all five countries of that region), which was implemented during the 1930s, relied on the Nordic *Sonderweg* (special way) to build a broad political consensus of state-regulated socially modified capitalism (Kuhnle and Hort, 2004). Even in a global COVID-19 environment, the five Scandinavian nations all ranked in the top ten happiest nations in the 2021 World Happiness Report (Helliwell et al, 2021). While the high literacy rate in these Nordic countries has been attributed to education provided by the Lutheran Church (after all, in order to read the Bible one first must be taught how to read), it is no coincidence that public social welfare provisions in Germany and Scandinavia share a history influenced by a Lutheran social imaginary of poor relief and social welfare (which, you will remember from Chapter 4, relied on a common community fund model), and were the earliest and most generous national approaches in Europe.[10]

Meanwhile, Roman Catholic France lagged behind Germany in developing its welfare state reforms (Nord, 1994), although the social welfare budget doubled between 1890 and 1910. The French system continued to rely on fraternal benefit societies alongside the continuing assistance historically provided by the Roman Catholic Church. The public health care system was reformed in 1893, accident insurance was enacted in 1898, a Department of Child Welfare was created in 1904, and in 1905 assistance for the aged and infirm was put in place. A voluntary national pension scheme was enacted in 1910, just before the outbreak of the First World War, although at the time the scheme was considered less generous than that of the Liberal scheme introduced in England. Legislation protecting children in abusive homes (1889), restricting women's working hours (1892), cash bonuses to women who breast-fed, and easing the financial burdens on large families (1913) were all designed to encourage the generation of healthy and

---

[10] It must be pointed out that some historians argue that the German *Sonderweg* was in the interests of the ruling elites and not those of the bourgeoisie, and the 'precocious development of the modern welfare state' eventually led to the rise of Nazism in the 1920s (McMillan, 2013, p 16); this point has in turn been challenged.

numerous progeny (Nord, 1994, p 828).[11] All of these so-called 'pronatalist' reforms were consistent with and broadly supported by the Roman Catholic Church. Wider social welfare provisions were introduced in France in 1945 as part of reconstruction following the Second World War.

As can be imagined, the Great Depression (1929–1933) affected global economies, and World War II (1939–45) had a radical impact on social welfare and social work in belligerent countries. As the various nations created policy responses or emerged from the devastation, they enacted broad social assistance programmes to assist in national recovery efforts. In the UK, following the Liberal reforms, the Local Government Act of 1929 abolished the workhouses for indoor relief and replaced them with the gentler-sounding Public Assistance Institutions. Sir William Beveridge (1874–1963) authored his reports *Social Insurance and Allied Services* (1942) and *Full Employment in a Free Society* (1944) as part of Britain's post-war recovery plan. In the report, he advocated a common attack on the 'giant social evils' encountered on the road to post-war reconstruction: Want, Disease, Ignorance, and Squalor (Beveridge, 1944, p 31). Importantly, and perhaps for the first time in a conceptualisation of social welfare reform, these reports focused on problems, not persons. The Beveridge reports led to the National Assistance Act, abolished and replaced all poor laws (after nearly 350 years), and introduced the National Health Insurance scheme with its universal health coverage.[12] We have already seen how the state had to fill in the service gap left by charities and churches that had been obliterated during the war. Prochaska (2006) argues that during the post-war period 'social policy had shifted from the local to the national, from the religious to the secular, and the parish and the congregation bowed to the constituency' (p 150). The state effectively reabsorbed all the charitable efforts that had emerged in response to the 1834 Poor Law reform (most of which had come from the religious sector). In a remarkable *volte-face* from the 19th-century COS founders and Christian Socialists, the Anglican Church declared at its decennial conference of bishops from around the world:

> We believe that the state is under the moral law of God, and is intended by him to be an instrument for human welfare. We therefore welcome

---

[11] Nord also notes the argument that these provisions also removed women from the labour force and advantaged union men and fathers.

[12] The old Poor Law Union workhouse infirmaries served as the first public clinics and hospitals under the new national scheme. These workhouses also served as the prototype for what we would now recognise as residential (and residential rehabilitation) care for older and disabled persons. The Cappadocian Fathers would no doubt have been pleased to see the 20th-century incarnation of their 4th-century creations.

the growing concern and care of the modern state for its citizens, and call upon Church members to accept their own political responsibility and to co-operate with the state and its officers in their work. (Lambeth Conference, 1948)

With this statement, the Church of England, the Established Church, handed back to the state the responsibility for the poor that had been given to the Christian Church by Constantine in the 4th century and declared its confidence in the state's ability to care for the poor and prevent poverty. In the UK, at least, it seemed that the detheologising of social work was complete.

Prochaska (2006) argues that this statement by the Anglican bishops marks the beginning of the decline of the Anglican Church at the end of the 20th century. By the 1960s, Britain was being described as a post-Christian society (Hall and Howes, 1965, p 272), even though social care[13] 'stems from her very title deeds' (p 261); the notion of 'post-Christian' emerged in an American context not long thereafter (Hertel and Nelsen, 1974). The Anglican bishops were clearly in tune with the prevailing opinion that only the state had the authority to conjure the resources and provide the kind of universal benefits necessary to ensure social reconstruction following the Second World War. In fact, the tradition of voluntarism represented by the COS and other charities looked increasingly 'provincial and amateurish' (Prochaska, 2006, p 152). The expansion of government was not without its critics, as under Beveridge's plan, government services pervaded most aspects of the lives of British citizens. A century earlier, de Tocqueville had observed that through social legislation 'the state serves the physical needs and regulates the affairs of its citizens but turns them into dependent clients and fixes them "irrevocably in childhood"' (Prochaska, 2006, p 157). Governments will look 'with ill favour on those associations that are not in its own power' (de Tocqueville, cited in Prochaska, 2006, p 158). Thanks, then, to the second World War, the Beveridge Report, and the willing complicity of the Anglican Church, the British state had become the sole social safety net, guardian, nanny, and ultimate arbiter of the wellbeing of its citizenry. Social workers became agents of the state who ensured social order. Calvin's Bible was exchanged for the beadle's wand.

Although the US was a late entrant to the Second World War, the Great Depression had hit the country very hard in 1929. Social workers played

---

[13] Hall and Howes (1965) use the term 'moral welfare', which is "essentially social work undertaken in the name and on behalf of the Church" (p 3). It was a term that arose during the inter-war period to designate social work in relation to sex, marriage, and the family, and particularly unmarried parents ('fallen women') and their children, and the authors trace the term's history specifically in relation to that population.

an early and active role in advocating for federal unemployment relief, but they were rebuffed by the sitting president Herbert Hoover, who used the familiar small-government arguments to oppose such relief.[14] Shortly after Franklin Roosevelt was elected president in 1933, a number of federal relief measures were enacted, including the Federal Emergency Relief Act and the Civil Works Administration as parts of the so-called New Deal recovery from the Great Depression. The most enduring of the New Deal legislation was the omnibus Social Security Act (SSA) and Aid to Dependent Children, both enacted in 1935.[15] While the New Deal measures were welcomed by those who most needed them, they were also seen by some as an affront to America's rugged individualism, self-determination, and individual liberty, ideals inherited from the Calvinist Puritan settlers. A key omission in the New Deal was the failure to include national public health insurance, which made (and continues to make) the US unique among developed nations.[16] The SSA was, in reality, an income transfer programme that taxed workers in order to support those who had aged out of the workforce or who were unable to work (in other words, the worthy poor). Unemployment compensation was limited, and since the SSA was supported by taxing those who worked, it did not include support for people who were not regularly employed. Nevertheless, the SSA remains one of the most important pieces of federal legislation in American history. The number of social workers doubled during the 1930s. At the same time, there was also a resurgence in the interest of social workers in public relief, the poor, and the vulnerabilised that attempted to compensate for the purely psychological orientation of the previous decade. During this period, social workers achieved increasing social acceptance as part of 'the machinery of the state, an important everyday function in a modern urban industrial society' (Trattner, 1984, p280). This language certainly suggests that New Deal social workers fell on the social control side of the spectrum.

Partly due to the increased prosperity and employment brought on by the Second World War, there were no major welfare policy innovations in

---

[14] Hoover declaimed that 'You cannot extend the mastery of government over the daily lives of the people without at the same time making it the master of their souls and thoughts' (in Trattner, 1999, p 277).

[15] A Social Security Act was passed in New Zealand in 1938 which transformed that country into a welfare state (Kia Piki Ake, 2018), and similar protections were enacted in Australia in 1942 (Ey, 2012); Canada introduced national unemployment protections in 1942.

[16] It was not until the Johnson Administration in 1965 that Medicare was enacted to protect over-65s (and people under 65 with end-stage renal disease), and income-based Medicaid was put in place to support state health assistance. The contentious Affordable Care Act was signed into law by Barak Obama in 2010 as a health insurance safety net.

the US as a direct result of the war.[17] Except for Pearl Harbour, Hawai'i, of course, American infrastructure had not been devastated by the war, as were European countries and Britain. In the post-war period, there was widespread prosperity, and poverty (again) became something that was perceived to affect only the 'undeserving' and 'idle'. As a consequence, individual states began to reinstitute policies that reduced the number of recipients of public relief (or welfare, as it was now called): the familiar tropes of residency, work requirements, and conforming to socially acceptable lifestyles were enforced by welfare workers who denied assistance to anyone who did not conform to social or policy expectations. The rising tide of the post-war 1950s prosperity did not, however, lift all boats, and poverty became a problem identified by President John Kennedy in 1961. His successor, Lyndon Johnson, a Democrat who had been Kennedy's vice president, announced an unconditional 'war on poverty' in 1964. The array of federal social legislation that sought to eliminate poverty and racism became known as Johnson's 'Great Society'. Great Society programmes arguably reduced absolute poverty from 19.5 per cent in 1963 to 2.3 per cent in 2017 (Burkhauser et al, 2021). The Great Society did not achieve its full vision under Johnson in part because congressional appropriations were nowhere near what was required to meet the ambitious goals (despite Democrat majorities in both houses of Congress). Underfunding was due in part to Vietnam-era cynicism about the ability of government to be successful but also to the now very familiar conservative plaints about the undeserving poor. As a result, not only were the poor increasingly marginalised but so were the social workers who worked with them. Casework was relegated in favour of targeted spending on in-kind and tangible services such as housing, rehabilitation, and drug treatment centres. The disenchantment of middle-class Americans, the so-called 'Silent Majority', resulted in a retrenchment of social services during the 1970s and the contraction of federal assistance to states.[18]

Some social workers began to recognise that individual casework was no longer an effective model and that advocacy for the vulnerabilised and

---

[17] This is not to say there were no reforms: the G.I. Bill of Rights (1944), the National Mental Health Act (1946), the Housing Act (1949), and the Vocational Rehabilitation Act (1954) were among the new targeted social welfare benefits programmes; however, a fundamental national transformation into a welfare state did not occur in the US in the way it had in European nations and the UK.

[18] Although a major increase in the prison population as a result of Nixon's 'War on Drugs' – largely meant a war on poor communities of colour. Even in 2021, the proportion of persons incarcerated in state prisons for drug offences who are Black and Latinx is 57 per cent, although these groups make up only 30.1 per cent (13.4 per cent Black, 16.7 per cent Latinx) of the current population (Georgetown Law Library, 2021).

marginalised was necessary. However, the political winds were strong, and in 1971, the federal government required all recipients of public assistance to register for work or education (except mothers of children younger than six years old). By now, we recognise this age-old requirement to work as a legacy of the old poor laws. The work requirement continued for decades in various forms and countries; it was revised as the Personal Responsibility and Work Opportunity Act (1966) under President Clinton in the US, or Workfare for short (Aid to Families with Dependent Children was replaced with Temporary Assistance for Needy Families); in Australia, it was Work for the Dole (1997–98). New Zealand (1997), the UK (1998), Singapore (2007), and Ireland (2011) also (re-)instituted work requirements in order to receive a public benefit.[19] Once again, Calvin and the 500-year-old poor law expectation of work, dominated. In the US, while casework continued to be delivered, social work now diverged across a number of specialist fields of practice.

Internationalisation

The period following the first World War saw unprecedented international activity to prevent future devastating conflicts. The first such effort was the League of Nations (LON), established in 1920 as a way to preserve world peace. At its height, it had 58 member states. It failed when Hitler broke with the LON in 1933, and it became painfully aware that the LON had no power to enforce its agreements and protocols. Northern European nations fell to Hitler in 1940; Switzerland grew anxious about hosting an organisation that might threaten its national neutrality, and the League dismantled its headquarters in Geneva. The LON ended in 1946, but its enduring legacy is the Geneva Protocol signed in 1929, which prohibits the use of chemical and biological weapons in international armed conflicts. The LON was succeeded by the United Nations, founded by 58 nations in October 1945 (it now has 193 member nations). The Universal Declaration of Human Rights (UDHR) (United Nations, 1948), which sets out an individual's basic rights and fundamental freedoms, was supported by 48 nations. The UDHR asserts that all human beings are born free and equal in dignity and rights (Article 1); it bans infringement of rights and freedoms based on personal characteristics or political or national status (Article 2); that every person has the right to life, liberty, and security of person (Article 3); it bans slavery and the slave trade (Article 4) as well as torture or inhuman treatment or punishment (Article 5); and details an array of other rights and freedoms

---

[19] These work-requirement programmes were also part of the neoliberal reforms of the era, which we will consider in a moment.

in its 30 Articles. The UDHR has formed the basis for human rights law around the world.

Social workers participated in the movement to establish international political collaborations and organisations. Following the first World War, social work, although a young discipline, recognised the need for international cooperation and collaboration. The first international conference of social work was held in Paris in 1928 and was attended by 2,400 delegates from 42 countries. From this meeting, the International Permanent Secretariat of Social Workers (IPSSW) and the International Conference on Social Work emerged. The IPSSW was dissolved during the Second World War, reformed in the 1950s, and became the International Federation of Social Workers in 1956 (Cox and Pawar, 2013; see also https://www.ifsw.org/). The International Conference on Social Work became the International Council on Social Welfare in 1966 (Zelenev, 2018). The International Association of Schools of Social Work (IASSW) began with 46 members from 10 countries (together with the International Labour Organisation) in Berlin in 1929; within a decade, there were 75 members in 18 countries. After a hiatus during the Second World War, the IASSW was revived in 1946 and continues today as international social work's education and research organisation. The International Consortium for Social Development (ICSD) began in the early 1970s to respond to concerns from an international multidisciplinary perspective (ICSD, n.d.). Most of these international bodies have regional groups as well as national affiliates. Lynne Healy has written extensively about the development of international social work both in respect of the history of these organisations and as a field of social work practice (see, for instance, Healy, 1995; 2008; 2014; Healy and Link, 2012).[20]

Neoliberalism

The promise of the welfare state in the UK did not endure. A series of global recessions between 1969 and 1982 brought about by international oil crises and domestic attempts to control inflation created a sense of insecurity and social upheaval. New technology jobs only partly replaced increasingly obsolete traditional sector jobs like manufacturing. Growing unemployment created demand on the welfare system at the same time fiscal pressures required the government to cut back on its welfare system; this 'required a fundamental reassessment of the welfare state and its provisions' (Winter and Connolly, 1996, p 30). The British welfare state worked to manage modest demand, but when unemployment was high (and therefore

---

[20] See also Cox and Pawar (2013) and Shwarzer et al (2016) for more about international social work as a field of practice.

taxes that supported the state welfare system were reduced) it could not meet the need. The state 'was forced to shed its welfare role' (Hall, cited in Winter and Connolly, 1996, p 30). In addition, stories emerged (now thoroughly documented) of children in the care of charitable organisations who were separated from their families, forced to migrate overseas and even groomed for sexual abuse (Jay et al, 2018). The deaths of three children were investigated, and social workers and child protection agencies were widely condemned. Into this tumultuous and uncertain environment, Conservative leader Margaret Thatcher (1925–2013) swept into power in May 1979 and began the longest UK premiership of the 20th century, not stepping down until November 1990.

Thatcher believed that underlying the social and economic distress and upheaval was moral decline associated in the first instance with over-reliance on the state and the loss of those virtues of self-help and thrift (Winter and Connolly, 1996, p 31). When the state could no longer keep up with the demand, the familiar tropes of individual responsibility were resurrected. The Enlightenment had brought with it the liberal value of the freedom of the individual to make their own choices, and to free the individual from the constraints of a rigidly stratified hierarchical society. Thatcherism held that the welfare state had become a new kind of constraint on the individual: briefly put, this neoliberalism held that not only should the individual be free to make their own choices but *only* the individual had the right and responsibility to make their own choices. The science of the Royal Commission's Poor Law reports was replaced by a return to a familiar theology of poverty. In a neoliberal economy, the state should have only the most minimal role. The freedom to make choices then came with the responsibility for families to look after their own needs, including supporting and protecting their children. Thatcherism therefore also promoted a set of neoconservative values that reasserted a particular notion of family (father as head, mother as caretaker of children, and children obedient, quiet, and tidy) as the way to promote so-called traditional social values and to protect the vulnerabilised of society. Thatcherism's core agenda included reducing public spending, privatisation, targeting public relief (replacing the wider welfare state model), and rising inequalities (Hills, 1998). This agenda was embraced by the British electorate, and Thatcher was re-elected with sizeable majorities in 1983 and 1987.

If Thatcherism sounds like a return to Calvinist theology, then you have been paying attention. What neoliberalism brought about was a retheologising of social work and social welfare policy. There is a not insignificant literature about Thatcher's political 'theology'. She was a politician, of course, not a theologian, but there can be little doubt that she was greatly influenced by her Wesleyan roots. As a child, she attended Finkin Street Methodist Church in Grantham (a town in Lincolnshire), where her father, a greengrocer, was also a lay preacher (Filby, 2015). She remained strongly connected to her spiritual roots throughout her life, and in her memoirs, she wrote that 'I believe in what are often referred to as Judaeo-Christian values: indeed my whole political philosophy is based on them' (quoted in Smith, 2007, pp 233–4). Yet Smith and others argue that Thatcherism was not a set of coherent beliefs or systematic theological ideology, but rather her speeches, memoirs, and policy statements resonated with Calvinist values. 'What is striking for a theologian reading the speeches and memoirs of Margaret Thatcher is the prominence given to Christian belief, the language of morality, and the idea of spiritual regeneration' (Smith, 2007, pp 240–1). Values such as economic independence, self-reliance, hard work understood as a virtue, and independence (themes she emphasised repeatedly in her speeches) are central to her political theology; prosperity not ostentatiously displayed was the outward and visible sign of industrious hard work. These values would have been heard in 18th- and 19th-century Calvinist and Wesleyan pulpits. Such values could be seen as selfish individualism, but Thatcher was not a disciple of Rand's Objectivism.[21] She also believed in charitable giving and the responsibility of the individual to family and community[22] – again, values familiar to Calvinists. Thatcher believed that the state, particularly in its most intrusive forms of socialism or communism, prevents individuals from reaching their creative and economic potential. Any agency, including, and perhaps especially the state, that removes choice impairs the ability of the individual to behave morally. At the heart of her conservatism is freedom for the individual to take responsibility for their own decisions. In 1989, she wrote 'Remove man's [sic] freedom and you dwarf the individual, you devalue his conscience and you demoralize him. That is the heart of the matter' (quoted in Smith, p 253). This belief meant for her that every human being must work out their own salvation, and find their own way to respond to God's grace. Here is her Calvinism resurgent and explicit. While the Established Church of Anglicanism had handed over their responsibility

---

[21] Objectivism is the highly individualistic economic philosophy promoted by Russian-born American writer Ayn Rand, who believed that 'man exists for his own sake, that the pursuit of his own happiness is his highest moral purpose, that he must not sacrifice himself to others, nor sacrifice others to himself' (cited by Freedland, 2017).

[22] Thatcher claimed that her often-cited 1987 statement 'And, you know, there's no such thing as society. There are individual men and women and there are families. And no government can do anything except through people, and people must look after themselves first. It is our duty to look after ourselves and then, also, to look after our neighbours' (cited by the Margaret Thatcher Foundation, n.d.) that appeared in the magazine *Women's Own* in an interview with Douglas Keay was misunderstood. She later wrote that her intention 'was to challenge the rise in welfare dependence caused by overreliance on the state as the "helper of first resort"' (Smith, 2007, p 244).

for the social care of the poor to the state after the Second World War, Thatcher's Calvinist (or at least Arminian) politics passed the responsibility for moral, political, and economic salvation back to the individual. If they were not up to the task, it was not up to the state to save them.

So what of social work during this period? After decades of being a part of the British welfare state, social workers were fighting something of a rear-guard action and were whipsawed about by major policy reversals and struggles between local and national government. In London, the tension between the Conservative-led national government and a left-wing Labour-led city government created an untenable situation as many non-governmental organisations, particularly in housing, saw their funding reduced in an attempt to bring community organisations to heel. The welfare state, previously understood as a progressive attempt to look after the poor was now being interpreted as a sign of Britain's national moral decline. Social workers and their training (or lack of it) came under attack for being incompetent, unaccountable, inexperienced, gullible, and anti-family (Winter and Connolly, 1996), particularly when they attempted to negotiate the competing rights of parents to control their children and children to be safe from violence. Legislation increasingly restricted the powers and authority of social workers (and the state) in order to preserve the institution of the family, understood in very traditional ways. The combined influences of neoliberalism and neoconservatism joined to constrain social work and to limit the capacity of social workers to do the work they expected to do. This meant that the broad scope of social work at the time led to 'professional indecision, conflict, flexibility and creativity – depending on one's point of view – over the 20th century' (Manthorpe et al, 2005, p 370).

Thatcherism's economic neoliberalism and neoconservatism struck a chord around a politically and economically conservative world largely informed by Ayn Rand's laissez-faire economic capitalism (Freedland, 2017). In America, Thatcher's ideological brother from another mother Ronald Reagan (1911–2004) was elected president in 1981 and served two terms until January 1989. Reagan's neoliberal economic platform, known as supply-side economics, or Reaganomics, was put in place in the early years of his tenure. While America had never understood itself as a welfare state, in the 1970s, neoliberal economic policy advocates had begun to advocate for smaller government and more personal responsibility in response to the economic and social impact of Roosevelt's New Deal. The New Deal redistributed government resources downward, that is, to the poor who needed assistance. Neoliberalism proposed that there was no alternative to a market economy, and the freer that marketplace the better. It also promised that a rising tide would lift all boats; that is, an improving economy that benefitted business would eventually trickle down to the average person (Abramovitz, 2012). Notably, in the 1980 campaign leading up to Reagan's election, presidential candidate George H.W. Bush called this supply-side economic ideology 'voodoo economics' before he was named as Reagan's vice president. Key features of the American neoliberal economic agenda included lower taxes for the wealthy (which transferred wealth upward), privatisation of government functions (reducing costs to the federal government and relying on presumed efficiencies of a less-regulated private sector), retransfer of social welfare programmes from the federal to the state governments, lower labour costs (by weakening unions and transferring production overseas), and deregulation of businesses, banks, and share markets.

As in the UK, the era of big government in the US, born in the New Deal, was over. Public assistance programmes were severely reduced, the number of people eligible to receive assistance was reduced, and overall poverty in the US increased from 11.1 per cent in 1973 to 15.3 per cent in 1983. However, poverty was not equally distributed: Blacks and Latinx had particularly high rates of poverty, at around 25 per cent each. Income disparity increased dramatically: by 2004 the top 1 per cent of US households owned one third of all net worth in the US, while the bottom 80 per cent owned only 15 per cent (Abramovitz, 2012).[23] Overseas outsourcing of production meant lower costs to industry but fewer domestic jobs. Neoliberalism was locked in place in the US when Reagan nominated Alan Greenspan (an admirer of Rand) to be chair of the Federal Reserve in 1987, where he continued until 2006.

At the same time as economic reforms were being promulgated, American neoconservatives who publicly proclaimed their evangelical Christianity (of a sort) advocated for restoring 'family values', and a colour-blind social order that would 'undo the gains of the women's liberation and civil rights movements' (Abramovitz, 2014, p 230). It would be drawing a very long bow to suggest that Reagan had any but opportunistic religious convictions. His sunny American civil religion was quite generic, and he was quite ready to create alliances with any religious groups useful to his election campaign and political agenda. In any case, the American political system is expressly designed to prevent the individual religious beliefs of its political leaders to inform the policy landscape. However, during this era, organisations like Jerry Falwell's fundamentalist Moral Majority (1979–89) and later Pat Robertson's[24] evangelical Christian Coalition (founded in 1988) espoused very conservative religious moral views (and in particular held strong positions against abortion, feminism, and homosexuality, and were in favour

---

[23] Economist Emmanuel Saez at the University of California Berkeley finds that the richest 0.1 per cent in the US earn over 196 times the bottom 90 per cent (2018 data; inequality.org, n.d.).

[24] Robertson himself was an unsuccessful candidate for president in 1987.

of prayer in public schools and so-called traditional family values); adherents of these groups worked to ensure Reagan's elections and were even formal parts of the Reagan election campaigns. Neoconservative (also described as the New Right, or 'neocon') organisations were vocal in US politics; in 1997 *Fortune* ranked the Christian Coalition of America[25] the seventh most powerful political organisation in America, right behind the National Rifle Association (Birnbaum, 1997). These organisations exerted considerable influence to promote their neoconservative agendas. It would be tempting but inaccurate to conflate the neocon agenda with the neoliberal agenda, although as in Thatcher's Britain, the two complemented each other. The neoliberal agenda used the neocons to promote the 'traditional' patriarchal family structure and the policing of sex (Foucault, 1976/2020), including and perhaps especially rights for gender and sexually diverse persons, as fundamental to its agenda of reducing demand on state resources. This agenda continues today among neoconservatives.

During this period, attention was turned to regulating social work and authorising social workers to receive third-party (either public or private insurance) payments for their services as parts of large healthcare organisations. Mental health social workers were far cheaper than psychiatrists, and thanks to Virginia Robinson, could address many front-line mental health issues. Eligibility to receive such payments effectively codified social work as a profession, and the notion of private practice social workers appeared. As in the UK, however, some American social workers began to realise that their attention should be focused on advocacy in the increasingly restrictive policy environment that was creating the poor, rather than on casework which could only patch up the impoverished, refer them to emergency housing and food banks (funded by churches, private charities, and some scarce public resources), and hope for the best. It was a world that would have been familiar to Octavia Hill, Helen Bosanquet, the Barnetts, and the Webbs.

In the neoliberal world, state assistance came with increased state control. Perceived social deviance – that is, anyone who was not white, cis-gendered, heterosexual, at least middle-income, and able to speak standard English – was met with state control. The political philosopher Loïc Wacquant dubbed the neoliberal state 'neo-Darwinist' because it 'erects *competition* and celebrates unrestrained individual responsibility – whose counterpart is collective and thus political irresponsibility' (2004/2009, p 5; italics in original). In a neoliberal state, Wacquant (2004/2009) argues, people who petition for and receive government assistance are demonised, and the state punishes these deviants through socialising (e.g., rehousing homeless persons, requiring that

---

[25] This was a successor organisation to Robertson's original Christian Coalition, which lost its bid to become a tax-exempt charity because of its political activities.

individuals undertake work or education, or undergo drug testing in order to receive assistance), medicalising (classifying persons with non-conforming behaviours as having a health or mental health disorder), or penalising (arresting and incarcerating) them under the guise of protecting the public good. All of these options make the problem of deviance disappear to the general public. (We recall Constantine's 4th-century expectation that the church would make the poor disappear in favour of maintaining social order.) When a politician advocates a tough-on-crime approach, social workers should be vigilant because the likelihood that their clients will be incarcerated will increase; poor communities of colour already know this. In the US, for instance, while African Americans were only 12 per cent of the population, they made up 40 per cent of the prison population (Hetey and Eberhardt, 2014); in California, as early as 1990, 40 per cent of African American males age 18 to 35 were behind bars or on probation or parole (Wacquant 2004/2009, p 63); in other jurisdictions, the proportion was even higher. In England and Wales, people from Black, Asian, and minority ethnic (BAME) backgrounds make up 14 per cent of the general population, but 25 per cent of the prison population and 41 per cent of the youth justice system (BBC News, 2017). Ethnic and cultural minorities are similarly overrepresented in incarcerated populations of other neoliberal states.[26] Rather than critically questioning these disparities, whites are more likely to use this information to reinforce their own racialised assumptions that Blacks and other communities of colour are more likely to be criminals (Hetey and Eberhardt, 2014). It is the tragic irony of neoliberalism (combined with neoconservatism) that the freedom espoused by its elites is grossly over-balanced by social control of the 'deviant', who are largely defined or created by those elites. The economic costs not merely in maintaining incarcerated populations but in lost productivity and the costs to the next generations are staggering. In the US, Wacquant claims that while national expenditures for public assistance declined steeply relative to need (although this claim does not necessarily include in-kind assistance such as Medicaid and food stamps; see also Blank, 1998), the budget for criminal justice increased 540 per cent between 1972 and 1990, and the budget for corrections itself increased 11-fold (Wacquant, 2004/2009, p 64). Increasing amounts of national corrections budgets have gone to private operators[27] (this is true not only in the US and UK but also

---

[26] In Aotearoa New Zealand, the indigenous Māori are 15 per cent of the population, yet make up 51 per cent of the prison population; in Australia, Aboriginal and Torres Straits Islanders make up 3 per cent of the population but 28 per cent of the prison population.

[27] These private companies include Serco, CoreCivic, the GEO Group, Management and Training Corporation (MTCNovo in the UK); in South Korea the private prison is operated by the religious Agape Foundation and houses inmates convicted of relatively minor offences.

in Australia, Brazil, Chile, Greece, Jamaica, Japan, Mexico, New Zealand, Peru, South Africa, South Korea, and Thailand; Israel's Supreme Court rejected private prisons as unconstitutional). As I have written elsewhere,

> It is essential that the human service practitioner, researcher and policymaker be aware of the increasing concentration of power in these élites, and to be aware that their clients, research participants or beneficiaries are largely artefacts of the powerful élites who created them. (Henrickson and Fouché, 2017, p 60)

Britain and America were not the only places where neoliberalism found accommodation. In Australia, neoliberalism (under the banner of economic rationalism or economic fundamentalism) was promoted by Prime Ministers Bob Hawke (1983–91) and Paul Keating (1991–96) of the Australian Labor Party and implemented with fervour by John Howard (1996–2007) of the Australian Liberal Party. Australian neoliberal reforms moved away from equity schemes and protectionism in favour of efficiency, self-reliance, and competitiveness. Notwithstanding this approach, Australian neoliberal governments moved away from promoting atomised competition among individuals to supporting communities and collective approaches in the formulation and delivery of services in the wide spaces of the regions (Cheshire and Lawrence, 2006). Keating later acknowledged that the neoliberal experiment had run its course, and the policies for which he had advocated had led the Australian economy into a dead end (Snow, 2017).

In Aotearoa New Zealand, so-called 'Rogernomics' (a term coined by a journalist for the economic policies of Roger Douglas, then-Labour Minister of Finance, in a deliberate attempt to draw parallels with America's Reaganomics) was promoted between July 1984 and November 1990, with effects lasting far longer. Radical reforms included deregulation of the financial markets, a floating dollar, removal of industrial subsidies, and reduced marginal tax rates. As a consequence, redundancies occurred in manufacturing, and state-owned enterprises such as New Zealand Post lost thousands of jobs. The number of people living in poverty grew by 35 per cent from 1989 to 1992 (Kelsey, 1999), and the child poverty rate (based on a threshold of 60 per cent of median income) grew from 11 per cent in 1986 to 29 per cent in 1994 (Boston, 2014); in 2020 the figure was still 18.2 per cent, down from 22.8 per cent in 2018 (Stats NZ/Tatauranga Aotearoa, 2021). At the same time, however, neoliberal advocates argued that inflation was controlled, income taxes were halved, and per capita income nearly doubled by 1990. Still, in 2015 income inequality in Aotearoa New Zealand was described as one of the worst in the world (Fyers and Kirk, 2015). One of the most controversial fields of social work practice in Aotearoa New Zealand is child protection. Māori and Pacific Islander children have a far greater likelihood of being reported to child protection services than tauiwi (European, or white) children, and Māori children had a rate of physical abuse almost five times that of European children (Rouland et al, 2019). In 2019, there were 82 babies taken into custody *before* they were born, of which 61 (74.4 per cent) were Māori, although Māori make up only 15 per cent of the total population (Maxwell, 2020). A report by the Office of the Children's Commissioner (2020) concluded that 'Māori are not well served by current systems, and the impacts of colonisation, socio-economic disadvantage and racism are well entrenched and still evident today' (p 105), and that 'The statutory care and protection system continues to reproduce inequities for pēpi [babies], tamariki [children] and rangatahi [teenagers] Māori' (p 16). In other words, the indigenous people of Aotearoa continue to endure the consequences of colonialism *and* the legacy of neoliberalism that has systematically disadvantaged them: vulnerablised and marginalised by the state and then punished for being vulnerable and marginal. State social workers are an integral part of supporting that system.

In September 2017, New Zealand Prime Minister Jacinda Ardern agreed that neoliberalism had failed, and the leader of the opposition conservative National Party agreed with her.

Although it is not my intention to consider the development of social welfare in every country, it is impossible to consider the impact of neoliberalism on social policy and the poor without acknowledging Latin America. Kingstone (2018) writes that neoliberal economic reform arrived in Latin America earlier than any other region of the world – specifically following the 1973–74 coup by Augusto Pinochet in Chile – as the result of the influence of economists educated at the University of Chicago. It is widely agreed even among the contemporary military, that there were devastating consequences of the coup, including egregious violations of human rights and thousands of dead, tortured, and disappeared *chileanos*. While publicly criticising Pinochet, the US continued to provide military assistance to his regime. The neoliberal economic agenda in Latin America furthered the American political agenda. Over the next decade, neoliberal reforms were implemented throughout Latin America, beginning with Chile, Uruguay, Colombia, and Peru in the 1970s, and Argentina, Mexico, Bolivia, Costa Rica, Guatemala, and Panama in the 1980s. In the 1990s, neoliberal economic reforms were introduced by Brazil, Venezuela, Honduras, Nicaragua, Ecuador, and El Salvador (Harris, 2003); the lone holdout was Cuba. The inability to service foreign debt is cited as a major reason why neoliberalism was adopted so widely in Latin American. Across the continent, governments devalued their currencies, refinanced their foreign debt, drastically reduced government expenditures, globalised, and restructured their economies, at the direction of the three major international financial institutions (International Monetary Fund, World Bank, and the InterAmerican Development Bank) (Harris, 2003).

The resulting social consequences were felt throughout the continent: the number of poor Latin Americans increased from 120 million in 1989 to 196 million in 1990; by 2002, the number had increased to 221 million, or 44 per cent of the region's population (González, 2003). In 1981–82, Chile suffered the worst economic crisis since the global Great Depression, and by 1983 more than one third of the workforce was unemployed (Harris, 2003). As a consequence of the pain of these reforms, between 1989 and 2002 across the region there were massive anti-neoliberal uprisings, work stoppages, and strikes,[28] particularly in Argentina, Bolivia, Ecuador, and Venezuela (Silva, 2009), where labour activists formed alliances with populists, socialists, and communists (and social workers) to protest free-market capitalism in favour of a more mixed-market economy and social welfare policies. In these nations, leftist populist governments replaced governments that advocated neoliberal solutions to the region's financial problems (even though authoritarian governments introducing these free-market reforms were themselves anything but free). These leftist governments retained some neoliberal structural reforms, and in some cases have become deeply problematic themselves. Latin America is an example of neoliberal reforms that failed on a continental scale but that few people outside the continent other than economists and policy wonks understood or took seriously. If they had, they would have seen the massive suffering that neoliberal reforms caused throughout Latin America and the political instability in many nations that continues to this day.

Summary

In this chapter, we have seen how social welfare reforms and the social imaginary of responses to the poor effectively came full circle during the 20th century. An increasingly empirical approach replaced religious dogmatism in the early part of the century. As a result of two world wars and a global depression, Calvinist-informed classical liberalism gave way to social liberalism, public social insurance, the welfare state in the UK, and an increased role for government assistance in the US. States with Lutheran-informed imaginaries developed as strong social welfare nations. During the reconstruction of the UK following the Second World War, the welfare state took over the functions of social assistance in much the same way as it had throughout Europe after the Great Plague of 1347–50; only the state had the authority to marshal the resources necessary to care

---

[28] These have been called 'austerity protests' (Green, 1995).

for the population and maintain social order. The Established Church acknowledged that reality (as it surely must have done more informally in the 14th century). The New Deal in the US also increased the role of the state in caring for the aged, the infirm, and employed the unemployed. After a series of economic crises, including oil shocks, demands on welfare systems beyond their abilities to cope, and international debt, neoliberalism emerged as the dominant economic philosophy throughout the world in the latter part of the century. States shrank their budgets, and the poor were left to their own devices. Neoliberalism and its companion social philosophy neoconservativism resulted in the retheologising of social assistance, a resurgence of the Calvinist influence in the US, UK, and other Anglophone nations, and was imposed throughout Roman Catholic Latin America. In the US, the state maintained its historic Calvinist orientation and beliefs about the poor. Order was maintained by enforcing conformity to dominant social values and liberal free-market solutions, up to and including the incarceration of anyone who was perceived as a threat to the dominant white, middle-class social norm.

While the state desire for social stability was common to both the 4th and 19th centuries (and every century in between, for that matter), the social imaginary about paupery and the poor was very different at the beginning and end of that period. That difference stemmed from a Calvinism reinterpreted by capitalism and free-market economies, individualism, and the Industrial Revolution. As poor relief had been taken up by secular authorities after the Great Plague of the mid-14th century, so the responsibility for establishing and maintaining social values had been taken up by states who used the power of poor relief to enforce appropriate morals and behaviour. The wealthy and emerging middle classes could do pretty much as they liked; the lives of the poor, however, were exposed and regulated.

Social workers have multiple roles in these new, sometimes dangerous and always complex environments. In most countries, social workers have evolved either from indigenous caregiving roles, religious workers, or well-meaning volunteer charity workers to highly educated and skilled practitioners, researchers, educators, and policy advocates. Conceptualisations of social work and social worker roles vary by country, context, locality, and field of practice. The occupation of social work in the UK and the US took quite different paths in those countries, particularly after the Second World War. So far we have focused mostly on the development of social welfare and social work in liberal humanist, Anglophone nations because that is where what we know as contemporary social work emerged and came to dominate globally. It would be a gross oversimplification to ignore the multifarious political, religious, social, and economic influences in each country (Aspalter, 2014), even in places where English is not the first or dominant language; regions have been influenced by one or another of these Anglophone nations (often referred to jointly as 'Western influences'):

- Hong Kong SAR, for instance, has been influenced by UK understandings of social work and social work education (Chui, 2014), while the Republic of Korea (Yan et al, 2020), the Philippines (Almanzor, 1966), and India (Gunavathy, 2007; Mandal, 1989) have been influenced by the American approach (although in some cases a Christian missionary or group was instrumental in formalising what became social work).
- Social work education appeared in African nations as early as the 1930s; African nations have been largely influenced by their colonial heritage, particularly their European coloniser nations (Mupedziswa and Sinkamba, 2014). Indigenisation of social work is occurring throughout the continent.
- In Latin America, much contemporary social work traces its roots to Spanish and Portuguese Roman Catholic missionaries and 20th-century liberation theologians (see for instance the works of Gustavo Gutiérrez, Leonardo Boff, Juan Luis Segundo, and Jon Sobrino, as well as educator Paulo Freire). Not surprisingly, then, social work throughout Latin America is more oriented to a community organising or community development approach through conscientisation (see, for example, Hinestroza and Ioakimidis, 2011).
- In post-Soviet Eastern Europe, social work programmes began in the early 1990s after they seceded from the USSR (Semigina and Boyko, 2014),[29] suggesting again the importance of the liberal humanist influence on social work in those nations (particularly from Canada and European nations).

Although Anglophone and other European influences have been seminal influences in the history of social work, they are not likely to be its future if social work expects to be truly global. As the axis of social work shifts to Asia and Africa – if for no other reason than from the sheer weight of population – we will find that there are many other ways of conceptualising 'helping' and other philosophical contexts that shape what we now call social work looks like around the world. How these different contexts fit together to form something of a global discipline, occupation, or profession is the task of the next part of this book.

---

[29] Some scholarship suggests that social work education was established in Poland, Hungary, Romania, and Bulgaria after the first World War but was closed down at the end of the second World War because the communist leadership associated social work with capitalism (Zaviršek, 2015). These programmes then re-emerged in the post-Soviet era.

8

Professionalising work with the poor

The British Poor Law Amendment Act of 1834 resulted in the re-emergence and coordination of church-informed private philanthropy (in the various Charity Organisations Societies (COS)), the first use of the term 'social work', and efforts to bring the elite and poor together to learn from each other and effect broader social and policy changes (in the Settlement House movements in the UK and US). Formal training programmes for charity volunteers were devised by the COS in the latter part of the 19th and early 20th centuries, didactic texts were developed, and eventually training and education became an expectation of everyone who carried out client-facing social work in the North Atlantic axis (although as we have seen, the political and social construction of poor relief was different in Lutheran and Roman Catholic nations). Social work became a paid occupation, and volunteers were redeployed to support activities within agencies rather than with clients.[1] The tension between social control and social care remained as social workers became established in various fields of practice and were designated by different titles in those different fields. As national policies evolved to respond to economic and social crises in the 20th century, social workers became crucial to the operations of both public and private charitable agencies. Paid, qualified social workers increased in number (although the kinds of work they did looked quite different in different national, institutional, and practice contexts), national and international social work associations emerged, and various codes of ethics were devised and promulgated. In some national or regional contexts, social work became a regulated designation. The obvious question arises: is social work a profession?

This vexed question has been addressed in a number of ways by social workers and others during the last century. In 1915, Abraham Flexner (Assistant Secretary of the General Education Board, an American NGO established in 1902 with a donation from John D. Rockefeller to promote medical and higher education in the US) responded to that question to a

---

[1] Here and throughout I use the word 'client' in the broadest and most generic possible way; a client can be an individual, family group, organisation, tribe, and so forth. It is the person or group whose interests the social worker has committed to uphold. I am aware that words like service user, consumer, and so forth, are also used in this way, but I will leave those discussions for others.

group of social workers who were still finding their way. I mention Flexner only because social workers spent so much time over the next several decades responding to his critique. He concluded that – in 1915 – social work was not a profession, since it had no unique method or technique that could be communicated by education, and merely conscripted the resources of a community and made them available to the needy (Trattner, 1999, p 257); this was something presumably anyone could do. Flexner's criteria for a profession included that it (1) involve essentially intellectual operations with large individual responsibility, (2) derive their raw material from science and learning, and (3) this material be put to a practical and definite end, (4) possess an educationally communicable technique, (5) tend to self-organisation, and (6) become increasingly altruistic in motivation (Flexner, 1915).[2] Mary Richmond's 1917 *Social Diagnosis* may have been intended as a response to Flexner's criticism about the lack of an educationally communicable technique. Social work in many places around the world has arguably met each of Flexner's criteria to varying extents, but simply asserting that social work as a discipline has met those century-old criteria does not resolve the question for the present day.

The question of whether social work is a profession has been explored and re-explored by numerous authors over the course of the 20th century.[3] In 1925, William Hodson, then-president of the American Association of Social Workers, clearly asserted that social work was a profession in his paper entitled 'Is Social Work Professional? A Re-Examination of the Question'. Five years later, Hazel Newton, a senior social worker in Boston, US, again answered the question with a clear 'Yes'[4] in her paper 'Miss Case-Worker Goes Scientific'. She cited the increasingly scientific and objective basis for social work, characteristics then conventionally associated with 'male professions' (Walkowitz, 1990). In the same year, social work was recognised as a distinct occupation for the first time in the US census. Careful readers will have noticed that I have avoided using the word *profession* about social work in the preceding chapters. Firstly, we must ask what a profession is and establish whether there is a difference between a profession, an *occupation*, or even a *trade*. Wilensky (1964, p 137n) notes that the Webbs (who we met in a previous chapter) predicted that trade unions 'will more and more assume

---

[2] It is worth noting that the American Medical Association was incorporated in 1897, reorganised its governance in 1901, and created a master file (or register) of qualified physicians in 1906. The notion of professionalisation was clearly an issue on the minds of more than one occupation during the first decades of the 20th century. Flexner also proposed that neither nurse nor pharmacists were professionals, but those practitioners must speak for themselves.

[3] These include Brown, 1935; Chambers, 1967; Ehrenreich, 1985; Leiby, 1978; Leighninger, 1987; Lubove, 1965; and in an international context by Weiss and Welbourne, 2007.

[4] Flexner did apparently hurt our feelings.

the character of professional associations' in order to raise the standard of competency in its occupation, improve the professional equipment, educate their masters, and endeavour to increase their status in public estimation. These goals, and particularly the last, may be one reason why so many social workers have argued for the recognition of social work as a profession in the last century.

In the liberal humanist West, occupations that have traditionally been designated as professions have usually been limited to medicine, law, and the clergy (some lists include engineers).[5] Not incidentally, these occupations have historically been male-dominated. We cannot avoid the issue of gender when we consider whether occupations that have traditionally been dominated by women, such as social work,[6] nursing, or teaching children, are professions since these occupations have been assessed on the basis of criteria associated with historically male-dominated professions which have an obvious interest in maintaining their social and political status. These criteria include objectivity, rationality, and a scientific approach to work, traits considered inappropriate, or unachievable for women in the early 1900s. In 1920s America at least, status for the female social worker 'came from the social worker's position of authority over lower-class clients, who were dependent on her judgment. To her middle-class peers, however, the lower-class background of such clients minimized the status of social worker' (Walkowitz, 1990, p 1058). In other words, while they gained some status among the poor, women who worked with the poor and the marginalised were themselves devalued among their own social class because of that work. This issue endures in the 21st century when designating (formally or informally) a job as 'female' diminishes its authority, even when men fill the role (Hedreen, 2019). Those of us who have worked in the fields of HIV, substance misuse, sex workers, or homeless persons – among many fields of practice with stigmatised and marginalised persons – have no doubt experienced the same kind of devaluing ('How can you work with those people?') because clients in those fields are constructed as somehow disreputable, unruly, and morally responsible for their stigmatised conditions. At the same time, social workers who work with 'innocents' – young children, for instance, who

---

[5] The *sciencia*, or knowledge base, of physicians is multidisciplinary, based on anatomy, biology, chemistry, and so forth, and phenomenological, observed experiences of diagnosis and treatment. The *sciencia* of lawyers is, of course, the law, which varies by jurisdiction. The *sciencia*, or knowledge, of the clergy is scriptures of various kinds; the question of whether the scriptures are scientific is irrelevant to this discussion because they and their commentaries contain a transmittable body of knowledge.

[6] In the US, for instance, 83 per cent of social workers are women (Salsberg et al, 2017); gender proportions will, of course, vary by country.

are unable to make moral choices, or who are perceived as victims of the poor choices of others – are ennobled by their peers ('That must be so rewarding!'). Social workers who believe that arguing about whether social work as a profession is a distinction without a difference must remember that this question is not merely about social work but about the status of women and the value of their work and also about marginalised persons, communities, and conditions. The question of profession sits squarely in the tradition of social care and social work.

Identifying the characteristics of a profession, informed as they are by dynamic social values, is itself hardly an objective or scientific endeavour. It is a socially constructed undertaking based on dominant values in particular social contexts. The notion of profession is itself a post-Enlightenment, liberal humanist Western one where fields of knowledge have become increasingly specialised and even isolated from one another. In non-Western societies, except where Western values have been widely imposed or adopted, the notion of professional as a class or descriptor hardly exists.[7] In societies where one's caste determines one's social rank and usually occupation, the notion of profession has no meaning. Still, the issue cannot be readily avoided; Weiss and Welbourne (2007, p 1) write that the drive for profession is consistent, and consistently controversial, as a feature of social work in all countries. Any proposals here will hardly settle the matter conclusively, but because of the global implications for the recognition of social work, social workers, and their clients, we cannot avoid the question.

What is a profession?

What we mean by profession must be quite carefully considered because in the 21st century most English speakers have become quite casual in the way they use the word. It is often used synonymously with the notion of *occupation*, that is, the way people earn their living. Occupation must in turn differ from the notion of *vocation*, which is generally understood as a calling to a particularly worthy or valued occupation (which may or may not be paid), or *trade*, which is an occupation that is primarily skills-based. Half a century ago, Wilensky (1964) also cautioned against the profligate use of the notion of professional, because if we make everything a profession then we may obscure newer structural forms that are emerging. If, as I shall propose later, social work in its various global manifestations meets the criteria for being a profession in some places and not in others, and is one

---

[7] Confucius, for instance, ranked the four principal occupations in descending order: scholar, farmer, worker, and merchant. Under Mao, the position of the worker was raised. See also Alford et al (2011), which focuses on the traditional three professions.

of the newer structural forms, reconceptualising profession in the same way that the structure of its 2014 *Global Definition* reconceptualised the idea of definition may accommodate regional and national variations.

As we have seen already, traditional notions of profession vary. At the most general level, they include that the occupation has a body of theories that also has a clear set of tasks, together with some accountability. A profession at its most basic traditionally requires a specialised education; specialised skills; a basic ethic of altruism; a code of ethics; and that it tends to self-organise. We have seen Flexner's criteria. Greenwood's classic paper on the attributes of a profession cites a systematic body of theory, professional authority, sanction of the community, a regulatory code of ethics, and a professional culture (Greenwood, 1957). More general, high-level criteria are found in Carter et al (1990) and Thompson (2016). Weiss and Welbourne (2007) add autonomy, a monopoly over specialist skills and service provision, and prestige and remuneration to Greenwood's list. There may be a continuum between occupation and profession (Carter, et al, 1990) and even, one could argue, a trade, as medicine once was. Even within recognised and established professions, there are segments that organise to keep the profession dynamic and evolving (Bucher and Strauss, 1961).

Wilensky (1964) proposes a process by which occupations have become professions.

> [T]here is a typical process by which the established professions have arrived: men [sic!] begin doing the work full time and stake out a jurisdiction; the early masters of the technique or adherents of the movement become concerned about standards of training and practice and set up a training school, which, if not lodged in universities at the outset, makes academic connection within two or three decades; the teachers and activists then achieve success in promoting more effective organization, first local, then national – through either the transformation of an existing occupational association or the creation of a new one. Toward the end, legal protection of the monopoly of skill appears; at the end, a formal code of ethics is adopted. (p 146)

Social work certainly appears to have followed this process over the last 150 years, at least in the North Atlantic axis and its spheres of influence. Within the association stage, a kind of internal hierarchy develops where some core tasks (such as, say, documentation or routinised follow-up) are delegated to specific sub-professional colleagues. There is also occasionally competition with similar occupations doing similar work (such as we have seen from time to time between social work and nursing or occupational therapy in respect of case management, for instance, or even social work and mental health counselling).

Wilensky proposes that a significant contemporary barrier to the professionalisation of an occupation is the increasing lack of autonomy; for instance, many physicians now work for large health care organisations whose bureaucratic policies may affect the autonomy of their decisions. This may be equally true of any traditionally autonomous professional, such as a lawyer who works for a corporation or political organisation, or an academic in some university settings. Certainly, this has been the case for social workers, who often work for bureaucratic government organisations (such as child protection agencies) whose actions are prescribed in law, or even for NGOs such as religiously affiliated organisations. The moment that NGOs accept funding from a public source, however, the NGO has itself become a kind of hybrid, and along with its employees, professional or otherwise, will be accountable to the funder as much or more than any occupational or professional standards. Wilensky notes that professionals within these hybrids can be divided into three types: Professional Service, who are highly identified with the profession, are oriented to *outside* the workplace or organisational group, and want to make full use of their professional skills; the Careerist, who is highly identified with the incumbent leadership *within* the organisation and is primarily motivated towards a career within the organisation and the career security it brings; and the Missionary, who is oriented to a social movement, is highly identified with that outside movement or group and sees the organisation as a vehicle for social change that is consistent with those goals (Wilensky, p 151).

Radical and critical social workers have eschewed the notion of professionalism in respect of social work, a critique that was particularly prominent during the 1990s (Thompson, 2016). The notion of an elite class making decisions for oppressed classes creates an unacceptable dissonance with a discipline that understands itself as emancipatory in the first instance. For much the same reasons, indigenous and cultural groups have often opposed the designation of people who attend to the needs of other people in difficulty as a professional group, or even a designated occupation, since it is the responsibility of every member of the community or tribe to provide care and assistance when necessary, and the community or tribe will designate someone to take up that role if required. Some resistance to the concept of social work as a profession has to do with the idea that a professionalised social worker may claim to hold expert knowledge, while the expertise should lie within the community. This argument recalls the different approaches of casework of the COS where expertise clearly lay with the social worker, and the Settlement House Movement, where it was the community that held the expertise in their own lives. Thompson (2016) critiques anti-professionalism views as undermining the confidence of social workers in their own work, social workers' pride in their identity, and their ability to challenge the pervasive bureaucracies of neoliberal, managerialist environments. He advocates what he calls an *authentic professionalism* where social workers recognise the importance of professional knowledge, skills, values, and accountability, and at the same time act consistently with social work values such as empowerment and emancipation. Authenticity can be achieved by working in partnership and co-creating expertise with clients who are, after all, the only experts in their own lives. This kind of postmodern approach to expertise means that clients, workers, agencies, theories, and even the discipline of social work itself, have interactive relationships with one another, and each can be changed and informed by the others. Social work may be the only occupation where the practitioner actively seeks to be changed by their interactions with their clients and to reflect on those changes with a supervisor.

Is social work a profession?

Considering whether social work is a profession is an especially difficult question when we consider the wide variety of practice contexts (Hugman, 1996), formal, informal, legal, and popular ways of designating who social workers are and what they do. Indeed, many social workers and social work education programmes boast of being 'generalist' – that is, preparing students with basic theoretical knowledge and skills, with the expectation that beginning practitioners will learn more advanced or practice-specific knowledge and skills in placements or on the job. Increasingly, social workers are regulated in some way (registered, licensed, certified, or similar) by various bodies using various designations, including title protection (legal protection that establishes that only people who have met specific criteria may use the designation 'social worker'). To complicate matters further, in some jurisdictions multiple titles are used to designate what is essentially social work: caseworker, community worker, mental health worker, navigator, support worker, welfare worker, youth worker, and so on (one website lists 48 synonyms for social worker; Power Thesaurus, 2021). It is hardly surprising that contemporary social work is known by so many different names and job titles since the discipline has inherited so many different historical roles, including those of deacon, monk/nun, priest, hospitaller, almoner, counsellor, and so forth. Some of these metronyms are historical legacies, some are attempts to reflect a job description, and some are attempts to avoid the connotations that accompany the title of social worker. No doubt some also attempt to evade regulatory (and salary) requirements that are incumbent on the designation 'social worker', even though fully qualified social workers may be doing those jobs. It is little wonder then that there is confusion in the public mind, and that qualified social workers of all genders are eager for clarification of their status, with clearly identified boundaries around who is and who is not a social worker, and who is entitled to use the title.

For the moment, then, let us take a conservative approach and consider how the broadest understanding of the common attributes of profession I discussed earlier may be applied to social work. These attributes include:

- a clearly defined and altruistic purpose;
- transmissible theoretical knowledge (which may be trans- or interdisciplinary);
- specialised skills or techniques;
- a commonly held values base and enforceable ethical code;
- a high degree of individual responsibility and autonomy in decision-making;
- self-governing association, with a credentialing process and accountability to others within the association; and
- public and political recognition as a distinct professional group (this includes prestige).

These seven characteristics draw together what appear to be the most consistently agreed criteria and are, therefore, perhaps more rigorous than strictly necessary. With all this in mind, let us assess whether social work meets the seven criteria I have proposed for a profession.

Altruistic purpose

I have placed altruism first because it is the defining characteristic between a profession and a business or trade whose work may benefit people, or create a public good (such as vaccine manufacturers), but whose motivation is profit. Profit here is distinct from income. To say that social workers are not altruistic because they are paid is not the point; social work is altruistic because there is an initial cost to the worker-self (the investment in education and skill-building), there is a delay in seeing the consequences of the interaction, and its primary motivation is not individual or collective profit.[8] Altruism in response to another's pain, need, or distress is phylogenetically ancient, as old as mammals and birds, and is therefore potentially a shared trait among all humans. However, in social work, altruism is a key trait, even a virtue. Frans DeWaal (2008), an evolutionary psychologist, proposes that the ideal mechanism to underpin directed altruism is empathy, which we will consider in a moment. While a full exploration of altruism is beyond our scope here, deWaal finds that empathy-induced altruism is important because the actor (or in our case, the practitioner) is feeling what the other (or client) feels,

---

[8] This is one reason why so-called social bonds, where a private investor invests money in an agency and is rewarded by a government payout when clients and workers meet performance goals are objectionable to many social workers.

and therefore the actor has 'an emotional stake in the recipient's well-being' (p 281). The social worker has an emotional investment in the client's wellbeing. It may be that it is not merely the kind of *general* altruism shared by all humans (and mammals) but the more specific *directed* altruism, a wish for the best possible outcome for the client, that motivates social workers. But certainly, it is altruism.

Crudely put, a social worker's purpose is to put themselves out of a job. That is, the purpose of the social worker from the moment of engaging with a client is (or should be) emancipatory, to support that client to be independent of the social worker. That purpose is inherently altruistic. Of course, it may not be realistic for some clients (such as the chronically unwell or impaired) to expect to be entirely independent, but they can (or should) be supported to make independent decisions. In rare cases, it may be the best decision temporarily to require a client who is a danger to themselves or others to undergo some kind of intervention. In any case, the goal of enabling clients to determine their own futures regardless of engagement with a social worker is altruistic.

Another reason to place altruism first is to address the issue of social control. Social control is broadly incompatible with the concept of altruism. Social control places the interests of the state or institutional authorities above the interests of the client. Although a stable society is arguably safer for its individual members, if that stability is coerced rather than voluntary, then long-term stability may not be sustainable or may require increasing state intervention. This means that most statutory services, such as forensic social work (corrections, probation, and youth justice) and even child protection are not in the strictest sense altruistic. They seek to enforce dominant social standards and codes rather than the welfare of a specific client. In most forensic models, the ultimate client of the social worker is the public, and if you can have your client arrested for non-compliance that is hardly altruistic. Whether social work meets this criterion of a profession, then, may depend on the context of practice.

Theoretical knowledge

The knowledge base of a profession does not need to be unique to that profession (as in the case of medicine, for example, which draws on a variety of disciplines, including anatomy, biology, chemistry, and so forth). In our increasingly specialised world of knowledge, it is almost impossible to have a proprietary knowledge base, although aspects of a knowledge base may be unique. In the 21st century, for a helping profession to isolate its knowledge from all other disciplines would be difficult, unusual, and possibly risky; there also would not be much point. For a physician to prescribe psychotropic medications without considering the knowledge base of human behaviour would be ill-advised; likewise, it would be ill-advised for a social worker to work with a severely mentally ill client without a referral to a physician to assess the appropriateness of such medication. By definition, social work draws on an array of knowledges including social work and the social sciences, the humanities, and indigenous knowledges,[9] and education and training courses around the world exist to teach them. There are journals and libraries filled with social work theories and knowledge in many languages around the world, and new knowledge emerges constantly.

Social workers must be mindful of the historical, political, and epistemological contexts in which they work, and have access to a wide array of theories. One of the critiques of social work has been that it does not have a theory of theories – that is, how do social workers choose which knowledge base to draw from in any given situation? The answer to this question is not as simple as 'if Situation A, then Intervention B'. Social work's heuristic is interactive, dialogic, and praxis-based; that is, as I suggested earlier, social workers and clients are co-creators of social work theory, and therefore practice. This heuristic not only dismisses the expertise objection to the professionalisation of social work but is also emancipatory. A social worker cannot say 'I have a hammer therefore I will treat everything as if it were a nail'. Social work must also take into account, and even privilege, indigenous and local epistemologies and cultures, while at the same time engaging with them from the standpoint of social work's agreed values[10] (Noble and Henrickson, 2014, p 7). In this sense, then, social workers exercise a degree of autonomous judgement. This dynamic approach to a theory of theories is as valuable as a static, unitary philosophy, and certainly takes into account the endless variety of clients and the cultures and contexts in which we encounter them. The body of laws in a given jurisdiction also act as theory (as it does for lawyers), and social workers can be employed to enforce or implement those laws: the scope of certain kinds of child protection, school truancy workers (and as noted earlier, forensic social work) are defined in law. Social work appears to meet this criterion.

---

[9] This is from the *Global Definition*; and please don't forget that 's' on indigenous knowledges; there is not just one indigenous knowledge, and to pretend this is a collective term is to erase or homogenise identities of indigenous and First Nations peoples.

[10] Social workers cannot simply accept uncritically local values that are oppressive, or that marginalise or criminalise any person or group based on an essential characteristic like ethnicity, gender, sexuality, or even chosen characteristics such as religious or political affiliations; the *Global Definition* states that respect for diversities is central to social work.

Skills

Of all the aspects of professionalism, the one that has received the most attention has probably been social work skills. Here, skills like empathy (usually first on most lists of social work skills), advocacy, assessment, awareness of others, boundary-setting, communications, cooperation, coordination, counselling, critical thinking, cultural competence, organisation, self-awareness – well, the list is as long as we want to make it. Social work requires skills in any practice context, and most of these can be taught (although being innately empathetic helps). As we saw a moment ago, deWaal (2008) proposes that it is empathy that underpins directed altruism, and learning to understand and use empathy to build a relationship with a client is a social work skill. There are bookshelves of texts and screeds of video resources that are available to teach empathy.

It is the skills of qualified social workers that are most in demand in practice contexts that are not expressly social work, such as forensic or other statutory contexts, where social control is a primary aspect of the work. It is also the dissonance between social control and empowerment, emancipation, and empathy that creates enormous tension (and often disillusionment) in the practitioner in these contexts. Social work education programmes have both practical components and field education practicums designed to develop the student's professional skill set. I think we may safely say that social work meets this criterion in all practice contexts.

Values and ethics

Again, whether social work has shared values and ethics seems quite straightforward. While codes of ethics may differ among different social work associations and countries, all the associations I know about have codes of ethics. Even if there were not a national or regional code, there is the *Global Social Work Statement of Ethical Principles* (*GSWSEP*) (International Association of Schools of Social Work and International Federation of Social Workers, 2018), which set out social work values and the principles social workers are expected to follow, and it acts as a kind of default code of ethics.

However, as usual, this criterion is not quite as straightforward as it seems. In some jurisdictions, codes of conduct replace or sit alongside codes of ethics.[11] Codes of conduct set out a minimum standard of how workers are to behave rather than how to make decisions. Codes of conduct are

---

[11] Sewpaul and Henrickson (2019) found, for instance, that codes of ethics and codes of conduct co-exist in England (and separate ones in Scotland and Wales), Aotearoa New Zealand, and a 68-page document in South Africa.

largely the product of risk-averse managerialism (Sewpaul and Henrickson 2019), tools of surveillance which, ironically may create more risk to the organisation since they cannot possibly consider all possible situations and all possible behaviours. Workers become anxious about transgressing prescribed behaviours, which focuses their attention on their conduct rather than on good practice with a client. Codes of conduct are viewed as having practical utility by governments and employers because with them social workers can be monitored, controlled, investigated, and disciplined. Where codes of ethics alone exist (even if only the *GSWSEP*) then we can say that social work meets this criterion. Where only a code of conduct or both codes of ethics and conduct exist, then it may not, as individuals are not at liberty to exercise their own professional judgement without negative consequences.

Individual responsibility

This attribute of social work came under Flexner's most withering criticism. Social workers are simply good people doing good in the same way that anyone in the community can, and should, do good (or put another way, they are human beings acting altruistically as mammals do). This critique is worth considering carefully. If an individual is acting as part of a legal duty or is mandated to take certain actions in a situation (and I am not here considering legal duty-to-warn or child mistreatment reporting mandates which usually apply to all the helping professions) then can they said to be acting on their own professional assessment and judgement? If social work is manualised – that is, if interventions are effectively determined by a procedural manual, which can be as basic as requiring a worker to cite the legal foundation of each decision – then can the practitioner be said to be acting from their own judgement? Statutory agencies in particular (and especially those where the public may be at risk, such as probation services) are especially risk-averse and are most likely to ensure that the actions of the workers are prescribed in advance. No agency wants the death of a child in its care, or the apparent mistakes of one of its staff plastered all over the media. To manage such risk, institutions are more likely to remove the decision-making responsibility of the individual worker rather than provide them with the orientation, education, supervision, and authority to make their own professional decisions. The message such organisations send is 'We hired you, but we don't trust you'. Still, no manual can address the complexity of the human condition in its infinitely diverse array of social contexts. On the other hand, a number of social work practice contexts rely heavily on the independent decision-making abilities of the worker; mental health work and particularly counselling and therapeutic settings where clients are seen privately in one-to-one or group settings are examples of this. Assessing social work professionalism against this criterion again seems to depend on the context.

Self-governance and credentialling

In places where there is more than one social worker, there will be at least one professional association, and possibly more. Social workers are reasonably good at creating associations and developing the infrastructure to support them. Indeed, from the earliest days of social work in the UK and US, there has been a variety of different kinds of social work associations mostly created around specific fields of practice. However, whether these associations are regulatory bodies varies considerably by jurisdiction. Regulation of professionals of all kinds in the 21st century is highly legislated, even when governments establish professionally led organisations to implement regulatory functions. This is as true for physicians in the US (White, 2014) as it is for social workers in England (Social Work England, 2021). Along with state regulation, however, come the benefits of title protection; that is, a person cannot legally use the title of the profession unless they have met the criteria of the regulatory body. This presumably protects the public from charlatans and practitioners who do not meet the ethical, fitness, or educational requirements of their profession. This means that today almost nowhere are professions in general, or social work in particular, entirely autonomous or self-governing. In Australia, however, there is no legislation protecting the title of social work or establishing statutory agency; the Australian Association of Social Workers sets professional education and practice standards (Healy, 2016). This means that (as of 2021) social work as an occupation in Australia is autonomous and self-governing but does not have legal title protection. A purely self-governing profession with title protection, therefore, appears unrealistic now, if it ever was, and we may need to modify this criterion or at least amend it to read 'professionally led' credentialing, rather than autonomous credentialing.

Public and political recognition

This is probably a *sine qua non*. If the public does not legitimise your occupation, they certainly will not recognise it as a profession. If the public and political authorities do not value the work social workers do, it will not matter how well they do it. In the 21st century, esteem for an occupation is often or usually measured by the way its practitioners are compensated,[12] and, as we saw, Weiss and Welbourne include remuneration and prestige among their criteria for profession. This is also not to suggest that, all other criteria being met, one could not be a volunteer (that is, unpaid) professional social worker.

---

[12] As little as that may be – I'm sure we've all heard the old saw 'social workers are in it for the outcome, not the income'.

There are places in the world where educated social workers are recognised in law but deliberately undervalued and underpaid (Iaskaia-Smirnova, et al, 2004) because they are seen as a threat to the state. There are places in the world where social work is not recognised as an occupation: Bangladesh, for instance, does not yet recognise the occupation of social work; in India, home to 16 per cent of the world's population, social work is not regarded by government as a profession (Nair, 2015) and remains of relatively low status (Gunavathy, 2007). There are places in the world where social work is still emerging but is well-recognised by political authorities as an occupation, and even profession, such as the People's Republic of China. In some places, such as Romania, social work has only relatively recently (2005) been recognised in law as an independent profession (Hussein, 2011). Social work as a title is not protected in Sweden; in Norway, it has been protected only for some parts of the profession; the title has been fully protected since 1975 in Iceland; in France, all social workers, regardless of employer, are provided with professional identification (Hussein, 2011). What social work looks like in different parts of the world will differ, certainly, because social work is so context-dependent, and, as we have seen, so shaped by the local historical context; but if the local manifestation is not recognised or valued then it cannot be a profession. Social work is recognised in some countries as an occupation, and not in others, as a distinct profession in some, but the title is not protected in others. All we can say even from these limited reports is, again, it depends.

So not a profession then

Not so fast. Using the conservative criteria we set out earlier, it appears that the best we can say is that social work is an emerging or quasi-profession in many countries and regions in the world but certainly not in all. In some practice areas, it meets the definition of altruism but not in all of them. It has a broad theoretical foundation, which may also include legal mandates that limit the independent decision-making of practitioners. There is a clear, and widely agreed, set of skills. There are codes of ethics in place, but these may be mitigated by codes of conduct that closely regulate the behaviour and independence of a social worker. In some contexts, some social workers may be reasonably autonomous, but this too is balanced against prescriptive, manualised social work in some practice contexts where there are legal mandates that prescribe or proscribe independent professional judgement. In very few jurisdictions is social work fully autonomous, and where it is, the title is not protected. In some countries, social work is not recognised even as an occupation. It would seem by the conservative criteria I have proposed that social work cannot be called a global profession today, although it appears to be an emerging or quasi-profession in some jurisdictions where it is a mature occupation. However, it may be an example of what Wilensky calls a 'newer structural form' of profession. This new form has the attributes of profession that we have set out – altruism, transmissible theoretical knowledge, specialised skills, values and ethical code, public and political recognition as a distinct professional group – in many (but not all) countries and regions. Social work, like other professions, is now regulated by governments in one way or another, but if we can agree that as long as this regulation and accreditation are with the advice and consent of qualified social workers and the regulatory processes are led by social workers, we could agree that this is one of the newer structural forms of profession. The criterion where there remains some question is the level of individual responsibility and autonomy in decision-making, and as we have noted earlier, whether or not social work meets this criterion may rely on the practice context. This may be true about medicine and law as well.

Another challenge to conceptualising social work as a profession is the social control function, where social work as an occupation is expected to act on behalf of the state. Social control, as we have seen, has been part of the inheritance of social care and social work from the era of Constantine. Is it possible to talk with any authority about the empowerment and emancipation of clients when social workers themselves are controlled by and control on behalf of the state? How can social work centralise principles of social justice and human rights (as set out in the *Global Definition*) when states themselves may be unjust or violate principles of human rights? How can social workers hold states accountable or even advocate on behalf of their clients when this advocacy circle is managed by states? I pose these as rhetorical questions because I do not think it is possible.

If states set curriculum standards, credential social workers, employ them, control eligibility standards and benefits for clients or communities, and the standards of safety in a community (and by safety I include everything from domestic violence through to environmental regulation), we must ask whether 'Is social work a profession?' is the right question. A more nuanced question may be 'Is social work capable of acting autonomously?' Social workers must be able to hold states accountable for injustices, violations of internationally agreed human rights, oppression against any kind of diversity, ensure safe drinking water, access to adequate food, without risk of sanction, imprisonment, torture, or worse. Social workers must be relatively independent actors (within their scopes of practice or expertise) whose voices will be heard, respected, and acted on by civil authorities and the public. There are places in the world where brave individuals who are social workers have done so, and continue to do so. Social work differs from the historical professions in that social work foregrounds social justice in its definition and human dignity in its ethics. No other occupation or profession does that. That makes social work quite unruly, and states may work to ensure its lower status in order to contain and control it.

Now what?

The discipline of social work may need to reconceptualise the idea of a profession in the same way that it has reconceptualised the idea of a unitary definition. The 2014 *Global Definition of Social Work* and the 2018 *GSWSEP* clearly establish that social work is contextual as well as transactional – that is the innovation in these documents. There is no expectation that there is only one way to do social work in all places around the world. Indeed, resistance to the professionalisation of social work, particularly among indigenous communities and in decolonising and non-Western nations, is based on antipathy to the notion of expert advice rooted in a hegemonic, liberal humanist epistemology and positivist science. As we have seen, social work in colonised and post-colonial nations has very much been rooted in such an epistemology, although this may be changing as a decolonisation agenda is furthered and different knowledges and systems of ethics are recognised and implemented.

In addressing the question as to whether social work is a profession globally is important to social workers, there are, I think, four options.

First, we can continue the current patchwork system, where globally social work is recognised or not recognised either as an occupation or a profession, regulated or not regulated, depending on the political context. This means abandoning the notion of a global profession, at least for the present. It is certainly easy to say that international social work bodies should not interfere with local development. However, this approach has a number of disadvantages, including putting social workers at risk in places where their work is not recognised; international recognition and mobility of social workers is restricted, social workers are undervalued in some nations, and access to social work services is limited. Since social work is most advanced in developed nations, it means those nations will also continue to dominate social work, colonial (and particularly Anglophone) discourses will continue to be replicated, and the voices of indigenous and developing communities and states will struggle to be heard. Continuing business as usual means that social work education programmes and access to research and project development funding will continue to be subsumed under other categories such as sociology, public administration, criminology, and so forth. This invisibility impairs researchers and practitioners who must compete for recognition and funding on an uneven playing surface and inhibits the development of new knowledge. All but the most persistent students will be lured into other occupations.

Second, social workers can modify the notion of autonomy and reconceptualise the notion of profession to allow (or encourage) government regulation of practitioners, scopes of practice, education, and practice standards, provided this regulation is led by qualified social workers. From a regulatory perspective, this new structural form would be largely equivalent to other recognised professions such as medicine and nursing. This option would also mean that this new structural form of profession should advocate for state recognition and regulation in nations and territories where such recognition does not currently exist, and for dedicated education, programme, and research funding categories. The risk to this approach in more undemocratic nations is that social workers may be compromised (or perceived as compromised) in any public debates where governments that regulate social workers must be held accountable for actions or values that contradict values that are important to social workers. There is a very real possibility, of course, that less democratic governments could develop criteria where social workers who challenge governments could be accused of misconduct or acting outside their scopes of practice, struck off their registers, or even criminalised.

Third, a more limited version of the state-regulated profession approach would mean delegating to states only the administrative processes that are required to ensure that states implement criteria for recognition of individual practitioners (education, supervised experience, continuing professional development, fitness to practice, and so forth) that are set by independent associations of social workers. This would require that there be robust and independent national and territorial social work associations. States would maintain registers of qualified practitioners, whose title would be protected in law.

Fourth, social workers can decide that only a fully independent status can ensure its core values of social justice and human dignity for the widow, the orphan, the *ger*,[13] and the poor, and reclaim regulatory authority from states. In most places, this would mean law changes, possible loss of title protection, and developing the infrastructure and resourcing to manage and set standards for itself. This may be an approach that is attractive to indigenous peoples who prefer to maintain a truly distant relationship with any external regulatory authority (and its colonial legacy) or any notion of a profession with expert knowledge. There is no question that this would be a very large undertaking over a period of many years but would establish beyond question that social work is entirely autonomous.

---

[13] From Chapter 2.

There may be other hybrid approaches, but if social work is to be an authentic and new structural form of profession, particularly one dominated by women, and which works with vulnerabilised and marginalised people, they must be feasible and practicable in every nation or region in the world, under all kinds of governments. The debate on social work's future as a profession (or not) must be led in collaboration by the international social work associations in close consultation with regional, territorial, and national associations. The entire community of social workers must come to a consensus on the way forward. International social work associations are historically reluctant to be seen to interfere with national or regional associations, and, therefore, this issue is likely to remain unresolved for some time. Nevertheless, the pathway forward has been laid out by the *Global Definition* and *GSWSEP* processes, and if social work wishes to become a truly global profession the issue must be prioritised on the international social work agenda.

9

A global perspective

So far we have focused on Western, or liberal humanist, traditions and their responses to the poor, the widow, the orphan, and the marginalised. I identified the rationale for this focus at the outset of our exploration. These cultures, and particularly Anglophone societies, have been instrumental in the development and global dissemination of what we now know as social care and particularly social work, even though contemporary post-colonial cultures and societies have struggled to recover from that dissemination. This focus has not been to suggest even for a moment that there are no other significant texts and traditions that address poverty and the poor, or that Western societies are the only ones that have provided social care over the millennia. A number of scholars[1] have contributed to understanding ways that global texts and traditions create cultural understandings of the poor and marginalised and propose responses consistent with those cultures. The literature on decolonising and indigenous[2] social work is growing at an extraordinary rate, which, while challenging for social workers in nations with a history of colonising, will only strengthen social work globally. The social imaginaries of these ancient religious, philosophical, and cultural traditions differ radically from those found in Judaeo-Christian and even Islamic traditions because of their assumptions about humanity, society, poverty, and even whether human life is linear or cyclical, are fundamentally different. Nevertheless, the ultimate goals of their interventions are aligned; each seeks to emancipate human beings from oppression, although understandings about the nature and source of that oppression are different. While Western notions of social care and contemporary social work have until now hegemonised responses to the poor around the world, it is impossible to conceive of a global future for social work without listening to, respecting, and learning from these other global responses.

---

[1] This is particularly notable in books such as *Poverty and the Poor in the World's Religious Traditions: Religious Reponses to the Problem of Poverty* (Brackney and Das, 2019) and through institutions such as the Asian Research Institution for International Social Work at Shukutoku University in Chiba, Japan.

[2] The word *indigenous* is capitalised in some contexts when referring to a specific people, and that is the usage I will follow.

This chapter considers social care in some of those global traditions and then considers how contemporary social work has (or has not) been responsive to those traditions. Some of these global traditions are ancient, and adherents have developed complexities that are far beyond the scope of the present study; such a consideration would be encyclopaedic. I write with the ignorance of someone who has studied and even taught but not lived these traditions; I can write about but not from these worldviews. I encourage serious students of South and East Asian, African, and indigenous cultures to undertake their own more in-depth explorations perhaps beginning with some of the resources included here.

South Asia

The Vedas (Rig Veda, Sama Veda, Yajur Veda, and Atharva Veda) are the earliest body of Indian scripture. They were composed in Vedic Sanskrit probably between 1500 and 700 BCE and formed the foundation of what is considered the world's oldest religion, Hinduism (or Santana Dharma, the 'eternal path'; Dash and Nagar, 2021). With an estimated 1.2 billion adherents, Hinduism is the religion of about 15 per cent of the world's population. Vyasi, also known as Krishna Dvaipānaya and Veda Vyāsa, is the traditional compiler of the Vedas (with their 20,379 mantras), although in the epic *Mahabharata* their origin is credited to Brahma. They were orally transmitted for centuries before being recorded in writing. The Vedas teach that the material body is an illusion and that this illusion is the source of suffering or *dukkha*, sometimes called 'un-satisfactoriness' (Inagaki et al, 2020, p 2). The material body and its extended social identities such as gender, caste, relationships, politics, citizenship, and the like have no connection with the actual life of the essential self (Wolf, 2003), but the body is intended to help the self on the journey to spiritual liberation (*mokṣa*) from the cycle of rebirth and the world (*saṃsāra*) and enlightenment. Caring for the individual from a Vedic perspective, therefore, is ancient, although the purpose of such care is primarily spiritual, and it would be ahistorical to say that this care was 'social work' any more than we could say that meeting the obligation of caring for the widow and orphan under the Code of Hammurabi or the First Testament was social work. Vedic social care is dualist: it assists the individual (or community or state) to understand and dispel the illusion that the material body is the self, or that the self is the corporeal body. The caregiver themself models detachment from externalities in order to connect with the essential self. That means that care provision was historically provided by advanced practitioners of faith in temples, monasteries, or religious houses (Zysk, 1991). Nevertheless, as in most models of social care, the caregiver encounters the person where they are; if they are hungry, then they must be fed, if they are naked, then they must be clothed. In addressing the material needs, the practitioner helps the person realise the true source of their *dukkha*, to eventually emancipate them from that *dukkha*.

A challenging aspect of Hindu tradition is caste. Caste stratification has been generally accepted as being at least 3,000 years old and divides Hindus into four *varnas* or categories, 3,000 castes, and 25,000 subcastes, based on occupation, and people who are outside caste, the Dalit. This system privileges the upper castes, marginalises or stigmatises the lower castes, and creates a rigid separation among castes. However, contemporary scholarship (Bayly, 1999; Chakravorty, 2019b) proposes that caste was of limited importance in India until the colonial period and that it was the British colonisers who viewed Indian society through their own imposed systems of religion, race, caste, and tribe. Under the Raj, these social identities were formalised because creating and enforcing divisions allowed a more governable society. Even as early as 1871, a census supervisor in Madras wrote that 'regarding the origin of caste we can place no reliance upon the statements made in the Hindu sacred writings' (in Chakravorty, 2019a). Indeed, in the 15th century, Sri Caitanya Mahaprabhu (d. 1534) emphasised *para-upakara*, welfare work for all regardless of caste or creed (Wolf, 2003), and Das and Nagar write that contemporary Hinduism 'preaches self-less social service, compassion, mutual aid and love for the community' (2021, p 166). Negative discrimination on the basis of caste is now banned in India and caste is not formally recognised by Muslims in India or nearby Muslim-dominated nations, although it remains implicit and controversial, and its legacy and other residual effects of colonialism remain throughout the region (see Patnaik, 2020).

In Hinduism, three concepts underpin activities related to social welfare. *Danam* is not merely charitable giving but a duty of those people who are able to give; importantly, *danam* upholds the dignity of the recipient of charity. Charitable giving that is done reluctantly, with disrespect to the recipient, or that is motivated by selfish desire is harmful to both the donor and recipient. *Dharma* is action that always considers the welfare of the other, lives life with compassion, and results in a harmonious society where the common welfare is a priority. *Yagna* is collective activity that is undertaken for the welfare of the larger social good. There are obvious parallels between the Hindu notions of *danam*, *dharma*, and *yagna* and the Greek and Roman notions of *philanthropia* and *euergesia*, which we considered in Chapter 3. Whether these values emerged from a common source culture or because the ancients serendipitously found common ways to live a common life is not important here. Giving in these cultures was motivated by compassion, carrying out one's responsibility to the common life of the community, and the poor. In Vedic social care, however, since Hinduism did not require the same process of legitimation as did the Christian church of the 4th century CE, there was no need to create a class of poor in order to justify an institution (although such classes were arguably created through the caste and *quom*[3] systems). Nevertheless, because of the shared values of *danam*, *dharma*, and *yagna*, Hinduism 'continues to act as an important agent of social control' (Dash and Nagar, p 166).

The dharmic faiths of Hinduism and its offshoot Jainism, as well as Sikhism (a non-Vedic monotheistic Indian faith founded in the 16th century by Guru Nanak Davanti) each have different understandings of poverty and how to respond to the poor, and within each tradition are yet further strands of belief that make different assumptions about poverty: poverty is a social fact which must be lived through or put up with; poverty is bad so it should be eradicated; or poverty is a virtue, something to be embraced. Yet in each faith, responding to the poor is accepted as essential to creating dharma, which contributes to the benefit of both the giver and the recipient. Anyone who has walked among the enormous steaming pots of dal in a vast Sikh temple kitchen as the faithful prepare to feed hundreds of people every day will recognise that caring for the poor and hungry in very practical ways is accepted as an integral part of Sikh daily life. However, it has not always been so for Hindus: Zysk (1991) notes that in the first millennium BCE medical practitioners and providers of social care were denigrated by higher castes because of their close association with impure (lower-caste) persons. As a consequence, healers often assimilated into Buddhist communities and contributed to the dissemination of healing knowledge throughout the Buddhist sphere of influence.

The Vedic reliance on a cyclical rather than a linear understanding of human existence means that poverty in the present life may not be a result of faults in the present life but that occurred in a past life. Likewise, in the present, one might accumulate *karma* so that the next life will be better (or, in a life not well-lived, poorer). This dogma acts as an explanation for the poor to accept their condition (Kumar, 2018). Further,

> Within the Vedic culture, therefore, poverty was recognized and accommodated within a socio-philosophical tradition that both explained, and furthermore justified, its existence with reference to the divine. This reinforced the legitimacy of the prevalent social inequalities, removed any moral imperative for structural reform, and was used by the ruling class to justify the imposition of further barriers to social mobility. (Walker, 2014, pp 7–8)

Nevertheless, Walker (2014) continues, the wealthy were encouraged to be grateful for their wealth and exhorted to give food directly to people who

---

[3] Social stratification in Pakistan.

had to beg because the wealthy might very well be the poor in the next incarnation. Feasts were offered by the wealthy and attended by the poor; during their observances, religious centres competed to provide food for the greatest number. In the same way, as we saw in early Constantinople and early Christianity, resources were transferred from the wealthy to the poor, often via the priest class.

Buddhism dates from around the 6th century BCE. The founder of Buddhism was Prince Siddhartha Gautama, an ascetic seeker who ultimately became the Buddha, the Enlightened One. As in the founder stories of any religion, it is difficult to separate the myths from the facts of the life of Gautama, but it appears that he was born into relative luxury ca. 563 (or 448) BCE in Lumbini, in what is today southern Nepal. The region where he was born appears to have been non-Vedic and even pantheistic, although Gautama apparently held some early beliefs consistent with Hinduism. The title of Buddha came into use about Gautama several centuries after his death (generally accepted as between 420 and 380 BCE). Despite his wealth and royal status, Gautama was concerned with the poor and the human condition in general. At some point, he left his palace on a quest to see the outside world and was shocked to see the extent of human suffering. Eventually, he left the palace permanently to become an ascetic in order to seek nobler truths that would alleviate suffering. He eventually discovered the Noble Eightfold Path[4] and gained insight into the Four Noble Truths.[5] His awakening into these truths allowed him to achieve *nirvana* (emancipation) and released him from the cycle of rebirth. He spent the rest of his life travelling and teaching in what is now Uttar Pradesh, Bihar, and southern Nepal and eventually settled in Sravasti, in Kosala, where he continued to provide instruction to monastic communities before he died.

As in Hinduism, a Buddhist approach to the poor proposes that having no attachment to things or people allows one to be truly free of worry and craving, and opens up the possibility for achieving emancipation from suffering by overcoming human emotions that cause problems: greed, hatred, and delusion (Baskerville and Hansen, 2018). In this construction, homelessness can even serve as a central metaphor for spiritual liberation, although it must be said that (as in medieval Europe) there is a difference between voluntarily giving up one's home and privileges and involuntarily being homeless and poor. Emperor Ashoka, called the Great (r. 268–232

---

[4] Right view; right resolve; right speech; right conduct; right livelihood; right effort; right mindfulness; right *samadhi* (meditation).

[5] *Dukkha* (suffering is a part of *saṃsāra*, the world); *samudaya* (the origin of *dukkha* arises from *taṇhā*, craving or attachment); *nirodha* (the ending of dukkha is attainable by renouncing *taṇhā*); *magga* (the Noble Eightfold Path that leads to the renunciation of *taṇhā*).

BCE), ruled almost all the Indian subcontinent and converted to Buddhism in pain and repentance (Lahiri, 2015) after witnessing the great slaughter and deportations of the Kalinga War he had waged (described in Rock Edict 13[6]). Ashoka renounced a traditional text on Indian statecraft, the *Arthashastra*, and is said to have sent out emissaries to introduce Buddhism throughout his empire, from Kandahar to Mesopotamia, and into (modern) Sri Lanka, Greece, and Egypt. He is generally acclaimed as one of India's greatest emperors. While Ashoka is often credited with building many hospitals during his time, and in Rock Edict II he orders the provision of medical facilities for 'men [sic] and beasts' (Strong, 1983/1989, p 4), there is no clear evidence that any hospitals as we would recognise them existed in India during the 3rd century BCE, or that Ashoka was responsible for commissioning the construction of any hospitals (Zysk, 1991, p 44), although there were certainly other structures and pillars attributable to him. In Rock Edict V he commissions officers to work for the welfare and happiness of the poor and aged, and in Rock Edict VI he commits constantly 'to promote the welfare of all beings so as to pay off his debt to living creatures and to work for their happiness in this world and the next' (Strong, 1983/1989, p 4). Regardless of what actually occurred during his reign, these legendary attributions are rock-solid evidence that caring for the sick, the poor, and the aged were valued by his contemporaries and Buddhist admirers, and Ashoka continues to serve as a beacon of social care in ancient India.

China

K'ung-tzu, better known today as Confucius (孔夫子, 551?–479 BCE), and his contemporary Laotzi (老子) each advocated for a relational approach to social order; that is, that the foundations of social order are based on each person knowing their place in relation to each other person within their cultural framework. These relationships were mostly hierarchical, with the social or political class 'above' and 'below' the person. This approach was developed to promote social harmony and stability and intended to call to mind the structure of the family.

Such a hierarchical approach and the goal of social harmony have implications for understanding poverty and the poor. Sometimes these approaches are called collectivist, but a more appropriate word would be relational (Baggini, 2018).[7] A Confucian approaches poverty first from a

---

[6] Ashoka's exploits and edicts are carved into rocks and pillars known as the Major and Minor Rock and Pillar Edicts. There are 14 Major Rock Edicts.

[7] 'Collectivist' (in English at least) implies a kind of amorphous social lump moving in a universally agreed direction; it would be hard to defend such a vision, since universal agreement on values and goals is unlikely at best in such very large societies. Using the

personal obligation perspective: 'One must first examine whether one has fulfilled his duties of one's role before blaming the social system as a cause to one's poverty. If one does not work hard and causes oneself to be poor, one should not expect any to help or show compassion' (Chan, 2018, p 54).

While a liberal humanist with a Calvinist or neoliberal-influenced perspective will focus on Chan's second sentence, which appears to emphasise the importance of self-determination and hard work, a Confucian approach will begin with the first sentence: it is by attending to the duties of one's relationships that one avoids poverty. If everyone attends to their relationships by showing compassion and helping where necessary, social harmony is maintained, and individual and social poverty is avoided. A Confucian perspective is the inverse of Maslow's hierarchy: the management of poverty focuses not so much on how to satisfy one's basic physical needs but on affirming the value of a person from a holistic perspective, in the context of their relationships. Unlike in the ancient Near East, or any of the examples we have seen in Western traditions, in a Confucian system it is the responsibility of the ruling authority to ensure social harmony by minimising the gap between the wealthy and the poor. In this way, the poor are protected but from entirely different motivations from those in Christian traditions. In the network of right relationships that characterises Confucianism, the notion of *ren* (仁), usually translated as 'benevolence' (Zheng, 2019), assumes that an individual is able to empathise or commiserate with, say, poor children because they cannot imagine their own children going without food.

Daoism (or Taoism) is a philosophical and spiritual system that relies on balance and harmony; the word Dao 道 means way, road, path, or flow. Together with Confucianism and Buddhism, Daoism is considered one of the three teachings that have shaped Chinese culture. The *Tao Te Ching* (prob. 4th century BCE) expounds on how human behaviour can maintain accord with the natural order of things; great things can be accomplished through small actions or even no action. Asians and non-Asians alike will be familiar with the *taijitu* (yin-yang) circular symbol of black and white (with a spot of each in the other for balance) that represents how the universe creates itself out of chaos and resulted in the balance of forces seen in nature. Daoism relies on naturalness, spontaneity, and individualism, and rejects the rituals, morality, and hierarchical social order of Confucianism (Maspero, 1981). Daoism has been called a religion with 'a spirit of charity and a heart of compassion' (Zhao, 2015, p 122). Zhao argues that Daoism is consistent with modern ideas of charity, including notions of human rights, conflict resolution, reconciliation, and the promotion of religious or racial harmony,

---

word 'relational' implies that attention is focused more on relationships than the aspirations of the individual self.

equality, and diversity. It emphasises the importance of personal wellbeing and also stresses harmonious relationships among individuals and between individuals and societies. To be 'poor' from a Daoist perspective does not merely refer to financial hardship but also the consequences of that hardship, including, for example, the inability to access education for employability or to function effectively in work or society. In modern social work terms, Daoism stresses the interconnectedness of the individual with the array of social institutions within their ecosystem. The central spirit of charity and heart of compassion of Daoism is strengthened by the Three Treasures.[8] Since humans share *qi* (气, life force) with all things, the principle of protecting the vulnerable and marginalised is integral to Daoism.

Although they appear ultimately to have dominated, Confucianism and Taoism were not the only philosophies of social care in China. While Confucianism held that one owed a stronger duty to one's family than to the emerging state, Legalism (promoted by Shang Yang 商鞅, d. 338 BCE, and Han Fei 韓非, d. 233 BCE) promoted a strong state. Legalists proposed to treat subjects of the state not as moral beings but as economic units (Fukuyama, 2011). Legalists, on whose foundation Mao Tse-Tung sought to construct his revolution two millennia later, delegitimised family morality, and instead relied on the strength of the ruler to bind the people together. Unlike India and the later Muslim world, however, China had no code of laws that stood independent of the emperor; care for the poor depended on the disposition and inclinations of elites. If peasants did not meet productivity quotas set by the land-owning lords, for instance, they were punished rather than assisted. It is hardly surprising, then, that Confucianism, with its relatively benign assertion of family loyalty, came to prevail for so many centuries.

Japan

Shintō (神道) is an indigenous, historic Japanese system of beliefs that acknowledges no founder, central authority, or specific texts. It is nonetheless Japan's largest system of beliefs. It has been described as polytheistic or even pantheistic and acknowledges *kami*, or divine entities that dwell in everything. Shintō seems to have emerged during the Yayoi period (300 BCE–300 CE) and became closely associated with Buddhism after Buddhism arrived in Japan. Its sources are also attributed to court rituals in the 7th century CE (Underwood, 1934/2013). Susumu (2009) writes that Shintō 'might be

---

[8] *Ci* (慈, kindness, or parental love), *jian* (俭, simplicity or thriftiness), and *bug an wei tian xia xian* (不敢为天下先, not leading the world, or restraint); some translations render these as compassion, moderation, and humility.

understood as a somewhat coherent system of practices and religious ideas united in the belief in the kami of the Japanese land' (p 99). In Shintō belief, *kami* are worshipped at household, family, and public shrines in order to maintain harmony between *kami*, humans, and the natural world. A *binbōgami* is a *kami* of poverty that brings poverty, illness, and misery to any household they visit or inhabit and are expelled through ritual.

During the isolationist Tokugawa (or Edo) period of early modern Japan (1603–1867 CE), poverty was a key source of instability and required a flexible and benign response from local rulers. Appropriate management of poverty was central to the stability of the regions throughout the country. During the Tokugawa period, regional rulers relied on an imported Confucian-style response to poor relief to their subjects in order to maintain social order (Ehlers, 2018). Strong social subgroups were formed based on, for example, village, block association, or occupation: not unlike many regions of Europe and the UK during the same period, a Japanese beggar was expected to belong to an approved group of beggars in order to beg. Confucian principles and responses to poverty are familiar from our previous considerations. The Meiji Restoration (1868–1912) that succeeded the Tokugawa era renovated Shintō beliefs to create what is now known as State Shintō. State Shintō, notes Susumu (2009), differs from historic Shintō and was formed by Meiji civil authorities as a way of disambiguating Shintō from Buddhism and Confucianism, uniting the Japanese people through emperor worship and a kind of national 'religion' and ritual. This is the period during which Shintō became generally regarded as a distinct system of belief. The history of the tension between the two forms of Shintō is complex and well-explored by Susumu and others.

African ubuntu and other indigenous cultural approaches

The indigenous sub-Sahara African notion of *ubuntu* – 'I am because we are' – has become so important to international social work that it became the focus of World Social Work Day (15 March) in 2021. *Ubuntu* is a notion that understands that social relationships are the primary good and the transcendent sources of value (Baggini, 2018, p 201). *Ubuntu* is inclusive and relies on consensus decision-making rather than majoritarian rule. The word *ubuntu* is not simply a static thing or quality, it is grammatically a 'gerundive', or an adjective based on action; it is being the self because of others and adapting to changing times. To express *ubuntu* is to affirm one's own humanity by recognising the humanity of others and by choosing the wellbeing of others over personal gain. *Ubuntu* is a moral quality of a person; one is not a person simply by virtue of one's birth but because one meets moral expectations, social obligations, and is connected to the community. Respect for both 'horizontal' relationships (those people, places, and traditions with whom we have connections in the present) and 'vertical' relationships (honoured ancestors who have come before and the children who will come after us) are evidence of *ubuntu*. In his reflections on South Africa's Truth and Reconciliation Commission, Nobel laureate Anglican Archbishop Desmond Tutu (2000) identified *ubuntu* as the essence of being human; *ubuntu* provides resilience and enables people to survive and emerge as human despite all efforts to dehumanise them. It not only takes a village to raise a child but to care for the entire family structure from birth to death and beyond. This relational approach to life is one reason why so many grandparents are caring for grandchildren orphaned because of HIV (Nkosinathi and Mtshali, 2015; Rutakumwa et al, 2015). *Ubuntu* has been identified as a way to address overwhelming and seemingly intractable poverty in southern Africa (Handongwe, 2017).[9]

Ubuntu also has a shadow side; conformity to dominant social norms (even when these norms were relatively recently imposed by colonising Europeans and their churches) is enforced by social sanction, stigma, gossip, and exclusion. People living with HIV, and gender and sexually diverse people know this only too well (Visser et al, 2009; Fletcher, 2016; Mohan, 2019). The treatment of mentally unwell persons in many African nations has also been the subject of local and international criticism (Adjovi, 2016). *Ubuntu* and its shadow also travel with diasporic African communities where these stigmas, particularly about HIV, remain powerful and controlling (Poindexter, 2013). In my own research, I spoke with a Black African woman of the diaspora who was living with HIV. She said she had to hide her medications under the floorboards in her bedroom for fear that neighbours or friends would come into her house at will (as they would expect to be able to do), come across the medications, and so learn of her HIV status. She could not bear the imagined consequences of social shame and stigma in her church and social community and so she concealed not only her medications but herself.

The notion of relationship as the foundation of a stable society, and in order to maintain social harmony (and not incidentally, social control) is not limited to Confucian-based, Daoist, and *ubuntu*-based cultures, of course. Indigenous cultures throughout the world foreground relationships, interdependence, mutual care, and maintaining social harmony. In Pasifika cultures, for instance, the *aiga* (Samoan) or *kāinga* (Tongan and Tuvaluan; other Pacific languages have cognates) refer not merely to the 'immediate' or nuclear family (as it would in most Western societies) but to the larger extended family, including in-laws and distant cousins (Filoiali'i and Knowles,

---

[9] The East African Regional Resource Centre at Makerere University in Kampala, Uganda was launched in June 2021 and promises to be an important resource for social workers and social work educators.

1983); the behaviour of one member reflects on the entire group. Rituals such as *ifoga* – adopted by other legal systems around the world as restorative justice – were developed in order to maintain peaceful relationships among *aiga*, villages, and islands. *Mihi whakatau* (introductions) in *pōwhiri* (welcome ceremonies) among Māori in Aotearoa New Zealand begin with identifying one's *whakapapa* (a kind of genealogy) that identify one's mountain, one's river, the canoe in which one's ancestors arrived, one's founding ancestors, one's *turangawaewae* (the land or place where one was born or brought up), and important *iwi* (tribal), *hāpū* (sub-tribal), and *whānau* (kin) affiliations: the speaker introduces themselves in relationship to the land, their ancestors, and their extended family. By locating themself in this nexus of relationships, the speaker identifies where and to whom they belong. Similarly, Indigenous Australians and Torres Straits Islanders identify the importance of land, culture, spirituality, ancestry, family, and community (Nasir et al, 2021) in maintaining what Westerns call mental health, and what others might call balance or harmony. As we noted in earlier chapters, it was colonisation and the accompanying missionisation that disrupted these relationships, separating indigenous peoples from their lands, roots, and peoples and creating imbalance. This imbalance allowed the colonial powers more easily to maintain control.

Decolonising social work globally

In the last several decades, social work has attended to these imbalances with liberal humanist models of intervention, often modelled on North Atlantic psychological principles. Hwang (2009) however, has noted that such mental health interventions are rooted in three core values:

> [F]irst, the egocentricity of the self, which conceptualizes individuals as autonomous and self-contained units of action whose behaviors are determined by one's configuration of personality traits and internal attributes; second, mind–body dualism, which separates psychological problems from physical problems; and, third, culture as a set of beliefs superimposed a posteriori on an invariant bedrock reality of biology. (p 932)

He notes that each of these values are not facts but culture-bound assumptions (he also calls these assumptions scientific racism) that may not apply in non-Western cultures. While Hwang was speaking of counselling in North America, he could just as appropriately be describing models of social work in liberal Western nations and cultures. Using Western theories (or diagnoses) to create Western interventions to address problems created by Western colonisers in indigenous communities is not an appropriate pathway forward.

Rather, restoring relationships to lands, roots, and extended families lies at the heart of social work with indigenous peoples in any post-colonial setting. The notion of working with an individual separate from their family group, for instance, is literally a foreign concept to relational cultures and results in disrupted communications, delayed decisions, and disappointing outcomes for all concerned. To reconceptualise a 'client' as an entire family group, however, also means reconceptualising notions of privacy, confidentiality, autonomy, self-determination, and other individuated values that liberal humanist social workers have valorised as essential. For a social worker educated in Western theories to step into a relational world means adopting entirely different epistemological, ethical, and even ontological ('I am because we are') frameworks. In post-colonial societies, most laws and social norms are still shaped by the legacies of European and North Atlantic colonial powers, and this disempowerment perpetuates colonial laws, expectations, and violence on indigenous peoples. What this means is that social workers in both colonising and colonised nations must undergo the difficult process of becoming aware of the invidious residue of colonialism and missionisation (Bennett, 2015; Huygens, 2011) and learn new ways of thinking, working, educating, and researching (Gray et al, 2013/2016; Watene, 2016; Ravulo et al, 2019; Mooney et al, 2020).

Much of this work is well underway in social work today but mostly in formerly colonised societies. There has been only incipient awareness in coloniser societies of the impact of their legacies. For instance, while social workers in European coloniser nations may claim that the notion of indigenous peoples is irrelevant to them, they ignore the reality that they have hegemonised indigenous peoples in their colonial pasts. By ignoring that reality, they sustain and perpetuate that colonial past into the present day.

In case you are not yet convinced of the urgency or relevance of this argument, let's look at some population data. Admittedly, population data are only estimates at moments in time, and estimates are influenced by any number of factors including population movements, politics, and most recently, COVID-19. But the numbers I've included in the tables that follow are consensus estimates compiled from readily available public sources.

To these estimates, we need to add an estimate of Black Africans, both in Africa (an estimated 81 per cent of 1.37 billion people on the continent, or about 1.11 billion people) and in the African diaspora (an additional 140 million), giving us an additional 1.5 billion. Finally, the World Bank estimates that there are about 500 million indigenous peoples around the world. All these estimates together (the totals of Tables 9.1 and 9.2, plus Black Africans, plus indigenous peoples) gives us a rough estimate of 5.59 billion people in these populations or 71.6 per cent of the estimated global population of 7.8 billion. That is a lot of people who do not share Western ways of knowing.

Table 9.1: Global non-Abrahamic religious adherents

Hindu	1.2 b
Sikh	30 m
Jain	6 m
Buddhist	535 m
Shintō	104 m
Taoist	12 m
Total	**1.88 b**

Table 9.2: Population estimate of Confucian-influenced countries

PR China	1.4 b
Chinese Taipei (ROC)	23.6 m
Hong Kong	7.5 m
Macau	0.64 m
Republic of Korea	51.7 m
Japan	126.3 m
Vietnam	96.5 m
Singapore	5.7 m
Total	**1.71 b**

Global social work today

The 2014 *Global Definition of Social Work* was the first major revision of how social work defines itself in over 20 years. There was extensive consultation over about four years in order to produce a concise and readily translatable statement. Regional and national social work associations were encouraged to meet and contribute what they felt were essential elements of a global definition and, in the end, a layered definition with a core, stable, high-level definition with opportunities for regional and national amplifications was adopted by the IASSW and IFSW. 'Indigenous knowledges' were acknowledged for the first time, and also for the first time 'social harmony' was included in a social work definition, in order to attend to the development of social work in Confucian-influenced East Asian societies and their cultural and political concerns (the full definition can be found in Chapter 1). An accompanying commentary explained the new language and provided a rationale for the changes (International Association of Schools of Social Work and International Federation of Social Work, 2014). The new *Global Definition* was not uncontroversial. Latin American social workers, for instance, felt that it did not go far enough to challenge oppressive state regimes, and German social workers felt that the idea of 'indigenous' was irrelevant to them and sought to exclude it entirely from their version.

The adoption of this new, layered definition of social work, together with the development of social work in East Asian and post-colonial and indigenous regions, required a new understanding of social work ethics and a new code of ethics that did not simply reflect Western values. Consultation occurred in much the same way as the 2014 *Global Definition*. The *Global Social Work Statement of Ethical Principles* (*GSWSEP*)[10] was approved (although in slightly different versions) in mid-2018 by the two international bodies. Traditional liberal humanist concepts such as self-determination, autonomy, and independence are de-emphasised in the *GSWSEP*, and, instead, human dignity was placed at the core. Since human dignity is mutable and often culturally determined, there is greater flexibility in cultural interpretation and practice than in previous ethics statements. The *Global Definition* and *GSWSEP* reflect an overall shift in international social work away from liberal humanist frameworks and ontologies, towards language and underpinning philosophies that are more readily adopted by non-Western cultures and nations. They recognise that the centre of gravity of social work has now relocated from the North Atlantic axis and Europe and become much more diffuse.

At the same time, Asian, African, indigenous, and other social workers in a post-colonial world must ask if these innovations went far enough. Is there sufficient scope even within the layered 2014 *Global Definition* to reflect the astonishing diversity of global worldviews that inform contemporary social work?

Even in nations where direct European colonisation did not occur, there is concern about the ways that contemporary social work and its definitions appear to replicate a colonising approach to impose a particular kind of social work. There is a contemporary movement in Asia to define a 'Buddhist social work' (Akimoto and Hattori, 2017; Gohori, 2019). One of the three working definitions of Buddhist social work reads,

> Buddhist Social Work is human activities to help other people solve or alleviate life difficulties and problems based on the Buddha-nature. Buddhist Social Work always finds causes to work on in the material, or social arena, as well as in the human, or inner, arena, working on both arenas in tandem. Its fundamental principles include compassion, lovingkindness, and mutual help, and interdependency and self-reliance.

---

[10] You'll need to look this up online at https://www.iassw-aiets.org/global-social-work-statement-of-ethical-principles-iassw/ or https://www.ifsw.org/global-social-work-statement-of-ethical-principles/ for the IFSW version; it is quite lengthy.

> The central value is the Five Precepts.[11] The ultimate goal is to achieve the well-being of all sentient beings and peace. (Akimoto, 2021)

This preferred working definition of Buddhist social work rejects 'Western-rooted professional social work' and perceives, as we have seen quite rightly, that in contemporary understandings and international definitions of social work (specifically, the 2014 *Global Definition*) one could read '"individualism", "modernism", and "Christianity" between the lines' (Akimoto et al, 2019, p 63). This argument holds that Buddhist monks have been 'doing the same or similar work for 2,500 years while [Western-rooted professional social work] has only done so for 150–200 years … although [Buddhist monks] haven't used the term "social work"' (p 65). This epistemological dissonance is a core issue at the heart of the challenge of creating a global social work. However, it must be said that Buddhist monks have been performing social care for 2,500 years in the same way that Jewish and ancient Near Eastern traditions have been performing social care for roughly the same time and Christians since the time of Constantine. None of these is social work as we understand it today, but all are a kind of social care, reaching out to the sick, the poor, the aged, the widow, the orphan, and the marginalised. Akimoto et al (2019) argue that any construction of social work as 'indigenous' is simply to put a local face on a discipline fundamentally shaped by Western epistemology. I am sympathetic to this point of view, but I am not yet prepared to abandon the notion of a global social care or social work undertaking. What social workers and their international organisations must now do is critically consider how we arrived at the current situation and what the forces are that shaped our current understandings of social work.

Even though our focus here is on global social work, these considerations cannot help but have flow-on effects on national, regional, and local social work practice. Contemporary discussions about racialisation and critical race theory, for instance, born from experiences of violent oppression and an emancipatory movement that challenges continuing internal national colonialism and privilege, are important sources of conscientisation for social workers at all levels and fields of practice. To be sure, most front-line social workers are mostly occupied with overly heavy caseloads or workloads and have little time or interest in a social work practice agenda beyond the borders of their own countries or regions. What national, regional, and international associations can do is support social work practitioners, educators, and researchers to lift their gazes beyond the immediate crises

---

[11] These are to refrain from taking life, to refrain from taking what is not given, to refrain from misuse of the senses or sexual misconduct, to refrain from wrong speech, and to refrain from using other intoxicants that cloud the mind.

in front of them, and to recognise that creating a comprehensive, global profession of social work will benefit not only them but more importantly the lives of the marginalised and vulnerabilised people they seek to serve.

I am confident in both the process and the outcome of the 2014 *Global Definition*; it was a lengthy and highly consultative process, which resulted in major changes to the definition of social work and created a layered approach, the very notion of a static, unitary definition. Nevertheless, the 2014 definition should only be seen as a temporary oasis, a waystation on a critical journey to greater inclusiveness. Social workers around the world now have the opportunity and the tools to interrogate their assumptions about social care and social work and to unpack the influences of the many theologies, philosophies, and anthropologies that have contributed to contemporary understandings of social care and social work. Research that replicates and reinforces a business-as-usual approach to social work is not sufficient to create a global understanding of social work. Modernist (and even post-modern) research is heavily skewed to liberal humanist knowledge, reviewed by reviewers who share that modernist mindset, most of it published in English-language journals of relatively limited circulation, in quite rigidly set formats, to which researchers and practitioners alike are required to conform or be silenced. Unless we are sufficiently talented to read multiple languages, it is unlikely that we read research or theoretical publications in any language other than our own primary language. This means that social work knowledge is largely self-replicating and self-reinforcing, and while there are doubtless innovations in the field, much work is produced mostly for an audience of academics or professional promotions panels rather than to further the emancipation of oppressed and marginalised persons from oppression and unsatisfactoriness in their lives. These processes only constrain the full potential of social care that has existed for thousands of years in all the societies we know about.

I am also very mindful that notions of emancipation and critical theory risk disrupting the social harmony advocated by the global perspectives we have been considering in this chapter. What the heroes of these philosophies have discovered is that the illusion of social harmony is not true harmony and can be maintained only through greater control and oppression. A benevolent ruler is flexible, tolerant, compassionate, inclusive, and attentive to the needs of even the poorest and most marginalised people. True social harmony does not need to impose social order. True social harmony values the humanity of every person even when every effort has been made to dehumanise them, and in that way can ensure social stability. Social stability is a shared goal of all systems of social care through the millennia.

10

Creating a global future

In these pages, we have travelled thousands of years and around much of the world to canvass the origins of social care and social work. A goal of this book has been to make the historical influences that implicitly inform contemporary Western social work explicit and available for critique. By understanding those influences, we can understand how we got to where we are now, and that understanding in turn can help social workers around the world to create the kind of social work we want for the future. Some social historians have argued that contemporary Western social work was enabled by the Reformation and the Enlightenment. I have contended that the seeds of social care were planted at least a millennium earlier in 4th century Byzantium, and two millennia earlier if we consider ancient Near Eastern codes and practices. Historically in the Christian West, at various times, both wealth and poverty have been theologically constructed as problems to be addressed. Social work in the 21st century has been informed by those histories. While the present study has focused mostly on the North Atlantic axis and (for better or worse) its global influence, beliefs and models from East and South Asian, Islamic, African, and other indigenous contexts must be more widely understood around the world, and particularly by social workers who practise from a North Atlantic axis-informed worldview. Different worldviews have much to learn from each other and can do so if each approaches the conversation with humility and respect and in good faith. Practitioners of social care of all sorts are informed by altruism, and, at the risk of over-generalising, I think all of us seek some form of just societies that ensure every member can access a full measure of the social benefits available in that society. In our increasingly globalised age, we need now to consider a 'global society' as much as we have in the past considered collections of local societies. The consequences of the extreme gap between the very wealthy and the very poor, sustainability, the climate crisis, and global pandemics have highlighted the urgency of the global challenges we face in the 21st century.

This chapter looks forward to the future of social work as a mature and perhaps global discipline. It is not my intention to be prescriptive here because many voices must be heard, and for a Western social worker to propose a direction for global social work would simply reproduce the very coloniality I have critiqued. Nevertheless, some obvious fundamentals must be addressed before we can establish a platform to consider a global future for social work. These fundamentals include the decolonisation agenda and dialogue between colonising powers and colonised territories; deciding whether social stability and individual emancipation can coexist as goals within the same discipline; and whether social work should (or can) evolve into a global profession. Asian, Islamic, African, and indigenous colleagues, along with many voices in the West have made it clear that social work practitioners, educators, and researchers can no longer simply graft a global veneer onto what are essentially Western social work epistemologies and methods and call them 'international'. Nor is it adequate to talk about international social work as if it were some kind of Hydra (the multi-headed beast of Greek mythology) – or its Chinese counterpart the *Xiangliu* – that appears and is practised differently in various countries and territories around the world. This Hydra approach is confusing to non-social workers and social workers alike, and particularly to politicians and international organisations. While such approaches may attempt to avoid the coloniality problem, in fact, they merely put it off. How can social workers explain to others what it is that we do, or what our disciplinary contribution is to knowledge and human wellbeing if what we do looks so very different around the world? How can social work have a credible voice at international organisations, or be invited to sit at their tables, if it is not clear what it is that social work as a discipline brings to those tables? Non-social workers with private agendas and perhaps less altruistic motivations move into the helping space – how hard can it be to dish out soup? – and prove Flexner right, that there is no unique knowledge base required to 'help people'. Polman (2010), for instance, shines a light on the way many international aid organisations respond to crises, using the publicity from these crises to generate income to support their own organisations and to create dependent local populations in post-crisis economies. Religious organisations promote their food banks, soup kitchens, shelters, and other social assistance programmes; they at least have historical precedent behind them, although they are unlikely to have the capacity to provide what we now understand as comprehensive social work services.

In large part, thanks to our history over the last 150 years, we know that the work of social workers (in the West) is to undertake a complete analysis of social and environmental inequalities, ensure that the policy context enables access to sufficient resources, and empower people to create and enact their own solutions. That we do many different things in many different contexts is both our greatest strength and our greatest weakness as a discipline. Our credibility as a discipline is at stake. Global definitions and statements of ethics are certainly steps in the right direction, but these remain contentious and should be considered as progress rather than as destinations. If social workers in one country can practise with no knowledge of what social workers in another country are doing, or worse, disregard or dismiss what they are doing, then how can they be part of the same undertaking? Ahead of us is the hard work of identifying, naming, and critiquing the implicit assumptions that shape the imaginary that social work has inherited from Christian-informed Western theologians, politicians, educators, innovators, and practitioners who have gone before. In that way, we will be prepared to engage with other epistemologies and worldviews.

What excites me is that I believe social work is now on the cusp of being able to have these discussions.

The origins of social care and social work

The origins of social care are ancient and began as the responsibility of the ruler and the political elites as a way of demonstrating political power and generosity by protecting the poor. This demonstration of power had the additional advantage to the state of maintaining social order. In the Christian West, beginning in the 4th century CE, Roman imperial authorities in Byzantium, and eventually throughout the empire, maintained social order through the expectation that the Christian Church would provide care to the widow, the orphan, the sick, the poor, and other marginalised persons, keep them out of the sight of the wealthy, and ensure they created no public disturbance through begging or rioting. In exchange for legitimacy and fiscal independence, the Christian Church created a category of poor, problematised wealth, and took up the responsibility for managing the poor for the next thousand years. Caring for the poor was caring for Christ. From the mid-14th century, civic authorities took on that responsibility because the church no longer had the resources to manage the massively increased numbers requiring assistance due to population mobility caused by the Great Plague. Those civic authorities adopted whole cloth the theology and methods of the church and largely retained the infrastructure of the delivery of care through the churches. The Christian Church in the West split in 1053 and fragmented further during the Reformation, and the new, reformed theologies of the poor became more punitive. With the rise of Calvinism, it was the glory of God through hard work and industriousness that were idealised, and wealth came to be understood as a divine blessing. The wealthy were deemed blessed, and poverty was problematised as divine disfavour. Social care evolved from an expectation during the first millennium CE to a kind of right for the worthy under European poor laws, and finally to a privilege that had to be earned, through work, good character, or good behaviour. Social control of the poor and enforcing moral norms remained key features of social care during these 1,500 years.

As the burden of caring for the poor increased and available resources were diverted to wars and profit-making, civic authorities increasingly adopted more restrictive approaches to social care, shaped by Reformed theologies. These theologies were exported from Europe around the world through global exploration, exploitation, and colonisation in the 17th and 18th centuries. Following the financial crisis in the UK brought about by the Napoleonic Wars in the early 19th century, the Oriel Noetics of Oxford University – virtue-driven rationalist political economists, politicians, and church leaders who were well known to each other – shaped the theoretical and economic foundations of the Poor Law Amendment Act. The origins of social work as we know it today in the West are found in the mid-late 19th century as the result of a counter-theological response to the 1834 reform. This response, ironically but not coincidentally, also emerged from Oxford University and its dons and theology graduates – F.D. Maurice, T.H. Green, and Samuel Barnett – and the women who shared their theological convictions – Octavia Hill, Helen Bosanquet, Henrietta (Rowland) Barnett, and Beatrice Webb – and who recognised from their first-hand experience that it was not laziness nor lack of virtue nor other individual failings that led to poverty but social inequalities. Helen Bosanquet is probably the first writer to use the term social work in her history of the Charity Organisation Society, but the belief that structural solutions to poverty lay in bridging the enormous divide between the elites and the poor informed the development of the COS and settlement houses in both the UK and US. The formalisation of the training and education of social workers meant that an occupation was born as volunteers were replaced by paid workers. Thanks to Virginia Robinson and her post-First World War advocacy for Freud's psychoanalytic approach, social work in the US took quite a different course than in the UK, a difference that was made even greater by the nationalisation of health and social services in the UK after the Second World War. The emergence and dominance of neoliberal economic policies in the Thatcher-Reagan era ensured that Reformed theologies about the poor were resurrected in social policies and social services not only in the UK and US but also in their economic spheres of influence around the world. Neoliberal constructions of the poor continue to dominate. In our own era of vast income inequalities, this perspective may be shifting once again to understanding that the concentration of global wealth in the private accounts of the 1 per cent may not be in the best interests of the other 99 per cent of humanity.

Teach and learn history

In order to create a global future for social work, social workers must understand the influences that shaped the theory and practice of the discipline. For many good-hearted progressives, social work has become a kind of screen on which is projected all their hopes for their versions of equitable and just societies. It cannot be so, for these two-dimensional projections can uncritically ignore the history of social work to fit individual agendas and local hopes. That has resulted in the current fragmented state of the discipline, which is inevitably dominated by Western, liberal humanist social imaginaries. We have seen that in the West, historical contexts have largely been shaped by the dominant Christian theologies of the time, whether Cappadocian, Calvinist, or Christian Socialist. Even the putatively secularist Enlightenment was formed in response to a Christian social imaginary. In other parts of the world, social care has been shaped by other social imaginaries, whether Hindu, Buddhist, Confucian, Taoist, Islam, ubuntu, indigenous, and others. Who provides care, who receives care, the extent of that care, and the nature of that care have evolved over history. In the West, those theologies have not disappeared; they have, however, become so much a part of our contemporary social imaginary, adopted by states from the church that we are no longer critically aware of them and we unmindfully reproduce them in our work and our global dialogues.

We can understand and critique contemporary social imaginaries by understanding how they evolved in history. The history of social care and social work should be an essential part of all social work and social policy curricula. Only by understanding that history will student social workers understand why politicians require people receiving public assistance to apply for work, undertake education, take and pass drug tests, prove that they are disabled, or that they are otherwise worthy poor, raise their children in certain ways, behave in socially acceptable ways, and act as grateful recipients of a social privilege. These are not new expectations: they emerged historically in response to particular theological constructions of individual salvation and worth and are sustained in civic theologies of the poor. Innovative responses to poverty and social inequalities such as a universal basic income are dismissed by policymakers today largely based on Calvinist and Noetic constructions of the poor as unworthy or lazy, and who must somehow prove their worthiness. In an era when social and global inequalities are unimaginably large, and the ownership of wealth is increasingly restricted to a very few elites, we need to consider whether we wish to perpetuate the Noetic response to the poor or to recall that the roots of contemporary social work are found in the practical critique of that response. These theological constructions are often generalised to entire nations whose poverty is seen as a failure of the people to be industrious and productive rather than as the result of, say, the plundering of the nation's resources and peoples by European traders, slavers, and colonial governments. We must choose whether to problematise poverty or problematise wealth. Understanding that history will help us to understand and make informed choices in the present.

Decolonise

Once we have understood how completely integrated a Reformed and even Evangelical Christian theology of the poor is into Western social imaginaries, civic theologies, and social policies, we can – and must – interrogate social work's relationship to these religious roots. Social workers cannot maintain these implicit theological assumptions in cultures where these assumptions have never been part of the social imaginaries. That is what happened during colonisation, when Europeans hegemonised local cultures, either by missionising them, imposing moral standards (such as the infamous Section 377 in British-occupied South Asian nations), race codes, reconstructed notions of caste, and forced local cultures into economically dependent relationships. Social work has been complicit in promulgating these hegemonic values. A decade ago, Dominelli (2012, p 51) wrote about social work's 'historical legacy of oppressing indigenous and other marginalised groups'. She proposed that one way to reverse that legacy is by developing a professional voice, independent of states or corporations. In order to counter that hegemonic legacy, of course, social work as a global discipline must agree that it should globalise, professionalise, and be independent of states and other influences.

Led by indigenous scholars and activists, the process of decolonising is underway in many parts of the globe, although decolonisation is not the same thing as indigenisation. Indigenisation must be led by indigenous peoples in indigenous contexts, although decolonisation will be an inevitable part of that process. Decolonisation is a process that can – and must – occur in both colonised and coloniser nations. Regrettably, the truly traditional histories of some colonised nations, history before European traders, colonisers, and missionaries, have become hazy, or suppressed because they were transmitted orally. These nations and peoples have adopted coloniser values as their own 'traditions' (the legal codes and moral stance of many post-colonial Pacific Island, South Asian, African, Caribbean, and even Arab nations towards gender and sexual diversity is an obvious example). But these traditional histories have not been entirely lost, and they are beginning to re-emerge. Nations with a history of colonising cannot say 'we have no indigenous people, therefore indigeneity is not our concern' as some European nations have. Facing the difficult parts of their colonial history is as much a responsibility of colonising and slaving nations as it is among colonised peoples. In some nations, truth and reconciliation commissions, tribunals, and other bodies are hearing testimony, offering apologies, making legislative changes where necessary, and restitution where possible.

Contemporary social work practitioners, educators, and researchers must attend to these decolonising processes, advocate for them, and participate in them in their own national settings. International, regional, and national social work associations need to consider how they can foreground decolonisation (and indigenisation) in their memberships, in their agendas, and in their ways of enacting those agendas. Capacity building, education, and development support cannot be provided without a clear understanding of how such activities can perpetuate colonialism or can work to address it, or as Buddhist social work scholars have said, being aware of colonialism, imperialism, and hegemonism. Well-intended support from educational institutions from the North Atlantic axis for social work programmes in developing nations must not simply export Western-style social work theories, practices, and research methods. We have seen that Western, individualist worldviews are not native to nearly three quarters of the global population. Yet Western nations control much of the financial and human resources and the global media that promote Western values, and it will take great courage to relinquish control of those resources in favour of local direction. Programmes and support should not be provided by international associations without also providing opportunities for developing countries to participate fully (not tokenistically) as equals on boards and planning bodies.

None of this will happen quickly, nor will it be a 'one-and-done' effort. Decolonising is an ongoing and iterative process. It will be painful as traditional leaders and their peoples recognise how much has been suppressed or lost. It must be done with courage, humility, and respect, and results may take a generation or more.

Social control

Another significant issue that must be considered by social workers and their international associations is how or whether social cohesion, empowerment, and liberation – specified in the 2014 *Global Definition* – can coexist as goals. Is it possible to talk about social cohesion without social control? Social cohesion, social stability, individual empowerment, and liberation can coexist, of course, but these words and ideas mean many things in different cultural contexts, and each could be understood as threatening to governments, economies, and social stability. Concepts such as human rights can be interpreted quite differently in relational cultures and belief systems that valorise the wider social good, or even the dignity and authority of ancestors over that of the individual. Whether social workers can legitimately act as agents of social control on behalf of states must be considered carefully. Of course, qualified social workers will have valuable skills that can be used by social control agencies such as prisons, probation, and child protection, but whether being employed by these agencies and acting on their behalf is consistent with empowerment and liberation must be assessed.

The issue of social control also requires that social work as a discipline address and resolve its relationship with states. Does the occupation of social work wish to be a servant of the state, ceding regulatory authority to states and accepting scopes of practice, codes of conduct, and educational and ethical requirements established by states? Or do social workers and their associations wish greater or complete autonomy in order to speak with an independent voice? Can social workers, for instance, claim title protection (enforceable only through state legislation and legal sanctions) and autonomy in the same breath? Can social workers employed by a state agency hold that agency accountable for obvious abuses of authority or negligence? What about so-called re-education camps, or governments that construct political dissent as a mental health problem? Recognition of an occupation or profession is usually construed as legitimacy, but that construction may not be shared by indigenous peoples for whom the authority of the tribe, clan, or moiety has a greater claim than that of the state. It may not yet be possible to have a consistent solution globally since social work as an occupation is at such different stages of development in countries and territories around the world. These legal, moral, and ethical questions will not be resolved quickly, but if we do not ask them, we will never get started on the answers.

The question of profession

We have also seen that contemporary social work is neither global nor is it everywhere a profession. In the admittedly conservative criteria I set out in Chapter 8, we saw that social work meets some of these criteria in some places around the world, most of them in a few places, and all of them in none. Social work is not even an occupation recognised in all countries. Is notionalising social work as a profession useful? I have proposed that it is, if only because of the implications for a women-dominated profession and a profession that deliberately seeks to work with marginalised and disempowered persons. It may be that social work is a new kind of profession that is a hybrid of existing ideas about what a profession is or looks like. This is a decision that must be considered internationally as well as nationally. I am not proposing that social workers should look the same and do the same thing everywhere; being professional or consistent does not mean being identical. Criteria for an internationalised profession of social work (and education that leads to that status) will need to be established in a way that balances local understandings and practices with key features of international social work documents and what is common across nations. If professionalising is a goal for one nation, it must be so for all. That will require an enormous, coordinated international effort.

The question about the professionalisation undertaking also raises questions about the nature of the occupation of social work. Should social work – as occupation or profession – be defined so carefully and narrowly that only a relatively few highly qualified persons in only a relatively few countries meet the criteria? That would expose the occupation to accusations of elitism and make a social work career available only to those who have the resources to access social work education programmes. Or must we define social work so broadly that eligibility workers, child protection workers, youth workers, community and social development workers, tribal and other community-designated workers as well as educationally qualified and accredited social workers are included in an umbrella notion of social work? How do such definitions fit into the idea of professionalisation? Cox and Pawar (2013, p 549) set out a thoughtful scheme of a three-tiered social work structure – a social work assistant, social work graduate, and senior social worker who provides leadership across the profession – and what issues need to be addressed at each stage of education for the three different tiers. Each would require a different structure of training or education. Yet it does not appear that this structure is in development, and there remains little consistency internationally in the social work curriculum. If we do not know where we are going, then anywhere will do. And nowhere in particular is where we are now.

Create a global future

In order to create a global future for social work, it will be necessary to marshal the resources and commitment of social workers, educators, and researchers around the world, and their local, national, regional, and international organisations. Only the existing international associations are likely to have the infrastructure and resources to do this. The precedent has been set for such collaborations in undertakings like the *Global Agenda for Social Work and Social Development* (International Association of Schools of Social Work, International Federation of Social Work, and International Council on Social Welfare, 2012) and its successor documents. In their work on the *Global Agenda*, the international associations attended to such critical international issues as social and economic inequality, the dignity and worth of peoples, environmental sustainability, and human relationships. These initiatives and collaborations have mostly been issue-focused, and they have been largely passive in that they set an agenda and encourage national and local organisations to take up the challenge.

To create a global future for social work these organisations will need to recover their founding purposes and principles and turn their attentions to the enterprise of social work itself. I am not suggesting that they move fast and break things, but they must move beyond the fear of moving too quickly. Over the next decade, international and regional organisations will need to enhance trust, create broad international and intersectional consensus, and establish a framework to address the questions I have identified earlier. They will need to reconsider a global definition of social work; address decolonisation and Western privilege; come to a consensus on the questions of professionalism, statements of ethics, and educational curricula; and tackle such thorny issues as gender equality, gender and sexual diversity, natural and human rights, and democracy (this is not an exhaustive list!), where there is now a great diversity of national law, cultural values, and other social presses that have stymied international consensus. Such a process should not be dominated by any theology, epistemology, groups, or individuals. Perhaps it should not even be carried out in English, the usual language of international proceedings, or any European language since these languages are freighted with Western assumptions. These consultations will need to include not only social workers but also other stakeholders, including regulatory and political authorities, people from communities who access social work services, and allied professions such as nursing, psychology, medicine, and occupational therapy (for example) to clarify how the scopes of practice and research of these disciplines interface with each other.

Such a process will be neither smooth nor swift. The process of developing the existing 78-word *Global Definition of Social Work* took four years, and the *Global Social Work Statement of Ethical Principles* was an even bumpier process. These processes will require open minds and open hearts. Everyone should expect to be heard, but inevitably all stakeholders will need to make compromises and concessions if the goal is a global future for social work.

This book has offered a way to understand why social work in the present looks as it does. With that understanding social workers can with greater awareness choose to retain what is valuable about the past, change or discard what is no longer useful, in order to create an intentional global future for social work. Social workers around the world are now positioned to create their own collective future, one based on its agreed values and principles, not one that uncritically perpetuates theologies or principles handed to them long ago by church or civic authorities. National social workers can continue along the diverse paths that have been shaped by their histories; or they can co-create a shared vision of a new kind of profession. A shared vision will allow social workers to create a richer, more diverse, and less hegemonic profession, and truly to engage people and structures to address life challenges and enhance wellbeing around the world.

References

Abramovitz, M. (2014) 'Economic crises, neoliberalism, and the US welfare state: trends, outcomes and political struggle', in Noble, C., Strauss, H., and Littlechild, B. (eds) *Global social work: crossing borders, blurring boundaries*, Sydney: Sydney University Press, pp 225-240.

Activist New York. (2016) *Houses of welcome: the Settlement House Movement 1886–1925* [Online]. Museum of the City of New York. Available from: https://activistnewyork.mcny.org/exhibition/immigration/settlement (Accessed 15 March 2021).

Addams, J. (1910/2011) *Twenty years at Hull House*, Seattle, WA: Pacific Publishing Studio.

Adjovi, L. (2016) *Gregoire Ahongbong: freeing people chained for being ill*, BBC News [Online]. Available from: http://www.bbc.com/news/magazine-35586177 (Accessed 11 April 2016).

Akimoto, T. (2021) Buddhist social work. *Asian Research Institute for International Social Work [ARIISW] 5th International Academic Forum on Decolonization, Indigenization, Spirituality and Buddhist Social Work: Social work academics resisting the globalization of Western-rooted social work.* Chiba, Japan.

Akimoto, T. and Hattori, M. (2017) The working definition of Buddhist social work, in Akimoto, T. and Hattori, M. (eds) *Working definition and current curricula of Buddhist social work*, Hanoi, Vietnam. Asian Research Institute for International Social Work.

Akimoto, T., Fujimori, Y., Gohori, J., and Matsuo, K. (2019) Objection to Western-rooted professional social work: to make social work something truly of the world indigenization is not the answer, in Gohori, J. (ed) 4th International Academic Forum on Buddhist Social Work, 2019 Tokyo, Japan. Asian Research Institution for International Social Work, pp 62–72.

Aldrich, R. (2003) *Colonialism and homosexuality*, London: Routledge.

Alford, W.P., Winston, K., and Kirby, W.C. (eds) (2011) *Prospects for the professions in China*, Oxford: Routledge.

Almanzor, A.C. (1966) 'The profession of social work in the Philippines', *International Social Work*, pp 27–34.

Ambrose (2002) *De Officiis*, Oxford: Oxford University Press.

Ambrosino, R., Ambrosino, R., Heffernan, J., and Shuttlesworth, G. (2008) *Social work and social welfare: an introduction*, Belmont, CA: Brooks/Cole.

Ames, G.J. (2008) *The globe encompassed: the age of European discovery, 1500–1700*, New York: Pearson.

Anstey, R. (1979) 'Slavery and the Protestant ethic', in Craton, M. (ed) *Roots and Branches: current directions in slave studies*, Toronto, ONT: Pergamon Press.

Armfield, F.L. (2014) *Eugene Kinckle Jones: the National Urban League and Black social work, 1910–1940*, Champaign, IL: University of Illinois Press.

References

Armstrong, K. (1993) *A history of God*, New York: Ballantine Books.

Aspalter, C. (2014) 'Introduction', in C. Aspalter (ed) *Social work in East Asia*, Abingdon: Routledge.

Avis, P. (2002) *Anglicanism and the Christian church*, Edinburgh: T&T Clark.

Baggini J. (2018) *How the world thinks*, London: Granta.

Bamford, T. and Bilton, K. (eds) (2020) *Social work: past, present and future*, Bristol: Policy Press.

Barnett, H. (1918) *Canon Barnett, his life, work and friends*, London: John Murray.

Baskerville, J. and Hansen, A.R. (2018) 'Poverty and the poor in the Buddhist tradition', in Brackney, W.H. and Das, R. (eds) *Poverty and the poor in the world's religious traditions: religious responses to the problem of poverty*, Santa Barbara, CA: Praeger/ABC-CLIO.

Bayly, S. (1999) *Caste, society and politics in India from the eighteenth century to the modern age*, Cambridge: Cambridge University Press.

BBC News. (2006) *Church apologises for slave trade* [Online]. Available from: http://news.bbc.co.uk/2/hi/uk_news/4694896.stm (Accessed 10 January 2021).

BBC News. (2017) *Bias against ethnic minorities 'needs to be tackled' in justice system* [Online]. Available from: https://www.bbc.com/news/uk-41191311 (Accessed 9 April 2021).

Bennett, B. (2015) '"Stop deploying your white privilege on me!" Aboriginal and Torres Strait Islander engagement with the Australian Association of Social Workers', *Australian Social Work*, 68, pp 19–31.

Bernard, G.W. (2011) 'The dissolution of the monasteries', *History*, 96, pp 390–409. doi: 10.1111/j.1468-229X.2011.00526.x

Beveridge, W.H. (1942) *Social insurance and allied services*, London: His Majesty's Stationery Office.

Beveridge, W.H. (1944/2015) *Full employment in a free society*, Oxford: Routledge.

Birnbaum, J.H. (1997, December 8) 'Washington's power 25', *Fortune*, 8, pp 144–58.

Blank, R.A. (1998) *Welfare, the family, and reproductive behavior: research perspectives*, Washington, DC: National Academies Press. Available from: https://www.ncbi.nlm.nih.gov/books/NBK230339/ (Accessed 12 April 2021).

Blaug, M. (1963) 'The myth of the Old Poor Law and the making of the New', *The Journal of Economic History*, 23, pp 151–84.

Blaug, M. (1964) 'The Poor Law reexamined', *The Journal of Economic History*, 24, pp 229–45.

Boffey, D. (2020, 30 June) 'Ship drawing sheds new light on Amsterdam's role in slave trade', *The Guardian* [Online]. Available from: https://www.theguardian.com/world/2020/jun/30/ship-drawing-sheds-new-light-on-amsterdams-role-in-slave-trade (Accessed 15 March 2021).

Bohstedt, J. (2015) 'Food riots and the politics of provisions in early modern England and France, the Irish Famine, and World War I', in Davis, M.T. (ed) *Crowd actions in Britain and France from the Middle Ages to the modern world*, London: Palgrave.

Bosanquet, H.D. (1914) *Social work in London, 1869–1912: a history of the Charity Organisation Society*, London: John Murray.

Boston, J. (2014) 'Child poverty in New Zealand: why it matters and how it can be reduced', *Educational Philosophy and Theory*, 46, pp 962–88. doi:10.1080/00131857.2014.931002

Bouwsma, W.J. (2020) *John Calvin* [Online]. Available from: https://www.britannica.com/biography/John-Calvin (Accessed 19 August 2020).

Bowpitt, G. (1998) 'Evangelical Christianity, secular humanism, and the genesis of British social work', *British Journal of Social Work*, 28, pp 675–93. doi:10.1093/oxfordjournals.bjsw.a011385

Bowpitt, G. (2007) 'Review of the book Christianity and social service in modern Britain: The disinherited spirit by F. Prochaska', *Social Policy & Administration*, 41(1), pp 105–7.

Brackney, W.H. and Das, R. (2019) *Poverty and the poor in the world's religious traditions: religious responses to the problem of poverty*, Santa Barbara, CA: Praeger/ABC-CLIO.

Brown, E.L. (1935) *Social work as a profession*, London: Russell Sage Foundation.

Brown, F., Driver, S.B., and Briggs, C.A. (eds) (1976) *A Hebrew and English lexicon of the Old Testament*, Oxford: Clarendon Press.

Brown, P. (2002) *Poverty and leadership in the later Roman Empire*, Hanover, NH: University Press of New England.

Brown, P. (2012) *Through the eye of a needle: wealth, the fall of Rome, and the making of Christianity in the West, 350–550 AD*, Princeton, NJ: Princeton University Press.

Brown, W. (1993) 'Wounded attachments', *Political Theory*, 21(3), pp 390–410.

Brueggemann, W. (2003) 'Inventing the poor', *The Christian Century*, 120(12), pp 30–31.

Brummel, L. (1980) 'Luther and the Biblical language of poverty', *The Ecumenical Review*, 32(1), pp 40–58. doi: 10.1111/j.1758-6623.1980.tb03252.x

Bucher, R. and Strauss, A. (1961) 'Professions in process', *American Journal of Sociology*, 66, pp 325–34. Available from: https://www.jstor.org/stable/2773729 (Accessed 20 January 2022).

Burkhauser, R.V., Corinth, K., Elewell, J., and Larrimore, J. (2019/2021) *Evaluating the success of President Johnson's war on poverty: revisiting the historical record using a full-income poverty measure* [Online]. Available from: https://www.nber.org/papers/w26532 (Accessed 19 January 2022).

Burwick, F. (2015) *British drama of the Industrial Revolution*, Cambridge: Cambridge University Press.

Campos Boralevi, L. (1984) *Bentham and the oppressed*, Berlin: Walter de Gruyter.

Carson, P. (2012) *The East India Company and religion, 1698–1858* (Vol. 7), Boydell and Brewer. Available from: https://www.jstor.org/stable/10.7722/j.ctt1x71sz (Accessed 20 January 2022).

Carter, M.J., Gebner, F., Seaman, J.A., and Foret, C. (1990) 'Occupation to profession continuum – status and future of HPERD', *Journal of Physical Education, Recreation & Dance*, 61(3), pp 106–19.

Chakravorty, S. (2019a) *How the British reshaped India's caste system* [Online]. Available from: https://www.bbc.com/news/world-asia-india-48619734 (Accessed 30 May 2021).

Chakravorty, S. (2019b) *The truth about us: the politics of information from Manu to Modi*, Abingdon: Hachette India.

Chambers, C.A. (1967) *Seedtime of reform: American social service and social action 1918–1933*, Minneapolis, MN: University of Minnesota Press.

Chan, C.-Y.J. (2018) 'Poverty and the poor in Chinese religions', in Brackney, W.H. and Das, R. (eds) *Poverty and the poor in the world's religious traditions: religious responses to the problem of poverty*, Santa Barbara, CA: Praeger/ABC-CLIO.

Cheshire, L. and Lawrence, G. (2006) 'Neoliberalism, individualisation and community: regional restructuring in Australia', *Social Identities*, 11(5), pp 435–45. doi: 10.1080/13504630500407869

Chi, I. (2005) 'Social work in China', *International Social Work*, 48(4), pp 371–9. doi: 10.1177/0020872805053456

Child, Sir Josiah. (1690) *Proposals for the relief and employment of the poor* [Online]. Available from: https://play.google.com/books/reader?id=eYwbHV80v6AC&hl=en&pg=GBS.PA3 (Accessed 14 December 2020).

Chilisa, B., Major, T.E., and Khudu-Petersen, K. (2017) 'Community engagement with a postcolonial, African-based relational paradigm', *Qualitative Research*, 17(3), pp 326–39. doi: 10.1177/1468794117696176

Chui, E.W.T. (2014) 'Social work in Hong Kong', in Aspalter, C. (ed.) *Social work in East Asia*, Oxford: Routledge.

Coit, S. (1892) *Neighbourhood guilds*, London: Swan Sonnenschein & Co.

Colledge, G.L. (2012) *God and Charles Dickens*, Grand Rapids, MI: Brazos Press.

Constantelos, D.J. (1968) *Byzantine philanthropy and social welfare*, New Brunswick, NJ: Rutgers University Press.

Corsini, C.A. and Viazzo, P.P. (eds) (1993) *The decline of infant mortality in Europe, 1800–1950: four national case studies*, Florence: International Child Development Centre.

Cowherd, R.G. (1960) 'The humanitarian reform of the English Poor Laws from 1782 to 1815', *Proceedings of the American Philosophical Society*, 104(3), pp 328–42.

Cox, D. and Pawar, M. (2013) *International social work: issues, strategies and programs*, Thousand Oaks, CA: Sage.

Cribelar, T. (2001) From sin to laziness: early modern views of the poor and poor relief [Online]. Available from: https://www.eiu.edu/historia/cribelar.pdf (Accessed 19 January 2022).

Crompton, L. (2003) *Homosexuality and Civilization*, Cambridge, MA: Harvard University Press.

Dabbagh, N.T. (2005) *Suicide in Palestine: narratives of despair*, London: Hurst & Company.

Dahood, M. (1979) *Psalms II: 51–100*, Garden City, NY: Doubleday & Co. Inc.

Dash, B.M. and Nagar, A. (2021) 'Relevance of Hinduism in social work', in Dash, B.M., Kumar, M., Singh, D.P., and Shukla, S. (eds) *Indian social work*, London: Routledge India.

Davenport-Hines, R. (2001) *The pursuit of oblivion: a global history of narcotics 1500–2000*, London: Weidenfeld & Nicolson.

Davis, A. (2008) *Celebrating 100 years of social work*, Birmingham: University of Birmingham. Available from: https://www.birmingham.ac.uk/Documents/college-social-sciences/social-policy/IASS/100-years-of-social-work.pdf (Accessed 20 January 2022).

Davis, D.B. (1988) *The problem of slavery in Western culture*, New York: Oxford University Press.

Davis, N.Z. (1968) 'Poor relief, humanism and heresy: The case of Lyon', *Studies in Medieval and Renaissance History*, 5, pp 217–75.

Day, P. and Schiele, J.H. (2013) *A new history of social welfare*, Boston, MA: Pearson.

Deane, J.K. (2011) *A history of medieval heresy and inquisition*, Plymouth: Rowman & Littlefield.

Denzin, N.K. and Giardina, M.D. (eds) (2007) *Ethical futures in qualitative research: decolonizing the politics of knowledge*, Walnut Creek, CA: Left Coast Press.

Depetris-Chauvin, E. and Weil, D.N. (2018) 'Malaria and early African development: evidence from the sickle cell trait', *The Economic Journal*, 128(610), pp 1207–34. doi: 10.1111/ecoj.12433

deWaal, F.B.K. (2008) 'Putting the altruism back into altruism: the evolution of empathy', *Annual Review of Psychology*, 59, pp 279–300. doi: 10.1146/annurev.psych.59.103006.093625

DeWitte, S.N. (2014) 'Mortality risk and survival in the aftermath of the medieval Black Death', *PLOS One*, 9(5), pp e96513. doi: 10.1371/journal.pone.0096513

Diamond, J. (1999) *Guns, germs and steel*, New York: Norton.

Dominelli, L. (2012) 'Globalization and indigenisation: reconciling the irreconcilable in social work?', in Lyons, K., Hokenstad, T., Pawar, M., Huegler, N., and Hall, N. (eds) *The Sage handbook of international social work*, London: Sage.

Downs, J. (2012) *Sick from freedom*, New York: Oxford University Press.

Dunkley, P. (1981) 'Whigs and paupers: the reform of the English Poor Laws, 1830–1834', *Journal of British Studies*, 20(2), pp 124–49. doi: 10.1086/385776

Easton, B.S. (2020) *Stranger and sojourner (in the Apocrypha and the New Testament), International Standard Bible Encyclopedia* [Online]. Available from: https://www.biblestudytools.com/encyclopedias/isbe/stranger-and-sojourner-in-the-apocrypha-and-the-new-testament.html (Accessed 20 March 2020).

Ehlers, M.A. (2018) *Give and take: poverty and social order in early modern Japan*, Cambridge, MA: Harvard University Asia Center.

Ehrenreich, J.H. (1985) *The altruistic imagination: a history of social work and social policy in the United States*. New York: Cornell University Press.

Esposito, E. (2019) *Mosquitos, malaria and the spread of slavery in the US* [Online]. Available from: https://wp.unil.ch/hecimpact/mosquitoes-malaria-and-the-spread-of-slavery-in-the-us/ (Accessed 15 March 2021).

Fensham, F.C. (1962) 'Widow, orphan and the poor in ancient near eastern legal and wisdom literature', Journal of Near Eastern Studies, 21(2), pp 129–139. Available from: https://www.jstor.org/stable/543887.pdf (Accessed 20 January 2022).

Filby, E. (2015) *God and Mrs Thatcher: the battle for Britain's soul*, London: Biteback Publishing.

Filoiali'i, L.A. and Knowles, L. (1983) 'The ifoga: the Samoan practice of seeking forgiveness for criminal behaviour', *Oceanea*, 53(4), pp 384–8. Available from: https://www.jstor.org/stable/40330698 (Accessed 20 January 2022).

Fletcher, J. (2016) *Born free, killed by hate – the price of being gay in South Africa* [Online]. BBC News. Available from: http://www.bbc.com/news/magazine-35967725 (Accessed 30 May 2016).

Flexner, A. (1915) *Is social work a profession?* The Social Welfare History Project [Online]. Available from: http://www.socialwelfarehistory.com/social-work/is-social-work-a-profession-1915/ (Accessed 24 December 2013).

Forrest, A. (1981) *The French Revolution and the poor*, New York: St. Martin's Press.

Fortescue, A. (2015) *The Greek fathers*, London: Aeterna Press.

Foucault, M. (1976/2020) *The history of sexuality, Vol 1*, New York: Penguin Random House.

Fowler, B. (2020) 'Pierre Bourdieu on social transformation, with particular reference to political and symbolic revolutions', Theory and Society, 49, pp 439–63. doi: 10.1007/s11186-019-09375-z

Frankopan, P. (2016) *The silk roads: a new history of the world*, New York: Alfred A. Knopf.

Freedland, J. (2017, 10 April) 'The new age of Ayn Rand: how she won over Trump and Silicon Valley', *The Guardian*, Available from: https://www.theguardian.com/books/2017/apr/10/new-age-ayn-rand-conquered-trump-white-house-silicon-valley (Accessed 15 April 2021).

Frumentariae leges (1875) [Online]. London: John Murray. Available from: http://penelope.uchicago.edu/Thayer/E/Roman/Texts/secondary/SMIGRA*/Frumentariae_Leges.html (Accessed 15 October 2021).

Fukuyama, F. (2011) *The origins of political order*, New York: Farrar, Straus and Giroux.

Fyers, A. and Kirk, S. (2015) *Income inequality: how NZ is one of the worst in the world, Stuff* [Online]. Available from: https://www.stuff.co.nz/national/politics/68600911/income-inequality-how-nz-is-one-of-the-worst-in-the-world (Accessed 9 April 2021).

Garvin, C.D., Gutiérrez, L.M., and Davis, L.E. (2020) *Social work luminaries: luminaries contributing to the founding of social work practice, policy, and research in the United States*, Oxford Bibliographies [Online]. Available from: https://www.oxfordbibliographies.com/view/document/obo-9780195389678/obo-9780195389678-0287.xml (Accessed 1 February 2021).

Georgetown Law Library. (2021) *A brief history of civil rights in the United States*, Georgetown University Law Library [Online]. Available from: https://guides.ll.georgetown.edu/c.php?g=592919&p=4172706 (Accessed 2 March 2021).

Gerbner, K. (2018) *Christian slavery: conversion and race in the Protestant Atlantic world*, Philadelphia, PA: University of Pennsylvania Press.

Gillingham, J. (2014) 'French chivalry in twelfth-century Britain?', *The Historian*, Summer, pp 6–10. Available from: https://www.history.org.uk/secondary/resource/7591/french-chivalry-in-twelfth-century-britain (Accessed 20 January 2022).

Gohori, J. (2019) 'From the ABC model to the definition of Buddhist social work', in Gohori, J. (ed) 4th International Academic Forum on Buddhist Social Work, Tokyo: Asian Research Institute for International Social Work, pp 5–8.

Gone, J.P. (2017) '"It felt like violence": indigenous knowledge traditions and the postcolonial ethics of academic inquiry and community engagement', *American Journal of Community Psychology*, 60(3–4), pp 353–60. doi: 10.1002/ajcp.12183

González, G. (2003) *Latin America: more poverty, fewer social services*, Inter Press Service [Online]. Available from: http://www.ipsnews.net/2003/01/latin-america-more-poverty-fewer-social-services/ (Accessed 10 April 2021).

Goodhew, D. (2018) 'Lambeth 2020 and African Anglicanism', Available from: https://livingchurch.org/covenant/2018/02/21/lambeth-2020-and-african-anglicanism (Accessed 15 April 2021).

Goodstein, L. (2009, 15 August) 'Believers invest in the gospel of getting rich', *The New York Times*. Available from https://www.nytimes.com/2009/08/16/us/16gospel.html (Accessed 15 October 2021)

Gopal, P. (2019) *Insurgent empire: anticolonial resistance and British dissent*, London: Verso.

Gottlieb, A. (n.d.) *The best books on the Enlightenment recommended by Jonathan Israel*, fivebooks.com [Online]. Available from: https://fivebooks.com/best-books/enlightenment-jonathan-israel/ (Accessed 15 December 2020).

Gowan, D.E. (1987) 'Wealth and poverty in the Old Testament: the case of the widow, the orphan and the sojourner', *Interpretation: A Journal of Bible and Theology*, 41(4), pp 341–53. doi: 10.1177/002096438704100402

Gray, D. (1986) *Earth and altar: the evolution of the parish communion in the Church of England to 1945*, Norwich: Alcuin Club.

Gray, M., Coates, J., Yellow Bird, M., and Hetherington, T. (eds) (2013/2016) *Decolonising social work*, Abingdon: Routledge.

Green, D. (1995) *Silent revolution: the rise of market economies in Latin America*, New York: Cassell.

Greensmith, C. and Giwa, S. (2013) 'Challenging settler colonialism in contemporary queer politics: settler homonationalism, Pride Toronto, and two-spirit subjectivities', *American Indian Culture and Research Journal*, 37(2), pp 129–48. doi: 10.17953/aicr.37.2.p4q2r84l12735117

Greenwood, E. (1957) 'Attributes of a profession', *Social Work*, 2(3), pp 45–55. doi: 10.17953/aicr.37.2.p4q2r84l12735117

Grell, O.P. and Cunningham, A. (1997) 'The Reformation and changes in welfare provision in early modern Northern Europe', in Cunningham, A. and Grell, O.P. (eds) *Health care and poor relief in Protestant Europe 1500–1700*. London: Routledge.

Griffin, E. (2015) *A short history of the British Industrial Revolution*, New York: Palgrave Macmillan.

Gunavathy, J.S. (2007) 'India', in Weiss, I. and Welbourne, P. (eds) *Social work as a profession: a comparative cross-national perspective*, Birmingham: Venture Press.

Hall, M.P. and Howes, I.V. (1965) *The church in social work*, Abingdon: Routledge and Kegan Paul.

Handel, G. (2009) *Social welfare in western society*, New York: Transaction/Routledge.

Handongwe, S. (2017) 'Ending poverty through ubuntu', *Psychology Research*, 7(11), pp 592–603. doi: 10.17265/2159-5542/2017.11.002

Hansan, J.E. (2011) *Poor relief in early America*, Virginia Commonwealth University [Online]. Available from: https://socialwelfare.library.vcu.edu/programs/poor-relief-early-amer/ (Accessed 26 January 2021).

Hare, J. (2006) 'The bishop and the prior: demense agriculture in medieval Hampshire', *The Agricultural History Review*, 54(2), pp 187–212. Available from: https://www.jstor.org/stable/40276195 (Accessed 20 January 2022).

Harper, T. (2020) *Underground Asia: global revolutionaries and the assault on Empire*, Cambridge, MA: Belknap Press.

Harris, K. (2002) *Evangelical Anglicans and their ambivalent involvement in middle-class education in nineteenth-century England*. Doctor of Philosophy thesis, Graduate School of Education, University of Western Australia, Perth, WA. Available from: https://research-repository.uwa.edu.au/en/publications/evangelical-anglicans-and-their-ambivalent-involvement-in-middle- (Accessed 20 January 2022).

Harris, R.L. (2003) 'Popular resistance to globalization and neoliberalism in Latin America', *Journal of Developing Societies*, 19(2), pp 365–426. doi: 10.1177/0169796X0301900209

Healy, K. (2016) 'Social work education and regulation in Australia', in *Encyclopedia of Social Work*, National Association of Social Workers Press and Oxford University Press. doi: 10.1093/acrefore/9780199975839.013.1169

Healy, L. (2008) *International social work: professional action in an interdependent world*, New York: Oxford University Press.

Healy, L.M. (1995) 'International social welfare: organisations and activities', in Edwards, R.L. and Hopps, J.G. (eds) *Encyclopedia of Social Work* (19th edn). Washington, DC: NASW Press

Healy, L.M. (2014) 'Global education for social work: Old debates and future directions for international social work', in Noble, C., Strauss, H., and Littlechild, B. (eds) *Global social work: crossing borders, blurring boundaries*, Sydney, NSW: Sydney University Press, pp 369–80.

Healy, L.M. and Link, R.J. (eds) (2012) *Handbook of international social work: human rights, development and the global profession*, New York: Oxford University Press.

Hedreen, S. (2019, 15 August) ' "Gendered" jobs are on the decline, but stereotypes remain', *Business News Daily* [Online]. Available from: https://www.businessnewsdaily.com/10085-male-female-dominated-jobs.html (Accessed 10 May 2021).

Helliwell, J.F., Layard, R., Sachs, J.D., De Neve, J.-E., Aknin, L.B., and Wang, S. (2021) *World Happiness Report 2021*. Sustainable Development Solutions Network. Available from: https://worldhappiness.report/ed/2021/ (Accessed 15 June 2021).

Henrickson, M. and Fouché, C. (2017) *Vulnerability and marginality in human services*, Abingdon: Routledge.

Hertel, B.R. and Nelsen, H.M. (1974) 'Are we entering a post-Christian Era? Religious belief and attendance in America, 1957–1968', *Journal for the Scientific Study of Religion*, 13(4), pp 409–19. Available from: https://www.jstor.org/stable/1384605 (Accessed 20 January 2022).

Hetey, R.C. and Eberhardt, J.L. (2014) 'Racial disparities in incarceration increase acceptance of punitive policies', *Psychological Science*, 25(10), pp 1949–54. doi: 10.1177/0956797614540307

Higginbotham, P. (2014) *Life in a Victorian workhouse*, Cheltenham: The History Press.

Hildegard of Bingen (2004) *The letters of Hildegard of Bingen*, Oxford: Oxford University Press.

Hills, J. (1998) *Thatcherism, New Labour and the welfare state*. London: Centre for Analysis of Social Exclusion, London School of Economics. Available from: http://eprints.lse.ac.uk/5553/1/Thatcherism_New_Labour_and_the_Welfare_State.pdf (Accessed 20 January 2022).

Himmelfarb, G. (1984, April) 'The idea of poverty', *History Today*, 34(4) [Online]. Available from: https://www.historytoday.com/archive/idea-poverty (Accessed 20 January 2022).

Hinestroza, C. and Ioakimidis, V. (2011) 'In search of emancipatory social work practice in contemporary Colombia: working with the despalzados in Bogotá', in Lavalette, M. and Ioakimidis, V. (eds) *Social work in extremis*, Bristol: Policy Press, pp 81–92.

Historic England. (n.d.) *Independent women: social work and environmentalism* [Online]. Available from: https://historicengland.org.uk/research/inclusive-heritage/lgbtq-heritage-project/workplaces-and-creativity/independent-women/ (Accessed 26 January 2021).

Holland, T. (2019) *Dominion: how the Christian revolution remade the world*, New York: Basic Books.

Holman, S.R. (2016) 'God and the poor in early Christian thought', in McGowan, A.B., Daley, B.E., and Gaden, T.J. (eds) *God in early Christian thought: essays in Memory of Lloyd G. Patterson*, Leiden: Brill.

Howard, M.C. (2011) *Transnationalism and society: an introduction*, Jefferson, NC: McFarland & Company.

Hugman, R. (1996) 'Professionalization in social work: the challenge of diversity', *International Social Work*, 39(2), pp 131–147.

Hussein, S. (2011) *Social work qualifications and regulation in European Economic Area (EEA)*, London: General Social Care Council. Available from: https://kar.kent.ac.uk/68359/ (Accessed 20 January 2022).

Huygens, I. (2011) 'Developing a decolonisation practice for settler colonisers: a case study from Aotearoa New Zealand', *Settler Colonial Studies*, 1(2), pp 53–81. doi: 10.1080/2201473X.2011.10648812

Hwang, K.-K. (2009) 'The development of indigenous counseling in contemporary Confucian communities', *Counseling Psychologist*, 37(7), pp 930–43. doi: 10.1177/0011000009336241

Iaskaia-Smirnova, E., Romanov, P., and Lovtsova, N. (2004) 'Professional development of social work in Russia', *Social Work and Society*, 2(1), pp 132–8. Available from: http://www.socwork.de/Iarskaia-Romanov-Lovtsova2004-1.pdf (Accessed 20 January 2022).

Ibrahim, M. (1982) 'Social and economic conditions in pre-Islamic Mecca', *International Journal of Middle East Studies*, 14(3), pp 343–58. Available from: https://www.jstor.org/stable/163677 (Accessed 20 January 2022).

Inagaki, M., Kikuchi, K., and Gohori, J. (eds) (2020) *Towards new horizon: beyond the Buddhist social work*, Tokyo: Gakubunsha.

Inequality.org. (n.d.) *Income inequality in the United States* [Online]. Available from: https://inequality.org/facts/income-inequality/ (Accessed 20 January 2021).

Inikori, J.E. (1987) 'Slavery and the development of industrial capitalism in England', *The Journal of Interdisciplinary History*, 17(4), pp 771–93. Available from: https://www.jstor.org/stable/204653 (Accessed 20 January 2022).

International Association of Schools of Social Work and International Federation of Social Work. (2014) *Global definition of social work* [Online]. Available from: https://www.iassw-aiets.org/global-definition-of-social-work-review-of-the-global-definition/ (Accessed 15 August 2014).

International Association of Schools of Social Work, International Federation of Social Work, and International Council on Social Welfare. (2012) *The global agenda for social work and social development: commitment to action* [Online]. Available from: http://cdn.ifsw.org/assets/globalagenda2012.pdf (Accessed 15 January 2020).

International Association of Schools of Social Work and International Federation of Social Workers. (2018) *Global social work statement of ethical principles* [Online]. Available from: https://www.iassw-aiets.org/2018/04/18/global-social-work-statement-of-ethical-principles-iassw/ (Accessed 15 January 2019).

International Consortium for Social Development. (n.d.) *About us* [Online]. Available from: https://www.socialdevelopment.net/about-us/ (Accessed 3 March 2021).

International Labour Organization. (2009) 'From Bismarck to Beveridge: social security for all', *World of Work* [Online]. 67. Available from: https://www.ilo.org/global/publications/world-of-work-magazine/articles/ilo-in-history/WCMS_120043/lang--en/index.htm (Accessed 17 February 2021).

Israel, J.I. (2001) *Radical enlightenment: philosophy and the making of modernity 1650–1750*, Oxford: Oxford University Press.

Jay, A.J., Evans, M., Frank, I., and Sharpling, D. (2018) *Child migration programmes investigation report*. Independent Inquiry Child Sexual Abuse. Available from: https://www.iicsa.org.uk/publications/investigation/child-migration/part-c-detailed-examination-institutional-responses/sending-institutions/24-national-childrens-home. (Accessed 15 July 2021).

Jennissen, T. and Lundy, C. (2011) *One hundred years of social work: a history of the profession in English Canada, 1900–2000*, Waterloo, ON: Wilfrid Laurier University Press.

Jones, J.D. (1995) 'The concept pf poverty in St. Thomas Aquinas's Contra Impugnantes Dei Cultum et Religionem', *The Thomist: A Speculative Quarterly Review*, 59(3), pp 409–39. doi: 10.1353/tho.1995.0018

Jordan, W.C. (1998) *The great famine: northern Europe in the early fourteenth century*, Princeton, NJ: Princeton University Press.

Joseph, S.J. (2018) *Jesus, the Essenes, and Christian origins: new light on ancient texts and communities*, Waco, TX: Baylor University Press.

Kahl, S. (2009) 'Religious doctrines and poor relief: a different causal pathway', in van Kersbergen, K. and Marrow, P. (eds) *Religion, class coalitions, and welfare states*, Cambridge: Cambridge University Press.

Kars, M. (2020) *Blood on the river: a chronical of mutiny and freedom on the Wild Coast*, New York: The New Press.

Kaufman, S.A. (1984) 'A reconstruction of the social welfare system of ancient Israel', in Barrick, W.B. and Spencer, J.R. (eds) *In the shelter of Elyon: essays on ancient Palestinian life and literature in honor of G.W. Ahlstrom*, Sheffield: T&T Clark.

Kaufman, T. (2017) 'Luther and the Jews', *Antisemitism Studies*, 3(1), pp 46–65. doi: 10.2979/antistud.3.1.03

Keane, J. (2016, 9 April). 'The 18th century Enlightenment and the problem of public misery', *The Conversation* [Online]. Available from: https://theconversation.com/the-18th-century-enlightenment-and-the-problem-of-public-misery-57541 2020 (Accessed 13 December, 2020).

Keefer, L.L. (1990) 'John Wesley, the Methodists and social reform in England', Wesleyan Theological Journal, 25(1), pp 7–20.

Kelsey, J. (1999) *Life in the economic test-tube: New Zealand 'experiment' a colossal failure* [Online]. Available from: http://www.converge.org.nz/pma/apfail.htm (Accessed 9 April 2021).

Kia Piki Ake/Welfare Expert Advisory Group. (2018) *A brief history of family support payments in New Zealand*, Ministry of Social Development [Online]. Available from: http://www.weag.govt.nz/weag-report/background-papers/ (Accessed 27 February 2021).

Kingstone, P. (2018) 'The rise and fall (and rise again?) of neoliberalism in Latin America', in Cahill, D., Cooper, M., Konings, M., and Primrose, D. (eds) *The Sage handbook of neoliberalism*, Thousand Oaks, CA: Sage.

Klaits, J. (1985) *Servants of Satan: the age of the witch hunts*, Bloomington, IN: Indiana University Press.

Klausen, J.C. (2016) 'Violence and epistemology: J.S. Mill's Indians after the "mutiny"', *Political Research Quarterly*, 69(1), pp 96–107. doi: 10.1177/1065912915623379

Knight, J. (2010) *Jane Addams: spirit in action*, New York: Norton & Co.

Krausman Ben-Amos, I. (2008) *The culture of giving: informal support and gift-exchange in early modern England*, Cambridge: Cambridge University Press.

Kuhnle, S. and Hort, S.E.O. (2004) *The developmental welfare state in Scandinavia: lessons for the developing world*, Geneva: United Nations Research Institute for Social Development.

Kumar, J.A. (2018) 'Poverty and the poor in the Hindu, Jain and Sikh religions of India', in Brackney, W.H. and Das, R. (eds) *Poverty and the poor in the world's religious traditions*, Santa Barbara, CA: Praeger/ABC-CLIO.

Lahiri, N. (2015) *Ashoka in ancient India*, Cambridge, MA: Harvard University Press.

Lambeth Conference. (1948) *Resolution 19- the Church and the Modern World* [Online]. Available from: https://www.anglicancommunion.org/resources/document-library/lambeth-conference/1948/resolution-19-the-church-and-the-modern-world-the-church-and-the-modern?author=Lambeth+Conference&language=English&year=1948&tag=Lambeth+Conference (Accessed 26 February 2021).

Leiby, J. (1978) *A history of social welfare and social work in the United States*, New York: Columbia University Press.

Liebescheutz, J.H.W.G. (translator) (2010) *Ambrose of Milan: Political letters and speeches*, Liverpool: Liverpool University Press.

Leighninger, L. (1987) *Social work: search for identity*, New York: Greenwood Press.

Linscome, S.A. (1972). 'Henry Houseley, versatile musician of early Denver', *The Colorado Magazine*, 49(1), pp 1–18.

Lloyd, A.G. (2007) *Emigration, immigration and migration in nineteenth century Britain* [Online]. Available from: https://www.gale.com/binaries/content/assets/gale-us-en/primary-sources/intl-gps/intl-gps-essays/full-ghn-contextual-essays/ghn_essay_bln_lloyd1_website.pdf (Accessed 1 February 2021).

Lohfink, N. (1991) 'Poverty in the laws of the ancient near east and of the Bible', *Theological Studies*, 52(1), pp 34–50.

Lubove, R. (1965) *The professional altruist: the emergence of social work as a career 1830–1930*. Cambridge, MA: Harvard University Press.

Macgregor, G.H.C. (1954) 'The Acts of the Apostles (Exegesis)', in Buttrick, G.A., Bowie, W.R., Scherer, P., Knox, J., and Terrien, S. (eds) *The interpreter's bible*, New York: Abingdon Press.

Mandal, K.S. (1989) 'American influence on social work education in India and its impact', *Economic & Political Weekly*, 24(49), pp 2710–12. Available from: https://www.jstor.org/stable/4395683 (Accessed 20 January 2022).

Mandler, P. (1990) 'Christian political economy and the making of the new Poor Law', *The Historical Journal*, 33(1), pp 81–103. Available from: https://www.jstor.org/stable/2639392 (Accessed 20 January 2022).

Mann, C.S. (1979) 'The organization and institutions of the Jerusalem church in Acts', in Albright, W.F. and Mann, C.S. (eds) *The Acts of the Apostles*, Garden City, NY: Doubleday & Co.

Manthorpe, J., Hussein, S., and Moriarty, J. (2005) 'The evolution of social work education in England: a critical review of its connections and commonalities with nurse education', *Nurse Education Today*, 25(5), pp 369–76. doi: 10.1016/j.nedt.2005.03.004

Margaret Thatcher Foundation. (n.d.) *Interview for Women's Own ('no such thing as society')* [Online]. Margaret Thatcher Foundation. Available from: https://www.margaretthatcher.org/document/106689 (Accessed 15 July 2021).

Marshall, P. and Ryrie, A. (eds) (2002) *The beginnings of English Protestantism*, Cambridge: Cambridge University Press.

Maspero, H. (1981) *Taoism and Chinese religion*, University of Massachusetts Press.

Maxwell, J. (2020) 'Oranga Tamariki reports looms from Children's Commissioner over Māori baby uplifts', *Stuff* [Online]. Available from: https://www.stuff.co.nz/national/politics/123430194/oranga-tamariki-report-looms-from-childrens-commissioner-over-mori-baby-uplifts (Accessed 9 April 2021).

McMillan, R.O. (2013) *Perceptions of poverty: the evolution of German attitudes towards social welfare from 1830 to World War I*, Fayetteville, AR: University of Arkansas.

Mendelsohn, I. (1948) 'The family in the ancient Near East', *Biblical Archaeologist*, 11(2), pp 24–40. Available from: https://www.jstor.org/stable/3209201?seq=1 (Accessed 20 January 2022).

Mikhail, A. (2020) *God's shadow: Sultan Selim, his Ottoman Empire and the making of the modern world*, New York: W.W. Norton & Co.

Millbank, A. (2017) 'Maurice as a resource for the church today', in Spencer, S. (ed), *Theology reforming society: revisiting Anglican social theology*, London: SCM Press.

Miller, T.S. (2011) 'Basil's house of healing', *Christian History*, 101 [Online]. Available from: https://christianhistoryinstitute.org/magazine/article/basils-house-of-healing (Accessed 15 February 2020).

Miller, T.S. (2016) 'Byzantine philanthropic institutions and modern humanitarianism', *The Review of Faith & International Affairs*, 14(1), pp 18–25.

Moffatt, K. and Irving, A. (2002) '"Living for the bretheren": idealism, social work's lost Enlightenment strain', *British Journal of Social Work*, 32(4), pp 415–27. doi: 10.1080/15570274.2016.1145475

Mohan, M. (2019) *The secret language of lesbian love: the wives mothers and friends who hide their sexuality*, [Online]. BBC News. Available from: https://www.bbc.co.uk/news/resources/idt-sh/secret_lesbian_language (Accessed 20 December 2020).

Mooney, H., Watson, A., Ruwhiu, P., and Hollis-English, A. (2020) 'Māori social work and Māori mental health in Aotearoa New Zealand', in Ow, R. and Poon, A. (eds) *Mental health and social work*, New York: Springer, pp 1–28.

Morris, J. (2017) 'F.D. Maurice and the myth of Christian Socialist origins', in Spencer, S. (ed.) *Theology reforming society: revisiting Anglican social theology*, London: SCM Press.

Muñoz-Guzmán, C., Mancinas, S., and Nucci, N. (2014) 'Social work education and a family in Latin America: a case study', in Noble, C., Strauss, H., and Littlechild, B. (eds) *Global social work: crossing borders, blurring boundaries*, Sydney, NSW: Sydney University Press, pp 113–25.

Mupedziswa, R. and Sinkamba, R.P. (2014) 'Social work education and training in southern and east Africa: yesterday, today and tomorrow', in Noble, C., Strauss, H., and Littlechild, B. (eds) *Global social work: crossing borders, blurring boundaries*. Sydney, NSW: Sydney University Press, pp 141–53.

Nair, T.K. (2015) *Social work in India: a semi-profession*. Social Work Foot Prints (Samajakarayada Hejjegalu), https://www.socialworkfootprints.org/articles/social-work-in-india-a-semi-profession

Nasir, B.F., Brennan-Olsen, S., Gill, N.S., Beccaria, G., Kisely, S., Hides, L., Kondalsamy-Chennakesavan, S., Nicholson, G., and Toombs, M. (2021) 'A community-led design for an Indigenous model of mental health care for Indigenous people with depressive disorders', *Australian and New Zealand Journal of Public Health*. doi: https://doi.org/10.1111/1753-6405.13115

National Archives. (n.d.) *Slave or free* [Online]. Available from: https://www.nationalarchives.gov.uk/pathways/blackhistory/rights/slave_free.htm (Accessed 27 May 2021).

Nixey, C. (2018) *The darkening age*, Boston, MA: Houghton Mifflin Harcourt.

Nkosinathi, M. and Mtshali, G. (2015) 'The relationship between grandparents and their grandchildren in the Black families in South Africa', *Journal of Comparative Family Studies*, 46(1), pp 75–83.

Noble, C. and Henrickson, M. (2014) 'Towards identifying a philosophical basis for social work', in Noble, C., Strauss, H., and Littlechild, B. (eds) *Global social work: crossing borders, blurring boundaries*. Sydney, NSW: Sydney University Press, pp 3–14.

Noble, C., Henrickson, M., and Han, I.Y. (eds) (2009) *Social work education: voices from the Asia-Pacific*, Melbourne, VIC: Vulgar Press.

Noble, C., Strauss, H., and Littlechild, B. (eds) (2014) *Global social work: crossing borders, blurring boundaries*, Sydney, NSW: Sydney University Press.

Norberg, K. (1985) *Rich and poor in Grenoble, 1600–1814*, Berkeley, CA: University of California Press.

Nord, P. (1994) 'The welfare state in France, 1870–1914', *French Historical Studies*, 18, pp 821–838. doi: 10.2307/286694

Office of the Children's Commissioner (2020, November) *Te kuuku o te manawa: Moe ararā! Haumanutia ngā moemoeā a ngā tūpuna mō te oranga o ngā tamariki*. Wellington: Office of the Children's Commissioner. Available from: https://www.occ.org.nz/publications/reports/tktm-report-2/. (Accessed 15 June 2021).

Oosterhoff, A.J. (1977) 'The law of mortmain: An historical and comparative review', *University of Toronto Law Journal*, 27(3), pp 257–334. doi: 10.2307/825569

Ordinance of Labourers (1349) [Online]. Available from: https://web.archive.org/web/20140701104840/http://britannia.com/history/docs/laborer1.html (Accessed 21 October 2021).

Palmer, A. (2014) *The East End: four centuries of London life*, London: Faber & Faber.

Patnaik, P. (2020) 'Caste among Indian Muslims is a real issue: So why deny them reservation?' *The Wire* [Online]. Available from: https://thewire.in/caste/caste-among-indian-muslims-real-why-deny-reservation (Accessed 20 April 2021).

Patterson, R.D. (1973) 'The widow, the orphan and the poor in the Old Testament and the extra-Biblical literature', *Bibliotheca Sacra*, 130, pp 125–32. Available from: https://www.martincwiner.com/wp-content/uploads/2010/11/Patterson_Widow_BSac.pdf (Accessed 20 January 2022).

Payne, L. (n.d.) 'Health in England (16th–18th c.)', in *Children and youth in history, Item #166* [Online]. Available from: https://chnm.gmu.edu/cyh/items/show/166 (Accessed 4 October 2020).

Payne, R. (1957) *The holy fire: the story of the fathers of the Eastern Church*, Crestwood, NY: St Vladimir's Seminary Press.

Pew Research Center. (2008) *Global Anglicanism at a crossroads* [Online]. Available from: https://www.pewforum.org/2008/06/19/global-anglicanism-at-a-crossroads/ (Accessed 15 April 2021).

Pinker, S. (2018) *Enlightenment now: the case for reason, science, humanism and progress*, New York: Viking.

Poindexter, C.C. (2013) 'HIV stigma and discrimination in medical settings: stories from African women in New Zealand', *Social Work in Health Care*, 52(8), pp 704–27. doi: 10.1080/00981389.2013.808726

Polman, L. (2010) *The crisis caravan: what's wrong with humanitarian aid*, New York: Henry Holt & Co.

Power Thesaurus. (2021) 'Synonyms for social worker', https://www.powerthesaurus.org/social_worker/synonyms

Pritchard, J.B. (ed) (1969) *Ancient near eastern texts relating to the Old Testament*, Princeton, NJ: Princeton University Press.

Prochaska, F.K. (2006) *Christianity and social service in modern Britain: the disinherited spirit*, Oxford: Oxford University Press.

Prodromou, E.H. and Symeonides, N. (2016) 'Orthodox Christianity and humanitarianism: an introduction to thought and practice, past and present', *The Review of Faith & International Affairs*, 14(1), pp 1–8. doi: 10.1080/15570274.2016.1145479

Ragab, I.A. (2016) 'The Islamic perspective on social work: a conceptual framework', *International Social Work*, 59(3), pp 325–42. doi: 10.1177/0020872815627120

Ravulo, J., Mafile'o, T., and Yeates, D.B. (eds) (2019) *Pacific social work: navigating practice, policy and research*, Oxford: Routledge.

Richardson, T.A. (2012) 'Disrupting the coloniality of being: toward decolonial ontologies in philosophy of education', *Studies in Philosophy and Education*, 31(6), pp 539–51. doi: 10.1007/s11217-011-9284-1

Richmond, M. (1917) *Social diagnosis*, New York: Russell Sage Foundation.

Richter, M. (1964) *The politics of conscience: T.H. Green and his age*, London: Weidenfeld and Nicolson.

Robinson, V.P. (1930) *A changing psychology in social case work*, Chapel Hill, NC: University of North Carolina Press.

Rogal, S.J. (1988) 'John Wesley's journal: prescriptions for the social, spiritual and intellectual ills of Britain's middle class', *Andrews University Seminary Studies*, 26(1), pp 33–42.

Rouland, B., Vaithianathan, R., Wilson, D., and Putnam-Hornstein (2019) 'Ethnic disparities in childhood prevalence of maltreatment: evidence from a New Zealand birth cohort', *American Journal of Public Health*, 109, pp 1255–7. doi: 10.2105/AJPH.2019.305163

Rutakumwa, R., Zalwango, F., Richards, E., and Seeley, J. (2015) 'Exploring the care relationship between grandparents/older carers and children infected with HIV in south-western Uganda: implications for care for both the children and their older carers', *International Journal of Environmental Research and Public Health*, 12(2), pp 2120–34. doi: 10.3390/ijerph120202120

Ryan, D. (2017) 'Octavia Hill: From theology to action', in Spencer, S. (ed), *Theology reforming society: revisiting Anglican social theology*, London: SCM Press.

References

Salsberg, E., Quigley, L., Mehfoud, N., Acquaviva, K., Wyche, K., and Sliwa, S. (2017) *Profile of the social work workforce*, Washington, DC: George Washington University Health Workforce Institute and School of Nursing.

Schlabach, T. (1969) *Rationality and welfare: public discussion of poverty and social insurance in the United States 1875–1935*, United States Social Security Administration [Online]. Available from: https://www.ssa.gov/history/reports/schlabach1.html (Accessed 31 January 2021).

Schwarzer, B., Kämmerer-Rütten, U., Schleyer-Lindenmann, A., and Wang, Y. (eds) (2016) *Transnational social work and social welfare: challenges for the social work profession*, London: Routledge.

Semigina, T. and Boyko, O. (2014) 'Social work education in the post-socialist and post-modern era: the case of Ukraine', in Noble, C., Strauss, H., and Littlechild, B. (eds) *Global social work: crossing borders, blurring boundaries*, Sydney, NSW: Sydney University Press, pp 257–69.

Sewpaul, V. and Henrickson, M. (2019) 'The (r)evolution and decolonization of social work ethics: the Global Social Work Statement of Ethical Principles', *International Social Work*, 62(6), pp 1469–81. doi: 10.1177/0020872819846238

Shave, S.A. (2017) *Pauper policies: poor law practice in England, 1780–1850*, Manchester: Manchester University Press.

Silva, E. (2009) *Challenging neoliberalism in Latin America*, Cambridge: Cambridge University Press.

Sivasundaram, S. (2020) *Waves across the South: a new history of revolution and empire*, London: William Collins.

Skinner, S.A. (2004) *Tractarians and the 'Condition of England': the social and political thought of the Oxford Movement*, Oxford: Clarendon Press.

Slack, P. (1984) 'Poverty in Elizabethan England', *History Today*, 34(1), pp 5–13. Available from: https://www.historytoday.com/archive/poverty-elizabethan-england (Accessed 15 October 2020).

Slater, M. (2009) *Charles Dickens*, New Haven, CT: Yale University Press.

Smith, A. (1759/2002). *The theory of moral sentiments*, Haakonssen, K. (ed.), Cambridge: Cambridge University Press.

Smith, A. (1776) *Wealth of nations*, Hoboken, NJ: Generic NL Freebook.

Smith, G. (2007) 'Margaret Thatcher's Christian faith: a case study in political theology', *The Journal of Religious Ethics*, 35(2), pp 233–57. Available from: https://www.jstor.org/stable/40014868 (Accessed 20 January 2022).

Sneed, M. (1999) 'Israelite concern for the alien, orphan and widow: altruism or ideology?', *Zeitschrift für die Alttestamentliche Wissenschaft*, 111, pp 498–507. doi: 10.1515/zatw.1999.111.4.498

Snow, D. (2017, 30 March) 'Paul Keating says neo-liberalism is at "a dead end" after Sally McManus speech', *Sydney Morning Herald* [Online]. Available from: https://www.smh.com.au/politics/federal/paul-keating-says-neoliberalism-is-at-a-dead-end-after-sally-mcmanus-speech-20170329-gv9cto.html (Accessed 15 June 2021).

Social Welfare History Project. (2011) *Stanton Coit (18571944) – founder of Neighborhood Guild, the first settlement house in the U.S. in 1886 and founder of the South Place Ethical Society in London in 1887*, Social Welfare History Project [Online]. Available from: http://socialwelfare.library.vcu.edu/people/coit-stanton/ (Accessed 31 January 2021).

Social Work England. (2021) *The Social Workers Regulations 2018* [Online]. Available from: https://www.socialworkengland.org.uk/about/what-we-do/publications/the-social-workers-regulations-2018/ (Accessed 21 October 2021).

Stats NZ/Tatauranga Aotearoa. (2021) *Latest release of child poverty statistics* [Online]. Available from: https://www.stats.govt.nz/news/latest-release-of-child-poverty-statistics (Accessed 9 April 2021).

Stol, M. (2016) *Women in the ancient Near East*, Amsterdam: Walter de Gruyter GMbH & Co KG.

Strong, J.S. (1983/1989) *The legend of King Aśoka: a study and translation of the Aśokāvadāna*, Delhi: Princeton University Press/Motilal Banarsidass.

Susumu, S. (2009) 'State Shinto in the lives of the people: the establishment of emperor worship, modern nationalism and shrine Shinto in late Meiji', *Japanese Journal of Religious Studies*, 36(1), pp 93–124. Available from: https://www.jstor.org/stable/30233855 (Accessed 20 January 2022).

Swan, J. 2011. 'Luther: women are made to be either wives or prostitutes', *Beggars all: Reformation and apologetics* [Online]. Available from: https://beggarsallreformation.blogspot.com/2010/01/luther-women-are-made-to-be-either.html (Accessed 17 August 2020).

Swan, K. and Vargas, J. (n.d.) *Lockean property rights* [Online]. Available from: https://www.csus.edu/faculty/s/kyle.swan/docs/Lockean%20property%20rights-revised.pdf (Accessed 8 December 2020).

Tannenbaum, N. and Reisch, M. (2001) *From charitable volunteers to architects of social welfare: a brief history of social work*, University of Michigan [Online]. Available from: https://ssw.umich.edu/about/history/brief-history-of-social-work (Accessed 9 February 2021).

Taylor, C. (2007) *A secular age*, Cambridge, MA: Belknap-Harvard University Press.

Tennant, M. (1989) *Paupers and providers: charitable aid in New Zealand*, Auckland: Allen & Unwin.

The Times of London. (1930) Miss Alice Gruner. *The Times [of London]*, January 7.

Thompson, J.W. (1928/1959) *Economic and social history of the Middle Ages (300–1300), Vol. I*, New York: Frederick Ungar.

Thompson, N. (2016) *The professional social worker*, London: Palgrave Macmillan.

Thomson, D. (1998) *A world without welfare*, Auckland: Auckland University Press.

References

Tierney, B. (1959) *Medieval poor law: a sketch of canonical theory and its application in England*, Oakland, CA: University of California Press.

Toplady, A.M. (1774) *Calvin's influence on the English Reformation [extract from The Historic Proof of the Doctrinal Calvinism of the Church of England, ch. 15]* [Online]. Available from: http://www.theologian.org.uk/churchhistory/calvinsinfluence.html (Accessed 19 November 2020).

Trattner, W.I. (1984) *From poor law to the welfare state: a history of social welfare in America* (3rd ed). New York: The Free Press.

Trattner, W.I. (1999) *From Poor Law to welfare state: a history of social welfare in America* (6th ed). New York: Free Press.

Tutu, D. (2000) *No future without forgiveness*, New York: Random House.

Tyacke, N. (2010) 'The Puritan paradigm of English politics, 1558–1642', *The Historical Journal*, 53(3), pp 527–50. doi: 10.1017/S0018246X10000108X

Underwood, A.C. (1934/2013) *Shintoism: the indigenous religion of Japan*, Redditch: Read Books.

United Nations. (1948) *Universal Declaration of Human Rights* [Online]. Available from: http://www.un.org/en/universal-declaration-human-rights/ (Accessed 20 January 2022).

van Kersbergen, K. and Marrow, P. (eds) (2009) *Religion, class coalitions, and welfare states*, Cambridge: Cambridge University Press.

van Nederveen Meerkerk, E. and Teeuwen, D. (2013) 'The stability of voluntarism: financing social care in early modern Dutch towns compared with the English Poor Law, c. 1600–1800', *European Review of Economic History*, 18(1), pp 82–105. doi: 10.1093/ereh/het014

Virginia Commonwealth University Libraries. (n.d.) *Mary Ellen Richmond (1861–1928) – social work pioneer, administrator, researcher and author*, Virginia Commonwealth University Libraries [Online]. Available from: https://socialwelfare.library.vcu.edu/social-work/richmond-mary/ (Accessed 1 February 2021).

Visser, M.J., Makin, J.D., Vandormael, A., Sikkema, K.J., and Forsyth, B.W.C. (2009) 'HIV/AIDS stigma in a South African community', *AIDS Care*, 21(2), pp 197–206. doi: 10.1080/09540120801932157

Vivier, R. (1921) 'La grande ordonnance de février 1351: les mesures anticorporatives et la liberté du travail', *Revue Historique*, 138(2), pp 201–14. Available from: https://www.jstor.org/stable/40943950 (Accessed 20 January 2022).

Wacquant, L. (2004/2009) *Punishing the poor*, Durham, NC: Duke University Press.

Walker, R. (2014) *The shame of poverty*, Oxford: Oxford University Press.

Walkowitz, D.J. (1990) 'The making of a feminine professional identity: social workers in the 1920s', *The American Historical Review*, 95(4), pp 1051–75. Available from: https://www.jstor.org/stable/2163478 (Accessed 20 January 2022).

Wallis, J. (2018) *The Bloody Code in England and Wales, 1760–1830*, Cham: Palgrave Macmillan.

Wandel, L.P. (1990) *Always among us: images of the poor in Zwingli's Zurich*, Cambridge: Cambridge University Press.

Watene, K. (2016) 'Valuing nature: Māori philosophy and the capability approach', *Oxford Development Studies*, 44(3), pp 287–96. doi: 10.1080/13600818.2015.1124077

Webb, S. and Webb, B. (1910) *English local government, Vol 10: English Poor Law policy*, Abingdon: Routledge.

Webb, S. and Webb, B. (1927) *English poor law history*, London: Frank Cass and Co.

Weber, M. (1930/2001) *The Protestant ethic and the spirit of capitalism*, London: Routledge Classics.

Weiss, I. and Welbourne, P. (eds) (2007) *Social work as a profession: a comparative cross-national perspective*, New York: Venture Press.

Weiss, J.H. (1983) 'Origins of the French welfare state: poor relief in the Third Republic, 1871–1914', *French Historical Studies*, 13(1), pp 47–78. doi: 10.2307/286593

Wessel, S. (2016) *Passion and compassion in early Christianity*, Cambridge: Cambridge University Press.

White, W.D. (2014) 'Professional self-regulation in medicine', *American Medical Association Journal of Ethics*, 16(4), pp 275–78. doi: 10.1001/virtualmentor.2014.16.4.hlaw1-1404

Wilensky, H.L. (1964) 'The professionalization of everyone?', *American Journal of Sociology*, 70(2), pp 137–58. doi: 10.1086/223790

Wilson, D.C.S. (2014) 'Arnold Toynbee and the Industrial Revolution: the science of history, political economy and the machine past', *History and Memory*, 26(4), pp 133–61. doi: 10.2979/histmemo.26.2.133

Winter, K. and Connolly, P. (1996) '"Keeping it in the family": Thatcherism and the Children's Act 1989', in Pilcher, J. and Wagg, S. (eds) *Thatcher's children?: politics, childhood and society in the 1980s and 1990s*, London: Falmer Press.

Wolf, D.B. (2003) 'The Vedic theory of clinical social work', *The Indian Journal of Social Work*, 64(3), pp 1–23.

Woodberry, R.D. (2012) 'The missionary roots of liberal democracy', *American Political Science Review*, 106(2), pp 244–74. doi: 10.1017/S0003055412000093

Woodroofe, K. (1977) 'The Royal Commission on the Poor Laws, 1905–09', *International Review of Social History*, 22(2), pp 137–64. Available from: https://www.jstor.org/stable/44581768 (Accessed 20 January 2022).

Wright, W.J. (2017) 'The influence of Renaissance humanism and skepticism on Martin Luther', *Oxford Research Encyclopedia of Religion*, Oxford: Oxford University Press, pp 137–64.

Yan, M.C., Lee, J., and Chan, E.K.L. (2020) 'Mechanisms of gatekeeping in the social work profession: lessons learned from Canada, Hong Kong and South Korea', *British Journal of Social Work*. doi: 10.1093/bjsw/bcaa146

Younghusband, E. (1981) 'The 1870s to 1900: What the pioneers discovered', in *The newest profession: A short history of social work*, Surrey: Community Care/IPC Business Press, pp 11–17. Available from: https://www.historyofsocialwork.org/1947_Younghusband/1981%20Younghusband%20newest%20profession%20OCR.pdf (Accessed 20 January 2022).

Zaviršek, D. (2015) 'Social work education in Eastern Europe: Can post-communism be followed by diversity?', in Noble, C., Strauss, H., and Littlechild, B. (eds) *Global social work: Crossing borders, blurring boundaries*, Sydney, NSW: Sydney University Press, pp 271–82.

Zelenev, S. (2018) *The ICSW at the forefront of conceptual thinking, social practice and transnational advocacy*, International Council on Social Welfare [Online]. Available from: https://www.icsw.org/index.php/about-icsw (Accessed 20 January 2022).

Zhao, Y. (2015) 'The spirit of charity and compassion in Daoist religion', *Sociology and Anthropology*, 3(2), pp 122–135. doi: 10.13189/sa.2015.030207

Zheng, A. (2019) 'Ren (仁), the benevolent thought of traditional Chinese medicine', *Chinese Medicine and Culture*, 2(3), pp 137–40.

Zufferey, C. (2013) '"Not knowing that I do not know and not wanting to know": Reflections of a white Australian social worker', *International Social Work*, 56(5), pp 659–73. doi: 10.1177/0020872812436624

Zysk, K. (1991) *Ascetism and healing in ancient India: medicine in the Buddhist monastery*, Oxford: Oxford University Press.

Index

References to tables appear in **bold** type.
References to footnotes show both the
page number and the note number (165n15).

A

Abram/Abraham 24–5, 26, 31
Abramovitz, M. 172
Act for the Abolition of the Slave Trade 1807 127, 135
Act for the Amendment and Better Administration of the Laws Relating to the Poor in England 1834 (New Poor Law) 1, 17, 122, 123, 127–53, 154, 155, 180, 217
Act for the Amendment of the Laws Relating to the Settlement, Employment and Relief of the Poor 1782 ('Gilbert's Act') 116, 118
Act for the Better Regulation of Lying-in Hospitals 1773 116
Act for the Regulation of Parish Vestries (Sturges Bourne Act) 1818 127–8
Act of Supremacy 97
Act of Toleration 1689 139n35
Acts (New Testament book) 33, 35, 37–8, 43
Addams, Jane 1, 147–8
 and female partners 147–8
Adern, Jacinda 176
Adler, Felix 149
Affordable Care Act 2010, US 165n15
Africa 8, 10, 15–16
 social work education 179
 ubuntu and indigenous cultural approaches to social work 206–8
agape 47
agriculture
 Middle Ages 68
 nineteenth century 121–3
Aid to Dependent Children, US 165
Akimoto, T. 211–12
Alexander (the Great) 25
Alfonso V, King of Portugal 84
Altituda Divini Consolii papal bull, 1537 (Paul III) 125
altruism, in social work 187–8, 193, 214
Ambrose, Bishop of Milan 54, 70
American Association of Social Workers 181
American Civil War (1861–65) 123, 147
American colonies 106, 108
 American Revolutionary War (1775–83) 146
Puritanism in 91, 99, 146
 see also New World; slavery; US
American Medical Association 181n2
Amos (First Testament book) 30
ancient Near Eastern texts 19–23, 214
Anglican Church *see* Church of England (Anglican Church)
Anstey, R. 126
Anthony ('the Great') of Egypt 55
Aotearoa New Zealand
 'blackbirding' 125
 exploration and colonisation 109
 Māori people 95, 174n26, 175–6, 208
 migration to 133
 neoliberalism 175–6
 Old Age Pension Act (1898) 158
 prisons and imprisonment 174n26
 Social Security Act 1938 165n15
 workfare policies 167
Aquinas, Thomas 56, 90
Arab cultures, pre-Islamic period 60
Argentina 177
Aristotle 47
Arminianism 91–2, 99, 126, 137, 152
Arminius, Jacobus (Jakob Hermanszoon) 91–2
Armstrong, K. 61–2
Ashley-Cooper, Anthony, Earl of Shaftesbury 136n29
Ashoka ('the Great'), Emperor of India 202–3
Asia 8, 10
 trade with 108
 see also South Asia
Askar 58
Augustine, Bishop of Hippo 54–5, 90
Augustine of Canterbury 58
Augustus Caesar 43
Australia
 'blackbirding' 125–6
 exploration and colonisation 109
 Indigenous Australians and Torres Straits Islanders 208
 migration to 133
 neoliberalism 175
 old age pensions 158
 welfare state 165n15
 workfare policies 167

Index

autonomy, in social work 185, 193, 194, 196, 221
Avis, P. 97

B

Babylonian Empire 10, 22, 25
Bangladesh 193
Baptists 96
Barbados 124
Barnett, Henrietta 1, 141, 143, 145, 147, 148, 217
Barnett, Samuel 1, 140, 141, 143, 144–5, 147, 148, 217
Basil ('the Great'), Bishop of Caesarea 49, 50, 70, 93
Bede (of England) 59
Benezet, Anthony 126
Bentham, Jeremy 107, 128, 129
Berbice slave rebellion, Dutch Guiana, 1763 123
Beveridge, William 163
Beveridge Report 164
biblical texts 10, 18–19, 41
  Christian scriptures (New Testament) 32–5, 41
    Acts 33, 35, 37–8, 43
    Corinthians 44, 124
    Ephesians 124
    the epistles 33, 35, 38–40
    Galatians 124
    the gospels and Acts 33, 35–9
    James 39
    John 33, 35
    Luke 20, 33, 35, 36–7, 53
    Mark 33, 35, 36
    Matthew 20, 32, 33, 35–6, 42, 48, 50–1
    Philemon 124
    Revelation 33
    Thessalonians 39–40, 42, 90, 94
    Timothy 38–9
  Hebrew scriptures (Tanakh; First or Old Testament) 23–6, 33
    Amos 30
    Deuteronomy 20, 27, 28
    Exodus 25, 27
    Genesis 18–19, 24–5, 60
    Hosea 30
    Isaiah 29–30, 37
    Job 30, 31
    Joshua 25
    Law (Torah) 24, 27–9
    Leviticus 27–8
    Micah 30
    Prophets (Nev'im) 24, 29–30
    Proverbs 30, 31
    Psalms 30–1
    Samuel 1 and 2 29, 36
    Writings (Ketuvim) 30–1
    Zechariah 30
Bishop, Henry 129, 130
Bismarck, Otto von 162
'blackbirding' 110–11, 125–6
Blackfriars Settlement 145
Blomfield, Charles James, Bishop of London 129, 130
Bolivia 177
Boniface 58
Boniface VIII, Pope 70
Book of Common Prayer 98
Booth, Charles 156n3
Booth, William 100
Bosanquet, Bernard 144
Bosanquet, Helen 137, 138, 139, 140, 143–4, 145, 156n3, 217
Bowpitt, G. 100, 102, 152
Bray, Thomas 110
Breck, James Lloyd 137
Bristol, and the slave trade 124
Britain 108, 109
  Middle Ages poor law 81–3
  roots of social work in 7–8
  see also England; UK
Brown, P. 49, 52
Brummel, L. 86, 87, 88
Bucer, Martin 98
Buddhism and Buddhist cultures 15–16, 201, 202–3
  Buddhist social work 211–12, 220
  Japan 205
  population data **210**
Burwick, F. 122
Bush, George H.W. 172
Byzantium 44–5, 49, 55, 57, 63, 83, 84, 214, 216
Byzantium/Byzantine Empire 73

C

Caitanya Mahaprabhu 200
Callixtus III, Pope 84
Calvin (Cauvin), John (Jehan/Jean) 90–1, 95–6, 97, 98
Calvinism 3, 12, 118, 155, 216, 218
  and neoliberalism 169, 170, 171, 178
Canaan 25
Canada 156, 158
capital punishment 117n30
capitalism 8
  and Calvinism 91
  critical Marxist perspective on 11
  and the poor 103–8
Cappadocians 49–55, 64, 65, 74, 83, 218
Captain Swing Riots, 1830 121, 128
Caribbean colonies 108
  see also slavery
Carson, P. 110
castes, in Hinduism 200

Catholic Church (Roman/Western
    church) 9n1, 33, 63–4, 66
  missionisation 58–9, 110
  persecution of witches 76
  rise of and feudalism 56–9
  see also Reformation; Roman
    Catholic Church
Central America, Roman Catholic
  missionaries 110
Chadwick, Edwin 129, 130
Chan, C.-Y.J. 204
Changing Psychology in Social Case Work, A
  (Robinson) 159–61, 217
Charity Organisation Societies *see* COSs
Charles V, Holy Roman Emperor 97
Chartism 134
Child, Sir Josiah 105–6
Children and Young Persons Act 1908 157
Children's Bureau, US 155
Chile 176, 177
China 11, 193, 203–5
Christian Coalition of America 172–3
Christian missionisation 109–11, 119
Christian Social Union 134, 152
Christian Socialism 123, 137, 141, 145,
    148, 152, 163, 218
Christianity 3, 18, 216
  early Christian Church and the
    state 42–6
  Great Schism, 1054 63, 64, 83
  Great Schism of 1054 63, 64
  and slavery 124–5, 126–7
  see also biblical texts; Catholic Church
    (Roman/Western church);
    Church of England (Anglican
    Church); Evangelical Christianity;
    Orthodox/Eastern church;
    Protestantism; Reformation; Roman
    Catholic Church
'Christians under the Cross' 87
Christmas Rebellion, 1831–1832,
  Jamaica 123
Church of England (Anglican
  Church) 89n26, 97, 163–4
  Black African majority of 10–11
  Religious Settlement, 1559 99
  and slavery 124, 126–7
Cistercian Order of St Bernard of
  Clairvaux 56
civil rights 112, 114
Clement V, Pope 70
Clementines (Clement V) 70
Clinton, Bill 167
Code of Hammurabi 20, 22–3
codes of conduct 190–1, 193, 211,
    215
Coit, Stanton George 148, 149–50
collective bargaining, prohibition of 122
College for Working Women 134

colonialism 2, 8, 108–11, 217
  resistance to 109, 115
  see also decolonisation
Columba of Ireland and Scotland 58
Columbanos 58
Columbia University, New York City 159
Columbus, Christopher 84
Combination Act 1799 122
Commonwealth, the 111
communalism 70
concubinage, in ancient Near East
  societies 20
confessionalisation of poor relief, Dutch
  Republic 117
confraternities, France 102
Confucius, Confucianism and Confucian
  cultures 15–16, 203–4, 205, 210
  population data **210**
Constantelos, D.J. 47
Constantine, Emperor (Flavius Valerius
  Aurelius Constantinus) 3, 44–5,
    46–7, 65, 93
conversion 100–1
Cook, James 111
Corinthians (New Testament
  book) 44, 124
Corpus Iuris Canonici ('The body of canon
  law') 70
COSs (Charity Organisation Societies)
  UK 1, 137–41, 145, 149, 152, 159, 163,
    164, 180, 185, 217
  US 150–1, 153, 156, 159
Coulson, Walter 129, 130
Council of Lambeth, 1281 76
Council of Nicea 46
Council of Trent (1545–63) 92
Counter-Enlightenment 113
Counter-Reformation 97
Cowherd, R.G. 118
Cox, D. 2, 4, 222
Cranmer, Thomas, Archbishop of
  Canterbury 98
creation stories 19
Crusades 68n1
Cunningham, A. 9, 10
Cyril 58
Cyrus the Great of Persia 25

D

danam (Hindu concept) 200, 201
Daoism (Taoism) 204–5
  population data **210**
Dark Ages 58, 68
  see also Middle Ages
Darwinism 12
Dash, B.M. 200, 201
David of Wales 58
Davis, N.Z. 92, 102
Day, P. 19, 59, 75, 146

Index

De Officiis (Ambrose) 54
De publica in pauperes beneficentia (Hyperius) 10
de Tocqueville, A. 164
Dead Sea Scrolls, Qumran 33–5, 37
Deane, J.K. 78
decolonisation 198, 208–9, **210**, 215, 219–20
Decretals (Gregory IX) 70
Decretum Gratiani (Gratian) 54, 67, 70, 71, 72, 74, 83
democracy, Enlightenment belief in 112, 119
denominalism 126
Dessalines, Jean-Jacques 123
Deuteronomy (First Testament book) 20, 27, 28
deviance, and neoliberalism 173–4
Devine, Edward 156
DeWaal, Frans B.K. 187–8
dharma (Hindu concept) 200, 201
Dickens, Charles 133, 152
Diet of Speyer 97
Diet of Worms 97
Diocletian Persecution 45
dishonourable professions 69
Disraeli, Benjamin 131
Dissolution of the Monasteries, 1536 89n26
Dives 53
Dominelli, L. 219
Dominic 56
Dominion: How the Christian revolution remade the world (Holland) 18
Douglas, Roger 175
Dublin, and the slave trade 123–4
Dum Diversas [Until Different] Papal Bull, 1452 (Nicholas V) 83–4, 124

E

East India Companies *see* EIC (British East India Company); VOC (Dutch Vereenigde Oostindische Compagnia)
East London slums 1, 17, 40, 144
Eastern Europe 179
Ecuador 177
Edict of Milan 45
Edict of Thessalonica 45
Edward VI, King of England 98
Egypt, pharaoh's responsibility for care of the poor 23
EIC (British East India Company) 107, 108, 109, 110, 127
Elizabeth I, Queen of England 99
Elizabethan Poor Law, 1601 1, 9, 40, 82–3, 103–4, 105, 115
empiricism 112, 114
Enclosure Movement 68–9, 121
Engels, F. 123

England
  hospitals, Middle Ages 73
  poor laws 92, 103, 119
    1555 reform 101
    1597 reform 103
    1601 Elizabethan Poor Law 1, 9, 40, 82–3, 103–4, 105, 115
    1662 Poor Relief Act 115
    1722 Workhouse Act 115–16
    1773 Act for the Better Regulation of Lying-in Hospitals 116
    1782 Act for the Amendment of the Laws Relating to the Settlement, Employment and Relief of the Poor ('Gilbert's Act') 116, 118
    1795 Poor Law Act 116
    1834 New Poor Law (Act for the Amendment and Better Administration of the Laws Relating to the Poor in England) 122, 123, 127–53, 154, 155, 180, 217
    Middle Ages 80, 81–3
  Protestantism in 97–102
  see also Britain; UK
Enlightenment, the 2, 3, 8, 12, 84, 111–19, 214
Ephesians (New Testament book) 124
Equiano, Olaudah 123
Erasmus (Desiderius Erasmus Roterodamus) 86, 89, 96n3
'Essay on the Principle of Population, An' (Malthus) 107–8
Essenes 33–5
Ethical Movement 149, 152
ethics, in social work 190–1, 193, 211, 215
ethnic minorities
  incarceration rates 166n18, 174
  income inequality in the US 172
euergesia/euergetism 47, 48, 200
Evangelical Christianity 9, 96, 97, 100–2, 137, 142, 152, 153
  missionaries 110
  and the New Poor Law 134
  and slavery 123, 126
Exodus (First Testament book) 25, 27

F

Fabian Society 130n23, 134
Falwell, Jerry 172
Federal Emergency Relief Act, US 165
Fensham, F.C. 21–2
feudalism 12, 13, 57–9, 68–9, 80
First World War 154, 160, 161, 162, 167, 168, 177, 179n9, 217
Flexner, Abraham 159, 180–1, 184, 191, 215
food riots 122
Fouché, C. 175

France 92
  17th century poor relief 102
  French Revolution 113, 121
  Middle Ages 80
  old age pensions 162
  post-revolutionary poor relief 116, 119
  Roman Catholic missionaries 110
  social work as a profession 193
  welfare state 162–3
Francis of Assisi 56, 67
Freud, Sigmund 159n8
Friedrich III, Elector of Saxony 85
Fry, Elizabeth 100
Fukuyama, F. 57, 58
Full Employment in a Free Society (Beveridge) 163

G

Galatians (New Testament book) 124
Garvin, C.D. 150–1
Gawler, Henry 129, 130
gender
  and professions 182–3, 197, 221
  see also men; women
Genesis (First Testament book) 18–19, 24–5, 60
Geneva Protocol 1929 167
ger, the, care of in Hebrew scriptures 26–31
Germany 211
  hospitals, Middle Ages 73
  welfare state, emergence of 161–2
'Gilbert's Act' (Act for the Amendment of the Laws Relating to the Settlement, Employment and Relief of the Poor 1782) 116, 118
Glasgow, and the slave trade 124
Global Agenda for Social Work and Social Development, 2012 (International Associations of Schools of Social Work, International Federation of Social Work, and International Council on Social Welfare) 222
Global Definition of Social Work 2014 (International Association of Schools of Social Work and International Federation of Social Work) 6–7, 9, 11, 16, 184, 189n9, 189n10, 194, 195, 197, 210–11, 212, 213, 220, 223
global perspective on social work 198–9
  Africa 206–8
  China 203–5
  current situation 210–13
  decolonisation of social work 198, 208–9, **210**
  Japan 205–6
  South Asia 199–203

global trade, and colonialism 108–11
globalisation of social work 1–2, 10–11, 15–16
Gopal, P. 115
Gowan, D.E. 21
Gratian 54, 59, 67, 70, 71, 72, 74, 83
Great Depression (1929–1933) 154, 163, 164–5
Great Famine (1315–76), Europe 76–8
Great Famine, Ireland 146–7
Great Plague (1347–53) 3–4, 12, 13, 78–9, 80, 81, 103, 177, 216
Great Schism, 1054 63, 64, 83
Great Society programmes, US 166
Greece, ancient, and philanthropy 46–7
Green, Thomas Hill (T.H.) 141–3, 145, 152, 217
Greenspan, Alan 172
Greenwood, E. 184
Gregory, Bishop of Nyssa 49, 51–2, 93, 124
Gregory I (' the Great') 58
Gregory IX, Pope 70
Gregory of Nazianzus 49, 51, 93
Gregory VII, Pope 75
Grell, O.P. 9, 10
Griffin, E. 122
Grosseteste, Bishop of Lincoln 76
Grüner, Alice 145
Gurteen, Stephen Humphreys 150–1
GWSEP (Global Social Work Statement of Ethical Principles) 2018 (International Association of Schools of Social Work and International Federation of Social Work) 11, 16, 190, 195, 197, 223

H

Haitian Revolution, 1791 123
Hall, M.P. 164n13
Handbook of Charity Organization, A (Gurten) 150–1
Handel, G. 44, 47, 58
Hart, Martyn 138
Hawke, Bob 175
Healy, Lynne 168
Hebrew scriptures *see* biblical texts, Hebrew scriptures
Hegira 62
Henry VIII, King of England 89n26, 97–8
heresy, and the Great Famine (1315–76) 77
hermits 55–6
Hildegard of Bingen 67
Hill, Octavia 1, 134–5, 139, 140, 143, 145, 147, 149, 156n3, 217
  and female partners 135
Hilton, Boyd 136
Himmelfarb, G. 131

Index

Hinduism and Hindu cultures 15–16, 199–202
  population data **210**
HIV, in Africa 207
Hobbes, Thomas 107n20
Hodson, William 181
Holland, Henry Scott 142
Holland, Tom 3, 18, 32, 46, 50, 55
Holman, S.R. 51
Holy Roman Empire 161
Homer 47
Hong Kong SAR 179
Hooker, Richard 142n39
Hoover, Herbert 165
Hopkins, Gerard Manley 142
Hosea (First Testament book) 30
hospitals
  India 203
  Middle Ages 72–3
Howard, John 100, 175
Howes, I.V. 164n13
Huguccio 71–2
Hull House, Chicago 1, 147, 148–9
human rights 167–8
humanism 3, 8, 9, 15, 84, 86, 89, 90, 92, 95, 96, 113, 114
Hume, David 107n20
Hundred Years' War (1337–1453) 81
Hwang, K.-K. 208
Hyperius, Andreas 10

I

IASSW (International Association of Schools of Social Work) *see* International Association of Schools of Social Work (IASSW)
Ibrahim, M. 60
Iceland 193
ICSD (International Consortium for Social Development) 168
Idealism 141
impotent (disabled) poor 81, 82, 104
India 179, 193, 199–203
  'Mutiny'/Indian Uprising, 1857–58 109
Indian Ocean cultures 109
indigenous cultures 8, 10, 15–16, 108–9, 110–11, 185, 198, 207–8, 209, 219
  population data 209, **210**
'indigenous knowledges' 6, 189, 210
individual responsibility in social work 191, 193
individualism 8, 96, 112
indoor relief 1, 13, 104–5, 130
  abolition of in UK 163
  US 146
indulgences, sale of 85, 95
Industrial Revolution and nineteenth-century period 121–3, 127–53
infant mortality, Britain 158

Inikori, J.E. 125
Institutes of the Christian Religion (Calvin) 90
international aid organisations 215
International Association of Schools of Social Work (IASSW) 168
  Global Agenda for Social Work and Social Development, 2012 222
  Global Definition of Social Work 2014 6–7, 9, 11, 16, 184, 189n9, 189n10, 194, 195, 197, 210–11, 212, 213, 220, 223
  GSWSEP (Global Social Work Statement of Ethical Principles) 2018 11, 16, 190, 195, 197, 223
International Conference on Social Work 168
International Consortium for Social Development (ICSD) 168
International Council on Social Welfare (ICSW) 168
  Global Agenda for Social Work and Social Development, 2012 222
International Federation of Social Work (IFSW) 168
  Global Agenda for Social Work and Social Development, 2012 222
  Global Definition of Social Work 2014 6–7, 9, 11, 16, 184, 189n9, 189n10, 194, 195, 197, 210–11, 212, 213, 220, 223
  GSWSEP (Global Social Work Statement of Ethical Principles) 2018 11, 16, 190, 195, 197, 223
International Permanent Secretariat of Social Workers (IPSSW) 168
international social work 1–2, 10–11, 15–16, 167–8, 215
IPSSW (International Permanent Secretariat of Social Workers) 168
Ireland 146–7, 167
Irving, A. 118–19
Isaiah (First Testament book) 29–30, 37
Islam and Islamic cultures 8, 10, 15, 66, 109
  emergence of 59–63
  hospitals 72–3
  Qur'an 24, 61–2
Islip, Simon, Archbishop of Canterbury 80
Italy 73, 80, 147

J

Jackson, John, Bishop of London 139
Jainism 201
  population data **210**
James (New Testament book) 39
Japan 205–6
Jarrett, Mary 160
Jean II, King of France 80
Jesus of Nazareth 32
  Second Coming of 40, 41, 42
  see also Christianity

Jex-Blake, Sophia 135
Job (First Testament book) 30, 31
John Chrysostom, Bishop of
    Constantinople 49, 51, 53, 93,
    124, 137
John (New Testament book) 33, 35
John XXII, Pope 67–8
Johnson, Lyndon 166
Jordan, W.C. 77
Joseph, S.J. 34, 35
Joshua (First Testament book) 25
Jowett, Benjamin 141, 145, 152
Julius II, Pope 84–5, 89

K

Kahl, S. 88, 92
Kant, Immanuel 111–12
Keane, J. 112
Keating, Paul 175
Keble, John 135
Kennedy, John 166
King, Edward 149
Kingstone, P. 176
Klaits, J. 75–6, 83, 84
Kopling Houses 161
K'ung-tzu (Confucius) 203

L

labour, and the poor 103–8
labour shortage, and the Great Plague
    (1347–53) 79–80
laïcisme *see* secularity
Laotzi 203
Latin America 210–11
    neoliberalism 176–7, 178
    Roman Catholic missionaries 110
    social work in 11, 179
law codes
    Code of Hammurabi 20, 22–3
    Law of Moses 43, 44
    Ur-Nammu 22
    Urukagina of Lagash 22
Law (Torah) 24, 27–9
Lazarus 53
League of Nations (LON) 167
Legalism 205
Leo IX, Pope 64
Leo the Great, Pope 55
Leo X, Pope 84, 85
levirate marriage 20–1
Leviticus (First Testament book) 27–8
Liber Sextus ('Sixth Book') (Boniface
    VIII) 70, 72
liberalism, Enlightenment belief
    in 112, 118
liberty, Enlightenment belief in 119
'list' widows 38–9
Liverpool, and the slave trade 124
Local Government Act 1929 163

Locke, John 107, 125
Lohfink, N. 22, 23, 26
LON (League of Nations) 167
London School of Economics 130n23
Louverture, Toussaint 123
Luke (New Testament book) 20, 33, 35,
    36–7, 53
Luther, Martin 85–9, 90, 94, 97, 98

M

Macauley, Thomas 109
Macrina 49, 50
Magellan, Ferdinand 111
Majority Report, Royal Commission on
    Poor Laws and Relief of Distress
    (1905–1909) 156–7, 158
Malleson, Elizabeth 134
Malthus, Thomas 107–8, 128
Mandler, P. 130
Mann, C.S. 33–4
Mao Tse-Tung 205
Māori people, Aotearoa New Zealand 95,
    174n26, 175–6, 208
Mark (New Testament book) 33, 35, 36
Martin of Tours 52, 55–6
Marx, K. 123
Mary I, Queen of England 98, 101
Matthew (New Testament book) 20, 32,
    33, 35–6, 42, 48, 50–1
Maurice, F.D. 133–4, 135, 141, 145, 217
Mecca 60–1
Medicare, US 165n15
medieval period *see* Middle Ages
Medina 62
men
    same-sex attracted, Middle Ages 75n10
    see also gender
mendicants 55–6, 89
Mesopotamia 19
    see also ancient Near East texts
Methodism 92, 96, 99–100, 126
Methodius 58
Micah (First Testament book) 30
Micronesian cultures 108–9
Middle Ages
    Christian church and theology of the
        poor 67–8, 69–76, 77, 81, 92
    end of 84
    poor laws 10, 13, 80, 81–3
migration
    from Britain 133
    challenges of 11
    to US 133, 146–7, 156
Mill, John Stuart 107
Millbank, A. 134
Minority Report, Royal Commission
    on Poor Laws and Relief of Distress
    (1905–1909) 156, 157
missionisation, Christian 109–11, 119

modernity, subtraction view of 12
Moffatt, K. 118–19
monasticism 55–6, 65, 67–8, 89, 136
  dissolution of the monasteries by Henry VIII 97
Moral Majority, US 172–3
'moral welfare' 164n13
Moravian Brethren 100
Morris, J. 134
Moses 25, 27
  Law of Moses 43, 44
Muhammad Ibn Abdallah (PBOH) 61–2
Muñoz-Guzmán, C. 11
'Mutiny'/Indian Uprising, 1857–58 109
mutual aid societies, France 102

N

Nagar, A. 200, 201
Nanak Davanti 201
Napoleonic Wars 121, 217
National Assistance Act, UK 163
National Conference of Charities and Correction, US 150
National Health Insurance Scheme, UK 163
National Relief Fund, UK 154
National Rifle Association, US 173
natural theology 129
Nazarenes 100
Neighbourhood Guilds 148, 149–50
neoconservatism, in the US 172–3
neoliberalism 8, 11, 154, 155, 168–77, 178–9, 217
Netherlands
  Christian missionaries 110
  exploration and colonialism 108, 111
  poor relief 104, 116–17, 119
New Deal, US 165, 171, 178
New Poor Law (Act for the Amendment and Better Administration of the Laws Relating to the Poor in England) 1834 1, 17, 122, 123, 127–53, 154, 155, 180, 217
New Testament *see* biblical texts, Christian scriptures
New World
  colonisation of 84
  see also American colonies
New Zealand *see* Aotearoa New Zealand
Newman, John Henry 135, 136
Newton, Hazel 181
NGOs (non-governmental organisations) 185
Nicene Creed 46
Nicholas V, Pope 83–4, 124
Nightingale, Florence 135, 135n28
Ninety-Five Theses (Luther) 85
Norberg, K. 102

North Atlantic axis 18, 214, 220
  roots of social work in 7–8
Norway 193

O

Obama, Barack 165n15
Objectivism 170
Old Age Pension Act 1898, New Zealand 158
old age pensions 158, 162
  UK 132–3, 157
Ordinance of Labourers 1349 (England) 79
Ordonnance sur la métier de la ville de Paris [Ordinance on the trades of the city of Paris], 1351 80
Oriel Noetics 128–9, 217
orphan children, care of 104
  ancient Near eastern texts 20–3
  Christian biblical texts 35–41, 44
  Hebrew scriptures 26–31
Orphanotropeion (Imperial/Great Orphanage) 49, 105, 491
Orthodox/Eastern church 33, 63–4, 66
Ostrogothic Kingdom 57
Ottoman Empire 83
outdoor relief 104, 105, 118, 131
  Dutch Republic 117
  US 146
Oxford House 145, 147
Oxford Movement 135, 136

P

Pacific Island Labourers Act 1901, Australia 125–6
Paine, Thomas 112, 114–15
Palestine 25
Panopticon 107
Pasifika cultures 207–8
Patrick of Ireland 58, 124
Patterson, R.D. 22, 26
Paul, Christian apostle 12, 35, 39–40, 43, 44, 90, 94, 101
Paul III, Pope 125
Pawar, M. 2, 4, 222
Peasant's Revolt 1381, England 80
Peasant's War (1524–25), Germany 86, 88
People's Republic of China *see* China
Personal Responsibility and Work Opportunities Act 1966, US 167
Phases of Charity (Gurteen) 150
philanthropia 46–7, 200
philanthropy
  ancient Greece 46–7
  Britain 103–4
  Middle Ages 72–3
  Roman Empire 46, 47–8
Philemon (New Testament book) 124
Philippines 179

Pietism 96
Pinochet, Augusto 176
Pinker, S. 113, 114
plague
 Britain 103n14
 see also Great Plague (1347–53)
Plato 46
political recognition of social work 192–3
Polman, L. 215
polygamy, ancient Near East societies 20
Polynesian cultures 108–9
Ponet, John, Bishop of Winchester 99
Poor Law Board (1847–71) 132
Poor Law Commission (1834–47) 129, 132
Poor Law Unions 131
poor laws 13, 14
 England 92, 103, 119
  1555 reform 101
  1597 reform 103
  1601 Elizabethan Poor Law 1, 9, 40, 82–3, 103–4, 105, 115
  1662 Poor Relief Act 115
  1722 Workhouse Act 115–17
  1773 Act for the Better Regulation of Lying-in Hospitals 116
  1782 Act for the Amendment of the Laws Relating to the Settlement, Employment and Relief of the Poor ('Gilbert's Act') 116, 118
  1795 Poor Law Act 116
  1834 New Poor Law (Act for the Amendment and Better Administration of the Laws Relating to the Poor in England) 1, 17, 122, 123, 127–53, 154, 155, 180, 217
  Royal Commission into the Operation of the Poor Laws, 1832–1834 128–30, 132, 152
  Royal Commission on Poor Laws and Relief of Distress (1905–1909) 156–7, 158
 Middle Ages 10, 80, 81–3
 Northern European countries, Reformation period 88–9
 secularisation of 13
 Switzerland
  Poor Law, 1525 89
Poor Relief Act 1662 115
population data, indigenous cultures 209, **210**
Portugal 108, 110
post-colonial societies and cultures 115, 198, 209
predestination 90, 96
Primitive Methodism 100
prisons and imprisonment 105, 107
 ethnic minorities 174
 and neoliberalism 174–5

prison reform 100
privatisation of prison services 174–5
 US 166n18, 174
Pritchard, J.B. 23
Prochaska, F.K. 155, 163
Prodromou, E.H. 64
profession(s)
 characteristics and criteria of 181, 182, 183–6
 and gender 182–3, 197, 221
 'newer structural form' of 194, 221
 social work as 180–3, 186–97, 221–2
progress, Enlightenment belief in 113, 118, 119
'pronatalist' policies, France 162–3
property held in common 70
Prophets (Nev'im) 24, 29–30
prosperity theology 96
Protestantism 8, 9, 68, 88, 91, 92, 94–5
 in England 97–102; *see also* Reformation
 missionaries 109–11
 New World colonies 91
 persecution of witches 75–6
 and slavery 126
Proverbs (First Testament book) 30, 31
Psalms (First Testament book) 30–1
psychoanalytical theory 217
 and social work 159–61
Public Assistance Institutions, UK 163
public recognition of social work 192–3
Puritanism 91, 97, 99, 106
Pusey, Edward Bouverie 135

Q

Quakerism 100
 and slavery 123, 126, 127

R

Rand, Ayn 170n21, 171
rationality, Enlightenment belief in 113, 118
Reagan, Ronald 171–2, 217
real widows 38–9
Reformation 68, 83–93, 94–7, 214, 216, 217
 see also Protestantism
refugees, challenges of transnational migration 11
regeneratio 96
Religious Settlement, 1559 99
Renaissance 84
Republic of Korea 179
Revelation (New Testament book) 33
Richmond, Mary 1, 151, 159, 181
Richter, M. 100, 142
Robertson, Pat 172
Robinson, Virginia 159–61, 217
Rogal, S.J. 126

Index

Roman Catholic Church 9n1, 84–5, 92
  France 102, 116, 162–3
  Germany 161
  missionaries 110
  Roman Catholic-dominated countries 9
  see also Catholic Church (Roman/Western church); Reformation
Roman Empire 3, 33, 84, 216
  early Christian Church and the state 42–6
  fall of 56–7
  philanthropy 46, 47–8
  and slavery 123
Romania 193
Roman/Western church *see* Catholic Church (Roman/Western church)
Romulus Augustulus 57
Roosevelt, Franklin 165, 171
Rowland, Henrietta 143
Royal Commission into the Operation of the Poor Laws, 1832–1834 128–30, 132, 152
Royal Commission on Poor Laws and Relief of Distress (1905–1909) 156–7, 158
royal responsibility for the care of the poor, ancient Near East societies 21–3
Rule *(Asketikon)* of St Basil 56
Rule of St Augustine 56
Rule of St Benedict 56
Ruskin, John 139n33

S

Salvation Army 100, 149
Samuel 1 and 2 (First Testament books) 29, 36
Scandinavian countries
  migration to US 146
  welfare state, emergence of 162
Schiele, J.H. 19, 59, 75, 146
science 112, 113, 114
Second Treatise on Government (Locke) 107
Second World War (1939–45) 154–5, 162, 163, 164, 165–6, 168, 171, 177, 178, 179n29, 217
Secular Age, A (Taylor) 11–13
secularism 11–13, 18
  secular/civic responsibility for care of the poor 68, 77–8, 81, 92, 93, 95, 96, 163–4, 216
Senior, Nassau William 128, 129, 130
Settlement House Movement 1, 141–5, 147–8, 152, 159, 185
  US 147–8, 149, 150
Sharpe, Sam 123
Shintō 205–6
  population data **210**
Siddhartha Gautama 202
Sikhism 201

population data **210**
Silk Roads 108
Singapore 167
Sivaundaram, S. 109
Sixtus IV, Pope 84
skills, in social work 190, 193
Skinner, S.A. 136
Slack, P. 9, 99
slavery 108, 111, 123–7, 135
  'blackbirding' 110–11, 125–6
  of Muslims in West Africa 84
  in the US 123, 147
Slavery Abolition Act 1834 127, 135
Smith, Adam 106–7, 114, 119, 122, 125, 128, 131
Smith, G. 170
Smith, Mary Rozet 148
social bonds 187n8
social control 3–4, 15, 73, 220–1
  and altruism 188
  social work as agent of the state 4, 5, 164, 194, 221
Social Diagnosis (Richmond) 1, 151, 159, 181
social harmony 3, 203, 204, 207, 210, 213
social imaginary
  change from vertical to horizontal 12–13, 14, 112
  contemporary 218
  Lutheran 161, 162
  Middle Ages 74–80
Social Insurance and Allied Services (Beveridge) 163
social liberalism period 154, 155–61
social order 158
Social Security Act 1938, New Zealand 165n15
Social Security Act (SSA), US 165
social stability 3–4, 73
social work
  20th century emergence of 1, 13–15, 159–60, 178–9
  as agent of the state 4, 5, 164, 194, 221
  altruism in 187–8, 193, 214
  autonomy in 185, 193, 194, 196, 221
  community and social development role 4
  and decolonisation 198, 208–9, **210**, 215, 219–20
  definition of 5–7
  and gender 182–3, 197
  global future of 214–16, 222–3
  individual responsibility in 191, 193
  internationalisation/globalisation of 1–2, 10–11, 15–16, 167–8, 215
  mental health services 4
  and neoliberalism 171, 173–4
  origins and history overview 216–18
  as a profession 180–3, 186–97, 221–2
  and psychoanalytical theory 159–61

public and political recognition 192–3
regulation of 186, 192, 196
self-governance and credentialling 192
skills in 190, 193
theoretical knowledge in 188–9, 193
title protection 192, 221
values and ethics 190–1, 193, 211, 215
Society for Ethical Culture 149
Society for the Promotion of Christian Knowledge (SPCK) 104, 110
Society for the Promulgation of the Gospel in Foreign Parts (SPG) 110, 124
Solly, Henry 139
sororate marriage 20–1
South Africa 133
South Asia 199–203
Spain 92, 108, 110
SPCK (Society for the Promotion of Christian Knowledge) 104, 110
Speenhamland System 121, 128, 130
SPG (Society for the Promulgation of the Gospel in Foreign Parts) 110, 124
SSA (Social Security Act), US 165
St Athanasius 64
St Marylebone Charity Organisation Committee 140–1
St Mary's Bryaston Square (Marylebone) 143, 144
St Peter's Basilica, Vatican 84–5
Starr, Ellen Gates 147
State Shintō 206
Statute of Artificers, 1388 82
Statute of Labourers, 1351 (England) 79–81, 82
Statute of Merton 1235 68–9
Stele of Hammurabi 10
Stover, Charles 149
Sublimus Dei papal bull, 1537 (Paul III) 125
subtraction view of modernity 12
Sumner, John Bird 129, 130
Surges Bourne, William 129, 130
Susumu, S. 205–6
Sweden 193
Switzerland
  Poor Law, 1525 89
  poverty levels, Middle Ages 69–70
  Reformation period 89–90
Symeonides, N. 64

T

Tale of Aqhat 23
Tao Te Ching 204
Tasman, Abel 111
Taylor, Charles 11–13, 74, 91, 110, 112–13
Taylor, George 129, 130
Ten Commandments 27
Teutonicus (Joannes Teutonicus Zemeke) 70, 72

Thatcher, Margaret 169–71, 217
Theatrical Representations Act of 1788 116
theoretical knowledge in social work 188–9, 193
Theory of Moral Sentiments, The (Smith) 114
Thessalonians (New Testament book) 39–40, 42, 90, 94
Thompson, J.W. 62
Thompson, N. 185–6
Thucydides 47
Tierney, B. 8, 10, 54, 55, 56, 57, 70, 72, 78, 79, 81–2
Timothy (New Testament book) 38–9
tithes 73n9, 122
title protection in social work 192, 221
Tolstoy, L. 147
Toynbee, Arnold 121n1, 122, 141, 143, 145
Toynbee Hall 1, 141, 144, 145, 147, 148, 149
Tractarians 134, 135–7, 141, 142, 145, 147, 148, 152, 153
trade unions 181–2
  prohibition of 122
Traill, James 129
transportation to colonies, as punishment 117n30, 128n19
Trattner, W.I. 156, 161
Trinitarianism 134
Tutu, Desmond 207
Tyacke, N. 99
typhus 77

U

ubuntu 206–7
UDHR (Universal Declaration of Human Rights) 167–8
UK
  ethnic minorities incarceration rates 174
  neoliberalism 168–71
  old age pensions 132–3, 157, 158
  social work, early developments 159
  twentieth-century 154–5
  welfare state 155, 163–4, 177–8
  workfare policies 167
  see also Britain; England
Unitarianism 139n35, 151
United Nations 167
universal basic income 105–6, 114–15
Universal Declaration of Human Rights (UDHR) 167–8
University of Chicago, School of Social Service Administration 159
University Settlement House, New York City 149
Ur-Nammu law code 22
Urukagina of Lagash, law code 22

Index

US
  anti-slavery movement 123
  Evangelical Christianity 9
  migration 133, 146–7, 156
  neoliberalism 171–3
  nineteenth-century developments 146–51, 153
  old age pensions 158
  social work
    early developments 151, 159–60
    twentieth-century 155, 156
  welfare state 177, 178
    emergence of 164–7
  workfare policies 167

V

vagrancy, Middle Ages 79, 81–2
values, in social work 190–1, 193, 211, 215
Vedas 199–202
Venezuela 177
Viking slave trade 23–124
Villiers, Thomas Hyde 128
VOC (Dutch Vereenigde Oostindische Compagnia) 108, 124
vocation 183
voluntary poverty 55–6, 65, 67–8, 89, 94
Vyasi (Krishna Dvaipānaya; Veda Vyāsa) 199

W

Wacquant, Loïc,173–174 105
Walker, R. 38, 201–2
Walkowitz, D.J. 182
Waltham Black Act 1723 (Bloody Code) 117n30
Wandel, L.P. 70, 92
wealth, and Calvinism 91
Wealth of Nations (Smith) 106–7
Webb, Beatrice 73, 130, 147, 156, 157, 158–9, 181–2, 217
Webb, Sydney 73, 130, 147, 156, 157, 158–9, 181–2
Weber, Max 91, 96, 106
Weiss, I. 183, 184, 192
Weiss, J.H. 116
Welbourne, P. 183, 184, 192
welfare state, emergence of 154, 161–7
Wesley, Charles 99

Wesley, John 91–2, 99–100, 126
White House Conference on Children, 1909 (US) 155
widows, care of
  ancient Near eastern texts 20–3
  Christian biblical texts 35–41, 44
  Hebrew scriptures 26–31
Wilberforce, William 127
Wilensky, H.L. 181–2, 183, 184, 185, 194
William of Wyckeham, Bishop of Winchester 80
Willibrord 58
witches, persecution of 75–6, 97
women
  gender, professionalisation and social work 182–3, 221
  persecution of as witches 75–6, 97
Women's Institute 154
Women's University Settlement 145
Woodberry, R.D. 110
Woodroofe, K. 157
work
  Calvin's theology of 90–1, 104, 105, 155, 167
  as prerequisite for public assistance 40, 167
  see also Statute of Artificers, 1388; Statute of Labourers, 1351 (England)
Work for the Dole (1997–98), Australia 167
Workhouse Act 1722 104, 115–16
workhouses, indoor relief in 1, 13, 104–5, 130
  abolition of in UK 163
Working Men's College 133–4
working poor, Middle Ages 69
Writings (Ketuvim) 30–1

Y

yagna (Hindu concept) 200, 201
Yorke, Harriot 135
Younghusband, E. 1, 17, 144

Z

Zechariah (First Testament book) 30
Zhao, Y. 204–5
Zotikus 1, 49
Zwingli, Ulrich (Huldrych) 89–90, 98
Zysk, K. 201

www.ingramcontent.com/pod-product-compliance
Lightning Source LLC
Chambersburg PA
CBHW051533020426
42333CB00016B/1904